Lecture Notes in Computer Science 1417
Edited by G. Goos, J. Hartmanis and J. van Leeuwen

Springer
*Berlin
Heidelberg
New York
Barcelona
Budapest
Hong Kong
London
Milan
Paris
Singapore
Tokyo*

Sudhakar Yalamanchili   José Duato (Eds.)

Parallel Computer Routing and Communication

Second International Workshop, PCRCW'97
Atlanta, Georgia, USA, June 26-27, 1997
Proceedings

 Springer

Series Editors

Gerhard Goos, Karlsruhe University, Germany
Juris Hartmanis, Cornell University, NY, USA
Jan van Leeuwen, Utrecht University, The Netherlands

Volume Editors

Sudhakar Yalamanchili
Georgia Institute of Technology
School of Electrical and Computer Science
Atlanta, Georgia, 30332-0250, USA
E-mail: sudha@ece.gatech.edu

José Duato
Facultad de Informàtica, Universidad Politécnica de Valencia
Camino de Vera s/n, E-46071 Valencia, Spain
E-mail: jduato@gap.upv.es

Cataloging-in-Publication data applied for

Die Deutsche Bibliothek - CIP-Einheitsaufnahme

Parallel computer routing and communication : second
international workshop ; proceedings / PCRCW '97, Atlanta, Georgia,
USA, June 26 - 27, 1997 / Sudhakar Yalamanchili ; José Duato
(ed.). - Berlin ; Heidelberg ; New York ; Barcelona ; Budapest ; Hong
Kong ; Lonson ; Milan ; Paris ; Santa Clara ; Singapore ; Tokyo :
Springer, 1998
   (Lecture notes in computer science ; Vol. 1417)
   ISBN 3-540-64571-3

CR Subject Classification (1991): C.2, C.1.2, B.4.3, C.4, F.2

ISSN 0302-9743
ISBN 3-540-64571-3 Springer-Verlag Berlin Heidelberg New York

This work is subject to copyright. All rights are reserved, whether the whole or part of the material is concerned, specifically the rights of translation, reprinting, re-use of illustrations, recitation, broadcasting, reproduction on microfilms or in any other way, and storage in data banks. Duplication of this publication or parts thereof is permitted only under the provisions of the German Copyright Law of September 9, 1965, in its current version, and permission for use must always be obtained from Springer-Verlag. Violations are liable for prosecution under the German Copyright Law.

© Springer-Verlag Berlin Heidelberg 1998
Printed in Germany

Typesetting: Camera-ready by author
SPIN 10637396   06/3142 – 5 4 3 2 1 0   Printed on acid-free paper

Preface

This workshop was a continuation of the PCRCW '94 workshop that focused on issues in parallel communication and routing in support of parallel processing. The workshop series provides a forum for researchers and designers to exchange ideas with respect to challenges and issues in supporting communication for high-performance parallel computing.

Within the last few years we have seen the scope of interconnection network technology expand beyond traditional multiprocessor systems to include high-availability clusters and the emerging class of system area networks. New application domains are creating new requirements for interconnection network services, e.g., real-time video, on-line data mining, etc. The emergence of quality-of-service guarantees within these domains challenges existing approaches to interconnection network design. In the recent past we have seen the emphasis on low-latency software layers, the application of multicomputer interconnection technology to distributed shared-memory multiprocessors and LAN interconnects, and the shift toward the use of commodity clusters and standard components. There is a continuing evolution toward powerful and inexpensive network interfaces, and low-cost, high-speed routers and switches from commercial vendors. The goal is to address the above issues in the context of networks of workstations, multicomputers, distributed shared-memory multiprocessors, and traditional tightly-coupled multiprocessor interconnects.

The PCRCW '97 workshop presented 20 regular papers and two short papers covering a range of topics dealing with modern interconnection networks. It was hosted by the Georgia Institute of Technology and sponsored by the Atlanta Chapter of the IEEE Computer Society.

We would like to thank the program committee members for their time and effort in organizing this workshop, and the reviewers for ensuring timely reviews under a very short time-line. We are grateful to L. Ni for the use of his web-based review system and D. Panda and C. Stunkel for enhancements to the same. These systems considerably simplified the review process. We are grateful to the efforts of Diana Fouts and D. Schimmel for the production of the proceedings. Special thanks are due to D. Fouts, Pam Halverson, and the Georgia Tech Department of Continuing Education for their contribution in handling the local arrangements and the numerous details.

As the result of the efforts of many people, we hope you find the workshop proceedings informative, stimulating, and useful in your endeavors.

June 1997 *Sudhakar Yalamanchili and José Duato*

Program Committee

Sudhakar Yalamanchili
Georgia Institute of Technology (Co-Chair)

José Duato
Universidad Politécnica de Valencia (Co-Chair)

Kevin Bolding
Seattle Pacific University

Rajendra Boppana
University of Texas at San Antonio

Suresh Chalasani
University of Wisconsin

Michael Galles
Silicon Graphics, Inc.

Lionel Ni
Michigan State University

Dhabaleswar K. Panda
Ohio State University

Timothy Pinkston
University of Southern California

David Schimmel
Georgia Institute of Technology

Kang G. Shin
University of Michigan

Larry Snyder
University of Washington

Referees

D. P. Agrawal
K. Bolding
R. Boppana
G. Byrd
S. Chalasani
J. Duato
M. Galles
C. Hyatt
C. T. King
L. Kucera
P. Lopez
N. Mckenzie
R. Melham
W. A. Najjar
L. Ni
D. K. Panda
T. Pinkston
D. Schimmel
J. Sengupta
K. G. Shin
A. Smai
L. Snyder
L. Thorelli
D. S. Wills
S. Yalamanchili

Table of Contents

Keynote Address
Approaches to Quality of Service in High-Performance Networks
    A. A. Chien
    University of Illinois and Hewlett Packard Laboratories, USA 1

Session I   *Routing I*
                  Session Chair: R. Bopanna
                  University of Texas at San Antonio, US

Integrated Multi-class Routing
    M. L. Fulgham and L. Snyder
    University of Washington, USA 21

Congestion Control in the Wormhole-Routed Torus with Clustering and Delayed Deflection
    C. Hyatt and D. P. Agrawal
    North Carolina State University, USA 33

Multicasting in Irregular Networks with Cut-Through Switches Using Tree-Based Multidestination Worms
    R. Sivaram, D. K. Panda and C. B. Stunkel
    Ohio State University, USA and IBM T. J. Watson Research Center, USA 39

Poster Session

CCSIMD: A Concurrent Communication and Computation Framework for SIMD Machines
    V. Garg and D. E. Schimmel
    Georgia Institute of Technology, USA 55

Arctic Switch Fabric
    G. A. Boughton
    Massachusetts Institute of Technology, USA 65

Session II   *Router and Network Architectures I*
                Session Chair: K. Bolding
                Seattle Pacific University, USA

STREAMER: Hardware Support for Smoothed Transmission of Stored Video over ATM
    S.-W. Moon, P. Pillai and K. G. Shin
    University of Michigan, USA 75

Preliminary Evaluation of a Hybrid Deterministic/Adaptive Router
    D. Miller and W. A. Najjar
    Colorado State University, USA 89

HiPER-P: An Efficient, High-Performance Router for Multicomputer Interconnection Networks
    P. May, S. M. Chai and D. S. Wills
    Georgia Institute of Technology, USA 103

Session III   *Router and Network Architectures II (Invited Presentations)*
                Session Chair: D. Pander
                Ohio State University, USA

ServerNet™ II
    D. Garcia and W. Watson
    Tandem Computers Inc., USA 119

Embedded Systems Standards
    C. Lund
    Mercury Computer Systems, USA 137

Challenges in the Design of Contemporary Routers
    C. B. Stunkel
    IBM T. J. Watson Research Center, USA 139

Panel Session 153
    Moderator: Dhabaleswar Panda
    Ohio State University, USA
    Panelists: Andrew Chien, University of Illinois and Hewlett Packard, USA
                    Al Davis, University of Utah, USA
                    Thorsten von Eicken, Cornell University, USA
                    Dave Garcia, Tandem Computers, USA
                    Craig Stunkel, IBM T. J. Watson Research Center, USA

Session IV *Messaging Layer Support*
D. E. Schimmel
Georgia Institute of Technology, USA

Evaluation of Communication Mechanisms in Invalidate-Based Shared Memory Multiprocessors
G. T. Byrd and M. J. Flynn
Stanford University, USA 159

How Can We Design Better Networks for DSM Systems?
D. Dai and D. K. Panda
Ohio State University, USA 171

Integration of U-Net into Windows/NT (Invited Presentation)
T. von Eicken
Cornell University, USA 185

Session V *Routing II*
Session Chair: T. Pinkston
University of Southern California, USA

Distance-Based Flow Control in Wormhole Networks
A.-H. Smai and L.-E. Thorelli
Royal Institute of Technology, Sweden 189

On the Use of Virtual Channels in Networks of Workstations with Irregular Topology
F. Silla and J. Duato
Universidad Politécnica de Valencia, Spain 203

Multicasting on Switch-Based Irregular Networks Using Multi-Drop Path-Based Multidestination Worms
R. Kesavan and D. K. Panda
Ohio State University, USA 217

Power/Performance Trade-offs for Direct Networks
C. S. Patel, S. M. Chai, S. Yalamanchili and D. E. Schimmel
Georgia Institute of Technology, USA 231

Session VI *Router and Network Architectures III*
Session Chair: J. Duato
Universidad Politécnica de Valencia, Spain

ChaosLAN: Design and Implementation of a Gigabit LAN Using Chaotic Routing
N. R. McKenzie, K. Bolding, C. Ebeling and L. Snyder
Mitsubishi Electric Research Laboratory, Seattle Pacific University
University of Washington, USA 247

Does Time-Division Multiplexing Close the Gap Between Memory and Optical Communication Speeds?
X. Yuan, R. Gupta and R. Melhem
University of Pittsburg, USA..261

Session VII *Deadlock Issues*
Session Chair: S. Yalamanchili
Georgia Institute of Technology, USA

Modeling Message Blocking and Deadlock in Interconnection Networks
S. Warnakulasuriya and T. M. Pinkston
University of Southern California, USA 275

On the Reduction of Deadlock Frequency by Limiting Message Injection in Wormhole Networks
P. López, J. M. Martínez, J. Duato and F. Petrini
Universidad Politécnica de Valencia, Spain and Università di Pisa, Italy........295

Author's Index 309

Keynote Address

Approaches to Quality of Service in High-Performance Networks

Andrew A. Chien[1] and Jae H. Kim[2]

[1] Department of Computer Science, University of Illinois
and Hewlett Packard Laboratories
1304 W. Springfield Avenue, Urbana, IL 61801
Email: achien@cs.uiuc.edu

[2] HAL Computer Systems, Inc., Scalable Server Division
1315 Dell Avenue, Campbell, CA 95008
Email: jkim@hal.com

Abstract. In recent years, the topic of quality of service (QoS) has garnered much discussion and research amongst network designers. QoS has many definitions, but here we focus on the notion of predictable communication performance such as guaranteed bandwidth and maximum latency. Such predictability not only supports continuous media (e.g. audio, video, virtual reality) and interactive response (e.g. client response time, real-time control), but also good parallel application performance. We discuss three major approaches for quality of service and evaluate their match for high performance system-area networks.

We classify the wealth of approaches to network quality of service into three classes: virtual circuits, physical circuits, and global scheduling. These approaches differ significantly in their assumptions about the network environment and in how they bind communication tasks to physical resources, how physical resources are multiplexed and scheduled, and what information is available to do so. These choices fundamentally affect the cost, complexity, and performance of each approach. Virtual circuit approaches attain the greatest flexibility, but require complex hardware for implementation. Physical circuit approaches reduce hardware complexity, but need research to understand to best exploit them to deliver quality of service. Finally, we discuss two promising avenues for combining external control with simple network switches to deliver both low cost and high performance (route based and time-based global scheduling). These approaches are in their infancy and many research questions remain about their capabilities and generality.

1 Introduction

Rapid decrease in the cost of computing and networking elements is producing an explosion in both the deployment and range of digital electronic applications. Low-cost systems support not only traditional applications such as word processors, spreadsheets, email, and databases, but also, newer networked applications such a teleconferencing, multimedia email, VRML, and other applications which make pervasive use of multimedia. Further, the explosive growth of the internet is producing a wealth of new applications with different mixes of computation, network and internal communication, and distributed coordination. In short, new applications are driving both an increased demand for network performance (quantitative change) and service requirement (e.g. predictability, qualitative change). In this paper, we divide these increasing demands into two categories, wide-area networking and intra-cluster networking for scalable servers.

Over the past twenty years, while a great deal of research has gone into the study of a wide variety of approaches and techniques for intra-cluster communication networks [6, 3, 13, 4, 18], little of that effort has focused on simultaneously addressing highest performance and performance predictability (quality of service). Traditionally, workloads have been viewed as requiring only best-effort, and optimization for maximum throughput and minimum latency for a wealth of traffic patterns and message size distributions has been the goal. However, recent study of such best-effort applications indicates that predictable communication performance can improve their performance [12]. Further, emerging use of cluster systems for online interactive applications – both as traditional information resources (online databases) and revolutionary information infrastructure (e.g. web servers, electronic commerce, etc.) – is now driving a different set of concerns. In these latency-sensitive applications, and scalable environments (the internet scales over eight decimal orders of magnitude), the need for controlled performance is critical; both to support good performance (low latency), continuous media data types (video, audio), and to make efficient use of cluster resources (memory, networking connections, etc.). Together, these requirements are driving a need for high performance cluster networks with predictable performance or quality of service.

In the paper, we address the issue of approaches to quality of service in high performance cluster interconnects, discussing the factors that have shaped the major approaches and their pros and cons across the environments. We categorize the major approaches into three categories – virtual circuits, physical circuits, and global scheduling. Each of these approaches represents a different view of network resource management for quality of service and is a product of differing network and technology assumptions. As a consequence, each approach has significantly different cost and performance characteristics. For example, virtual circuits multiplex links independently, requiring significant buffering and link scheduling at each network switch. The physical circuits and global scheduling approaches do not virtualize communication links, permitting simpler switches. Examining these, we illustrate the tradeoffs in approach, and discuss some performance analysis results and some of the challenging open research problems which remain.

1.1 Organization

The remainder of the paper is organized as follows. Section 2 defines Quality of Service, clarifying the context and goals. Virtual and physical circuits are covered in Sections 3 and 4 respectively. Section 5 discusses a new approach, global scheduling. Finally, Section 6 summarizes the paper, and puts the results in perspective.

2 Background

To some applications, the quality rather than quantity of network services is more important. For instance, to some commercial database applications, reliability is essential rather than high-bandwidth, low-latency communications. Also, whereas efficient utilization of network bandwidth improves many data-oriented communications, it may be unnecessary for smooth delivery of audio/video stream data, only increasing buffer space requirement.

Quality of Service (QoS) has many definitions, ranging from reliability, availability to performance predictability. Of course, different applications require different QoS. For instance, to audio/video communications, reliable packet delivery is less important because they can tolerate packet dropping to a large extent. To these applications, some minumum amount of bandwidth for continuous delivery of large amount of data and maximum delay bounds for human interactivity should be guaranteed.

In the paper, we focus on the notion of predictable communication performance such as guaranteed bandwidth and maximum latency. This completely different service requirement demands different resource management from quantity-oriented networks, which is the main topic of the following sections.

3 Virtual Circuit Approach

Network resource control for QoS has long been a critical issue in real-time communication communities and its needs have been exploding with recent growth of multimedia applications which demand minimum bandwidth and worst-case delay guarantees.

In this section, we focus on mechanisms based on end-to-end virtual circuits. This approach was developed for the wide-area network environment (WAN), and therefore makes the weakest assumptions about network environment, indeterminate length links, heterogeneity, unstructured topology, etc. The resulting flexibility has allowed this approach to be widely accepted, but its resulting complexity produces implementation and cost challenges.

3.1 Concept

The basic idea is that, in order to control network services to each communicating pair in a distributed physical network, communication paths are virtualized and controlled locally at switches. For each communicating pair, a separate virtual circuit is established before actual communication for which network resources (buffer, link bandwidth, etc) are reserved depending on required communication QoS. Each local switch schedules arriving packets to allocate reserved resources, which eventually guarantees required QoS to end-to-end communication pairs.

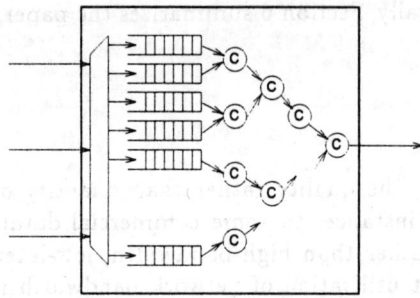

Fig. 1. A switch model for virtual circuit-based QoS control.

Figure 1 illustrates the basic structure of a switch for virtual circuit approach. In order to decouple traffic for different communications and service packets in other than their arrival orders, separate queues are provided one for each virtual circuit and they are scheduled based on service requirement such as reserved bandwidth or required delay bounds.

While sharing this basic structure, suggested algorithms vary significantly depending on the detailed queueing and scheduling mechanisms.

3.2 Examples

A well-known example of the virtual circuit approach is *Virtual Clock* (VC) [21]. Each virtual circuit keeps a *virtual clock* value which, for each packet arrival, increases by the expected inter-arrival time (the inverse of bandwidth reserved for the virtual circuit). By giving higher priority to the packet with a lower virtual clock value, VC guarantees the reserved bandwidth to each virtual circuit, independent of packets' arrival order.

Several algorithms share the basic idea with VC, including *Fair Queueing* [5] and *Packet-by-Packet General Processor Sharing* (PGPS) [15]. Also, many researchers presented more practical algorithms which reduce implementation complexity by approximating QoS, for instance, SCFQ [7, 16] and FFQ [19].

With network efficiency sacrificed, network QoS can be achieved at a much lower complexity. *Stop-and-Go* (SG) [8] is a well-known example of such simple, *non-work-conserving* service disciplines. During each frame interval, the source for each virtual circuit is strictly limited to inject at most as many packets as reserved packet slots and each switch transmits *all* and *only* packets which have arrived during the last frame time. This strict regulation of traffic flow rate dramatically reduces switch complexity by removing the needs for queueing and scheduling logic at the switch completely. Unfortunately, this approach wastes precious network bandwidth, so can support limited applications (e.g., pure CBR traffic) only.

Recently, the authors presented a compromising approach, called Rotating Combined Queueing (RCQ) [11, 10]. RCQ is also work-conserving but requires only a small number of queues independent of the number of supported virtual circuits and also reduces scheduling complexity using a larger control granularity (frames). Compared to other work-conserving virtual circuit algorithms, RCQ provides similar QoS to end users for most multimedia applications. More detailed surveys on virtual circuit-based algorithms can be found in [20, 10].

3.3 QoS Performance

Many existing networks and most networks in the near future need to support a wide range of applications which will require different traffic characteristics and communication services. In this section, we present a simulation result which typically shows how network QoS can be affected by different scheduling mechanisms.

Several 4x4 mesh networks with different scheduling mechanisms are simulated under an integrated traffic load in which nearly equal amounts of network load from each traffic type (CBR, VBR and ABR) are intermixed. Each message consists of 35 packets (32 bytes/packet). The source-destination pair of each connection (virtual circuit) is randomly selected. The worst-case message delays of CBR traffic are measured to observe the impacts of other traffic types on the QoS given to this simple traffic type.[3]

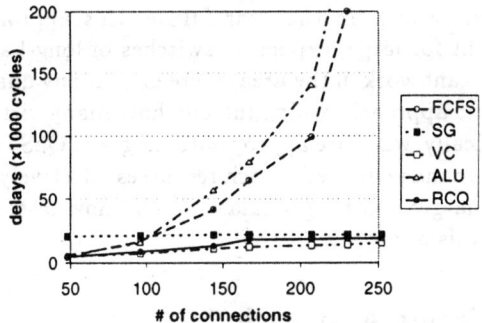

Fig. 2. Observed worst-case message delays of CBR traffic under intermixed traffic loads for different scheduling algorithms: First-Come-First-Serve (FCFS), Stop-and-Go (SG), Virtual Clock (VC), ALU-biasing (ALU), and Rotating Combined Queueing (RCQ).

Figure 2 compares the worst-case message delays of CBR traffic. We first observe that FCFS and ALU networks (this scheduling algorithm is discussed

---

[3] More general interactions of different traffic types for a range of scheduling algorithms are presented in [10].

in Section 4) provide significantly larger delay bounds than others, increasing in proportion to load rates. In these networks, CBR packets can be blocked by packets from bursty traffic coupled via shared physical links and buffers. So, these relatively simple algorithms have limitations in providing guaranteed services to the CBR traffic in integrated-service networks. In contrast, the VC and RCQ networks provide much smaller worst-case delays bounded by those of the SG network, showing that they can guarantee service qualities to CBR traffic regardless of the existence of other traffic types.

3.4 Perspective

Since end-to-end virtual circuits are treated as the basic scheduling unit, this approach provides flexible quality of services to end users. Each traffic stream can reserve network resources for its own required network service independent of other traffic streams, and can actually receive the reserved resources unless network resources are over-booked.

However, this approach requires large buffer pools and complex scheduling mechanism.[4] The complexity of virtual circuit-based switches increases linearly with the number of supported virtual circuits. For a large number of virtual circuits, these schemes are infeasible due to high implementation costs and large run-time overheads. While many algorithms have been suggested for simpler implementations, it is still difficult to implement this approach in low-cost switches. Until more improved, lower-complexity (in terms of cost, speed, and size) algorithms replace existing ones in the near future, this approach is expected to remain as the best fit for large, expensive switches of long-haul networks.

In spite of significant work in the area, there exist many unanswered questions on the virtual circuit approach, which include how many virtual circuits should be supported practically, what are appropriate ranges of QoS to be supported in a switch, how can we manage limited switch resources effectively (packet dropping, circuit merging, or larger control granularity), and how fast and cheap switches can we build from this approach.

4 Physical Circuit Approach

While the virtual circuit approach provides QoS to long-haul networks, QoS requirements are not unique to long-haul networks. As the market of multi-computer architectures (clusters) expands to support commercial applications including audio/video data serving and management, the needs for more flexible network resource control increase for short-haul, multicomputer networks (system-area networks) as well. These networks assume short links (a few 10's of meters), homogeneous networks, and irregular topologies. Because local-area bandwidth is mostly limited by router and link speeds, simplicity in design can be traded against efficient link management.

---

[4] Simple, non-working-conserving mechanisms are not considered because they have limited applications.

Recently, Tandem introduced the ServerNet routers [9], which implement a novel architecture for network-resource control called *ALU-biasing arbitration*. While sharing the basic architecture with most existing multicomputer networks (wormhole-routed and packet switching), ServerNet uses a unique arbitration, qualitatively different from round-robin or FCFS of most existing quantity-oriented networks.

4.1 ALU-Biasing Arbitration

The basic idea of ALU-biasing arbitration is that, by simply allocating different amounts of output link bandwidth to different input links at routers, we can control accumulated bandwidth between communicating end nodes.

In the ServerNet routers, output-link bandwidth is distributed to different input links by the following algorithm:

ALU-Biasing Arbitration

Preliminaries:
1. Input port i is given:
2. $\quad I_i$: Increment value (the larger, the more bandwidth reserved).
3. $\quad C_i$: Counter (initially zero).
4. $\quad S$: Sum of all increment values of input ports contending for the same output link.
5. $\quad S_i = S - I_i$.

Arbitration Algorithm:
1. When multiple input ports are contending for an idle output link, repeat 2-5.
2. $\quad$ Winner input port = input port with the largest C_i.
3. $\quad$ If won, $C_i = C_i - S_i$.
4. $\quad$ If lost, $C_i = C_i + I_i$.
5. $\quad$ If idle, $C_i = C_i$.

The bandwidth allocated to each input link is proportional to its increment value. More specifically, the reserved bandwidth is *at least* equal to its increment value divided by the sum of the increment values of all input ports. The bandwidth allocated to a source-destination path is determined by multiplying bandwidth fractions allocated to input links along the path.

Note that in this case, there is no end-to-end virtual circuit concept at the router. Since the scheduling complexity is determined by the number of input ports (physical links) of a router, this approach permits much simpler implementation of network resource control for QoS.

4.2 Benefits

Bandwidth guarantee of ALU-biased networks is provable. Its analysis and simulation study results on bandwidth guarantee are not provided here due to space limitation, but can be found in [10]. Instead, this section discusses additional benefits of such a low-complexity scheduling mechanism, focusing benefits for traditional multicomputer applications.

Uniform resource utilization and fairness ALU biasing arbitration can be used to allocate network resources uniformly to each node, which not only improves the overall system performance, but also enhances network quality by providing fair services to end nodes regardless of network topologies.

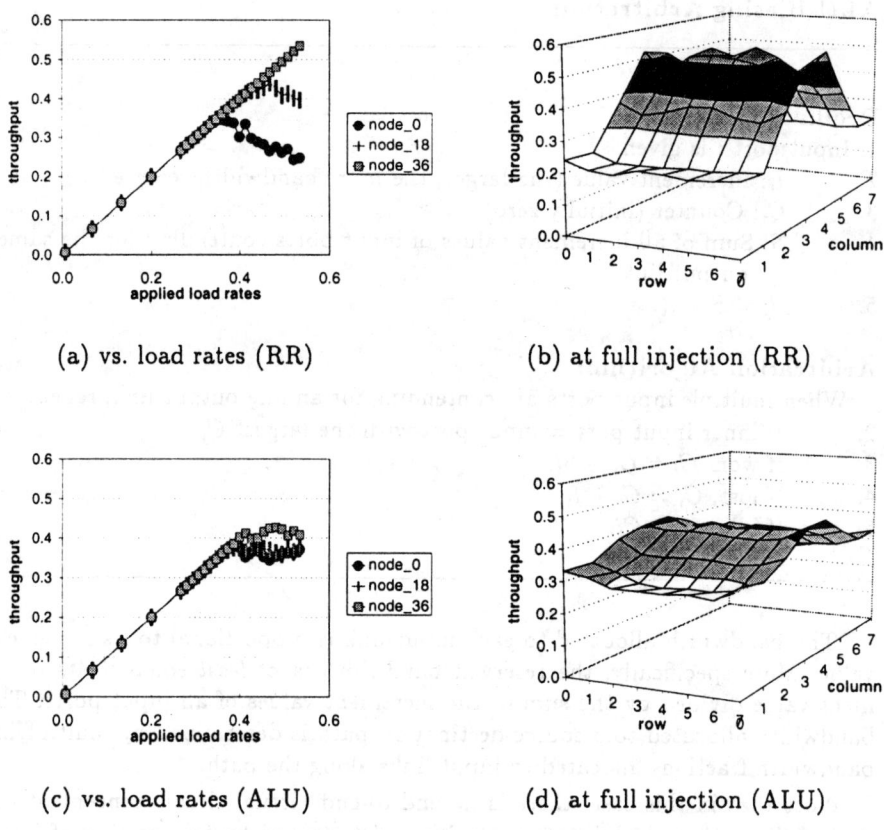

Fig. 3. Node throughput in 8x8 mesh networks with round-robin (RR) and ALU-biased (ALU) arbitration mechanisms.

Figure 3 shows simulation results which compare throughput distribution of round-robin networks ((a) and (b) in the figure) to ALU-biased networks ((c) and (d) in the figure). Under uniform traffic where destination is randomly selected for each packet, throughput is measured separately for each source node in 8x8 mesh networks. Applied load rates are normalized with respect to the full injection rate (i.e., link capacity) and varied from 0 (idle) to 1 (full injection). The ALU-biased routers are programmed to distribute (reserve) network bandwidth equally to all possible source-destination pairs. In this way, each router is programmed to allocate more bandwidth to input ports with more expected traffic amounts.

In Figure 3(a), we first observe in round-robin networks how each node throughput changes depending on its location. Node throughput is shown for three different nodes: node 0 (the corner), node 36 (the center), and node 18 (halfway between the corner and center). The figure shows that node 0 obtains much less peak-throughput than nodes in the center. Moreover, as network loads increase, its throughput drops because nodes in the center take more fractions of available link bandwidth.

Figure 3(b) shows the throughput of all source nodes when the applied load rate is increased to the full injection rate (load rate = 1.0). We observe that the center nodes' throughput is more than twice that of edge nodes (the ratio of the maximum to minimum is 2.61). This is because mesh networks are asymmetric, so link utilization is inherently unbalanced; links in the center are utilized more than links at the edge, forming a bottleneck. The round-robin scheduling simply gives more bandwidth of these highly utilized links to nodes in the center, saturating nodes at the edge at much lower load rates.

In contrast to round-robin networks, ALU-biased networks provide each node similar and stable throughput (see Figures 3(c)). At the full injection rate, the ratio of the maximum node throughput to the minimum is only 1.62, reducing an imbalance to 1.6 times smaller than that in the RR network (see Figures 3(d)). The ALU-biased router allocates much more bandwidth of the center links to passing traffic than injection traffic, because bandwidth is reserved for each input link based on the anticipated amount of its through traffic. Consequently, each source node shares the center links (bottlenecks) uniformly, thus giving much more balanced throughput.

Network efficiency The scheduling policy in the router also has an influence on the overall network efficiency because each traffic flow in the network has different impacts on other traffic.

Figure 4 shows measured average link utilization under uniform random traffic loads in mesh networks when each node injects messages at the maximum rate. In the figure, we first observe that link utilization of round-robin networks drops as the mesh network size increases. For instance, 32x32 round-robin mesh networks provide about 30% less link utilization than 4x4. This is because center links are congested with packets crossing the bisection, whose bandwidth share decreases exponentially with mesh scales, so they block other packets longer.

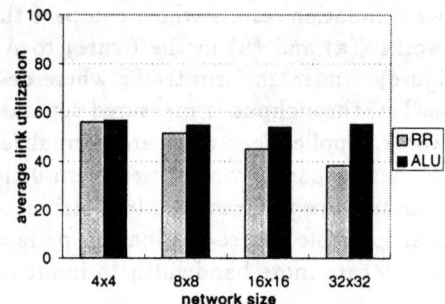

Fig. 4. Average link utilization in round-robin (RR) and ALU-biased (ALU) mesh networks.

In contrast, ALU networks provide nearly constant link utilization independent of the mesh size. This is because ALU can allocate more bandwidth to the input links which have more impact on the overall link utilization, that is, which more links are dependent on. Consequently, ALU biasing improves network efficiency about 50% better than round-robin arbitration for 32x32 mesh networks.

4.3 Perspective

Compared to the virtual circuit approach developed for long-haul networks, the physical circuit approach dramatically reduces control complexity and implementation costs for queueing and scheduling at switches, making the concept feasible in low-cost, high-performance networks. While providing additional communication services, this simple approach allows the routers to provide raw performance comparable to other multicomputer routers. Also, it is simple enough to be feasible in a single ASIC chip router. Hence, it could be adopted in many networks as a practical compromise of flexibility requirements and low-cost router implementation.

In addition to uniform resource utilization and improved efficiency that we observed above, physical circuit-based network resource control provides many additional benefits over simple arbitration of existing multicomputers such as:

- Different amounts of bandwidth can be reserved and guaranteed for different communication paths. This can be used to support new applications with bandwidth guarantee requirements or support irregular topologies efficiently.
- With routing control, this approach can also provide latency guarantee, which can be used to reduce communication protocol overheads or reduce variance in communication delays which can improve parallel applications performance.

However, compared to the virtual circuit approach, this low-cost approach has limitations in providing QoS. Because multiple communication streams are merged at a physical link and they are not virtualized, this approach causes coupling between communications sharing paths. Consequently, it is not so simple as in the virtual circuit approach to manage network resources and guarantee required bandwidth and delay bounds. Either QoS given to a communication path depends on other traffic streams to some extents or an excessive amount of bandwidth is required to compensate the coupling effect. This coupling effect makes fine-grain traffic control difficult, especially in large-scale networks [10].

The physical circuit approach is a novel concept, which opens many interesting research issues such as how can we eliminate coupling effects with routing or rate control in order to fully exploit the benefits of the router controllability, how can we apply or improve this simple approach to provide tight delay bounds, what are the optimal topologies and scales for the approach, and what are appropriate switch architectures (the number of ports, resource coordination of outputs, etc) to support this approach.

5 Global Scheduling

While virtual and physical circuits approaches augment the network switches additional mechanisms for scheduling or prioritization, the global scheduling approach depends on external coordination to achieve predictable high performance. This approach exploits the observation that cluster networks are typically uniform and closed – with well-defined sources and sinks for traffic. Thus, coordination amongst those sources is possible to manage resource conflicts. In fact because the number of nodes is typically moderate (tens to hundreds, rather than millions), route-based coordination is possible. Further, because cluster networks generally have limited physical extent (tens of meters versus 1000's of kilometers for WANs), time-based coordination is also possible. For global-scheduling approaches, the high level implementation architecture is as shown below.

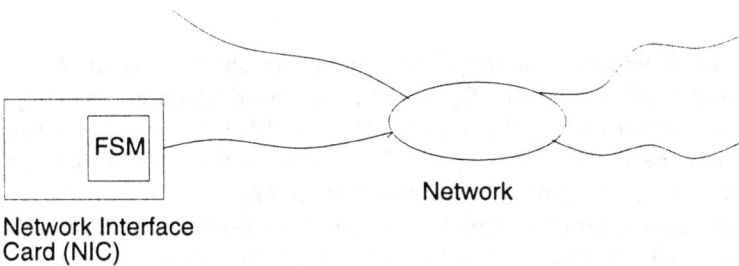

Fig. 5. Each NIC includes a finite-state machine which implements the traffic schedule. They may also support negotiation for resources amongst NIC's.

In Figure 5, traditional NIC's are augmented with special hardware which enforces routing or timing of packets injected into the network. The special hardware in one NIC may negotiate with that on other NICs explicitly or implicitly to acquire and use network resources.

5.1 Route-Based

Route-based approaches to global scheduling use the mapping of logical connections onto physical resources to control network performance [17, 9]. While this is conceptually similar to virtual circuits, route-based global scheduling differs in that physical network links are not virtualized by the switches. Rather, the sharing is controlled by selecting routes at the network interface. Thus, this approach has significant limitations, and it is most effective in richly connected networks with relatively sparse actual communication patterns.

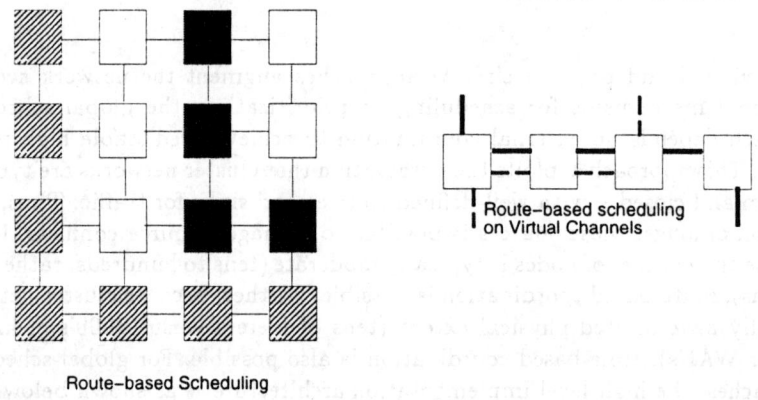

Fig. 6. Route-based scheduling can be used to control the interference between connections. Here it is illustrated for a mesh network.

Figure 6 depicts route-based scheduling on a mesh network, and on a network section with virtual channels. By choosing independent paths, the coupling between two connections can be reduced. Note that if there is another connection which cross the paths of both flows, it may cause them to be coupled. Thus, global scheduling is required to achieve decoupling.

Route-based scheduling can be combined with enhanced local arbitration techniques such as ALU-biasing to improve the guarantees achievable. For example, when large numbers of connections are "trunked" onto a shared path, the ALU biases can be set appropriately to ensure a large share of the network resources for those connections. This idea is similar to that described in Section 4.2.

5.2 Time Based

Time-based approaches to global scheduling map the logical connections onto physical resources, controlling resource sharing conflicts with temporal alignment. Essentially, the idea is to use time-division multiplexing of a physical link to create logical resources which can then be scheduled for logical connections without network conflicts. Time-based approaches require a network-level tight synchronization mechanism. Note that this multiplexing again differs from virtual circuits because in time-based approaches, the scheduling is done cooperatively by the network endpoints, not independently by individual switches. Further, the virtualization is created with respect to the network's global time base, so network switch complexity is not increased.

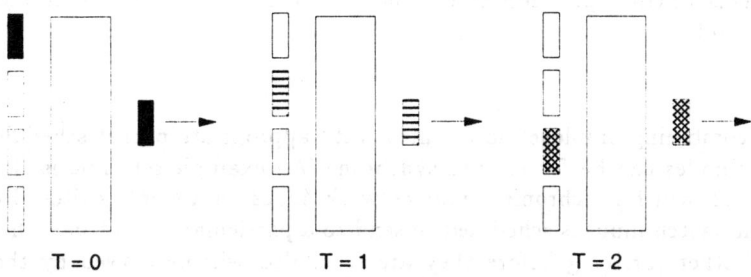

Fig. 7. Time-based scheduling can be used to control the interference between connections. Here it is illustrated for a single switch in a network.

Time-based global scheduling requires both a mechanism to derive a network time base and a management system for scheduling resources based on the network virtualization possible with that time base. Hardware clocks, software-based clock synchronization, and network feedback are all possible techniques for deriving a global time base. We describe an approach based on network feedback called *self-synchronizing schedules* in the following section.

With a network time base, the network's physical resources can be virtualized via time-division multiplexing, and those virtual resources are managed to avoid network resource contention. An important point here is that if the network has some link-level flow control, the network time synchronization can have significant skew. For example, in the FM-QoS scheme described below, the clock synchronization required is within a packet transmission time, potentially a few to tens of microseconds.

Example: FM-QoS We are building a time-based global scheduling system which delivers communication quality of service for cluster networks, called FM-QoS. This system builds on the API for low-overhead cluster communication called Fast Messages (FM) [14], but exploits novel low-level mechanisms to provide network synchronization. To provide network synchronization, FM-QoS uses a mechanism called feedback-based synchronization (FBS), which exploits link-level flow control to determine whether the local clock is too fast.

	Node A	Node B	Node C	Node D
Time = 1	A→A	B→B	C→C	D→D
Time = 2	A→B	B→C	C→D	D→A
Time = 3	A→C	B→D	C→A	D→B
Time = 4	A→D	B→A	C→B	D→C

Fig. 8. A 4-node cyclic schedule with equal bandwidth for all source-destination pairs. This schedule produces tight synchronization in a network with link-level flow control.

By combining link-level flow control with appropriate packet schedules, the network nodes can be forced into synchrony. An example schedule is shown in Figure 5.2, which synchronizes four network nodes on a single switch. Because only one switch input is scheduled to send to a particular output in each packet period, others arriving before they are scheduled will be slowed by the link-level flow control. This feedback can be used to adjust synchronization across nodes, allowing a time division multiplexing approach to sharing the network without contention. The example shown, if repeated can tightly synchronize four contending network inputs; however, if that were the only schedule ever executed, network bandwidth allocations would be restricted to fair. However, the key insight is that self-synchronizing schedules need only be run periodically to maintain tight synchronization. The remaining time can be scheduled flexibly (ensuring no output contention), enabling flexible use of most of the network capacity.

To demonstrate the viability of this approach, we are building a prototype[5] which works in the context of Myrinet [1]. This prototype has already demonstrated self-synchronization at the granularity of two kilobyte packets and can preserve this synchronization at a traffic overhead of less than 1%. More specifically, delivery can be guaranteed with a latency of approximately 20 microseconds, application to application. For more information on this approach see [2].

5.3 Perspective

Compared to both virtual circuit and physical circuit approaches, global scheduling reduces the hardware requirements for network switches. Simplicity may enable faster or cheaper switches, and further requiring no additional hardware

---
[5] The prototype for FM-QoS is being built by Kay Connelly and Andrew Chien

may make backward compatibility possible (e.g. providing QoS on switches not designed for it). The complexity of quality of service is reflected to the network interface cards, requiring a finite-state machine to implement the network schedule, and perhaps hardware support for connection negotiation (though handling this negotiation at the host processor level is also possible).

Because global scheduling is new, numerous open questions exist about its practicality, scalability, and performance. Our FM-QoS prototype is addressing questions of practicality for time-based coordination and has demonstrated that global scheduling systems can be built, deliver quality of service with low overhead, and deliver high performance. Scalability questions focus on larger switches, cascaded switches, increased buffer depth, and higher clock rates. These remain interesting open research questions. Finally, the primary questions of performance focus around deliverable quality of service via global scheduling approaches. This too is a rich space for inquiry.

6 Summary

The fundamental issue in delivering quality of service in network communication is resource management. Choices here affect the cost and capabilities of each approach. In this paper, we have discussed three approaches: virtual circuits, physical circuits, and global scheduling. Virtual circuits admits the most flexible application of switches, but also requires the most complex switch hardware. Physical circuits reduce switch cost, but fail to deliver precise guarantees for large numbers of connections. Finally, global scheduling moves the complexity from the switches out to the network interfaces, allowing fast, simple switches. However, questions about the cost of synchronization and scheduling in the network interfaces have yet to be answered.

Acknowledgements

The research described in this paper was supported in part by DARPA Order #E313 through the US Air Force Rome Laboratory Contract F30602-96-1-0286, ARPA Order #E524/00 through the US Air Force Contract F30602-97-2-0121, NSF grants MIP-92-23732, and NASA grant NAG 1-613. Support from Intel Corporation, Tandem Computers, Hewlett-Packard, Microsoft and Motorola is also gratefully acknowledged. Andrew Chien is supported in part by NSF Young Investigator Award CCR-94-57809. FM-QoS is part of joint research with Kay Connelly.

References

1. Nanette J. Boden, Danny Cohen, Robert E. Felderman, Alan E. Kulawik, Charles L. Seitz, Jakov N. Seizovic, and Wen-King Su. Myrinet—a gigabit-per-second local-area network. *IEEE Micro*, 15(1):29–36, February 1995. Available from http://www.myri.com/research/publications/Hot.ps.

2. Kay Connelly and Andrew Chien. FM-QoS: Real-time communication using self-synchronizing schedules. In *Proceedings of Supercomputing Conference*, San Jose, CA, November 1997.
3. W. Dally and C. Seitz. Deadlock-free message routing in multiprocessor interconnection networks. *IEEE Transactions on Computers*, C-36(5):547–53, May 1987.
4. W. J. Dally. Virtual channel flow control. *IEEE Transactions on Parallel and Distributed Systems*, 3(2):194–205, 1992.
5. A. Demers, S. Keshav, and S. Shenker. Analysis and simulations of a fair queueing algorithm. In *Proceedings of ACM SIGCOMM*, pages 3–12, Austin, TX, 1989.
6. T. Feng. A survey of interconnection networks. *IEEE Transactions on Computers*, C-14(12):12–27, Dec. 1981.
7. S. Golestani. A self-clocked fair queueing scheme for broadband applications. In *Proceedings of IEEE INFOCOM*, pages 636–646, Toronto, Canada, 1994.
8. S. J. Golestani. Congestion-free communication in high-speed packet networks. *IEEE Transactions on Communications*, 39(12):1802–1812, Dec. 1991.
9. R. Horst. TNet: A reliable system area network. *IEEE Micro*, pages 37–45, February 1995.
10. J. H. Kim. *Bandwidth and Latency Guarantees in Low-cost, High Performance Networks*. PhD thesis, University of Illinois at Urbana-Champaign, Urbana, Illinois, January 1997.
11. J. H. Kim and A. A. Chien. Rotating combined queueing (RCQ): Bandwidth and latency guarantees in low-cost, high-performance networks. In *Proceedings of the International Symposium on Computer Architecture*, pages 226–236, Philadelphia, PA, 1996.
12. R. Mraz. Reducing the variance of point-to-point transfers for parallel real-time programs. *IEEE Parallel & Distributed Technology*, pages 20–31, Winter 1994.
13. J. Ngai and C. Seitz. A framework for adaptive routing in multicomputer networks. In *Proceedings of the 1989 ACM Symposium on Parallel Algorithms and Architectures*, pages 1–9, Santa Fe, NM, 1989.
14. S. Pakin, M. Lauria, and A. Chien. High performance messaging on workstations: Illinois Fast Messages (FM) for Myrinet. In *Proceedings of Supercomputing*, San Diego, CA, Dec. 1995. Available from http://www-csag.cs.uiuc.edu/papers/myrinet-fm-sc95.ps.
15. A. Parekh and R. Gallager. A generalized processor sharing approach to flow control in integrated services networks – the single node case. In *Proceedings of IEEE INFOCOM*, pages 915–924, Florence, Italy, 1992.
16. J. Rexford, A. Greenberg, and F. Bonomi. Hardware-efficient fair queueing architectures for high-speed networks. In *Proceedings of IEEE INFOCOM*, San Francisco, CA, 1996.
17. S. Scott and G. Thorson. Optimized routing in the Cray T3D. In *Proceedings of the Parallel Computer Routing and Communication Workshop*, pages 281–294, Seattle, Washington, 1994. Springer-Verlag Lecture Notes in Computer Science No. 853.
18. C. Seitz. Myrinet – a gigabit-per-second local-area network. In *Proceedings of the IEEE Hot Interconnects Symposium*, Palo Alto, CA, 1994.
19. D. Stiliadis and A. Varma. Design and analysis of frame-based queueing: A new traffic scheduling algorithm for packet-switched networks. In *Proceedings of SIGMETRICS*, pages 104–115, Philadelphia, PA, 1996.
20. H. Zhang. Service disciplines for guaranteed performance service in packet-switching networks. *Proceedings of the IEEE*, 83(10), Oct. 1995.

21. L. Zhang. Virtual clock: A new traffic control algorithm for packet switching networks. In *Proceedings of ACM SIGCOMM*, pages 19–29, Philadelphia, PA, 1990.

Biographical Information

Andrew A. Chien is currently an Associate Professor in the Department of Computer Science at the University of Illinois at Urbana-Champaign, where he holds a joint appointment as an Associate Professor in the Department of Electrical and Computer Engineering and as a Senior Research Scientist with the National Center for Supercomputing Applications (NCSA). Andrew received his B.S. in Electrical Engineering from the Massachusetts Institute of Technology in 1984 and his M.S. and Ph.D., in Computer Science, from the Massachusetts Institute of Technology in 1987 and 1990, respectively. He is the recipient of a 1994 National Science Foundation Young Investigator Award, the C. W. Gear Outstanding Junior Faculty Award (1995), and the Xerox Senior Faculty Award for Outstanding Research (1996).

Jae H. Kim is a computer architect in the Scalable Server Division at HAL Computer Systems, Inc. where he is involved in developing the next-generation Mercury interconnects. He received the B.S degree in Electrical Engineering in 1990 from the University of Maryland at College Park and the M.S. and Ph.D. degrees in Electrical and Computer Engineering from the University of Illinois at Urbana-Champaign in 1993 and 1997, respectively.

Session I

ROUTING I

Thursday, June 26, 1997
10:00 - 11:30

Session Chair:

R. Boppana
University of Texas at San Antonio

Integrated Multi-class Routing

Melanie L. Fulgham and Lawrence Snyder

Department of Computer Science and Engineering, Box 352350
University of Washington, Seattle, WA 98195-2350 USA

Abstract. In this paper we describe a class of routing algorithms called multi-class algorithms. Multi-class algorithms support multiple classes of routing simultaneously, thereby allowing different applications, and even different messages, to select the most advantageous kind of routing. For example some applications prefer the smaller latency variance of oblivious routing, while others prefer the higher throughputs achieved by adaptive routing. Typical systems provide a single class routing algorithm, but applications benefit from the flexibility of multiple classes.
Integrated multi-class routers have two characteristics. First, they provide an integrated algorithm where routing classes share resources such as buffers. Each class is not an independent routing algorithm on an independent network, but rather to reduce costs, each class is implemented by a single algorithm on a shared network. Second, multi-class routers help increase performance by providing routing flexibility and network services which help simplify the network interface or system software.
The idea of multi-class routing is perhaps obvious and it has appeared before. Our contribution, however, lies in defining multi-class routers, describing their advantages, providing an appropriate method for evaluating such routers, and by demonstrating their usefulness though examples.

1 Introduction

Communication performance continues to be a critical factor in application performance. Communication time is composed of three components: the software overhead to send and receive messages, the time in the network interface to move messages between the processor and the network, and the latency in the interconnection network. In recent years, message overhead and network interface times [25, 6, 2, 22, 3] have improved substantially, transforming network latencies to a majority component of the total communication time [5]. This has focused attention on network issues such as routing and flow control which have substantial impact on the throughput and latency achieved by a network. Furthermore, as the demand for end-to-end services such as in-order delivery and quality of service increase, more attention is directed toward the router to provide services that otherwise would be implemented in the network interface or software.

This work was supported in part by the National Science Foundation Grant MIP-9213469 and by an ARPA Graduate Research Fellowship.

We present and describe multi-class routing. A multi-class router has two functions. First it should provide several classes of routing. This is useful since no single class of routing is suitable for all applications. Second, multi-class routers should simplify the network interface or system software by providing services with the routing that might otherwise be implemented in these layers. Nevertheless, nearly all known routers support a single class of routing, and few provide services such as in-order delivery required by many applications.

2 Motivation

Oblivious routing continues to be the routing algorithm of choice. Oblivious routers are simple and provide in-order delivery of messages, which is helpful for supporting efficient synchronization, checkpointing, memory consistency, and determinism in parallel computations. Since oblivious routers have no adaptivity, they perform poorly in congested networks and fail when faults are present in the network.

Minimal adaptive routers are more complex than oblivious designs, but can achieve higher throughputs, even with small amounts of congestion. Minimal adaptive algorithms provide some fault-tolerance, though they rarely provide in-order delivery since the flexibility in route selection allows messages to pass one another. Minimal adaptive algorithms often suffer from severe throughput degradation in heavy congestion.

Non-minimal algorithms can provide the highest throughputs because they tolerate large bursts of traffic and heavy congestion. Like minimal adaptive routers, delivery is rarely in-order. Non-minimal routers are also fault-tolerant, but are more complex due to livelock protection requirements. In cases of extreme congestion, non-minimal routers occasionally experience large increases in latency due to the overuse of non-minimal routes.

There are performance-complexity trade-offs to consider when selecting a class of routing. If performance of the simplest oblivious algorithm is sufficient then the choice is easy. Otherwise, an adaptive routing algorithm is preferable. The price of adaptivity is increased complexity and out-of-order delivery. In-order delivery, however, is necessary to support efficient synchronization [26], checkpointing [19], memory consistency [18] (e.g. via cache coherency algorithms or barriers), and determinism in parallel computations. Furthermore, providing in-order delivery for adaptive algorithms requires special hardware to avoid the substantial latency costs of a software solution. Although a few such network interface designs have been demonstrated [3, 22], there is reluctance to provide such a complex solution.

Multi-class routing provides an alternative method to provide the benefits of adaptive routing and is beginning to gain acceptance, as evidenced by the routing algorithms in the Cray T3E [24] and the lastest IBM SP2 routers [1]. Furthermore, since no router supports the needs of all applications, applications would benefit from a router that supports several kinds of routing simultaneously.

Applications also benefit if services like in-order delivery are provided by routers. At present, almost all routers provide a single kind of routing.

3 Overview

An integrated multi-class router is not simply a combination of several routers, but rather is an integrated router that shares resources to provide multiple kinds of routing. Multi-class algorithms should also simplify the network interface or system software by providing services in the router. This can simplify the network interface and reduce latencies for services that would otherwise be provided in the network interface or system software. Although the idea of a multi-class routing algorithm is perhaps obvious, and several routers have some of these features, the advantages of multi-class routing have not been promoted and multi-class performance has been ignored. Thus, our contribution lies in defining this notion, describing the methodology to evaluate such routers, demonstrating their usefulness, and by presenting a few examples of multi-class routing algorithms. Although we consider point-to-point networks in a parallel (multi)computer context, the idea of multi-class routing is applicable to other types of networks as well.

The remainder of the paper is organized as follows. Section 4 describes multi-class routers in more detail. Section 5 describes the methodology to evaluate multi-class routers, and Section 6 presents an example system that benefits from multi-class routing. Related work is found in Section 7, and conclusions are in Section 8.

4 Multi-class Routing

A multi-class router is a router designed specifically to provide routing for several classes of traffic, where each class of traffic requests distinct algorithmic constraints. Furthermore, different classes may reside in the network at the same time.

The key to an integrated multi-class router is the unification of the classes or modes of traffic it provides. Each routing class shares resources, such as buffers, with other classes thus reducing the cost and complexity of multiple classes. Although classes share resources, different classes of messages can exist in the network simultaneously. The typical method to distinguish messages of different classes only requires adding a few bits to the message header.

For example, consider the multi-class Triplex algorithm [11]. It provides three classes of routing: oblivious Triplex, minimal adaptive Triplex, and non-minimal adaptive Triplex. In-order delivery is provided by the oblivious class, which is considered the most restrictive class of the three. By providing support for an oblivious class, Triplex is an adaptive router that does not require a special network interface to re-order messages. Examples of other multi-class routers can be found in Section 7.

5 Evaluation

Evaluating a multi-class routing algorithm is difficult because its advantages include both quantifiable properties such as improved throughput, as well as more qualitative properties such as in-order delivery. Obviously, a multi-class router's single class performance cannot exceed the best known single class router; otherwise, a faster router for the class would have been discovered[1]. The goal, however, is to be competitive for a combination of all the traffic classes. Conversely, if the ability to select routing classes significantly degrades performance from single class routing, then perhaps the versatility is not worth the price.

5.1 Single Class Performance

One figure of merit we use is the amount by which a multi-class router's performance departs from the best router for each class. This is a rather stringent criterion, unless a single class router provides sufficient performance or a single class of traffic is expected at any given time. Nevertheless, this comparison gives an indication of the quantitative costs of multi-class routing by estimating the performance range of the router.

For example consider the multi-class Triplex algorithm. For single class evaluation, Triplex is compared with competitive algorithms in the oblivious and minimal adaptive modes, using the Dally-Seitz oblivious dimension-order algorithm [7] and the Duato minimal fully adaptive algorithm [8, 13]. A corresponding non-minimal deadlock-avoidance algorithm does not exist. See Figure 1 for the throughput and latency of these algorithms under the bit reversal traffic pattern.

The graph shows that the maximum difference between the oblivious and oblivious Triplex algorithms is .7 percent of the normalized throughput, a 5 percent throughput degradation. For Duato and minimal Triplex, Triplex meets or slightly exceeds the throughput of Duato. So, by examining single mode routing, the performance range of the multi-class router can be described for this traffic pattern. When all the traffic requires in-order delivery, there is a small throughput penalty, and when traffic is only fully adaptive, there is a small potential benefit for increased throughput. A similar analysis can be done on the latencies. In this case, the maximum difference in oblivious latencies is 70 cycles, a 14% latency increase for oblivious Triplex[2]. But with adaptive routing, Triplex experiences equivalent or lower latency than Duato. Specific details and additional traffic patterns can be found in [11].

5.2 Estimates of Mixed Traffic Performance

This is not the complete picture though. A more complete evaluation considers the performance of mixed classes of traffic, i.e. when several classes of messages

---
[1] This may occur, however, when comparing a new multi-class router with an existing single class router.
[2] Triplex is charged an extra cycle for node latency.

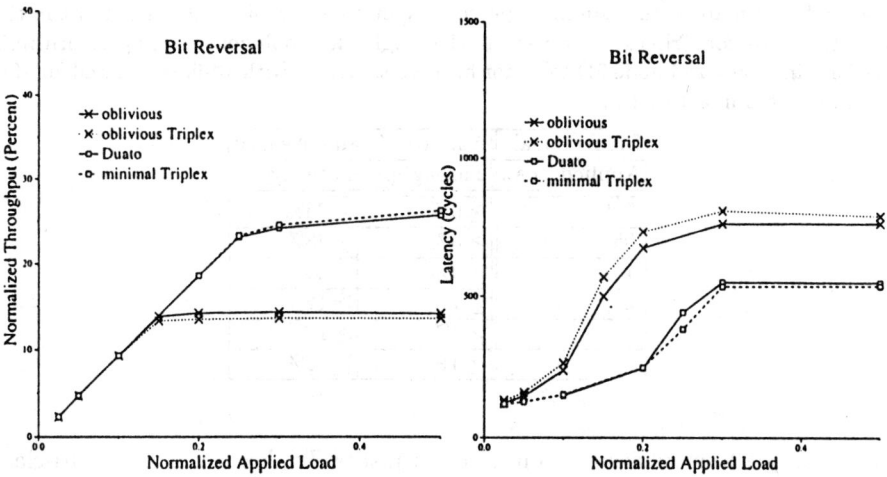

Fig. 1. Wormhole throughput and latency on a 256-node 2D torus with 40-flit and 400-flit messages in a 10:1 ratio.

reside in the network simultaneously. Even if several classes of traffic can be used by the application, a single class router would need to provide the most restrictive kind of routing required. Therefore with mixed class traffic, the multi-class routing algorithm is compared with the most restrictive single class routing algorithm necessary.

Because the performance space is so large, the first approach is to estimate mixed class performance. Mixed traffic performance can be estimated by computing the average of the single class performance results of the multi-class routing algorithm. The average is simply weighted to reflect the traffic mix of interest. With the mixed class traffic performance estimates, it is then possible to compute an estimate of the range of traffic mixes for which the multi-class routing algorithm maintains its advantage over the most restrictive single class routing algorithm.

Continuing with the example, Table 1 shows the estimate of the traffic mix, presented as the minimum percentage of adaptive traffic needed for which Triplex is the same or better than the oblivious routing algorithm's throughput and latency. In this case, estimates indicate multi-class Triplex matches or exceeds the throughput of the oblivious router for mixed workloads, provided that at least 14% of the traffic is adaptive. For all but the smallest loads, the latency estimates show that Triplex has the same or better (lower) latency than the oblivious router for mixed workloads when at least 24% of the traffic is adaptive. Thus, despite the throughput and latency degradation of oblivious Triplex, Triplex is still able to maintain an advantage for a large range of traffic loads and mixes. We give

Table 1. Estimate of the minimum percentage of mixed traffic that needs to be in the adaptive class for Triplex to win or tie the single class oblivious routing algorithm's performance on a 256-node 2D torus for bit reversal traffic with 40-flit short and 400-flit long messages in a 10:1 ratio.

Bit Reversal	Adaptive Traffic Needed	
Applied Load	Throughput	Latency
.025	$\geq 0\%$	$\geq 73\%$
.05	$\geq 0\%$	$\geq 38\%$
.1	$\geq 0\%$	$\geq 24\%$
.2	$\geq 14\%$	$\geq 12\%$
.3	$\geq 6\%$	$\geq 17\%$
.5	$\geq 4\%$	$\geq 10\%$

this example to emphasize a point, not to justify Triplex. Even if a multi-class router pays a rather significant penalty for its flexibility, it is quite possible that it will still maintain its advantage for a large range of traffic conditions. Nevertheless, even if this range is small, as long as it matches the expected traffic, the multi-class router may be advantageous.

5.3 Mixed Traffic Performance

Experiments with mixed traffic can also be simulated. This gives a more accurate representation of performance, since each class of traffic actually shares router resources while the estimates do not assume this. Such experiments allow comparisons of the performance of the most restrictive single class router with the performance of the multi-class router under mixed loads. Although it may be tedious to determine the range of loads and traffic mixes for which the multi-class router is superior to using only the most restrictive single class router, representative experiments can at least verify the estimates.

The graphs in Figure 2 compare the estimated and experimental results of Triplex for a range of traffic mixes. The graphs show that for the particular load shown, Triplex performs close to the estimates. This demonstrates that with this multi-class router, examining the single class traffic can help provide a reasonable prediction of mixed traffic behavior despite the shared resources of the multi-class router.

The next set of graphs in Figure 3 show the advantage of Triplex over the oblivious algorithm at a particular load. The graph on the left represents the difference in throughput between Triplex and the oblivious algorithm, while the graph on the right displays the difference in latency between the oblivious algorithm and Triplex. At very small loads there is no performance advantage (actually a penalty). But the graphs show that the performance advantage of the multi-class router increases as the percentage of adaptive traffic in the traffic mix increases. These results also show that it is possible for a multi-class router to provide superior performance over a single class router, even when the single

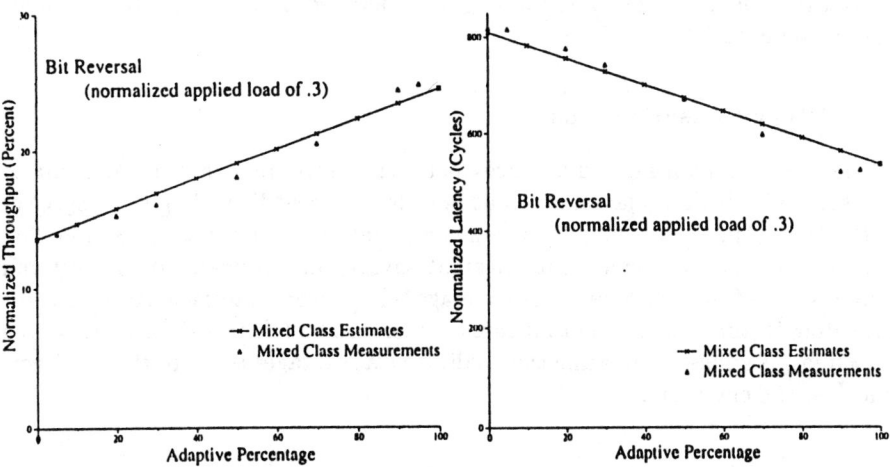

Fig. 2. Triplex mixed class throughput and latency on a 256-node 2D torus with 40-flit and 400-flit messages in a 10:1 ratio.

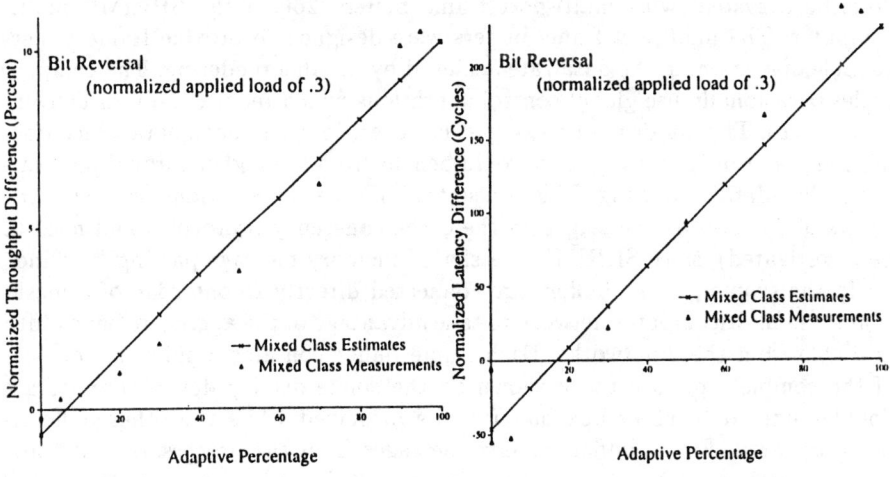

Fig. 3. The throughput and latency advantage of Triplex over the oblivious algorithm on a 256-node 2D torus with 40-flit and 400-flit messages in a 10:1 ratio.

class performance of each mode of the multi-class router does not match or exceed that of the single-class router. More detailed information about Triplex can be found in [10].

5.4 Other Considerations

There are also qualitative differences between the routers that are difficult to measure. This includes factors such as in-order delivery. Providing these services with the routing helps simplify the network interface or software. Simplifying the network interface can result in great savings in hardware complexity and may result in faster, cheaper, more manageable network interface. Alternatively, providing features in routers that might otherwise be left to software provides a big latency savings. Evaluating the qualitative advantages is left to the architects and systems engineers.

6 Example Application

As we alluded to before, a particularly useful class of multi-class routers is one that provides in-order delivery as well as fully-adaptive routing. Fully-adaptive routers generally achieve higher throughputs and saturate at higher loads than deterministic routers, while in-order delivery is usually assumed by programmers and helpful for providing efficient, low cost synchronization tasks.

We make this more concrete by providing the following example where we describe a system with multi-port frame buffers [26] on the SHRIMP multi-computer. The multiport frame buffers were designed to provide frame buffers capable of sustaining the data rate achieved by parallel rendering. The compute nodes occasionally use global control operations which require in-order delivery of messages. The majority of messages, however, contain image data which does not require in-order delivery and would benefit from the higher throughputs sustained by adaptive routing. This is also true of other applications (although the effects of out-of-order messages on the cache coherency protocol would need to be investigated), since SHRIMP is a shared memory message passing machine.

In the system, frame buffers are connected directly to one edge of a mesh-connected multicomputer network to take advantage of the aggregate bandwidth available from these networks. Each frame buffer contains a subframe or part of the complete picture to be shown on the single display device. Frames are double-buffered to allow one buffer to be displayed while the other buffer is being updated. Frame buffers receive messages from the processors containing data representing a small part of the image called the horizontal span, as well as requests to do tasks such as updating image buffers or aiding synchronization by receiving a special message called a *flush* message.

The frame buffers are multi-ported making synchronization a problem, since the order that messages arrive at a frame buffer are lost. Furthermore arrival at a frame buffer does not convey information about the order in which messages where sent with respect to other processors, since a path used by one processor may be shorter or less congested than a path to the frame buffer used by another. Synchronization is necessary for global control operations such as swapping the display frame when an updated frame is completely received. Synchronization overhead needs to be small compared with the time to send a frame, otherwise the full bandwidth of the network cannot be utilized.

Because the network provides in-order dimension-order routing, it is possible to implement low-cost barrier synchronization at the frame buffers with only a few messages being sent to the frame buffers by all the processors in a single column. The algorithm works by using flush messages to sweep all messages sent before the synchronization point into their appropriate frame buffers. If a multi-class routing algorithm is used, it also requires processors in a single row to send sweeping messages. By contrast in the most general case, the solution requires each processor to send a message to each frame buffer. This requires special counting hardware which is prone to deadlock or error if the counters are not initialized properly. Another expensive alternative, in this case, is to provide hardware support for barrier synchronization.

7 Related Work

A large number of single class k-ary n-cube routing algorithms have been developed [7, 17, 20, 9, 13, 12, 4, 21, 23, 16]. Each balances algorithm flexibility against resource requirements and router complexity.

Only a few routers provide in-order message delivery. The Dally Seitz oblivious algorithm [7] is one and requires two virtual channels per channel. Messages follow a dimension-order path by correcting dimension from the lowest to highest. Another is the Compressionless router [15]. Compressionless routing, which uses an abort and retry technique, is designed for small diameter networks with minimal buffering since it requires a message to own the entire path between its source and destination before sending is completed. Thus, if messages are sent in-order at the source, they arrive in-order at their destination. This method suffers from high contention in large congested networks, and wastes bandwidth on padding required for short messages when the network diameter is large but achieves adaptivity and fault tolerance without the use of virtual channels.

Even fewer routers offer several classes of routing. The planar-adaptive router [4] is a partially adaptive wormhole routing algorithm that sacrifices algorithm adaptivity to reduce the crossbar complexity required by fully adaptive algorithms. The algorithm restricts routing to two dimensions (a plane) at a time. The highest dimension in one plane is the lowest dimension in the next plane. By tagging messages and sending them on a dimension-order path, messages can also be delivered in-order.

The Cray T3E router [24] is a fully adaptive (in theory, not implementation) packet routing algorithm. The router uses a modified version of Duato's technique and provides four virtual channels for oblivious routes and a fifth virtual channel for adaptivity. Using packet-switching (either store-and-forward or virtual cut-through [14] as in the T3E) simplifies the routing and flow control requirements of using Duato's technique. For the T3E, the oblivious route is direction-order instead of dimension-order. Direction-order routes the positive directions in dimension-order and then the negative directions in dimension-order. A message can be restricted to oblivious routes to avoid faults in the network. Oblivious routes can also be used to provide in-order delivery, as in the planar-adaptive router.

The Triplex router [11] is a non-minimal fully-adaptive wormhole algorithm for the torus, that supports oblivious, minimal fully-adaptive, and non-minimal fully-adaptive routing. It uses three virtual channels per channel. Unlike the T3E, Triplex supports wormhole flow-control. Triplex uses a deadlock-avoidance technique of Schweibert and Jayasimha [23] that allows cyclic channel dependencies in the channels. This yields extra adaptivity over traditional adaptive algorithms since there is no set of virtual channels that are restricted to messages taking acyclic routes.

8 Conclusions

In this paper we promote the idea of multi-class routers which allow applications, or different messages within applications, to use different classes of routing. Multi-class routers are useful because not all applications have the same network requirements. Applications can achieve greater performance if they are allowed to use a class of routing which is most advantageous. Typically systems provide a single class one-size-fits-all routing algorithm. This generally provides routing which is overly restrictive for some messages.

Furthermore, this paper describes how to evaluate multi-class routers. Comparing the multi-class router against the best single class algorithm for each of its modes is not sufficient. Despite the costs of flexibility, multi-class routers can be advantageous for a large combination of traffic classes because all the traffic is not forced to use a single class of routing.

Although we have mentioned a few routers that provide multi-class routing, finding a competitive multi-class algorithm that provides oblivious, minimal-adaptive, and non-minimal adaptive routing is still an open problem. (For wormhole or packet routing, Triplex provides performance competitive with single class routers, but the non-minimal mode does not improve performance.) Another interesting multi-class router would be one that includes a class or two for quality of service or priority based routing.

References

1. Y. Aydogan, C. Stunkel, C. Aykanat, and B. Abali. Adaptive source routing in multistage interconnection networks. In *Intl. Parallel Processing Sym.*, pages 258–67, 1996.
2. M. Blumrich, K. Li, R. Alpert, C. Dubnicki, and E. Felten. Virtual memory mapped network interface for the SHRIMP multicomputer. In *Proc. of the Intl. Sym. on Computer Arch.*, pages 142–153, 1994.

3. G. Buzzard, D. Jacobson, M. Mackey, S. Marovich, and J. Wilkes. An implementation of the Hamlyn sender-managed interface architecture. In *Proc. of the Sym. on Operating Sys. Design and Implementation*, pages 245–259, 1996.
4. A. Chien and J. Kim. Planar-adaptive routing: Low-cost adaptive networks for multiprocessors. In *Proc. of the Intl. Sym. on Computer Arch.*, pages 268–277, 1992.
5. D. Culler, R. Karp, D. Patterson, A. Sahay, K. Schauser, E. Santos, R. Subramonian, and T. vonEicken. LogP: Towards a realistic model of parallel computation. In *Proc. of Sym. on Prin. and Prac. of Par. Prog.*, May 1993.
6. W. Dally. The J-machine system. In P.Winston and S. Shellard, editors, *Artificial Intelligence at MIT: Expanding Frontiers*. MIT Press, 1990.
7. W. Dally and C. Seitz. Deadlock-free message routing in multiprocessor interconnection networks. *IEEE Transactions on Computers*, C-36(5):547–553, May 1987.
8. J. Duato. A new theory of deadlock-free adaptive routing in wormhole networks. *IEEE Transactions on Parallel and Distributed Systems*, 4(4):466–475, Apr. 1993.
9. J. Duato. A necessary and sufficient condition for deadlock-free adaptive routing in wormhole networks. *IEEE Transactions on Parallel and Distributed Systems*, 6(10), Oct. 1995.
10. M. Fulgham. *Practical Multicomputer Routing*. PhD thesis, University of Washington, Seattle, 1997.
11. M. Fulgham and L. Snyder. Triplex: A multi-class routing algorithm. In *Sym. on Parallel Alg. and Arch.*, to appear, 1997.
12. C. J. Glass and L. M. Ni. The turn model for adaptive routing. *JACM*, 41(5):874–902, 1994.
13. L. Gravano, G. Pifarré, P. Berman, and J. Sanz. Adaptive deadlock- and livelock-free routing with all minimal paths in torus networks. *IEEE Transactions on Parallel and Distributed Systems*, 5(12):1233–1251, 1994.
14. P. Kermani and L. Kleinrock. Virtual cut-through: A new computer communication switching technique. *Computer Networks*, 3:267–286, 1979.
15. J. Kim, Z. Liu, and A. Chien. Compressionless routing: a framework for adaptive and fault-tolerant routing. In *Proc. of the Intl. Sym. on Computer Arch.*, pages 289–300, 1994.
16. S. Konstantinidou and L. Snyder. The chaos router. *IEEE Transactions on Computers*, 43(12):1386–97, Dec. 1994.
17. A. K.V. and T. Pinkston. An efficient, fully adaptive deadlock recovery scheme: DISHA. In *Proc of the Intl. Sym. on Comp. Arch.*, pages 201–210, 1995.
18. A. Landin, E. Hagersten, and S. Haridi. Race-free interconnection networks and multiprocessor consistency. In *Proc. of the Intl. Sym. on Computer Arch.*, pages 106–115, 1991.
19. K. Li, J. Naughton, and J. Plank. An efficient checkpointing method for multicomputers with wormhole routing. *International Journal of Parallel Programming*, 20:159–80, 1991.
20. D. H. Linder and J. C. Harden. An adaptive and fault tolerant wormhole routing strategy for k-ary n-cubes. *IEEE Transactions on Computers*, C-40(1):2–12, Jan. 1991.
21. Z. Liu and A. Chien. Hierarchical adaptive routing: A framework for fully adaptive and deadlock-free wormhole routing. In *Sym. on Par. and Distr. Processing*, pages 688–695, 1994.

22. N. McKenzie, K. Bolding, C. Ebeling, and L. Snyder. CRANIUM: An interface for message passing on adaptive packet routing networks. In *Lecture Notes in Computer Science*, volume 853, pages 266–80, 1994.
23. L. Schwiebert and D. Jayasimha. A universal proof technique for deadlock-free routing in interconnection networks. *Journal of Parallel and Distributed Computing*, 32(1):103–17, 1996.
24. S. Scott and G. M. Thorson. The cray T3E network: Adaptive routing in a high performance 3D torus. In *Proc. of the HOT Interconnects IV*, 1996.
25. T. von Eicken D.E. Culler, S. Goldstein, and K. Schauser. Active messages: a mechanism for integrated communication and computation. In *Proc. of the Intl. Sym. on Computer Arch.*, pages 256–266, May 1992.
26. B. Wei, G. Stoll, D. Clark, E. Felten, and K. Li. Synchronization for a multi-port frame buffer on a mesh-connected multicomputer. In *Proc. of the Parallel Rendering Symposium*, pages 81–88, 1995.

Congestion Control in the Wormhole-Routed Torus with Clustering and Delayed Deflection

Craig Hyatt and Dharma P. Agrawal

North Carolina State University
Raleigh, NC 27695-7911 USA
Department of Electrical and Computer Engineering
Tel: 919-515-3984 Fax: 919-515-5523
E-mail: {echyattldpa}@eos.ncsu.edu

Abstract. Although asynchronous transfer mode (ATM) is used for wide-area network applications such as video-on-demand, video conferencing, and live audio rebroadcasting, asynchronous wormhole networks are a lower-cost alternative to ATM for local area networks. This work compares the simulated performance of torus networks with wormhole routing, WICI routing, and WICI routing augmented by delayed deflection for congestion control. Simulation results show that WICI routing with delayed deflection continues to show good throughput even at traffic levels that would saturate a basic wormhole network.

1 Introduction

Network applications such as video-on-demand, video conferencing, and live audio rebroadcasting require high bandwidth, low latency communication networks. These requirements are met by asynchronous transfer mode (ATM) for wide area networks, but the high cost of ATM and its longer path setup time are drawbacks for local area networks and, especially, supercomputer processor interconnects.

Wormhole routing can be implemented more cheaply than ATM, and it has low latency and buffering requirements, but such networks tend to saturate easily [1,2]. Two alternatives to wormhole routing are virtual cut-through [3], in which packets are buffered when blocked, and WICI routing [4] which is a hybrid of wormhole and virtual cut-through. These latter methods perform better when the network is heavily loaded at a cost of additional buffering and switch complexity.

Congestion control algorithms [5] also help to overcome saturation in wormhole networks. *Deflection routing*, deflects a message to an alternate channel when the preferred channel is busy, thus routing traffic around a congested area. *Delayed deflection routing* buffers flits on the premise that the preferred channel might become available within a few flit times, so that the selection of longer alternate paths is minimized.

What we seek is a network design with a good trade-off between buffer requirements, complexity and speed of switching circuits, deadlock and livelock protection, freedom from blocking, fault tolerance and overall throughput. We conclude in this paper that a WICI-routed network augmented by delayed deflection for congestion control has many of these desirable properties.

2 Network Performance

Adding delayed deflection routing to the WICI torus network improves performance. We chose the torus for our experiments because it is scalable and easily partitioned [4]. For our performance experiments, the torus is partitioned into clusters of approximately the same size and overlapping border nodes communicate between clusters. Balanced cluster size is assumed for better load balancing and network modularity. For each dimension, border nodes are assigned the same dimensional address. Corresponding channels are termed *outcluster* channels and all other ports are termed *incluster* channels. Refer to Fig. 1 for an example of the torus and a partitioning scheme.

We measure performance as average latency *versus* load. In our experiments message size is fixed, and we define latency as the average elapsed time from the header flit leaving the source node until the tail flit reaches the destination node. Load is the flit injection rate into the network. We assume a Poisson process, and so the average load is λ. For simplicity, we assume uniform traffic and we assume that each hop counts as one time unit.

Virtual channels are used in all of our experiments in order to avoid deadlock. The strategy proposed by Dally and Seitz in [6] is to switch virtual channels when crossing a dimension boundary so that cycles and the resulting deadlock are eliminated. Livelock is eliminated because a random channel is selected if the deflection buffer overflows before the preferred channel becomes available.

For our experiments, the deflection buffer capacity is half the fixed message length. If the deflection buffer size were greater than the maximum message length, then the network performance would be equivalent to virtual cut-through with some additional performance gain from the congestion control algorithm.

Delayed deflection routing reduces the number of times that a non-preferred channel is chosen and so reduces the average path length and blocking as opposed to the static WICI self-routing strategy. The performance difference is more pronounced as the network load increases (Fig. 2).

3 Node Complexity and Cost

Node complexity affects both the cost and switching speed of the network. In wormhole routing, node complexity is relatively small because of the small buffer requirements and the network's self routing property. If deflection routing is added, then channel selection becomes dynamic and switching complexity increases. Also, a deflection buffer must be added for the delayed flits. The use of virtual channels for deadlock avoidance increases node complexity because switching logic and channel buffers are replicated for each virtual channel.

The slight decrease in switching speed and buffer requirements is offset by increased tolerance to network congestion and by improved fault tolerance. In our simple experiments, we do not account for the slower switching speed expected in our hybrid design because we expect the increase in switch complexity due to adding deflection routing to WICI to be relatively small. In future work, we plan to take this timing difference into account.

We measure the average number of messages queued in network routers and divide by the number of nodes in the network to give average buffer use. We use the product of average buffer usage and average latency to compute a node cost measure that is independent of network size (see Fig. 3). Adding a small delayed deflection buffer increases memory cost slightly compared to WICI routing without delayed deflection.

4 Simulation Experiments

We use a custom simulator, modified from the one used in [4], to compare the performance of wormhole, WICI, and WICI plus delayed deflection networks. Following is a summary of our experimental setup:

- The network is a 16×16 torus with 256 nodes.

- The network is partitioned into four clusters, each 8×8, with 64 nodes per cluster, similar to the strategy shown in Fig. 1. Wormhole routing is used within clusters and virtual cut-through is used between clusters.

- The message size is fixed at 20 flits per message.

- Virtual channels with dimension-order routing are used to avoid deadlock. Random channel selection is used to avoid livelock.

- Each node has a single delayed deflection buffer of 10 flits (half the message size).

- Each hop is equivalent to a simulation time step. All flits that are not blocked advance simultaneously in a given time step. Statistics are delayed to eliminate warmup effects.

- Traffic is globally uniform; destinations are chosen randomly from all nodes.

5 Future Research

Future research will examine the performance with varying message and deflection buffer sizes. As mentioned earlier, the increased switch complexity and resulting slower switch speed must be accounted for in simulation models. We also plan to examine the performance of other network types (*e.g.* non-torus networks and unidirectional networks such as the MSN [7]). Because of the importance of client-server arrangements in the real world, additional experiments with unbalanced traffic must be performed on our proposed network implementation. Network congestion can be caused by network faults, and future research will address link and node faults directly.

6 Conclusion

In this brief contribution, we focus on the performance of WICI-routed torus networks with delayed deflection. Wormhole networks have been proposed as an inexpensive alternative to ATM for LAN and supercomputer applications, but the basic wormhole implementation saturates under load and has problems with deadlock and congestion.

Our simulation results show that WICI routing reduces the saturation problem, and that delayed deflection further reduces congestion. Deadlock is handled by virtual channels and livelock is handled by random port selection inherent in the deflection algorithm. Our conclusion is that a WICI network with delayed deflection is cost-effective (low buffer requirements and simple switches) and has desirable performance characteristics such as good throughput under load, low latency, and freedom from deadlock and livelock.

References

[1] J. Ngai, *A framework for adaptive routing in multicomputer networks*, PhD thesis, California Institute of Technology, 1989.

[2] C. Seitz, *et al*, "Wormhole chip project report", tech. rep., Department of Computer Science, California Institute of Technology, 1985.

[3] P. Kermani and L. Kleinrock, "Virtual cut-through: a new computer communication switching technique," *Computer Networks*, v 3, pp 267-286, 1979.

[4] H. Park and D. P. Agrawal, "WICI: an efficient hybrid routing scheme for scalable and hierarchical networks", *IEEE Transactions on Computers*, v 45, n 11, Nov 1996.

[5] E. Leonardi, *et al*, "Congestion control in asynchronous, high-speed wormhole routing networks," *IEEE Communications*, v 34, n 11, pp 58-69, Nov 1996.

[6] W. J. Dally and C. L. Seitz, "Deadlock-free message routing in multiprocessor interconnection networks," *IEEE Transactions on Computing*, v C-36, pp 547-553, May 1987.

[7] N. Maxemchuk, "Routing in the manhattan street network," *IEEE Transactions on Communications*, v COM-35, n 5, pp 503-512, May 1987.

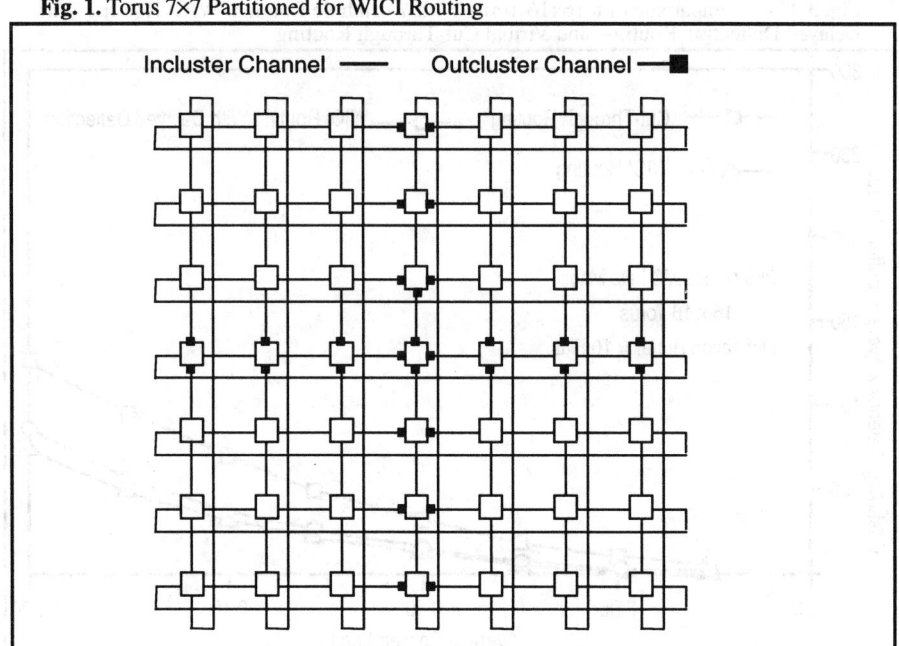

Fig. 1. Torus 7×7 Partitioned for WICI Routing

Fig. 2. Performance Comparison of a 16x16 Torus With Wormhole Routing, WICI Routing With Delayed Deflection Routing, and Virtual Cut-Through Routing

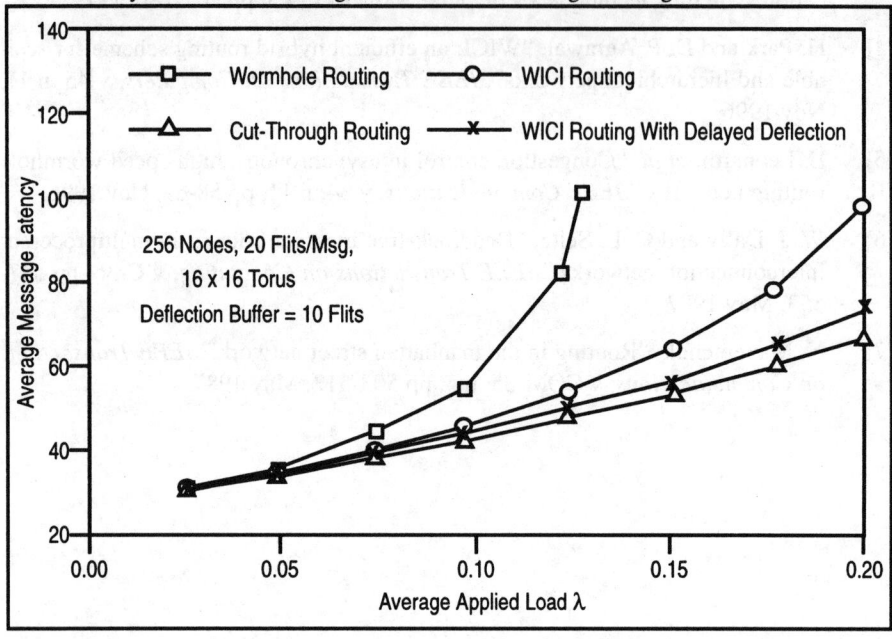

Fig. 3. Cost Comparison of a 16x16 Torus With Wormhole Routing, WICI Routing With Delayed Deflection Routing, and Virtual Cut-Through Routing

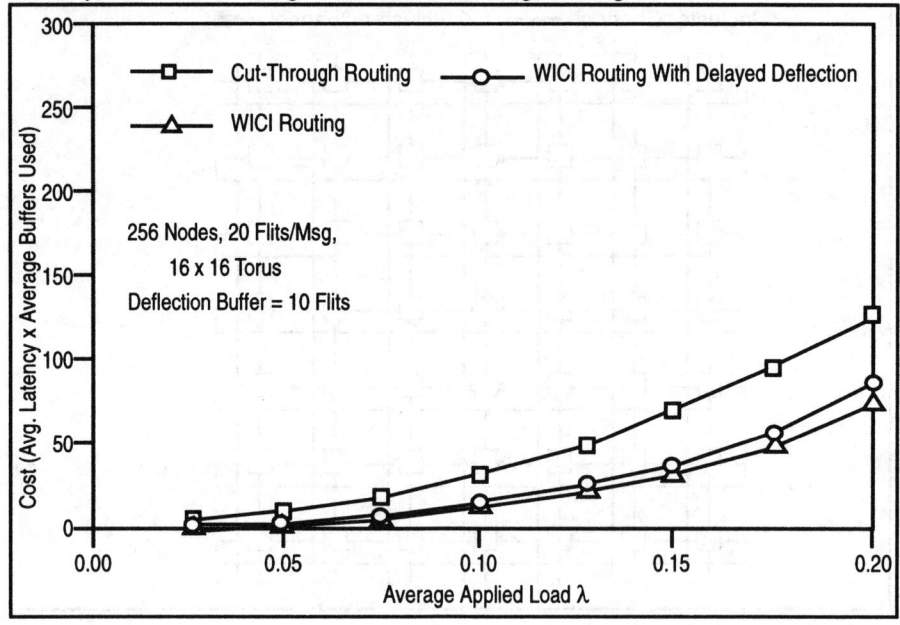

Multicasting in Irregular Networks with Cut-Through Switches Using Tree-Based Multidestination Worms*

Rajeev Sivaram[†] Dhabaleswar K. Panda[†] Craig B. Stunkel[‡]

[†]Dept. of Computer and Information Science
The Ohio State University, Columbus
Ohio 43210
{sivaram,panda}@cis.ohio-state.edu

[‡]IBM T. J. Watson Research Center
P. O. Box 218, Yorktown Heights
New York 10598
stunkel@watson.ibm.com

Abstract. Multidestination message passing has been proposed as a mechanism to achieve efficient multicast in regular direct and indirect networks. The application of this technique to parallel systems based on irregular networks has, however, not been studied. In this paper we propose two schemes for performing multicast using multidestination worms on irregular networks and examine the extent to which multidestination message passing can improve multicast performance. For each of the schemes we propose solutions for the associated problems such as, methods for encoding and decoding multidestination headers, alterations to the setup algorithm run by the switches, logic to perform header manipulation, etc. We perform extensive simulations to evaluate our schemes under a variety of changing parameters: software startup overhead per message, system size, switch size, message length, and degree of connectivity. Our results establish that even a very naive multicasting algorithm using multidestination message passing can result in considerable performance gains over the best unicast based multicasting schemes.

1 Introduction

Parallel computing on networks of workstations is fast emerging as a cost-effective alternative to MPPs. These systems are typically interconnected by switches in an irregular topology [1, 11]. Because of this, many of the problems that have been solved for regular topologies have to be solved anew for these systems.

To perform communication with low latency these systems typically use cut-through switching (routing) due to inherent advantages such as low latency. Much recent research has focussed on the problem of deadlock-free cut-through routing in irregular networks of workstations [9, 10].

It has been established that efficient multicast is crucial to the operation of a parallel system. This is because multicast, in addition to being used in other collective operations, is also used in system level operations such as for cache-invalidations in a Distributed Shared Memory (DSM) system [3]. Both,

---

* This research is supported in part by NSF Grant MIP-9309627, NSF Career Award MIP-9502294 and an IBM Cooperative Fellowship.

systems using the Distributed Memory, and systems using the DSM programming paradigms, make use of multicast/broadcast for various application and system level data distribution functions.

A lot of research has therefore focussed on methods for efficient multicast in parallel systems. These methods have predominantly been proposed for regular networks and fall into two broad categories: unicast-based and multidestination-based multicast. Unicast based multicast typically follows a multi-phase binomial tree based approach [15]. A unicast message is sent by the source to a destination in the first phase of this multicast. In every successive phase, the source and the multicast destinations covered up to the beginning of that phase send one message each to one of the remaining destinations. Such a multicast requires at least $\log_2 \lceil (d+1) \rceil$ phases to cover d destinations. Such unicast based multicasting schemes have been recently proposed for irregular networks [4].

Multidestination routing has been proposed for parallel systems based on regular networks. Originally proposed for direct (router-based) networks [5, 7], this scheme has been recently extended to regular switch-based parallel systems [12, 14]. However, the problem of how multidestination routing can be extended to irregular networks has not yet been addressed. Similarly, the extent to which such a multidestination message passing based multicast will benefit multicast performance in an irregular network has also not been evaluated.

In this paper we study the problem of performing multicast in irregular networks with cut-through routing using multidestination worms. We propose two schemes that are at the opposite ends of the spectrum of multidestination worm based multicasting. The first scheme, called the *Multiphase Multicast using Single Switch Replication* (MPM-SSR) scheme, uses a predominantly software based multi-phase approach to perform multicast to arbitrary destination sets along with the ability of a switch to replicate worms to multiple output ports. The second multicasting scheme, called the *One Phase Multicast* (OPM) scheme, carries out multicast in a single phase and is predominantly hardware based.

We then perform simulations to evaluate the *extent* of performance gain that can be achieved by using the two proposed schemes. Our simulations isolate the effect of increasing software startup time, system size, switch size, message length, and degree of connectivity on multicast performance of both schemes by varying one of these parameters at a time. The performance of our schemes is compared with a best possible unicast-based multicast implementation—an extremely optimistic estimation of the performance achievable using unicast-based multicasting schemes.

Our results show that even a naive multicasting algorithm in conjunction with minimal hardware support for multidestination routing (the MPM-SSR scheme) can result in considerable gain in performance over the best unicast based solutions with performance gains by factors of up to 2.6 being realizable. Our results also confirm that the single phase multicast (OPM) scheme scales across destination set sizes, system sizes, switch sizes, message lengths, and system connectivities, providing almost constant latency multicast with variation in all these parameters. This scheme provides performance improvements by factors of up to 7 over the best unicast based scheme in a 128 node system.

The remaining portion of this paper is organized as follows. In Sec. 2 we present our assumptions about the system and review a method for deadlock free unicast message passing. Section 3 reviews the various factors that affect tree-based multidestination routing in switch-based parallel systems. We then present the MPM-SSR scheme in Sec. 4 and the OPM scheme in Sec. 5. Simulation results are presented in Sec. 6 and our conclusions are presented in Sec. 7.

2 Irregular Networks

2.1 Topology and System Model

In an irregular network, processing nodes are connected to switches which are interconnected arbitrarily. An example of such a topology is shown in Fig. 1(a). The figure shows a 32 node system consisting of eight 8 port switches. The processing elements are typically workstations. The switches in the network are interconnected using bidirectional links. The network is assumed to support cut-through routing. To achieve cut-through routing, switches are equipped with buffers. We assume an input buffer based replication architecture [12, 14].

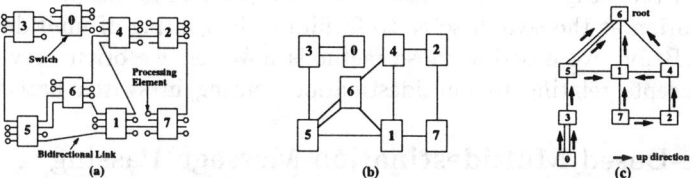

Fig. 1. (a) An example of an irregular network, (b) a graphical representation of the network, and (c) the direction of links after running the setup algorithm for up*/down* routing.

For the purposes of our experimental study, we assume that half of a switch's ports are connected to processing nodes. This is not a limitation of the methods proposed in this paper but is merely an assumption made for our performance evaluation. The remaining ports are either connected to other switches or left unconnected. The number of ports that are left unconnected is varied to obtain networks with different degrees of connectivity.

2.2 Unicast Routing in Irregular Networks

Recently, a number of approaches have been proposed for routing packets in irregular networks [1, 9, 10, 11]. An important issue in networks with cut-through routing is the avoidance of deadlock due to cyclic waiting among packets. Each of the proposed routing solutions tries to address this deadlock problem either by eliminating the possibility of cyclic wait [1, 9, 10] or by allowing cycles but by providing paths for messages to escape from cyclic wait scenarios [11]. For the purposes of this paper however, we will adopt the approach outlined in [10]. This approach, called up*/down* routing, is described next.

In the up*/down* routing scheme, the switches of the network first run a setup algorithm. In this algorithm, a common (breadth first) spanning tree is formed among the switches of the network from a commonly agreed upon root switch. The spanning tree is then used to assign directions to each of the unidirectional links in the network as one of 'up' or 'down'. A link is assigned an 'up' direction if the switch at which it ends is higher up in the tree (closer to the root switch) when compared to the switch from which it originates or if the switch at which it ends is at the same level of the tree but has a lower ID. Links are marked as 'down' links otherwise. In addition to assigning directions to links, the setup procedure also results in every switch being aware of the entire network topology after which routing tables are set up at every switch. The up*/down* scheme used to perform deadlock-free routing can be summarized as follows: a message is routed on zero or more 'up' links followed by zero or more 'down' links to reach its destination. Once a message takes a 'down' link, it is prohibited from taking an 'up' link again. Figure 1(b) shows a graphical representation of the irregular network of Fig. 1(a). The directions assigned to the links of the network after running the setup algorithm for up*/down* routing are shown in Fig. 1(c). The arrows indicate the 'up' links in each of the bidirectional links: the 'down' links are in the opposite direction.

The methods described in this paper make use of the information that is gathered by the setup procedure described above, adding to this procedure to set up information at the switch so as to facilitate the routing of multidestination messages. Before we describe those methods however, we briefly review some of the concepts relating to multidestination routing in switch based parallel systems.

3 Tree-Based Multidestination Message Passing

Multidestination message passing is a technique that has recently been proposed for routing messages from a single source to multiple destinations. Proposed originally in the context of parallel systems based on direct (router-based) networks [5, 7], this work has been extended recently to switch-based networks [12, 14]. A tree-based multidestination worm covers multiple destinations in a switch-based network by replicating at the switches on its path. The copies of the multidestination worm formed by replication at a switch are forwarded to other switches or nodes depending on whether the output ports to which they are replicated are connected to switches or nodes. There are three main issues w.r.t. implementing tree-based multidestination worm based multicast in a switch-based parallel system. These are described in the next three paragraphs.

Encoding and Decoding Multidestination Worm Headers: The set of ports to which a multidestination worm is to be forwarded may be determined either *statically* at the source or *dynamically* by the switches on the worm's path using the worm header. In the former case, the header encodes a route to the set of destinations that it covers. The switches on the worm's path use this route information (possibly after some decoding) to decide the set of output ports to which the multidestination message must be forwarded. Route table information is stored at the processing nodes. The switches in the network just require the ability to decode the header. In the latter case, the multidestination worm header typically encodes the set of destinations to which the worm is directed. Under this scheme, the switches in the network must store enough routing information to decide which output ports must receive a copy of the worm for it to reach all of its destinations.

Replication Mechanism: Multidestination routing in switch-based parallel systems requires an efficient replication mechanism at the switches [6]. In this paper, we assume that switches adopt the deadlock-free input-buffer-based asynchronous replication mechanism of [14]. Under such a replication mechanism, an arriving multidestination worm at an input buffer of a switch is read by multiple output ports. Furthermore, the various output ports proceed independently of each other so that blocked branches do not inhibit other non-blocked branches. A count value associated with packet units known as *chunks*, is initialized to the number of output ports to which the multidestination worm is to be forwarded. Every output port decrements the count value associated with a chunk as soon as it is read. A chunk is deleted once it has been read by all destination output ports.

Routing: Although many static encoding schemes encode the entire path of a multidestination worm, dynamic encoding schemes do not restrict the path of a multidestination worm in any way (except in requiring that the multidestination worm's destinations be eventually covered). The Base Routing Conformed Path (BRCP) model restricts multidestination worms to paths that are valid for unicast worms in the system [7]. By restricting tree-based multidestination worms to such paths, deadlock problems can be avoided without making special rules for multidestination messages. In this paper we assume that multidestination worms conform to the up*/down* routing in the following sense: no branch (copy) of the worm takes an 'up' link after it has taken a 'down' link.

4 Multiphase Multicast Using Single Switch Replication (MPM-SSR)

A simple method for multicasting can use the replication mechanism described above at a *single* switch. In this method, a multidestination worm covers a set of destinations that are all connected to the same switch. If the multicast destination set spans multiple switches, a multinomial tree based approach is used for multicast [12]. Under this approach multicast proceeds in multiple phases with the recipients of a multicast in any given phase acting as secondary sources in the next phase of the multicast. This scheme is discussed in detail in the following subsections.

Figure 2(a) shows the irregular network of Fig. 1 with the multicast destinations highlighted and a multidestination worm that replicates at a single switch.

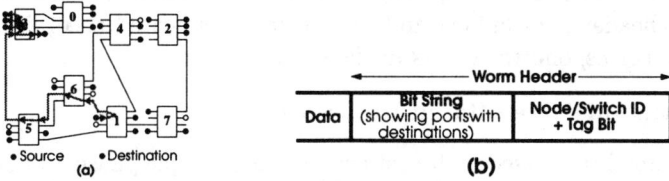

Fig. 2. (a) The path followed by a sample worm, and (b) the format of a multidestination packet header under the MPM-SSR scheme.

4.1 Encoding and Decoding Multidestination Headers

Before presenting the multinomial tree based algorithm for performing multicast to arbitrary destination sets, we first present a simple method for encoding and decoding the headers of the multidestination worms of the MPM-SSR scheme. Since replication is only allowed at a single switch, a simple method of encoding the multidestination header is to store information that the intermediate switches can use to route it to the destination switch (whose nodes are the destinations of the multidestination worm). In addition, the header must also encode the list of the destination switch's nodes that are recipients of the multicast.

A representation of such a header is shown in Fig. 2(b). The first portion of the header consists of a node or switch ID along with a 1 bit tag to denote whether the message is a unicast or a multidestination message. The choice of whether a node or a switch ID is used can be made depending on whether or not the system allows messages to be directed to switches (as allowed in Autonet [10]). If a node ID is used, this field may carry the ID of any one of the worm's destinations attached to the destination switch. The second field consists of a p bit string where p is the number of output ports in a switch: the ith bit in this string is set to '1' if output port i of the destination switch leads to a multicast destination.

For decoding the multidestination header, the information set up for routing unicast messages is sufficient. Let us first consider the case where the first field of the multidestination header encodes a node ID. A switch on the worm's path examines the first field of the header and the tag bit. If the tag bit is off (a unicast packet), the worm looks up its routing table to decide the port to which the worm is to be forwarded. If the tag bit is on (a multidestination packet), the switch first examines if the destination is one of the nodes connected to it. If so, the second field is read to determine the output ports that should receive copies of the packet. Otherwise, the worm is forwarded to an appropriate output port as determined from the switch's routing tables just as if it were a unicast message. Since the routing table lookup and the determination of whether a destination is connected to a given switch can potentially be performed concurrently, the multidestination header causes no additional decoding overhead (in terms of latency) at the intermediate switches.

If the first field of the header carries a switch ID, decoding can become even simpler. An intermediate switch examines the switch ID field with its own ID and forwards the message to an appropriate output port in the case of a mismatch. If the switch ID field matches its ID, the tag field is used to determine whether the packet must be consumed by the switch or whether it is a multidestination packet intended for nodes connected to the switch. In the latter case, the second field of the header is examined and the worm is replicated accordingly to the ports which correspond to '1' bits in the string.

4.2 Multinomial Tree Based Multicast

The multinomial tree based multicast proceeds in multiple phases. The multicast performance depends on the number of phases in the multicast and the amount of contention within each of these phases. Given a multicast destination set and an irregular network, the destinations covered by each of the multidestination worms in the MPM-SSR scheme can be easily inferred. However, because of contention, differing distributions of the multidestination worms into the various phases of the multicast can result in differing multicast performance. Given a multicast destination set (and hence the set of multidestination worms), finding the optimal distribution of worms into various phases (to minimize multicast latency) is an open problem. In this paper however, we adopt a simple, greedy method that focuses exclusively on the reduction of the number of phases. This method has been found to perform well for regular networks [12]. The method is described next.

Given a set of destinations, determine their associated switches. Arrange these switches in descending order of size according to the number of destinations in each switch. Since a worm can cover all the destinations associated with a single switch, we can associate one worm with each of these switches. Given this list of multidestination worms, in the first phase the largest multidestination worm is sent from the source. In the second phase of the multicast the source and the destinations covered in the first phase send out one multidestination worm each from the ordered list of worms. At any given phase the destinations covered up to the end of the previous phase and the source send out one worm each from the ordered list of (remaining) worms. This process continues till all worms have been sent. As can be inferred from the above description, if on the average p of the multicast destinations belong to the same switch, then multicast to d destinations using this approach requires $\lceil \log_{p+1}(d+1) \rceil$ phases. Such an approach will require fewer phases to cover a given multicast destination set than the number of phases required by the best known software multicasting algorithm [4] if $p > 1$. If $p = 1$, then the number of phases required by the MPM-SSR scheme and the best known software scheme are equal.

We have described a simple multi-phase approach for multicast in irregular networks. In the next section, we describe a method that accomplishes multicast in a single phase. However, it requires enhancements to the information stored and the decoding logic used at every switch in network.

5 One Phase Multicast Using Bit-String Encoding (OPM)

The feasibility of using bit-string encoded headers was first shown in [2]. An efficient, single phase multicasting scheme using a multidestination worm with a bit-string encoded header was proposed in [8, 14]. Key to the efficient implementation of this multicast is the presence of reachability strings at each of the network switches. Although such reachability strings are fairly easy to determine in regular networks, determining such reachability strings in irregular networks is more difficult. Furthermore, multiple paths exist from a given switch to a given destination, a property not present in many regular networks such as many of the unidirectional and bidirectional MINs. One contribution of this paper is to outline a method for setting up these reachability strings as an enhancement of the setup procedure used for the up*/down* routing algorithm in irregular networks. Another contribution is the presentation of simple header modifying logic that prevents multiple copies of a worm from being forwarded to a destination along different paths. Before examining these however, we briefly review the strategy adopted for encoding such multidestination worms.

5.1 Encoding Multidestination Headers

Bit string encoding is an example of a dynamic encoding scheme. In this form of encoding the header carries an N-bit string where N is the number of nodes in the system. The ith bit of this string is set to 1 if node i is a multicast destination; otherwise the bit is set to 0. In addition, a bit (called the *up-down bit*) may be added to the header to indicate whether the worm is currently traveling along the 'up' or 'down' direction. This bit is initially set to '1' to indicate that the worm is traveling in the 'up' direction. It is reset when the worm begins traveling 'down'-wards.

To decode such a header efficiently, the switches of the system must possess information about the nodes that are reachable from each of their 'down' output ports. This information can be efficiently captured using bit strings similar to the one described above, called *reachability strings* [8]. Every 'down' output port has a reachability string associated with it. Bits that are '1' in this string represent nodes that are reachable through the output port. In addition, every switch maintains a *total reachability string* that captures the set of nodes reachable through *all* of its 'down' output ports. Given these *reachability strings*, decoding a bit string header reduces to a simple logical operation.

5.2 Setting up Reachability Information

The setup procedure used for the up*/down* routing algorithm assigns a direction as one of 'up' or 'down' to every link in the system. From the root switch, the 'down' links along with the other switches form a Directed Acyclic Graph (DAG). This implies that more than one of the switch's 'down' links may lead to a given set of destinations. Furthermore, two different switches may lead to the same set of destinations (following 'down' links alone). If reachability strings captured all the destinations reachable through a given switch's ('down'-ward) output ports, we may end up forwarding a multidestination worm to more than one output port to cover the same set of destinations—this set of destinations will receive multiple copies of the message. To prevent this we can restrict the reachability strings at a switch so that only one 'down' port leads to a given destination. We call these reachability strings *restricted reachability strings*.

However, even this does not prevent multiple copies of the worm from reaching some of the destinations. There are two methods by which this can be prevented. The first method is to restrict multicasts so that they adhere to a strict (common) spanning BFS tree. A second alternative is to modify the headers of multidestination worms so that the worm copies carry only the subset of the multicast destinations that are reachable through the restricted reachability strings.

In this paper, we choose to modify multidestination headers. Although this method requires additional logic to perform the header modification, it has the important advantage that multicast need not be restricted to one common tree.

We provide a possible implementation for performing this header modification, in the next section. We have also developed a procedure to set up the restricted reachability strings at a switch given the network topology (found as a result of the setup algorithm for up*/down* routing), but have been unable to include it due to space limitations. Interested readers are requested to refer to [13] for further details.

5.3 Decoding Multidestination Headers

Basic Idea: For the purposes of this paper, the decoding method adopted is as follows. If an arriving multidestination worm has its up-down bit set to '1', the worm's header is compared with the total reachability string associated with the switch (a bit-wise AND is performed of the two strings). If all the worm's destinations are reachable from the switch's 'down' output ports (the fore-mentioned bit-wise AND operation results in a string that is identical to the bit-string header), the up-down bit is set to '0' and the header is compared with the (restricted) reachability strings of each of the switch's output ports that lead to 'down' links (another bit-wise AND). If the output port leads to any of the worm's destinations (the result of the bit-wise AND is non-zero), the worm is replicated to the specified output port. Before being forwarded to the specified output port, the worm header has to be modified as mentioned above. If a multidestination worm arrives at a switch with its up-down bit set to '0', the worm's header is directly compared with each of the 'down'-ward ports' restricted reachability strings.

If all the multidestination worm's destinations are not reachable from the switch's output ports that lead to 'down' links, the worm is routed to any one of the switch's output ports that lead to 'up' links. The choice may be made adaptively depending on local traffic conditions or may be made arbitrarily (for example, round robin among the output ports that leads to 'up' links). The worm should eventually arrive at a switch from which all its destinations are reachable. Note that this is a property that exists because of the up*/down* routing algorithm and the method followed for assigning 'up' and 'down' directions to the links (the set-up procedure).

Header Decoding and Modification Logic: As described above, to prevent multiple copies of a worm from arriving at the multicast destinations we have decided to alter the bit-string header that is forwarded to each output port (along the 'down'-ward path). An implementation that achieves this function in a switch with 4 output ports is shown in Fig. 3. The implementation consists of *reachability registers* that store the restricted reachability strings that are set up as described previously. A reachability register is associated with every one of the switch's output ports (although the restricted reachability strings are only stored for those output ports that lead to 'down' links—the other registers are initialized to zero). An additional register (the *header register*) stores the bit-string encoded header. The modified header for each of the output ports is obtained by a simple bit-wise AND of the reachability registers and the header register. This modified header is stored in a set of *result registers*. If the result in any of the registers is non-zero, a request is made for the corresponding output port. If the output port is free it begins forwarding the worm starting with the modified header in the corresponding result register. The bit-wise AND of the header register and each of the reachability registers can be carried out in parallel and completed in a single cycle. This logic may be replicated for every

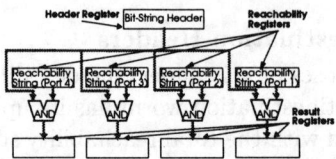

Fig. 3. An example implementation for modifying the multidestination headers.

input port. Alternatively, it may be more cost-effective to have shared logic for all input ports.

In this paper however, we assume that the logical unit shown in Fig. 3 is replicated for each input port. We conservatively assume that the above header modification takes 4 cycles (40.0 nanoseconds) for our experiments, as discussed in the next section.

6 Performance Evaluation

We performed simulation experiments using a C++/CSIM based simulator to measure the performance of the schemes proposed in the previous section. The flit-level simulator is flexible enough to model different regular and irregular topologies. We studied the impact of the following system parameters on single multicast performance: message startup time, system size, switch size, message length, and the percentage connectivity among the switches of the network. We assumed that half the number of switch ports are connected to processors/workstations. Networks were generated so that they were better connected by leaving fewer of the remaining switch ports unconnected. The interconnection between switches was randomly generated.

In each of the experiments, we measured multicast latency for different destination set sizes varying one parameter at a time to isolate its impact. Every point in the graphs that follow represents the average performance for the corresponding multicast set size over 20 repetitions each for 10 different randomly generated networks (i.e. an average over 200 multicasts). The default parameters assumed for the experiments are as follows: software startup overhead $(t_s) = 10.0$ μsecs., link propagation time for a single flit $(t_p) = 10.0$ nanoseconds, multidestination header decoding/modification time $(t_{route}) = 40.0$ nanoseconds, unicast header decoding and message routing time $(t_{route}^{unicast}) = 10.0$ nanoseconds, switch propagation time $(t_{sw}) = 10.0$ nanoseconds, and injection channel and consumption channel propagation time per flit $(t_{inj}$ and $t_{cons}) = 10.0$ nanoseconds. Our default system consisted of 64 nodes interconnected by 8 port switches with 75% network connectivity.

To estimate the impact of our proposed schemes we compare them with the currently prevalent software point to point messaging based mechanisms. We present a *lower bound* estimate of the performance of such a multicast. This estimate was obtained as follows. A software multicast using point to point communication primitives requires $\lceil \log_2(d+1) \rceil$ phases. Ignoring contention, each of these phases incurs the software overhead for a single communication and the propagation time for the entire message over *at least* the injection channel, consumption channel and one switch. The estimate we used for a multicast to d destinations is given by: $((t_s + t_{inj} + t_{route}^{unicast} + t_{cons} + l \times t_{cons}) \times \lceil \log_2(d+1) \rceil)$ μsecs, where l is the message length in flits. As shown in [4], contention free unicast based multicast is not always possible in irregular networks. Furthermore, messages may pass through multiple switches and links, so that the propagation cost of these messages may be higher. Actual multicast latency using unicast messages will therefore be higher than our lower bound estimate.

Effect of Startup Time: We first study the impact of startup overhead on the multicast performance. As shown in Fig. 4 the performance of the MPM-SSR scheme shows some variation with startup overhead. For startup times of 10.0 and 20.0 μsecs., the MPM-SSR scheme shows up to a factor of 2 improvement over the best unicast based solution. For a low startup time of 5 microseconds, the performance gain of the multicast under the MPM-SSR scheme reduces to a factor of 1.4. This is due to increased contention among the worms of the multicast at low values of startup. The single phase OPM multicast has the same factor of gain over the best unicast based multicast across the range of startup times. The main component of the multicast under this scheme is the single startup overhead.

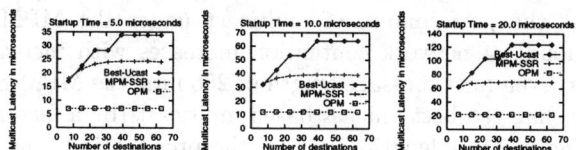

Fig. 4. Multicast latency vs. number of destinations for three different communication startup times: 5.0, 10.0, and 20.0 microseconds.

Effect of System Size: The performance of the OPM scheme is dominated by the single startup overhead. As shown in Fig. 5 it performs uniformly well across a range of destination set and system sizes, incurring approximately constant multicast latency. The performance gain due to the OPM multicast therefore increases with system size, from a factor of up to 5 for a 32 node system to a factor of up to 7 for a 128 node system over the best unicast based multicast scheme (a factor of up to 3–5 over the MPM-SSR scheme). Under the MPM-SSR scheme the amount of network contention increases as the multicast set size increases lowering the performance gain from a factor of up to 1.7 for a 32 node system to a factor of up to 1.5 for a 128 node system.

Effect of Switch Size: Since the multidestination worms under the MPM-SSR scheme can cover the destinations attached to a single switch, the number of destinations covered by each of them varies directly with the switch size.

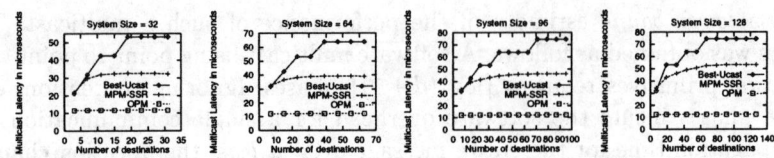

Fig. 5. Multicast latency vs. number of destinations for four different system sizes: 32, 64, 96, and 128 nodes.

Therefore, for a given system size, the number of phases required for multicast under the MPM-SSR scheme reduces directly with increasing switch size and multicast performance therefore improves (as shown in Fig. 6). Compared to the best unicast based multicast performance, multicast using the MPM-SSR scheme results in gains by factors of up to 1.6 for a 64 node system with 8 port switches and in gains by factors of upto 2.6 for a similar system with 32 port switches. Again, the OPM multicast incurs approximately constant latency across the range of destination sets and switch sizes.

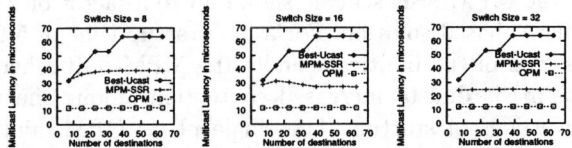

Fig. 6. Multicast latency vs. number of destinations for three different switch sizes: 8, 16, and 32 ports.

Effect of Message Length: As shown in Fig. 7, increasing message length adversely affects the performance of multicast under the MPM-SSR scheme because the amount of network contention increases with increasing message length. However, even for a message length of 256 flits, the MPM-SSR multicast performs better than the best unicast based multicast (by a factor of 1.15). Although increasing message lengths increase the propagation time for the OPM multicast, the difference in performance is very small because of the dominance of the single startup overhead.

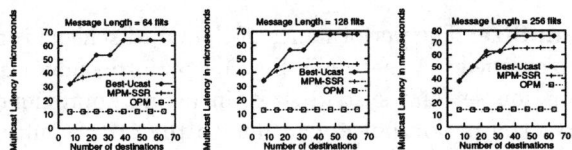

Fig. 7. Multicast latency vs. number of destinations for three different message lengths (payload sizes): 64, 128, and 256 flits.

Effect of Percentage Connectivity: Increased network connectivity in general improves the performance of both MPM-SSR and OPM multicast, although by a very small amount (as shown in Fig. 8). The reason why increase in network connectivity does not have a more pronounced effect on our performance figures is that we did not restrict the worms to minimal paths, and the up*/down* routing does not provide as much adaptivity as some of the more recent schemes ([1, 9, 11]).

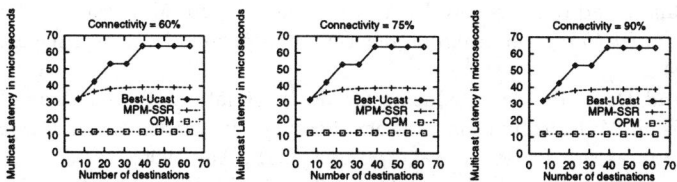

Fig. 8. Multicast latency vs. number of destinations for three different degrees of connectivity: 60, 75, and 90%.

7 Conclusion

We have presented two schemes for multicast using multidestination worms. The MPM-SSR scheme is predominantly software based and just uses the ability of a switch to replicate an arriving worm to multiple attached nodes. Under this scheme, multicast to arbitrary destination sets proceeds in multiple phases with destinations receiving the message in one phase acting as sources in succeeding phases. We have presented a header encoding and decoding method for the multidestination worms of this scheme that requires no additional information at the switch than what is already present for routing unicast messages. The second scheme, called the OPM scheme, is predominantly hardware-based and carries out multicast efficiently in a single phase. However it requires additions to the setup algorithm and modifications to the switch to support header modification and decoding. We have developed this addition to the setup algorithm as well as an implementation for carrying out header modification.

Our simulation results have shown that even the naive multicasting algorithm used in the MPM-SSR scheme can result in considerable performance gains over a unicast based multicasting scheme. Furthermore, our results confirm that a hardware multicasting scheme, such as the OPM scheme, can result in scalable multicast; multicast latency under this scheme is almost constant across a range of destination set sizes, system sizes, switch sizes, message lengths and network connectivities. These schemes therefore show considerable promise for being applied to parallel systems based on networks of workstations to achieve efficient multicast.

The methods developed in this paper are general and applicable to any network, although enhancements can be made to improve performance in networks where the topology is regular (such as unidirectional and bidirectional MINs). We are currently studying the effect of multiple multicast traffic on the performance of the proposed schemes. We are also investigating methods for other collective operations such as barrier synchronization and reduction in irregular networks.

Additional Information: A number of related papers can be obtained from: http://www.cis.ohio-state.edu/~panda/pac.html.

References

1. B. Abali. A Deadlock Avoidance Method for Computer Networks. In *Proceedings of the First International Workshop on Communication and Architectural Support for Network-Based Parallel Computing (CANPC '97)*, pages 61–72, February 1997.

2. C. M. Chiang and L. M. Ni. Multi-Address Encoding for Multicast. In *Proceedings of the Parallel Computer Routing and Communication Workshop*, pages 146–160, May 1994.
3. D. Dai and D. K. Panda. Reducing Cache Invalidation Overheads in Wormhole DSMs Using Multidestination Message Passing. In *International Conference on Parallel Processing*, pages I:138–145, Chicago, IL, Aug 1996.
4. R. Kesavan, K. Bondalapati, and D. K. Panda. Multicast on Irregular Switch-based Networks with Wormhole Routing. In *Proceedings of the International Symposium on High Performance Computer Architecture (HPCA-3)*, pages 48–57, 1997.
5. X. Lin and L. M. Ni. Deadlock-free Multicast Wormhole Routing in Multicomputer Networks. In *Proceedings of the International Symposium on Computer Architecture*, pages 116–124, 1991.
6. Lionel Ni. Should Scalable Parallel Computers Support Efficient Hardware Multicasting? In *ICPP Workshop on Challenges for Parallel Processing*, pages 2–7, 1995.
7. D. K. Panda, S. Singal, and R. Kesavan. Multidestination Message Passing in Wormhole k-ary n-cube Networks with Base Routing Conformed Paths. Technical Report OSU-CISRC-12/95-TR54, The Ohio State Univeristy, December 1995. *IEEE Transactions on Parallel and Distributed Systems*, to appear.
8. D. K. Panda and R. Sivaram. Fast Broadcast and Multicast in Wormhole Multistage Networks with Multidestination Worms. Technical Report OSU-CISRC-4/95-TR21, Dept. of Computer and Information Science, The Ohio State University, April 1995.
9. W. Qiao and L. M. Ni. Adaptive Routing in Irregular Networks Using Cut-Through Switches. In *Proceedings of the International Conference on Parallel Processing*, pages I:52–60, Chicago, IL, Aug 1996.
10. M. D. Schroeder et al. Autonet: A High-speed, Self-configuring Local Area Network Using Point-to-point Links. Technical Report SRC research report 59, DEC, Apr 1990.
11. F. Silla, M. P. Malumbres, A. Robles, P. Lopez, and J. Duato. Efficient Adaptive Routing in Networks of Workstations with Irregular Topology. In *Proceedings of the First International Workshop on Communication and Architectural Support for Network-Based Parallel Computing (CANPC '97)*, pages 46–60, February 1997.
12. R. Sivaram, D. K. Panda, and C. B. Stunkel. Efficient Broadcast and Multicast on Multistage Interconnection Networks using Multiport Encoding. In *Proceedings of the 8th IEEE Symposium on Parallel and Distributed Processing*, pages 36–45, Oct 1996.
13. R. Sivaram, D. K. Panda, and C. B. Stunkel. Multicasting in Irregular Networks with Cut-Through Switches using Tree-based Multidestination Worms. Technical Report OSU-CISRC-4/97-TR20, The Ohio State Univeristy, March 1997.
14. C. B. Stunkel, R. Sivaram, and D. K. Panda. Implementing Multidestination Worms in Switch-Based Parallel Systems: Architectural Alternatives and their Impact. In *Proceedings of the 24th IEEE/ACM Annual International Symposium on Computer Architecture (ISCA-24)*, pages 50–61, June 1997.
15. H. Xu, Y.-D. Gui, and L. M. Ni. Optimal Software Multicast in Wormhole-Routed Multistage Networks. In *Proceedings of the Supercomputing Conference*, pages 703–712, 1994.

Poster Session

CCSIMD: A Concurrent Communication and Computation Framework for SIMD Machines

Vivek Garg and David E. Schimmel

School of Electrical and Computer Engineering
Georgia Institute of Technology
Atlanta, GA 30332-0250
e-mail:{vivek,schimmel}@ece.gatech.edu

Abstract

Communication in data parallel architectures has been limited considerably due to the properties of conventional SIMD communication networks. In this study, we illustrate the degree of concurrency available in several data parallel applications. However, this concurrency can not be exploited in traditional SIMD machines. We investigate the communication properties and alternate communication mechanisms which may be used effectively to exploit this available concurrency. Some preliminary results are presented.

1.0 Introduction

SIMD machines have been and continue to be an important class of machines. The recent introduction of small scale SIMD paradigm in Intel's MMX architecture shows renewed interest in SIMD. The data parallel programming model is very attractive when algorithms require similar manipulation of large amounts of data. Example applications include image processing, quantum chromodynamics, seismic signal processing, climate modeling, finite element analysis, etc. All of these applications involve massive amounts of data parallelism, and require extensive amounts of near neighbor (local) communication.

Data parallel architectures typically have PEs with private memories. As a result any sharing of data between the PEs must be explicitly communicated. This implies that a significant fraction of the execution time is consumed as communication overhead. The goal of this work is to explore alternatives for efficient communication in the SIMD class of machines, and investigate mechanisms which exploit available concurrency to reduce communication latencies for both regular and irregular communication.

In this paper we identify the types of communication concurrency found in data parallel algorithms. Exploiting this concurrency can lead to significant decrease in communication latencies. To accomplish this we propose a framework which extends conventional SIMD architecture, which we denote as concurrently communicating SIMD.

1.1 Related work

There have been several research efforts which have addressed the exploitation of concurrency between communication and computation and within communication. The

SLIM [3] architecture allows a single bit memory plane to be shifted to the nearest neighbor concurrently with computation. The Execube [7] is a SIMD/MIMD architecture which uses processors with memory integrated on-chip along with DMA support to overlap communication with computation and other communication. The transputer based design by Atiquzzaman [1] has MIMD nodes connected with bidirectional communication ports to allow overlap between communication and computation and other communication. We note that each of these studies consider the concurrency for either coarse-grained parallelism or a SIMD/MIMD architecture. Our focus is to address the exploitation of communication concurrency in fine-grained SIMD architectures.

2.0 Communication in SIMD

SIMD communication operations are classified as either scalar or parallel. A scalar communication involves data objects in the array controller (scalar variable) and one or more PEs. Parallel communication involves data objects in the PE array (parallel variables). Parallel communication is supported via an interconnection network and often a global communication mechanism. Parallel communication can be either local or global in nature. Communication with the near-neighbor PEs is considered to be local communication, while communication with PEs relatively far away may be considered global. The efficiency of the communication mechanism is dependent on the regularity of the communication, the average distance to the destination, and the inherent architectural properties of the communication network.

The topology of nearest neighbor network is typically a k-ary n-cube. Global network topologies vary from hypercubes to multistage switch based networks such as Benes, Omega, Delta, Expanded Delta, etc. Since the addition of hardware support for global connection can be very expensive, a clustering approach is often used to share a port into this network among several PEs. While it provides the capability for more general types of traffic patterns, it typically requires a much longer time to complete a communication than a regular pattern on the interconnection network.

2.1 Communication network properties

A typical SIMD communication network is controlled centrally by the control unit, routes messages synchronously, and is circuit switched. The communication channels utilized in the network are half-duplex.

SIMD algorithms are executed in a lock-step manner, and as a result all active PEs execute the instruction being broadcast by the controller. The lock-step execution limits the PEs to either execute a communication or a computation operation, but not both. Since no overlap between computation and communication is possible, the PE architecture is designed to share hardware resources between computation and communication operations. An example of this is the MasPar MP-1 PE floating point unit which uses the mantissa unit for serially shifting the messages in or out of the PE during communication.

Due to the synchronous nature of the network, PEs can only communicate in the direction specified by the control unit in a given cycle, i.e. every PE participating in the communication operation must send or receive the messages to or from the same direction. For example, a data exchange between two adjacent PEs must be split up into two communication phases, one in which a PE sends the data to the other PE, and another to allow the other PE to send the data to the first PE. Unidirectional communication implies that physical links in the interconnection networks are managed as half-duplex, and circuit switching is the transport mechanism of choice for messages with uniform lengths and communication direction.

2.2 Message properties

In this section we present some definitions related to properties of messages in SIMD, and their interaction with other messages. We refer to the communication pattern implied by a SIMD communication instruction as a message set. A message set is a collection of communication primitives originating from all the PEs in the active set[1] and terminating at other active or passive PEs in the processor array. The membership of the message set may consist of one to N, src-dest PE pairs, where N is the total number of PEs in the processor array. In strict lockstep SIMD, at most one message set may occupy the network at a time. Every communication instruction has a corresponding message set which can be routed via the interconnection network or the global router.

We define a message set to be *simple* if the routing of its member messages does not produce any contention for physical links. A *complex* message set, on the other hand, results in contention for physical links. A physical link set corresponding to a message set is defined to be the set of physical links required to route that message set. We define two message sets to be *mutually exclusive* if the intersection of their physical links is null. Two message sets are *interfering* if they are not mutually exclusive. Two message sets are *conflicting* or *data-dependent* if one or more src-dest PE pairs are common to both message sets and the communicated data for those pairs is destined for the same variable. For a more formal treatment of these issues, see [5].

3.0 Concurrency in SIMD communication

There are three types of concurrency that can be exploited in data parallel algorithms: communication and computation overlap, inter-communication concurrency, and intra-communication concurrency. This parallelism is available only in parallel communication for both local and global message patterns.

3.1 Concurrency between computation and communication

Overlap of communication and computation is a type of concurrency which can be utilized to hide all or part of the communication phases of data parallel applications. An example of this type of concurrency is illustrated in Figure 1(b). The exploitation of this type of concurrency requires the ability to resolve data dependencies between the com-

---

1. The membership of the active set represents PEs which are to execute the current instruction being broadcast by the control unit.

munication and computation phases, and the PEs ability to execute both communication and computation simultaneously.

Techniques such as loop unrolling and software pipelining may be necessary to enhance the utilization of the communication resources concurrently with computation. Most SIMD algorithms are written to fit the current SIMD paradigm which requires strict lock-step execution. This implies that most programs have an implicit dependency between the communication and computation phases and vice versa. With the ability to hide the latency of communication, these programs can be manipulated by compiler or scheduling techniques to transform the data dependencies and hence decouple the communication and computation phases of the algorithm.

3.2 Inter-Communication Concurrency

Occasionally SIMD applications have communication patterns that are specified in multiple phases. This implies that the SIMD instruction stream can have one or more communication operations occur consecutively. If the associated message sets are mutually exclusive, they may be routed at the same time. With the overlapping of multiple communications, say j, the effective time spent on communication for one phase is given by

$$T_{Comm} = \left(max\left\{ T^i_{Comm} \right\} + O_{contention} + j - 1 \right) \quad \forall (1 \leq i \leq j), \tag{1}$$

```
forall {
    tmp = getN[1].value
    sum += tmp
    tmp = getE[1].value
    sum += tmp
    tmp = getW[1].value
    sum += tmp
    tmp = getS[1].value
    sum += tmp
    sum = sum / 5
}
```
(a)

```
forall {
    tmp = getN[1].value
    tmp1 = getE[1].value            sum += tmp
    tmp = getW[1].value             sum += tmp1
    tmp1 = getS[1].value            sum += tmp
    sum += tmp1
    sum = sum / 5
}
```
(b)

```
forall {
    tmp = getN[1].value;tmp1 = getE[1].value;tmp2 = getW[1].value;tmp3 = getS[1].value
    sum = tmp + tmp1
    sum += tmp2
    sum += tmp3
    sum = sum / 5
}
```
(c)

Figure 1. 5-pt averaging algorithm; (a) SIMD implementation; (b) overlapped communication and computation; (c) inter-communication concurrency. The get DIR [DIST].ADDR instruction represents a communication operation which fetches a value from the PE DIST hops away in the DIR direction from the register ADDR.

where $O_{contention}$ is the overhead incurred due to contention from multiple messages in the network. Depending on the significance of the incurred overhead, it is possible to completely mask out the communication times for all but the communication pattern with the longest routing time, and the time required to issue the other communication instructions in the network. An example of inter-communication concurrency is illustrated in Figure 1(c).

3.3 Intra-Communication Concurrency

Communication phases involving local communication are typically represented as a series of explicit communication steps specified with directional control by the programmer. As a result intra-communication concurrency does not exist in these patterns. Global communication on the other hand is typically specified as simply source destination pairs, and the global transport mechanism schedules the communication based on some routing protocol. We expect to find increased levels of intra-communication concurrency in global message patterns, which when exploited can reduce latency for global communication significantly. Let us consider the transpose communication pattern as a case study for this type of concurrency. A global router with full connectivity such as a crossbar may be able to route this pattern in a single cycle. Other types of global routers may take longer depending on the degree of connectivity and the router architecture. Yet another method of dealing with the transpose communication pattern is to decompose it into a series of non-conflicting message sets, as illustrated in Figure 2. The transpose in the figure has been decomposed into three phases, where in the ith phase the PEs i away from the diagonal exchange messages.

4.0 Concurrently Communicating SIMD (CCSIMD)

We propose a generalization of SIMD called Concurrently Communicating SIMD (CCSIMD), which decouples the communication and computation circuitry, and introduces autonomy into the communication network. This enables the architecture to exploit the types of concurrency discussed in Section 3.0. Communication and computation instructions may be overlapped provided there are no data dependencies among them. The communication network can be treated as an autonomous and independent entity. As a result, communication instructions may be boosted [8], barring any data dependencies, and can be combined in the network to take advantage of available network bandwidth

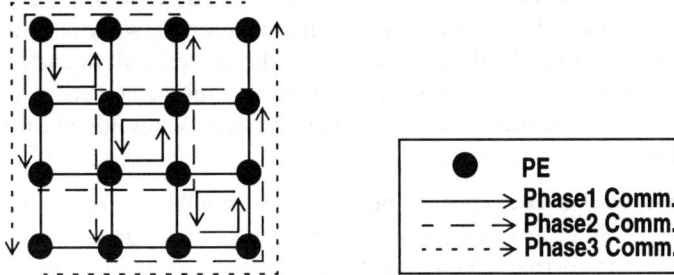

Figure 2. Decomposition of transpose into non-conflicting message sets.

and further hide communication latencies. We note that these mechanisms do not significantly change the SIMD execution model; furthermore, with a moderate hardware investment, communication latency can be significantly reduced or eliminated.

4.1 Communication model

A Concurrently Communicating SIMD (CCSIMD) machine allows concurrent execution of multiple communication instructions and overlapped execution of communication and computation. CCSIMD decouples the communication from computation in the same sense as the MasPar MP-1 decoupled memory access from execution; the final result is consistent with the SIMD execution model [2].

In CCSIMD there is no theoretical limitation on the number of message sets concurrently present in the network, i.e. the number of message sets in the network is only bounded by the number of simultaneous communication instructions available in the SIMD code and the available bandwidth in the network. For example, consider two consecutive communication instructions in the code with corresponding message sets C_i and C_{i+1}. In lockstep SIMD execution, if C_i is injected into the network at time t, then C_{i+1} is not injected into the network until time $t + \Delta t$, where Δt is the time required to route C_i. In CCSIMD the scheduling of these message sets depends on whether they are mutually exclusive or interfering, or conflicting. If the message sets are mutually exclusive, both can be injected into the network concurrently. For interfering message sets, concurrent existence in the network is only possible if the network can handle contention. If the message sets are conflicting, they must complete in order, to ensure data consistency.

4.2 Issues in CCSIMD Design

The ability of CCSIMD to take advantage of communication concurrency leads to an increase in complexity of handling communication instructions, and additional hardware costs. Data dependencies must be analyzed to ensure conflict-free concurrent dispatch of communication and computation instructions. Furthermore, the combining of communication instructions in the network require scheduling and synchronization primitives, which may add to the cost and/or timing of the system.

Superscalar Dispatch

Concurrent execution of communication and computation instructions requires the controller to dispatch multiple instructions simultaneously. The control unit must now track the execution status and the state of the communication network concurrently. This requires addition of some hardware resources in the control unit to enable tracking of multiple message sets in the network, and to determine their completion. The PEs must also separate the communication and computation circuitry, resulting in the addition of buffer resources.

The dependency analysis can either be performed at compile time (static) or during execution (dynamic). Static analysis can be used to insert synchronization instructions in the code to ensure hazard-free handling of the instructions by the hardware. While this approach requires some extra time during compilation, it is relatively inexpensive in terms of hardware resources and its effect on the cycle time. Dynamic analysis requires dependency checking logic, but may be able to schedule more efficiently than the static case.

Multiple Message Sets

The decision to combine message sets in the network depends on the available bandwidth in the network, number of injection channels, and the register file bandwidth. The combination of communication instructions may be performed either in hardware or software or both. Combined communication instructions also require that the membership of the active PE set be updated to include the PEs corresponding to the instructions, and that the PEs know which communication to participate in.

Message sets in the network may be deterministic or non-deterministic. In the case of several deterministic message sets active in the network, the control unit can determine the completion of the message sets. However, some message sets may be destined to PEs further away than others. As a result, the control unit must track the status of each message set to determine when it has reached the destination. This is necessary to ensure timely ejection of message sets, and relinquishment of the network resources to incorporate other message sets.

Synchronization techniques for complex message sets is highly dependent on the routing and transmission mechanisms invoked by the network for such communication. The non-deterministic message sets require global synchronization schemes, since the control unit can not determine the completion time of the communication. Global OR has been traditionally used to perform such synchronizations, for example in the MasPar MP-2. For circuit oriented routing schemes, tear-down may be performed by the message tail flits, as in the CM-5.

The ability to concurrently transmit multiple message sets in the PEs requires extra buffers and communication channels. The buffer requirements in a function of the number of dimensions and the maximum number of messages being transmitted via a PE. The flexibility of the PE to communicate with multiple directions also affects the switching complexity used for the communication buffers. The increase in communication channel resources can result in more wires and/or pins per PE.

4.3 Proposed mechanisms for the implementation of CCSIMD

The CCSIMD paradigm represents a class of architectures with the basic requirement of concurrent execution of communication with other communication and/or computation. Since the amount of available concurrency in parallel applications can vary substantially between different types of applications, varying amounts of hardware support to exploit this concurrency may be utilized to implement cost-effective networks.

Upon careful consideration of data-parallel applications, it is apparent that three principal types of message set combining are relevant. The first is combining of parallel or orthogonal simple message sets. This is common in parallel applications utilizing row or column exchanges or broadcasts. Applications using NEWS communication can benefit

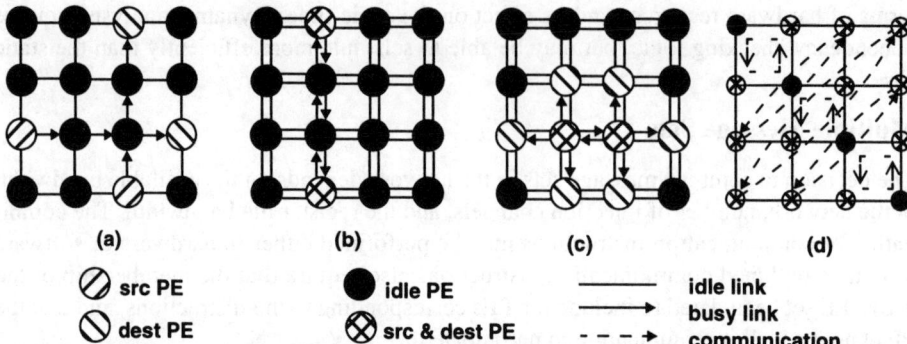

Figure 3. Combination of Message sets in CCSIMD; (a) Orthogonal Simple Message sets; (b) Parallel Simple Message Sets; (c) NEWS Message Sets; (d) Complex Message sets

from combining simple message sets destined for the four different directions into a single pattern. Finally for exploiting concurrency in applications with global communication, a mechanism for combining complex message sets is desirable. Based on this observation, we propose the following mechanisms to exploit the varying degrees of concurrency in data-parallel applications. The relative costs are shown in Table 1.

- O-CCSIMD allows concurrent routing of simple message sets in orthogonal directions (Figure 3a).
- P-CCSIMD allows concurrent routing of simple message sets in parallel (but opposite) direction (Figure 3b).
- NEWS-CCSIMD allows concurrent routing of simple message sets in all four directions (Figure 3c).
- G-CCSIMD allows arbitrary combining of all message sets simple or complex (Figure 3d).

Table 1. Additional PE hardware resources required for CCSIMD.

Hardware	O-CCSIMD	P-CCSIMD	NEWS-CCSIMD
Comm. Buffers	2	2	4
Switching Complex.	4-2:1 MUX	4-4:1 MUX	8-2:1 MUX
# of wires/PE	2c[a]	4c	4c
# of pins/PE	4c	8c	8c

a. c represents the communication channel width.

5.0 Preliminary results

The results presented in this section provide preliminary evidence that alternate communication strategies in SIMD may be used to reduce communication latencies and consequently enhance the performance of SIMD applications. In this section we will present the best-case benefit obtained by exploiting the overlapped communication and computation and inter-communication concurrency for the 5-pt averaging, and Cannon's matrix multiplication algorithms.

5.1 5-pt Averaging

The effects of exploiting the two types of concurrency on the 5-pt averaging algorithm is illustrated in Figure 1. Let us now consider the cycle times for the MasPar MP-2 (shown in Table 2), and compute the performance improvements possible by exploiting the com-

Table 2. Normalized Cycle times on the MasPar MP-2

Operation	Add	Comm[1]	Divide
# Cycles	1	1.5	2

munication concurrency. Based on the MP-2 cycle times, it can be easily deduced that the SIMD implementation requires 12 cycles. Exploiting the overlapped communication and computation concurrency reduces the execution time to 9 cycles yielding a speedup of 1.33. Exploiting inter-communication concurrency can further reduce the execution time to 6.5 cycles resulting in a speedup of 1.85.

5.2 Cannon's matrix multiply algorithm

A data parallel implementation of Cannon's algorithm is shown in Figure 4. The communication instructions in the preskew phase can overlap each other reducing the communication time by a factor of two. Similarly, the communication time in the compute phase can be reduced by a factor of two. Furthermore, we also have the ability to perform communication concurrently with computation, so the communication time can be completely overlapped with the time required for the multiply-add operation. As a result, the

```
for x = 0 to P-1              // Preskew matrices A and B
begin
    if (row > x)
        xnetW[1].a = a ;
    end if
    if (col > x)
        xnetN[1].b = b ;
    end if
end
c = 0 ;
for x = 1 to P                // Compute matrix C
begin
    c = c + a * b ;
    xnetW[1].a = a ;
    xnetN[1].b = b ;
end
```
Figure 4. Cannon's matrix multiply algorithm.

total communication time of the matrix multiplication algorithm can be reduced to 25% of the total communication time required for a SIMD implementation. It is evident from this example that there is a tremendous potential to speedup the SIMD implementations even further by exploiting instruction level parallelism in the form of concurrent communication and overlapped communication and computation.

6.0 Conclusions

There is considerable evidence that significant improvements in communication latency and consequently SIMD performance can be achieved by adopting alternate communication strategies in a SIMD environment. Although the nature of these results is preliminary and do not account for the hardware and software overhead involved in exploiting the available concurrency in SIMD communication, we believe that after accounting for such items, adoption of such communication strategies will prove to be fruitful and worthwhile.

7.0 References

[1] Atiquzzaman, M., "Enhancing the throughput of mesh-type multiprocessor systems," *Proceedings of the Third International Conference on Image Processing and its Applications*, Coventry, U.K., July 18-20, 1989, pp.487-491.

[2] Blank, T., "MasPar MP-1 architecture," *Proceedings of COMPCON Spring '90 - The Thirty-Fifth IEEE Computer Society International Conference*, San Francisco, CA, pp. 20-24.

[3] Chang, H.M., Sunwoo, M.H., and Cho, T.-H., "Implementation of a SLiM Array Processor," Proceedings of the 10th International Parallel Processing Symposium, Honolulu, Hawaii, April 15-19, 1996, pp.771-775.

[4] Fox, G.C., "What Have We Learnt from Using Real Parallel Machines to Solve Real Problems?," *Caltech Report C^3P-522*, December 1989.

[5] Garg, V., "Mechanisms for Hiding Communication Latency in Data Parallel Architectures," *A Proposal for Doctoral Thesis*, Dec. 1996.

[6] G.H. Golub, and C.F. Van Loan, *Matrix Computations*, Second Edition, Johns Hopkins Univ. Press, MD., 1989.

[7] Kogge, P.M. and Agrawal, P.A., "EXECUBE - a new architecture for scalable MPPS," *Proceedings of the 23rd International Conference on Parallel Processing*, Raleigh, N.C., August 15-19, 1994, vol. 1, pp. 77-84.

[8] Smith, M., Lam, M., and Horowitz, M., "Boosting Beyond Static Scheduling in a Superscalar processor," *17th International Symposium on Computer Architecture*, Seattle, WA, May, 1990, pp. 344-354.

Arctic Switch Fabric*

G. Andrew Boughton

Massachusetts Institute of Technology, Laboratory for Computer Science, Cambridge
Mass 02139, USA

Abstract. The Arctic Switch Fabric technology is a scalable network technology based on the Arctic router chip. Switch Fabrics are fat tree networks that are capable of providing high performance even under a heavy load of large (96 byte) packets. They have a number of diagnostic features that make them well suited for experimental computer systems. Switch Fabrics will be used in the StarT-Jr, StarT-Voyager, and Xolas computer systems at MIT. This paper describes the overall characteristics of Switch Fabrics and describes the three layers of Fabric components. These are the 16-leaf network, the four-leaf board, and the Arctic router chip.

1 Introduction

The Arctic Switch Fabric technology is a scalable network technology based on the Arctic router chip [2]. An Arctic Switch Fabric is a fat tree network which supports 150 MB/sec bandwidth in each direction at each endpoint and has a bisection bandwidth equal to 150 MB/sec times the number of endpoints divided by two. A Switch Fabric is currently being tested on the PC-based StarT-Jr multiprocessor. In the next six months Switch Fabrics will be used in a number of other multiprocessor systems at MIT including the nine node (72 processor) Xolas and the 32 processor StarT-Voyager.

Switch Fabrics provide high performance and reliability for large systems. The fat tree structure allows traffic to be evenly distributed. The buffering and crossbar scheme of the Arctic chip allows high utilization of network links. A Switch Fabric is capable of accepting high bandwidth packet flows from all of its inputs simultaneously, even when a large fraction of the packets are big (96 bytes). A differential signaling scheme is used on the interchassis cables to provide reliable data transmission. Each network link has extensive error detection circuitry including a 16-bit CRC circuit which verifies the accurate transmission of each packet and Manchester code checking circuits which verify the accurate transmission of each control signal.

The Switch Fabric technology includes powerful diagnostic features. A Switch Fabric has a dedicated Ethernet-based maintenance system which accesses each router through its JTAG port and is thus independent of the status of the network link cables. The maintenance system has access to six 36-bit counters in

---

* The research described in this paper was supported in part by the Advanced Research Projects Agency under Office of Naval Research contract N00014-92-J-1310 and Ft. Huachuca contract DABT63-95-C-0150.

each router output port which are used to monitor traffic through the port. It can disable and enable links, flush packets, inject packets, and reconfigure the routing algorithm in each router. It can also run verification tests on each router.

2 16-Leaf Fat Tree Network

The basic building block of the Fabric technology is a 16-leaf fat tree network. As shown in Figure 1, the network provides 16 leaf ports and 16 root ports. The leaf ports can be attached by cables to either endpoints or other (logically lower) networks. The root ports can be attached by cables to other (logically higher) networks. Thus arbitrarily large systems can be constructed.

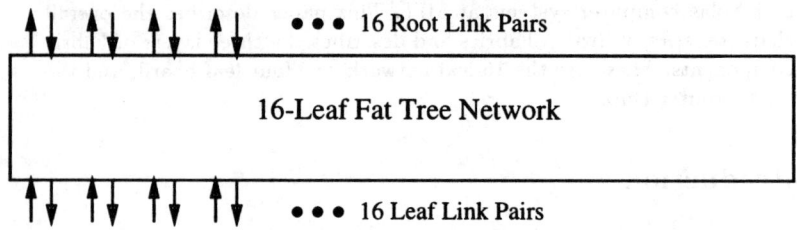

Fig. 1. 16-Leaf Fat Tree Network

The 16-leaf fat tree network is constructed from eight four-leaf boards as shown in Figure 2. Each four-leaf board provides four single ended GTL (low voltage swing CMOS) ports and four differential ECL ports. The GTL ports are used for the internal links of the network and the ECL ports are used for the external links.

Two 16-leaf fat tree networks fit in a single card cage as shown in Figure 3. The internal links of each network are implemented using backplane traces. A 32-leaf network (with no root ports) can be formed by cabling together the root ports of the two 16-leaf networks. Alternatively each 16-leaf network can be cabled to other 16-leaf networks in other cages as discussed above. Arbitrarily large fat tree networks can be constructed in this fashion.

Each card cage has an associated controller which is a small PC running the Linux operating system. The controller provides access to the maintenance systems of the cage's two networks.

3 Four-Leaf Board

Each board is a four-leaf fat tree network constructed from four Arctic router chips as shown in Figure 4. The board has four GTL ports attached to backplane

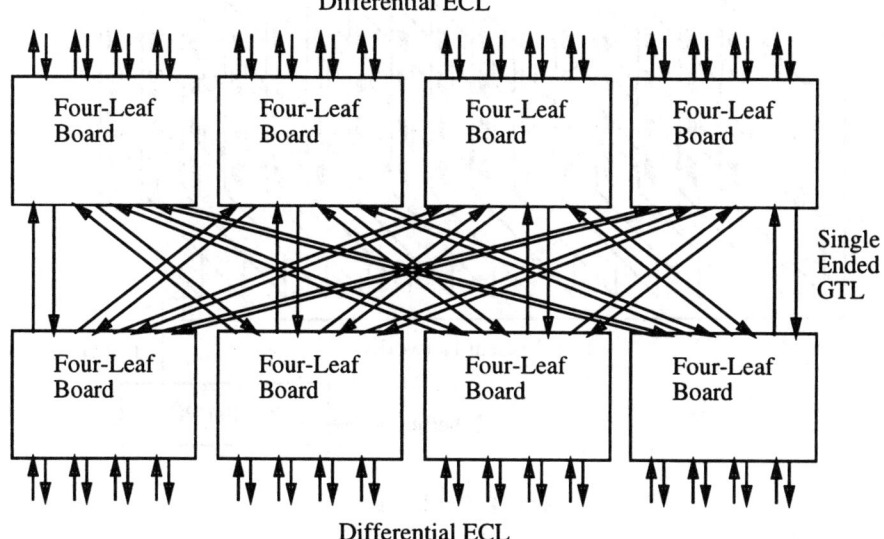

Fig. 2. Structure of the 16-Leaf Network

connectors and four ECL ports attached to cable connectors. Each port has both incoming and outgoing data lines.

Each differential ECL port is connected to a single ended GTL Arctic router port through an interface circuit. In addition to converting between logic families, the circuit registers both data coming out of Arctic and data going into Arctic. Arctic provides outgoing data at 77 Mbits/sec/line, and provides two complimentary 38.5 MHz clocks with the data. The interface circuit uses a PLL to generate a 77 MHz clock from these clocks. It uses the 77 MHz clock to register the data and outputs the clock on the ECL port with the registered data. Incoming data on the ECL port has an associated 77 MHz clock which the interface circuit uses to register the data and to generate, with a simple divide by two circuit, the appropriate 38.5 MHz input clocks for Arctic. The interface circuit sends these clocks with the registered data into Arctic.

The four-leaf board has a single maintenance port which is attached to a backplane connector. This port provides access to a scan chain which includes the JTAG ports of the four Arctics on the board.

4 Arctic Router Chip

Arctic [2] is a four input four output packet router implemented on a Motorola H4CP178 gate array chip in a 324 CBGA package. Arctic uses approximately 105,000 of the 178,000 available gates; roughly 44,000 are used for memories. Arctic supports two priority levels, packet sizes from 16 to 96 bytes, and exten-

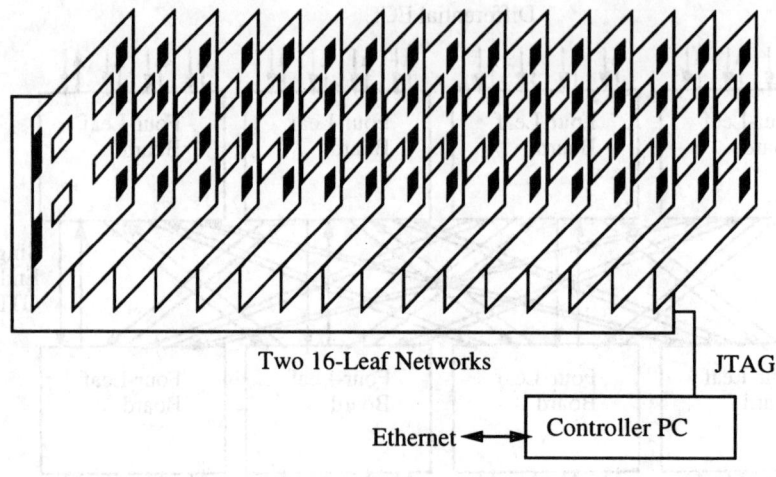

Fig. 3. Card Cage

sive error detection; it has limited error handling, keeps statistics, and provides significant testing support. The overall structure of Arctic is shown in Figure 5.

Arctic uses a sophisticated buffer management scheme that greatly increases the effectiveness of its buffers and the utilization of network links. This scheme is similar to that developed by Joerg for the PaRC routing chip [5, 6] of the Monsoon multiprocessor. All buffering in Arctic is located in the input sections. Each input section contains three buffers; each capable of storing a maximum size packet. Each buffer is capable of storing either a priority packet or a normal packet. The last empty buffer is reserved for a priority packet; this ensures that normal packets can not block priority packets. The head of a packet can be transferred out of a buffer before the end of the packet has been received (virtual cut-through with partial cut-throughs allowed). (The head of an unblocked packet will leave Arctic roughly 150 ns after it has entered Arctic.) The crossbar has 12 inputs and 4 outputs. Each of the packet buffers in the chip is directly connected to the crossbar. The scheduling scheme used in Arctic ensures that if any buffer in the chip contains a packet destined for a given output then a packet will be transferred to that output as soon as the output becomes available. Any four of the 12 input buffers can be simultaneously transferring to output sections. Packets received on a given input and destined for a particular output are transferred in the same order as they were received, thus in order delivery of packets is maintained along a given network path. Packets received on different inputs and destined for a particular output are scheduled using a round-robin scheme which guarantees that no packet is starved for service. All priority packets waiting for a particular output are transferred before any waiting normal packet is transferred to that output.

Each Arctic port has an incoming 16-bit data path and an outgoing 16-bit data path. Two clock lines, a frame line, and a (reverse direction) flow control line

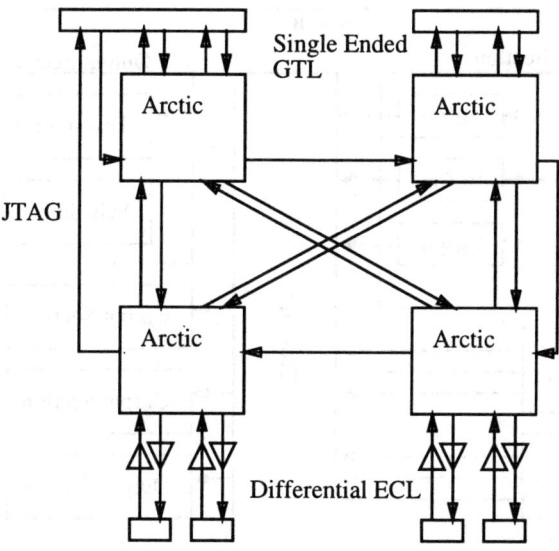

Fig. 4. Four-Leaf Board

are associated with each data path. Each data bit is transmitted using a single ended GTL driver at 77 Mbits/sec. This technology supports printed circuit board links that are one meter long. A 16-bit CRC is sent with each packet. The frame and flow control signals are Manchester encoded. Link errors are detected using a CRC check circuit for data and a Manchester check circuit for the frame and flow control signals. Since the two Switch Fabric link technologies (interchassis ECL and intrachassis GTL) have been designed for high reliability, Arctic does not provide link level packet retry. In the unlikely event of a CRC error, Arctic will record the error and will forward the packet, marked with a bad CRC, toward a Fabric endpoint.

Arctic uses source based routing; the course of a packet through a Switch Fabric is completely determined by routing information placed in the packet header by the source. Arctic can be configured to implement any of a wide variety of source based routing schemes. Each Arctic input port is configured with two masks, two reference values, and three bit extraction operations. For each incoming packet, Arctic uses the two masks to select two subfields of the packet's header and compares these subfields to the reference values. Based on the results of the comparison, Arctic selects an extraction operation and applies it to the header. The result of this operation determines the output port for the packet. Most Switch Fabrics will be configured for fat tree routing. For fat tree routing each packet header is divided into two fields. The source places a random bit string in the first and the destination address in the second. As the packet travels from the leaves to the root, each Arctic checks the appropriate prefix of the destination address to determine if the packet must travel farther from the

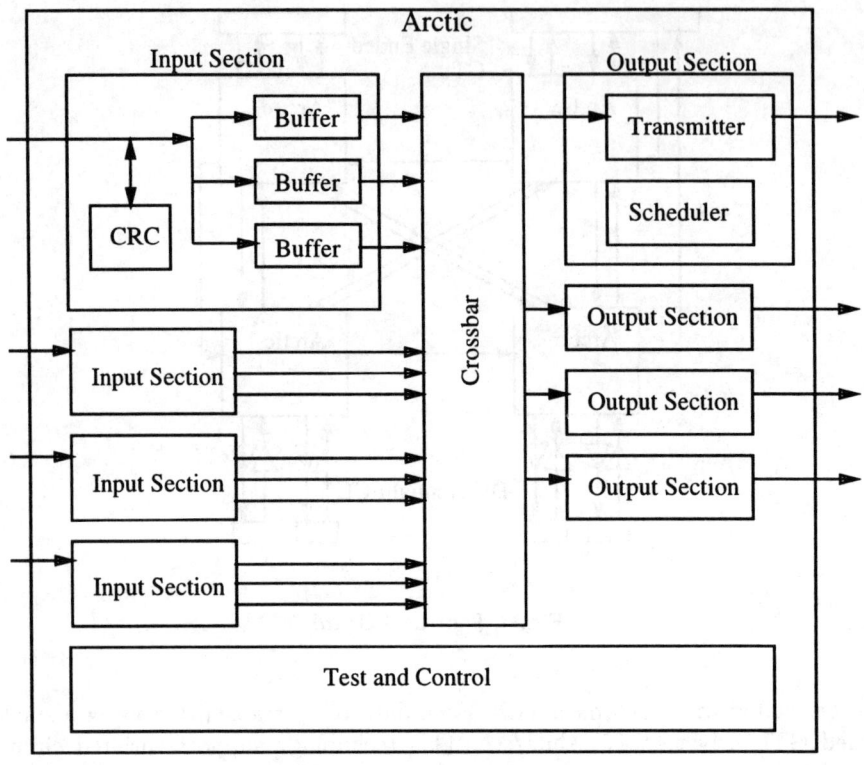

Fig. 5. Arctic Block Diagram

leaves. If this is the case then, since there are multiple acceptable paths away from the leaves, the Arctic uses a portion of the random bit string (the first header field) to choose an appropriate output port (away from the leaves). Otherwise the Arctic uses a portion of the destination address (the second header field) to determine the appropriate output port toward the leaves. The use of a random bit string generated at the source provides a more globally random distribution of traffic than would be produced if each Arctic dynamically routed packets based on local flow control information. Also since this string is generated at the source, a variety of modifications can easily be made to this fat tree routing algorithm.

Arctic has an extensive maintenance system which is accessed through its JTAG port. The maintenance system provides configuration data to Arctic including the routing algorithm for each input port. The maintenance system has real time control of Arctic. It can disable and enable each port, and can flush packets. It has access to the five error counters in each input port which record link errors, and to the six 36-bit counters in each output port which monitor packet traffic.

The maintenance system is capable of performing several off line test operations. It has access to Arctic's boundary scan ring. The boundary scan ring supports EXTEST operations which can be used to test the continuity of printed circuit board traces. The boundary scan ring also supports INTEST operations which can be used to run off line verification tests on Arctic through its I/O cells. The maintenance system has off line access to Arctic's manufacturing test rings which contain nearly all of Arctic's state elements. Thus the maintenance system allows ATPG generated manufacturing tests to be run on Arctic without a manufacturing tester. These tests verify the integrity of almost all of Arctic's internal circuitry.

Arctic's maintenance system allows test packets to be injected into the Switch Fabric. Packets are injected by taking Arctic off line, using the boundary scan ring to inject the packets into Arctic, and then placing Arctic back on line with the injected packets.

A more detailed description of the Arctic router chip can be found in the PCRCW 94 paper [2].

5 Status

A prototype Fabric circuit board has been constructed and successfully tested with StarT-Jr nodes. As shown in Figure 6, this prototype board includes one Arctic chip and one interface circuit. It has one ECL port cable connector, three GTL port cable connectors, and a maintenance port connector. Four copies of this board are being used in a four endpoint Switch Fabric. ECL links are being used to connect the prototype Fabric boards to StarT-Jr NIUs and GTL links are being used to interconnect the prototype Fabric boards.

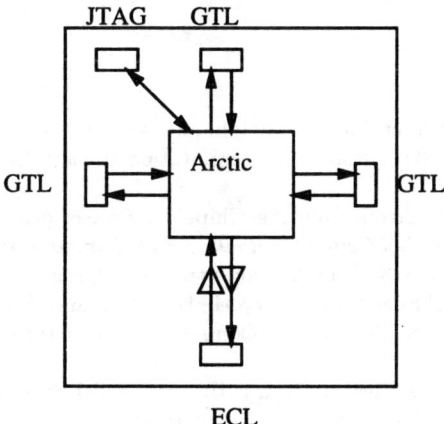

Fig. 6. Prototype Fabric Board

The four-leaf Fabric board is a simple extension of this prototype board. The design of the four-leaf board is currently being completed and fabricated four-leaf boards are expected in September. A Fabric card cage should be available in October.

Related work on network interfaces is being done by other members of our group. The StarT-Jr network interface [4] has been available for over a year. It is PCI-bus based and includes an embedded I960 microprocessor. The StarT-X network interface [3] is also PCI based but has a more direct hardware implementation and provides higher performance. While StarT-X has a more limited functionality than StarT-Jr, it provides the most important message passing functions including DMA. StarT-X boards will be available in August. The StarT-Voyager Network Endpoint System (NES) [1] is a much higher performance memory-bus based network interface. The NES contains an embedded PowerPC 604 service processor. The NES provides direct hardware support for four different types of messages and programmable support for cache coherent distributed shared memory. NES boards are expected in October.

6 Acknowledgments

I want to thank everyone who has contributed to the Arctic Switch Fabric project. Greg Papadopoulos, Bob Greiner, and Chris Joerg inspired many of the concepts used in the Arctic router chip. Many people have contributed to the detailed design of the Arctic router chip, the Fabric boards, and the support software. These include Jack Costanza, Doug Faust, Tom Durgavich, Ralph Tiberio, Richard Davis, Elth Ogston, Michael Sy, and Chen Chi Ming Hubert. Finally, I want to give special thanks to Arvind for providing his support and managerial guidance to the project.

References

1. Boon S. Ang, Derek Chiou, Larry Rudolph, and Arvind. Message Passing Support on StarT-Voyager. CSG Memo 387, Computation Structures Group, LCS, MIT, July 1996.
2. G. Andrew Boughton. Arctic Routing Chip. In *Proceedings of the 1994 University of Washington Parallel Computer Routing and Communication Workshop*, May 1994. Also CSG Memo 373, Computation Structures Group, LCS, MIT.
3. James Hoe. Functional Specification for a High-Performance Network Interface Unit on a Peripheral Bus. CSG Memo 389, Computation Structures Group, LCS, MIT, June 1997.
4. James C. Hoe and Mike Ehrlich. StarT-JR: A Parallel System from Commodity Technology. In *Proceedings of the 7th Transputer/Occam International Conference*, November 1996. Also CSG Memo 384, Computation Structures Group, LCS, MIT.
5. C. F. Joerg. Design and Implementation of a Packet Switched Routing Chip. TR 482, Laboratory for Computer Science, MIT, 1990.
6. C. F. Joerg and G. A. Boughton. The Monsoon Interconnection Network. In *Proceedings of the 1991 IEEE International Conference on Computer Design*, October 1991. Also CSG Memo 340, Computation Structures Group, LCS, MIT.

Session II

ROUTER AND NETWORK ARCHITECTURES I

Thursday, June 26, 1997
1:00 - 2:30

Session Chair:

K. Bolding
Seattle Pacific University

STREAMER: Hardware Support for Smoothed Transmission of Stored Video over ATM

Sung-Whan Moon, Padmanabhan Pillai, and Kang G. Shin

Real-Time Computing Laboratory, Dept. of EECS
The University of Michigan, Ann Arbor MI 48105
{swmoon, pillai, kgshin}@eecs.umich.edu

Abstract. We propose a hardware design which provides support for smoothed transmission of stored video from a server to a client for real-time playback. The design, called Streamer, resides on the network interface and handles the transmission scheduling of all streams over a single link connected to an ATM network. Streamer minimizes the interaction needed with the server CPU, while supporting very fine grain scheduling of cell transmissions for a large number of streams. Throughput is also maximized by streaming data directly from the storage medium to the network interface buffer over the I/O bus. We observe that the scheduling mechanism can be modified to operate at 2.1 Gbps link speeds and the Streamer as a whole can provide cell-granular, interleaved scheduling with full utilization of 155 Mbps and 622 Mbps links.

1 Introduction

Asynchronous Transfer Mode (ATM) networks use fixed size cells and a connection-oriented scheme to deliver information across a high-speed network. Because of their ability to deliver high-bandwidths and per-connection QoS guarantees, ATM networks are well-suited for real-time multimedia applications, such as delivering stored video for continuous playback at the client. In this application, a client requests delivery of some stored video (i.e., a video clip or an entire movie) from a remote server. The large amount of data versus relatively small buffer capacity on a typical client, coupled with the burstiness of compressed video, makes it difficult to deliver QoS guarantees for uninterrupted playback. Network resource allocation based on peak rates becomes expensive, resulting in under-utilization of resources and limited number of connections. Requiring very large client-side buffer capacity to absorb the bursts also becomes unrealistic due to cost considerations. A solution to this problem involves reducing the rate variability by using smoothing techniques [10][17]. Based on the buffer capacity of the client, these algorithms determine a transmission schedule which results in smoother transmission and decreased peak rate, without starving or overflowing the client buffer.

The work reported in this paper was supported in part by the National Science Foundation under Grant MIP-9203895. Any opinions, findings, and conclusions or recommendations expressed in this paper are those of the authors and do not necessarily reflect the view of the NSF.

Although these algorithms have been shown to increase network utilization [17], they still do not provide an end-to-end solution. These algorithms assume the video server will be able to put data into the network based on the smoothed transmission schedule. For a single stream a server CPU scheduling approach might suffice, but for a large number of streams utilizing close to full capacity of the link, such a server-based approach will not deliver the results obtainable with smoothing. Several researchers [5][6][8][9][14][15][16][18] have argued that the network I/O on current end systems, such as servers, is the main bottleneck in providing applications with the high-bandwidths available to them. In a video server application, Saha [16] recognizes a substantial penalty with a server-initiated transmission due to the cost of moving data from a storage device to the network interface via the server CPU. In this scheme, data is copied multiple times, from storage to the kernel's memory space inside the server's main memory, then to the application's memory space and back to the kernel, and finally to the network interface which sends the data out on the network link. Due to the overhead of multiple copying, the actual bandwidth available to the applications is substantially less than the link bandwidth. A common solution proposed is to reduce the number of data copies so that data can be moved from the source to the network interface with one copy.

In these single-copy schemes [5][6][18], the data that is to be transmitted is copied directly from the application's memory into the network interface's buffer. This copying is done either by the server CPU or by the network interface. Scheduling of transmissions is also done by the server CPU, which notifies the network interface of a transmission via some type of request mechanism. Unfortunately, in a video server application, data is usually on a separate storage medium (e.g., hard disk) and not in main memory. So, another method of copying data from the source to the network interface is required. Saha [16] proposes a streaming approach where the source of the data acts as an autonomous device which can send data without constant interaction with the server CPU. Once initiated, the autonomous device will continuously send data to the destination device. In his experimental platform, the autonomous device is the MMT adaptor, which captures real-time video and audio and then outputs compressed digitized video and audio streams. The MMT adaptor will then copy the data into the network interface over an I/O bus. Dittia *et al.* [8] propose a similar approach where data is streamed from the source to the network interface. Their approach consists of an interconnection of special chips (APIC), with each chip connecting to a single I/O device. This interconnection replaces the traditional I/O bus, with the first APIC connected to the network interface and main system bus. Data from an I/O device destined for the network will simply travel down the chain of APICs till it reaches the network interface.

In order to provide smoothed transmission of stored video, smoothing techniques and data streaming by themselves are not enough. Smoothing techniques can only calculate a smoothed transmission schedule. There is no explanation as to how to achieve such a smooth transmission. Data streaming techniques use a single copy approach to increase throughput available to applications and I/O devices. Although throughput is important, link scheduling is also needed in order to conform to the smoothed transmission schedule. Saha [16] proposes a scheduler based on round-robin scheduling implemented using a processor. This approach has the drawback that fine grain scheduling is limited by how fast the processor can determine the next stream to transmit. The APIC [8] solution is to simply limit the burst size and burst interval for each source of data. Because data travelling down the chain of APICs is continuously buffered at each APIC before reaching the network interface, such a mechanism cannot guarantee any smoothness in the transmission.

In this paper, we propose an integrated solution for smoothed transmission of stored video using both the smoothing schedule and data streaming. Since the I/O device can only control the rate at which it sends data to the network interface, actual link scheduling needs to be done on the network interface. Software scheduling on the server involves the server telling the network interface when to send data, how much data to send and from which stream. For a large number of streams, this approach will potentially stall the transmission due to delay associated with context switches, interrupt handling, other OS overheads, and issues dealing with CPU scheduling [11][12]. This may happen when trying to do fine grain scheduling where each stream transmits a small number of ATM cells at a time. Also, with the software scheduled method, a large number of messages need to be sent from the server CPU to the network interface. This decreases the bandwidth available to the devices for copying data to the network interface. Since the overall goal is to be able to transmit a large number of video streams as smoothly as possible, such a server CPU scheduled approach will not work. A hardware scheduler on the network interface, on the other hand, can off-load the scheduling and multiplexing of stream transmissions from the server, allowing the server to do other tasks. This also reduces traffic between the network interface and server CPU, while allowing for fine-grain scheduling at the ATM cell level. This in turn, allows for a large number of video streams to be transmitted onto the network, with each stream closely following its smoothed transmission schedule, and for better utilization of the link's bandwidth.

In this paper we propose such a hardware design, which facilitates both the streaming of stored video data from storage directly to the network interface, and the transmission scheduling of these video streams based on smoothing algorithms. Our hardware design, which we refer to as the Streamer, takes on the functionality of the transmitter unit on a network interface. The Streamer is responsible for buffering cells from various streams, scheduling the transmission of these cells, and retrieving these cells from the buffer for transmission. Parts of the smoothed transmission schedule are cached inside a buffer on the Streamer, and are used to determine which stream gets access to the link next. We argue that caching of the transmission schedule is very reasonable due to the small size of the schedule itself. The Streamer also allows unused link bandwidth to be used for best-effort traffic.

This paper is organized as follows. Before describing the Streamer, we first describe the smoothing algorithm assumed in our design, and the basic functionality of network interfaces. In Section 3 the Streamer architecture and operations are explained. Evaluation of our implementation and future work are presented in Section 4. Conclusions are presented in Section 5.

Schedule Segment #	Start Interval Frame #	End Interval Frame #	Transmit Size
1	a1	a2 - 1	B1
2	a2	a3 - 1	B2
...	...	...	...
M	aM	N	BM

Schedule Segment #	Chunk Interval	# of Chunks	Chunk Size	Last
1	I1	N1	C1	0
2	I2	N2	C2	0
...	...	...	...	...
L	IL	NL	CL	1

(a) Smoothed transmission schedule using frame intervals output by smoothing alorithm

(b) Possible format for smoothed transmission schedule using chunk intervals

Fig. 1. Smoothed transmission schedules

2 Background

Before describing our hardware design (Streamer), we will first look at smoothing algorithms and network interface issues, which are the main components of our design. We will first describe the smoothing algorithms presented in the literature, and then make extensions to the schedule for the purposes of our design. Basic architecture and functionality of a network interface are introduced, with emphasis on ATM networks. We then describe how the Streamer fits into the network interface, and explain the operations that are supported and not supported by our design.

2.1 Smoothing Algorithms

Although optimization criteria differs among various researchers, the main goal of smoothing algorithms [10][17] is to reduce the rate variability of stored variable bit rate video. Stored video consists of frames, which are just images, captured 10-30 times a second. Compression techniques, such as MPEG, take advantage of the inherent redundancy to compress the video data, and reduce the total storage required. Such compression, though, results in burstiness due to the varying frame sizes. For real-time playback across a network, such burstiness causes problems in network resource allocation and QoS guarantees when transmitting frames every 10-30 msecs. Smoothing algorithms take advantage of the fact that *a priori* knowledge of the video stream is available for stored video, and determine transmission schedules based on the buffer capacity of the client. The resulting smoothed schedule is characterized by small rate variations, and a fairly constant transmission rate.

The smoothed transmission schedule determines the amount of data to be sent at each of the N frame intervals. For a 30 frames per second video stream, the interval is 33 msecs. Instead of transmitting a different amount of data at each frame interval, the smoothing algorithm generates several constant rate schedule segments. During each schedule segment, which lasts for several frame intervals, the same amount of data will be transmitted at each frame interval. This amount will change slightly between different schedule segments. Fig. 1(a) shows the format for the final schedule. Based on the results reported in [10, 17], the number of these constant rate schedule segments (in the 100s to the 1000s) is considerably less than the total number of frames (in the 100,000s) in a video clip or movie, and decreases with an increase in the client's receive buffer (typically around 1 MB). The typical amount of data transmitted at each frame interval is in the range of 1-5 KB based on Salehi *et al.* [17], and 5-12 KB based on Feng [10].

Considering that each ATM cell's payload is 48 bytes, a 5 KB transmission requires around 105 ATM cells, while 12 KB requires a little over 250 ATM cells. Instead of transmitting these cells in a burst at each frame interval, we assume a schedule which is modified in three ways. First, the transmission size is assumed to be in units of ATM cells. A method for calculating such a schedule is described in [17]. Second, time is specified in units equal to the time required to transmit one ATM cell. In our design, we targeted a 155 Mbps ATM link. Third, frame intervals are further divided into chunk intervals, and the cells that need to be transmitted for the frame interval are divided up evenly and sent at each chunk interval, further smoothing out transmission. On a 155 Mbps link, each cell takes 2.7 μsecs to transmit, hence over 12000 cells can be transmitted within the typical 33 msec frame interval. So instead of bursting, say 200 cells, for a half msec every 33 msecs, chunk intervals can be used to burst 20 cells every 3.3 msecs. Such spread-out transmissions can be seen as more favorable from the network's point of view. We assume that this chunk interval schedule is derived from the frame interval schedule produced by the smoothing algorithm above, and will not result in client buffer overflow or underflow. Here we also make the obvious assumption that if the smoothed transmission schedule is observed, then the network will be able to provide certain guarantees for uninterrupted playback at the client side.

Fig. 1(b) shows the chunk interval schedule that our hardware design assumes. Chunk intervals (I1, I2, ..., IL) are specified in cell transmit time units, while the schedule segment duration is specified by the number of chunk intervals (N1, N2, ..., NL). Chunk size (C1, C2, ..., CL) is given in number of cells. For example, during the first schedule segment, there will be N1 transmission bursts of C1 cells each, with these bursts occurring every I1 cell transmit time units. The "Last" field flags the last schedule segment, and indicates the end of the stream. Each schedule segment can be encoded using a small number of bytes (6-8), so the entire schedule for a movie stream can be encoded with just a few KBytes (1-8). Since each schedule segment lasts for many frame intervals, the time between schedule segment changes will be in the range of 5-50 secs, which is an eternity for hardware.

2.2 Network Interface Architecture and Functions

The function of the network interface is to transmit data from the host to the network, and similarly transfer data received from the network to the host. As shown in Fig. 2, the network interface will typically interact with the rest of the host over the host's I/O bus. When an application on the CPU needs to send data, the necessary software will transfer the data to the network interface buffer. The transmit control on the interface will then handle the necessary overhead associated with transmitting each cell. For ATM, these tasks include segmenting the application data into cells, adding ATM cell headers, and performing CRC generation. The physical layer then handles all the physical medium specific functions, such as cell delineation, framing, and bit timing. When

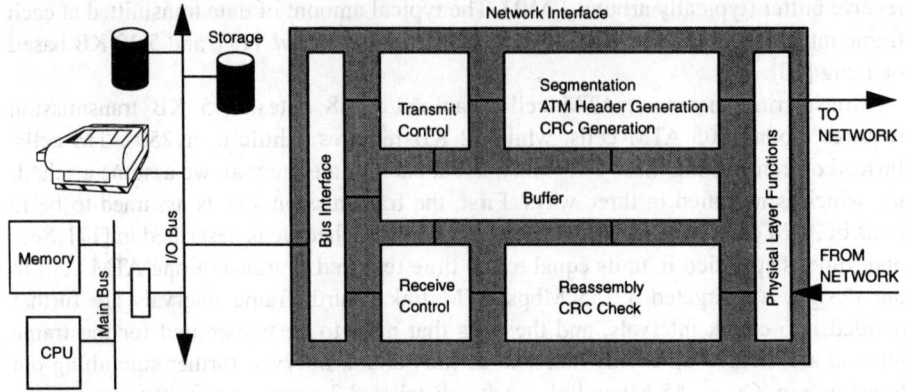

Fig. 2. Generic host system with I/O devices and the ATM network interface.

cells arrive at the interface, the receive control reassembles the cells into application data units before delivering them to the application. Commercial ATM network interface products [2][3][4] follow this general model.

As mentioned earlier, a single copy approach can improve throughput as seen by the application. Various solutions fall under one of two categories. The first consists of allowing the application to write directly into the network interface's buffer [5]. Actual transmission is initiated by sending a special control signal. The other approach is to first send a message to the network interface, which then copies the data directly from the application's memory into its own buffer [6][18]. In either case, the CPU is actively involved in each transmission. For a video server application, where a large amount of data resides on a hard disk, streaming of the data is more appropriate. In this scheme, the CPU simply initializes the hard disk to send data to the network interface. The hard disk is assumed to have enough intelligence to know when to pause and resume data flow based on feedback from the network interface. This streaming scheme is assumed for our design.

Our hardware design, the Streamer, proposed in this paper fits into the transmit control section in Fig. 2. One of the functions of the transmit controller is to determine which of the connections ready for transmission gets access to the link and for how long. Instead of simple FIFO link scheduling, Streamer is a hardware scheduling mechanism which allows for smoothed transmission scheduling of video streams. Streamer does this by maintaining scheduling information for each of the active video streams, storing cells from the hard disks into the buffer, determining which active stream needs to transmit and how much, and removing cells from the buffer for transmission. From product information we were able to obtain, several commercial products also offer some type of link scheduling on the network interface. [2] mentions independent transmit scheduling for each virtual circuit and support for MPEG-2 transport delivery. [7] mentions an ATM adapter with support for pacing of MPEG streams for smooth transmission of data. [4] describes a rate-based traffic shaping scheduler that provides interleaved stream scheduling. It uses a static round-based schedule to divide up link bandwidth among active connections. During each round, data for the corresponding connection is transmitted only if the traffic shaping permits it to do so. In contrast, Streamer dynamically schedules streams, requiring no adjustments for rate changes caused by the smoothed schedule, and also uses a dedicated priority queue mechanism to arbitrate among the active streams. Details of the Streamer are given in Section 3.

3 Streamer

We have discussed the potentials of ATM networks for the transmission of real-time video, the problems and inefficiencies of bursty video traffic in the context of guaranteed service reservation, and the existence of smoothing algorithms that alleviate these problems. We have also established that scheduling the transmission of smoothed video streams in real-time requires hardware support if link utilization is to be kept high. Addressing all of these issues, we have designed a hardware solution to real-time link scheduling of smoothed video streams that avoids CPU and memory bottlenecks by streaming data directly from storage devices to the network interface. The Streamer network interface allows for effective implementation of smoothed video multimedia servers as it can handle many simultaneous streams. We therefore extend the work done with smoothed video streams by providing the hardware link scheduling needed for efficient smoothed video streaming in a multimedia server.

3.1 Operation

The Streamer operates as follows. When the server receives a request for a new video stream, it checks for sufficient resources on the server to handle this new stream. This admission control mechanism takes into account such factors as storage device bandwidth and latency, and available buffer space on the network interface in addition to the conventional admission control on the network. Only then is the appropriate signalling performed to establish the new connection. Based on the client buffer, a smoothed transmission schedule is calculated on-line or is retrieved from storage. The server CPU then downloads the first few schedule segments and the cell header into the Streamer, and allocates sufficient number of buffers in the network interface to avoid buffer starvation.

The server CPU then signals the appropriate storage device to begin streaming data to the network interface. We assume that the storage devices are controlled by bus-mastering capable controllers. Once initialized by the host CPU, these controllers will stream data to the Streamer network interface with little or no further dependence on the host CPU. The devices are assumed to have sufficiently higher throughput than required by the video streams, and enough caching on the controllers to avoid buffer starvation at the network interface. We also assume that a file system optimized for video data stores the streams linearly in the storage devices to facilitate the autonomous retrieval by the bus-mastering controllers and to avoid seek latencies. Furthermore, we assume that the data has been preprocessed for transmission and is fragmented into ATM cells, taking into account overhead for error correction and ATM

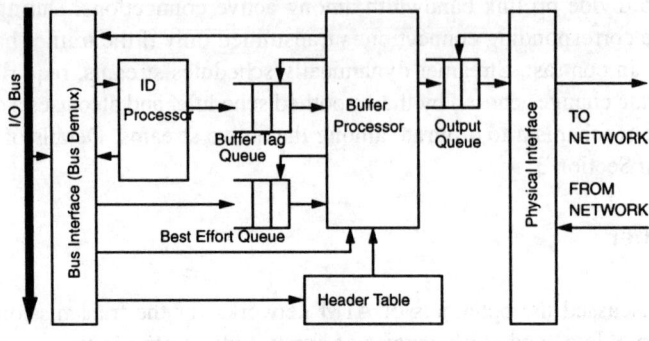

Fig. 3. Streamer.

Adaption Layer information, and is stored as a sequence of 48 byte cell payloads. This last assumption allowed us to focus on the smoothed scheduling support without worrying about the extra ATM cell processing.

Once the initialization has been completed, a control signal is sent to the Streamer to begin transmitting the particular stream. Scheduled transmission continues without host CPU intervention except to supply additional smoothed transmission schedule segments and to handle any errors that may occur.

3.2 Architecture

The basic architecture of the Streamer network interface is shown in Fig. 3. The Streamer board is not a complete network interface as it does not provide segmentation, CRC generation, or any receive functionality. Though a minimal design, it can provide fine-grained (down to cell level) interleaved transmission of up to 255 simultaneous streams based on independent traffic smoothing schedules.

3.2.1 Bus Interface (Bus Demux)

The bus demultiplexor provides the bus interface for the Streamer. In addition to decoding addresses and generating internal control signals, the bus demux also provides simple feedback to the data storage devices in order to prevent buffer overflows. As bus-mastering drive controllers stream data to the Streamer board, the bus demux determines if buffer space is available (based on a per-stream allocation and a table maintained in conjunction with the buffer processor). If buffer space for the particular stream is not currently available, it uses a device-not-ready mechanism to force the drive controller to relinquish the bus and try again later. The bus demux can also generate interrupts when the ID processor or the buffer processor needs servicing from the server CPU.

3.2.2 ID Processor

The ID processor (Fig. 4) is the heart of the Streamer board. This module performs

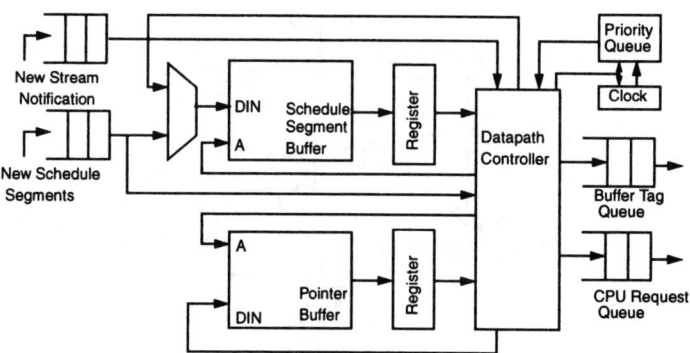

Fig. 4. ID Processor

scheduling among the active streams and generates a sequence of buffer tags, which are control structures that indicate a stream ID and a cell count, and are used to tell the buffer processor what to transmit. For each stream, the ID processor stores up to 4 segments of a smoothed transmission schedule. These segments indicate traffic shaping parameters such as burst length and burst interval to be applied to a specified number of cells. As each segment expires, the ID processor will place a request for more through the CPU request queue.

Scheduling is performed by keeping the departure time for the next chunk of data for each stream in a hardware priority queue [13]. The hardware priority queue allows single cycle insertion, and allows arbitrary interleaving of streams to produce a precise schedule for transmission, unlike the imprecise schemes used elsewhere [4], that are essentially round-robin schemes modified to take traffic shaping into account. Furthermore, the priority queue approach is fully dynamic, and works well with streams that have changing data rates, unlike the round-robin variants, which require the recomputation of a static schedule to reflect each data rate change. The priority queue produces the proper ordering of transmission from the active streams, while a cell counter, acting as a clock, ensures proper time intervals are maintained between subsequent transmissions. When the clock indicates that the stream at the top of the priority queue is ready to transmit, the entry is removed from the queue. Based on the stream's scheduling segment data, a buffer tag is generated indicating the stream ID and the number of cells to transmit. The number of remaining transmissions left for the particular schedule segment is updated, while the departure time for the next burst of data for the stream is computed and inserted into the priority queue. This entire operation can be accomplished in constant time (less than 10 cycles). If it is not time to send video stream data, delay slots can be introduced in the output by producing a special buffer tag that indicates either a best-effort traffic cell or an idle cell should be released instead of data from the video streams.

3.2.3 Buffer Processor

The buffer processor (Fig. 5) is essentially a combined buffer memory and manager

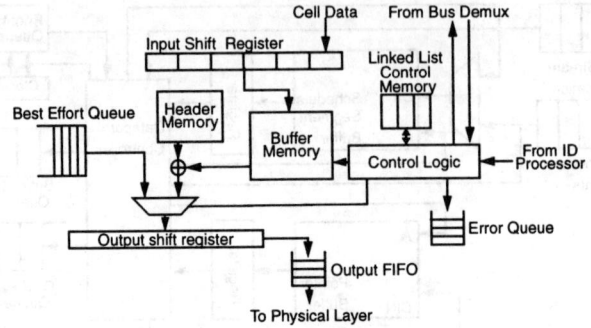

Fig. 5. Buffer Processor

with the added responsibility of sending cells to the physical layer interface. The buffer memory is organized as a bank of 48-byte cell buffers. Buffer allocation and management is performed through simple linked list mechanisms on a per-stream basis. A separate linked-list control memory maintains the buffer pointers for each stream as well as the list of free buffers. For simplicity of control and timing, the different data structures (cell buffers, header table, linked-list pointers) are stored in separate, parallelly accessible memories. Individual streams are limited to a specified allocation of buffers, which is determined during admission control. This is enforced in conjunction with the bus demux through a table that indicates the number of buffers that remain available to each stream. An input shift register decouples the buffer processor operation from the six cycle latency in transferring a cell payload over a 64-bit I/O bus. On the output end, as buffer tags are received from the ID processor, the indicated number of cells for the indicated stream ID are prepended with the ATM 5 byte header from a table of headers, and are transferred octet-by-octet to the physical layer through a shift register and a FIFO queue. This transfer mechanism is based on the ATM Forum Level 1 UTOPIA specifications [1]. If an insufficient number of cells are buffered for the stream, an error is reported in an error queue that causes an interrupt to be signaled. If the special idle tag is received from the ID processor, the next cell in a best-effort traffic FIFO queue is sent, or if that queue is empty, an idle cell is sent to the physical layer to ensure that proper cell timing is maintained.

4 Evaluation and Future Work

Streamer has been implemented in Verilog HDL using both behavioral and structural descriptions. Several Verilog simulations were performed to verify the correctness of our design. Due to the interactive nature of the network interface with the rest of the system, special behavioral Verilog code had to be written to emulate the functioning of the storage devices, I/O bus, and server CPU. Due to the extreme complexity involved in trying to do a precise simulation of these components in Verilog, we used simplified models of their behavior, focusing instead on the interaction with our network interface. These extra behavioral models allowed us to easily create test situations under which our design could be observed.

As expected, we observed that the hardware scheduling ran at significantly greater speeds than the transmission link, and as a result was idle most of the time waiting for the physical layer to catch up. This is expected since each ATM cell requires 2.7 μsecs to transmit, while scheduling of cells, based on a 33 MHz system clock, can be done within 10 clock cycles, or around 300 nsecs. Without modification our hardware priority queue scheduler is therefore capable of scheduling 3.3 million cells per second, corresponding to a link speed of 1.4 Gbps. As the hardware priority queue has already been shown to work at 64 MHz [13] using static CMOS technology, and since 15-20ns access time SRAMs are common, the scheduler can be trivially modified to operate off of a 50 MHz clock, and work with up to 2.1 Gbps links.

In contrast, a software-based scheduler using a dedicated processor on the adapter board will not scale as easily with increasing link speeds. If the processor were to handle only the scheduling of cells, an efficient implementation of the 255 entry priority queue would require between 200 and 300 instructions to schedule a single cell (depending upon the instruction set of the processor: 275 on HP PA-RISC, 290 on SPARC, 232 on RS/6000). This requires an effective throughput of 73 to 110 MIPS to provide cell-granular scheduling on a 155 Mbps link. Higher link speeds require proportionally higher instruction throughput. To put this in perspective, a 100 MHz RISC processor, capable of sustaining one instruction per cycle on the optimized priority queue code with 250 instructions executed per cell scheduled, would be capable of scheduling 1 cell every 2.5 μsecs. This is just within the 2.7 μsec transmission time of cells on a 155 Mbps link. So, even without taking into account other functions the onboard processor may need to perform, this processor is already incapable of providing full link utilization for rates over 170 Mbps. In other words, for very high link speeds a software-based scheduling at cell level granularity will require a very high performance, expensive microprocessor implementation.

As stated above, our scheduling module can be readily adapted to 2 Gbps operation. In our current implementation, the buffer management and transmission unit, based on the 33 MHz clock and the 8-bit wide UTOPIA[1] standard, is limited to 264 Mbps. By removing the 33 MHz and 8-bit wide limitations, faster throughput is attainable. Since the update of the buffer management structures can be performed in 6 cycles, and since two updates occur for each cell transmitted, the buffer management can handle 5.5 million cells per second (over 2.3 Gbps) with a 66 MHz clock. By using a 66 MHz, 32-bit wide interface to the physical layer, the buffer processor can support a 2 Gbps link.

In Streamer, the scheduling is done in parallel with the transmission of previously-scheduled cells, so the link can be kept fully utilized whenever there are cells to transmit. This is assuming that both schedule segment data and video data are present in the network interface buffers. As was mentioned in Section 2.1, each schedule segment will typically last several seconds and this combined with the fact that we store a few schedule segments ahead, allows large server CPU delays to be tolerated when additional scheduling segments are needed.

However, the transfer of video data across the I/O bus and into the cell buffers will restrict throughput and link utilization. Due to the simple data transfer model, in which the storage devices continuously try to push data to the network interface, and the fact

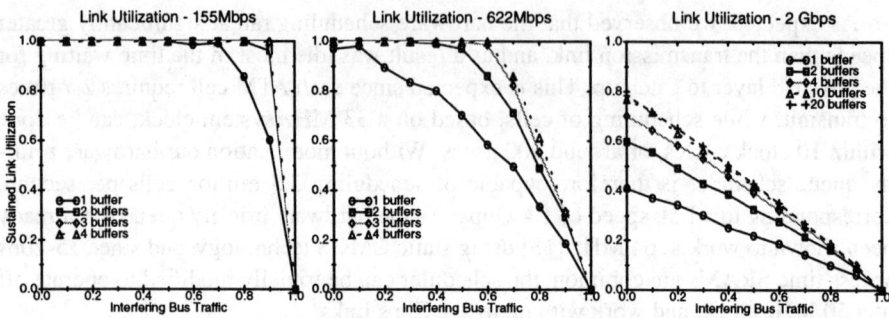

Fig. 6. Sustained Link Utilization

that multiple devices contend for the use of the shared bus, buffer starvation may occur beyond some throughput level. We performed simulations that quantify this effect. We model a Streamer network interface modified to operate at up to 2 Gbps and support more than 256 streams, and a PCI standard server I/O bus, based on the proposed 64-bit, 66 MHz implementation, with a peak throughput of 4.2 Gbps. We assume that bus arbitration results in a round-robin traversal of devices contending for bus access. To isolate the effects of the bus, we assume that each storage device has an internal cache and serves just one stream, so retrieval latencies are hidden and more than sufficient bandwidth is available. We also model interfering traffic on the I/O bus by granting a fraction of the bus accesses to a dummy device. We ran this simulation repeatedly with random sets of streams (mean stream data rate of 2 Mbps, 50% of streams between 1.8 and 2.2 Mbps) corresponding to various link utilizations, and determine the point at which buffer starvation begins to occur. We repeat the simulations, varying the fraction of interfering bus traffic, the number of cell buffers on the network interface for each stream, and the link speeds. The results are summarized in Fig. 6. The storage devices are granted bus access in round-robin fashion, and at each access, the device will send data corresponding to 1 ATM cell, but will abort its access if the corresponding stream's buffers are all full or if the Streamer buffer management is busy (within 4 clock cycles of the start of a cell transmission to the physical layer). As the Streamer does not accept data on the bus when it starts the transmission of a cell, and since the transmission rate is greater for the high speed links, the probability that a storage device will be forced to abort (even though buffer space is still available for the stream) on any particular bus access increases with link speed. With a large number of streams, there is a good chance that some devices will abort repeatedly on consecutive accesses, resulting in buffer starvation for the associated stream. Increasing the per stream buffering helps avoid starvation, as shown by the large jump in sustainable utilization when more than one buffer per stream are used on the 622 Mbps and 2 Gbps links. However, beyond the first few buffers per stream, there is little further increase in sustained utilization. This is apparent in the nearly identical results for 10 buffers and 20 buffers per stream on the 2 Gbps link.

Based on these observations, Streamer in both its original 155 Mbps implementation and in a 622 Mbps version does provide support for a large number of streams, fine grain interleaved link scheduling, full link utilization, low CPU overhead, and potentially improved network utilization resulting from the smoothed transmissions. To maintain all of these benefits at the full potential of 2 Gbps of the hardware priority queue scheduler, further refinements are required. We plan to study the Streamer concept further, and in particular, we would like to vary the operation of the bus interface, the major limitation in the current design. We are considering replacing the current "data push" model of operation, in which the storage device continuously try to send data to the network interface, with a "data pull" approach, in which data is requested by the Streamer only when necessary. This may improve link throughput and bus utilization, at the expense of increased hardware complexity. Another potential modification is to transfer data in blocks larger than the current 48 byte cell sized units and possibly reduce the bus overheads incurred. More significant changes may include entirely replacing the I/O bus with some form of internal network, which may allow for scalable use of multiple Streamer devices in the same system. We plan to develop a detailed, flexible simulator in order to quantitatively evaluate performance, determine optimal values for parameters such as buffer requirements, and characterize quality-of-service provided by the various architectural changes in the Streamer design. Such simulations will also allow us to easily vary the components of the video server and therefore determine system requirements under different scenarios.

5 Conclusion

In order to take full advantage of the features provided by ATM networks and bring them to the end systems, improvements need to be made within the end system. For the video server application, we proposed and described a hardware solution which would do just that. The main idea behind our design is to combine smoothed transmission scheduling with data streaming support on the network interface. This results in high sustained throughput from the server to the network, and also results in better utilization of network resources due to smoothing of bursty data streams. By moving the scheduling away from the server CPU and onto the network interface in the form of a hardware priority queue based scheduler, the server is free to do other work. Communication between the server CPU and network interface is also significantly reduced, and fine grain link scheduling becomes possible. Such fine grain scheduling at the cell level is possible in hardware because, unlike a software scheduler, the hardware scheduler can operate much faster than the cell transmission rate on the network link. We implemented our design using Verilog HDL, and based on Verilog simulations, showed functional correctness and potential performance gains. We also evaluated any limitations on scaling the current design to faster link speeds and indicated some potential future improvements.

References

1. ATM Forum Level 1 UTOPIA Specification 2.01, 1994.
2. ATM-155+ Mbps SAR Controller Module, http://www.chips.ibm.com/products/commun/a155.html, 1996.
3. SunATM Adapter, http://www.sun.com/products-n-solutions/hw/networking/jtf_sunatm.html, 1996.
4. TranSwitch SARA II TXC-05551 Product Preview: Document Number TXC-05551-MB, http://www.transwitch.com/iocd.html, 1996.
5. C. Dalton, G. Watson, D. Banks, C. Calamvokis, A. Edwards, and J. Lumley. Afterburner. *IEEE Network*, pages 36–43, July 1993.
6. B. S. Davie. The architecture and implemtation of a high-speed host interface. *IEEE Journal on Selected Areas in Communications*, 11(2):228–239, February 1993.
7. M. Day, S. Luning, and D. Spence. White paper: IBM mediaStreamer Solutions, A Technical Overview. http://www.rs6000.ibm.com/solutions/videoservers, February 1997.
8. Z. D. Dittia, J. R. Cox, and G. M. Parulkar. Design of the APIC: A high performance ATM host-interface chip. In *Proceedings of IEEE INFOCOM*, pages 179–187, 1995.
9. P. Druschel, M. B. Abbott, M. Pragels, and L. L. Peterson. Network subsystem design. *IEEE Network*, pages 8–17, July 1993.
10. W.-C. Feng, *Video-On-Demand Services: Efficient Transportation and Decompression of Variable Bit Rate Video*, PhD thesis, The University of Michigan, 1996.
11. A. Mehra, A. Indiresan, and K. G. Shin. Resource management for real-time communication: Making theory meet practice. In *Proceedings of IEEE Real-Time Technology and Applications*, pages 130–138, 1996.
12. A. Mehra, A. Indiresan, and K. G. Shin. Structuring communication software for Quality-of-Service guarantees. In *Proceedings of IEEE Real-Time Systems Symposium*, 1996.
13. S.-W. Moon, J. Rexford, and K. G. Shin. Scalable hardware priority queue architectures for high-speed packet switches. In *Proceedings of IEEE Real-time Technology and Applications Symposium*, pages 203-212, 1997.
14. G. W. Neufeld, M. R. Ito, M. Goldberg, M. J. McCutcheon, and S. Ritchie. Parallel host interface for an ATM network. *IEEE Network*, pages 24–34, July 1993.
15. K. K. Ramakrishnan. Performance considerations in designing network interfaces. *IEEE Journal on Selected Areas in Communications*, 11(2):203–219, February 1993.
16. D. Saha, *Supporting Distributed Multimedia Applications on ATM Networks*, PhD thesis, The University of Maryland, 1995.
17. J. D. Salehi, Z.-L. Zhang, J. F. Kurose, and D. Towsley. Supporting stored video: Reducing rate variability and end-to-end resource requirements through optimal smoothing. *Performance Evaluation Review*, 24(1):222–231, May 1996.
18. C. B. S. Traw and J. M. Smith. Hardware/software organization of a high-performance ATM host interface. *IEEE Journal on Selected Areas in Communications*, 11(2):240–253, February 1993.

Preliminary Evaluation of a Hybrid Deterministic/Adaptive Router

Dianne Miller and Walid A. Najjar

Department of Computer Science, Colorado State University, Ft. Collins, CO 80523
USA

Abstract. A novel routing scheme is proposed for virtual cut-through routing that attempts to combine the low routing delay of deterministic routing with the flexibility and low queuing delays of adaptive routing. This hybrid routing mechanism relies on a pipelined implementation where different paths and stages of the router are used for different routing modes. A simulation based experimental evaluation of these three schemes shows that the hybrid scheme does indeed achieve its objectives.

1 Introduction

This paper reports on the preliminary results of the evaluation of a hybrid deterministic and adaptive routing algorithm. The objective of this new approach to routing is to combine the advantages of both models.

In deterministic, or dimension-order, routing, a message is routed along decreasing dimensions with a dimension decrease occurring only when zero hops remain in all higher dimensions. Virtual channels are included in the router to avoid deadlock [5]. However, deterministic routing algorithms can suffer from congestion since only a small subset of all possible paths between a source and destination are used.

In adaptive routing, messages are not restricted to a single path when traveling from source to destination. Moreover, the choice of path can be made dynamically in response to current network conditions. Such schemes are more flexible, can minimize unnecessary waiting, and can provide fault-tolerance. Several studies have demonstrated that adaptive routing can achieve a lower latency, for the same load, than deterministic routing when measured by a constant clock cycle for both routers [12, 14].

The delay experienced by a message at each node can be broken down into: *routing* delay and *queuing* delay. The former is determined primarily by the complexity of the router. The later is determined by the congestion at each node which in turn is determined by the degrees of freedom the routing algorithm allows a message. The main performance advantage of adaptive routing (besides its fault-tolerance) is that it reduces the queuing delay by providing multiple path options.

However, the routing delay for deterministic routers, and consequently their corresponding clock cycles, can be significantly lower than adaptive routers as pointed out in [3, 1]. This difference in router delays is due to two main reasons:

- *Number of virtual channels:* Two virtual channels are sufficient to avoid deadlock in dimension ordered routing [5]; while adaptive routing (as described in [8, 2]) requires a minimum of three virtual channels in k-ary n-cube networks.
- *Output channel selection:* In dimension-ordered routing, the output channel selection policy is very simple: it depends only on information contained in the message header itself whereas in adaptive routing the output channel selection policy depends also on the state of the router (i.e the occupancy of various virtual channels) causing increased router complexity and thereby higher routing delays.

The results reported in [3, 1] show that the router delays for adaptive routers are about half to more than twice as long as the dimension-order router for worm-hole routing. These results, however, do not account for the advantage of adaptive routing in reducing queuing delays in the nodes between source and destination. Furthermore, the various routing algorithms evaluated, both deterministic and adaptive, require a variable amount of resources such as buffer area or physical channels between nodes. In [9], the advantage of adaptive routing in reducing queuing delays in the nodes between source and destination is accounted for in worm-hole routing.

In this paper we propose a novel routing scheme for virtual cut-through routing that attempts to combine the low routing delay of deterministic routing with the flexibility and low queuing delays of adaptive routing. This hybrid routing mechanism relies on pipelined implementation where different paths and stages of the router are used for different routing modes. The experimental, simulation based results show that the hybrid scheme does achieve, under most conditions, the low latency of the deterministic approach as well as the high saturation point of the adaptive one.

The deterministic and adaptive routing algorithms are described in Section 2 along with the model of the routing delay for virtual cut-through routing. The hybrid routing scheme is described in Section 3 along with simulation results for the three types of routing for k-ary n-cube networks and for various message sizes. Concluding remarks are given in Section 4.

2 Deterministic and Adaptive Routing

The interconnection network model considered in this study is a k-ary n-cube using virtual cut-through switching [13]: message advancement is similar to worm-hole routing [15], except that the body of a message can continue to progress even while the message head is blocked, and the entire message can be buffered at a single node. Note that a header flit can progress to a next node only if the whole message can fit in the destination buffer. For simplicity all messages are assumed to have the same length.

2.1 Routing Models

In the deterministic routing scheme [4, 5], a message is routed along decreasing dimensions with a dimension decrease occurring only when zero hops remain in all higher dimensions. By assigning an order to the network dimensions, no cycle exists in the channel-dependency graph and the algorithm is deadlock-free.

The adaptive routing scheme considered here is described in [7, 8, 2] (also known as the *-channels algorithm). In this algorithm, adaptive routing is obtained by using virtual channels along with dimension-order routing. A message can be routed, adaptively, in any dimension until it is blocked. Once a message is blocked, it is then routed using the dimension-order routing. This algorithm has been proven to be deadlock-free as long as the following routing restrictions are imposed: when the message size is greater than the buffer size (i.e. size of the the virtual channel), deadlock is prevented by allowing the head flit of a message to advance to the next node only if the receiving queue at that node is empty. If the message size is less than the buffer size, then deadlock is prevented by allowing a message to advance only as long as the whole message fits in the receiving queue at that node. This algorithm requires a minimum of three virtual channels per dimension per node for each physical unidirectional channel. Therefore, the number of virtual channels grows linearly with the size of the network.

2.2 Switching Models

In this study, both the deterministic and adaptive routing schemes use one *unidirectional physical channel* (PC) per dimension per node. Figure 1 shows a schematic for each of the routers simulated here for the 2D case. In the deterministic routing case, both high and low virtual channels (VC) of each dimension are multiplexed onto one physical channel. In the adaptive routing case, the deterministic and adaptive VCs are multiplexed onto one PC. For both cases there is only one PC for the sink channel. Once this channel is assigned to a message, it is not released until the whole message has finished its transmission.

The deterministic router uses storage buffers associated with output channels, while the adaptive router uses storage buffers associated with input channels. When using output buffers, the routing decision is made before buffering the message. This type of routing is ideal for deterministic routing because only one choice is available for an incoming message. When a message comes into a node, it can be immediately placed into the appropriate buffer.

When using input buffers, the routing decision is made after buffering the message in the buffer associated with the input channel. This strategy lacks the problem of early commitment of output channels. Since a message can usually be routed on several possible output channels in adaptive routing, this buffering strategy was used for the adaptive router.

The input/output selection policy used for adaptive routing is as follows: a round-robin policy is used for message selection first among all adaptive buffers and then among all deterministic buffers. Output channel selection is performed in each dimension with decreasing number of hops until a free channel is found. By using this output channel selection policy, the greatest amount of adaptivity for a message is retained which reduces blocking.

2.3 Modeling Router Delay

In this section we describe a router delay model for the virtual cut-though deterministic and adaptive routers. The model is based on the ones described in [3, 1, 9]. These models account for both the logic complexity of the routers as well as the size of the crossbar as determined by the number of virtual channels that are multiplexed on one physical channel. These models were modified to account for the varying buffer space used in virtual cut-through routing. The parameters of these models are:

Symbol	Variable (delay)
T_{AD}	Address decoding
T_{ARB}	Routing arbitration
T_{CB}	Crossbar
T_{FC}	Flow control
T_{SEL}	Header selection
T_{VC}	Virtual channel controller
P	Max. no. of IP or OP ports in crossbar
F	Degrees of freedom (OP choices of a message)
C	No. of virtual channels
B	Buffer size (in number of flits)

The address decoding term (T_{AD}) includes the time for examining the packet header and creating new packet headers for all possible routes. The time required for selecting among all possible routes is included in the routing arbitration delay (T_{ARB}). The crossbar delay (T_{CB}) is the time necessary for data to go through the switch's crossbar and is usually implemented with a tree of gates. The flow control delay (T_{FC}) includes the time for flow control between routers so that buffers do not overflow. T_{SEL} is the time for selecting the appropriate header. Finally, the virtual channel controller delay (T_{VC}) includes the time required for multiplexing virtual channels onto physical channels.

For all dimension-order routers simulated here, the number of degrees of freedom (F) equals the number of switch crossbar ports (P). This results because a deterministic router routes a message in either the same dimension on which the message came (on either the low or high channel) or routes it to the next dimension. For all of the adaptive routers, $F = P - 2(n-1)$ where n equals the number of network dimensions. This relationship holds because adaptive routing can use the adaptive channels in all the dimensions while only two virtual channels per physical channel can be used in dimension-order (to avoid deadlock). Note that this relationship includes the delivery port.

Delay equations for the routers are derived, using the above parameters. The constants in these equations were obtained in [3] using router designs along

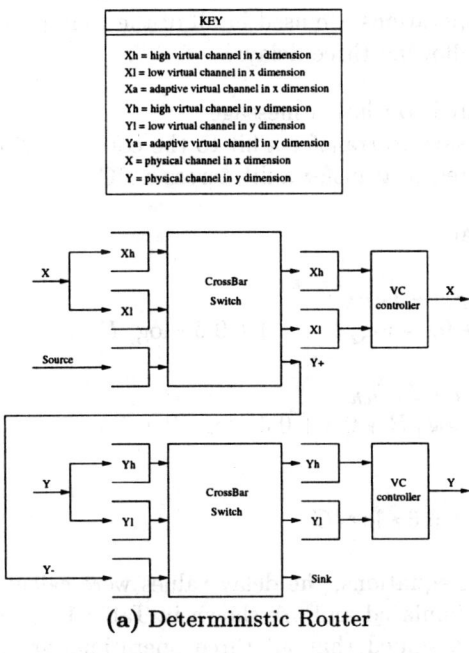

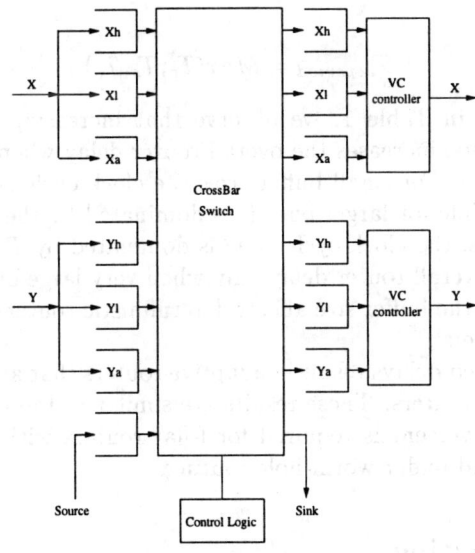

Fig. 1. Schematics of two routers for the 2D case

with gate-level timing estimates based on a 0.8 micron CMOS gate array process. Three main operations are used in all of the routers simulated here which contribute to the following three delays:

- T_r: Time required to route a message
- T_s: Time necessary to transfer a flit to the corresponding output channel
- T_c: Time required to transfer a flit across a PC

The equations are:

$$T_r = T_{AD} + T_{ARB} + T_{SEL}$$
$$T_r = 2.7 + 0.6 + 0.6 * \log_2 F + 1.4 + 0.6 * \log_2 F$$

$$T_s = T_{FC} + T_{CB} + T_{Latch}$$
$$T_s = 0.8 + 0.6 * \log_2 B + 0.4 + 0.6 * \log_2 P + 0.8$$

$$T_c = 4.9 + T_{VC}$$
$$T_c = 4.9 + 1.24 + 0.6 * \log_2 C$$

Using the above equations, the delay values were calculated for each of the router algorithms simulated and are shown in Table 1. To decrease the overall router delay, it is assumed that all three operations are overlapped through pipelining as described in [9], and therefore the clock period is determined by the longest delay:

$$T_{ccperiod} = Max(T_r, T_s, T_c)$$

From the data in Table 1, we observe that increasing the buffer size, in deterministic routers, increases the overall router delay when moderate to large buffer sizes are used. For small buffer sizes the clock cycle is dominated by the transfer time T_c while for larger ones it is dominated by the switching time T_s. In adaptive routers, the clock cycle time is dominated by T_r. Increasing buffer size increases the overall router delay only when very large buffer sizes are used. Finally, changes in the buffer size affects deterministic routers' clock cycles more than adaptive routers'.

All of these added delays result in adaptive routers that are 13 to 30 % slower than deterministic routers. These results are similar to the results in [1] where 15% to 60% improvement is required for f-flat routers with similar number of virtual channels and under worm-hole routing.

3 Hybrid Routing

A typical comparison of deterministic versus adaptive routing latencies is shown in Figure 2: at low traffic and for short to moderate message sizes, the latency of deterministic routing is smaller. However, the flexibility of adaptive routing provides smaller queuing delays and a much higher saturation point. The objective

B	T_r	T_s	T_c	CC Period
8	6.60	5.15	6.74	6.74
16	6.60	5.95	6.74	6.74
24	6.60	6.42	6.74	6.74
32	6.60	6.75	6.74	6.75
48	6.60	7.22	6.74	7.22
64	6.60	7.55	6.74	7.55
96	6.60	8.02	6.74	8.02

a- Deterministic router for
k-ary 2-cube and 3-cube networks
($C = 2$ and $P = F = 3$ for all)

B	T_r	T_s	T_c	CC Period
8	7.80	6.19	7.09	7.80
16	7.80	6.99	7.09	7.80
24	7.80	7.46	7.09	7.80
32	7.80	7.79	7.09	7.80
48	7.80	8.26	7.09	8.26
64	7.80	8.59	7.09	8.59
96	7.80	9.06	7.09	9.06

b- Adaptive router for
k-ary 3-cube networks
($C = 3$ and $P = 10$ and $F = 6$ for all)

Table 1. Deterministic and adaptive router delays (all values in $nsec$)

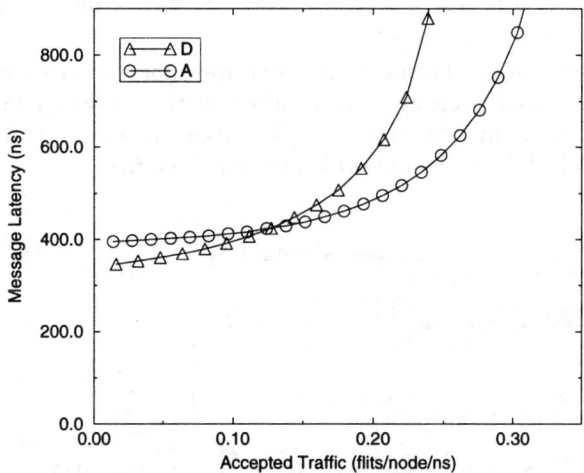

Fig. 2. Latency of dimension-order and adaptive routing on a 10-ary 3-cube network under random uniform traffic for buffer area = 48 flits and L = 8 flits.

of the hybrid routing mechanism is to combine the short latency of deterministic routing for low traffic with the shorter queuing delays of adaptive routing at high traffic. In this section we describe the mechanism of the hybrid routing scheme and present the preliminary results of its performance evaluation.

Hybrid Router Model. The hybrid router, shown as a schematic in Figure 3, consists of three logically independent message paths: Fast Deterministic Path

(FDP), Slow Deterministic Path (SDP), and Adaptive Path (AP)[1]. The FDP requires two stages for a header flit and one clock cycle for a data flit. The SDP and AP both take three clock cycles for a header flit and two clock cycles for a data flit.

These paths are shown in flow chart format in Figure 4 along with their respective pipeline stages. In this scheme, a header flit entering on a deterministic channel that is also able to leave on a deterministic channel of the same type (low/high) and dimension, goes through the router on the FDP. If a deterministic channel of the same type is not available or a message is being switched to a different type or dimension, then the message is sent through the SDP. A header flit entering on any adaptive channel, is first routed to a deterministic path if possible. Otherwise it is routed to an adaptive channel. In either case, the message goes through the AP.

Since the routing decision and switching logic for routing along the FDP is simpler than traditional deterministic routing, the FDP router requires only two stages. Also, the clock cycle times used for the hybrid router are equal to or larger than those of a purely adaptive router. Therefore more "work" can be accomplished within a clock cycle[2].

Note that this routing scheme is deadlock free: for any given message, the choice of paths selected is always a true subset of those that could be selected by the adaptive algorithm described in [8]. Since the adaptive algorithm has been proven deadlock free, the hybrid is also deadlock free.

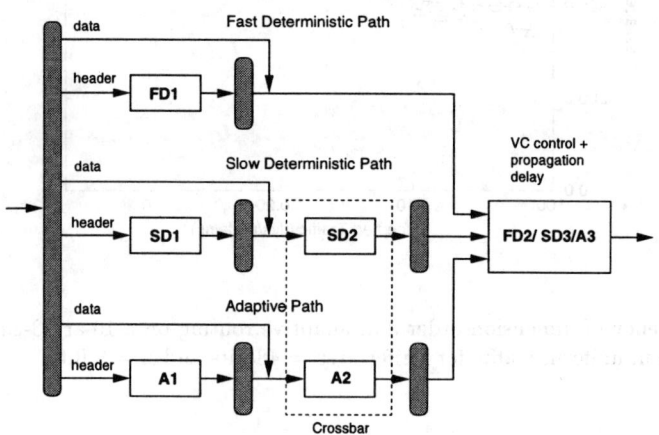

Fig. 3. Logic schematic of the hybrid router.

---

[1] Physical stages are actually shared among these logically independent paths.
[2] As always, it might be necessary to modify this pipeline organization to accommodate a specific physical implementation.

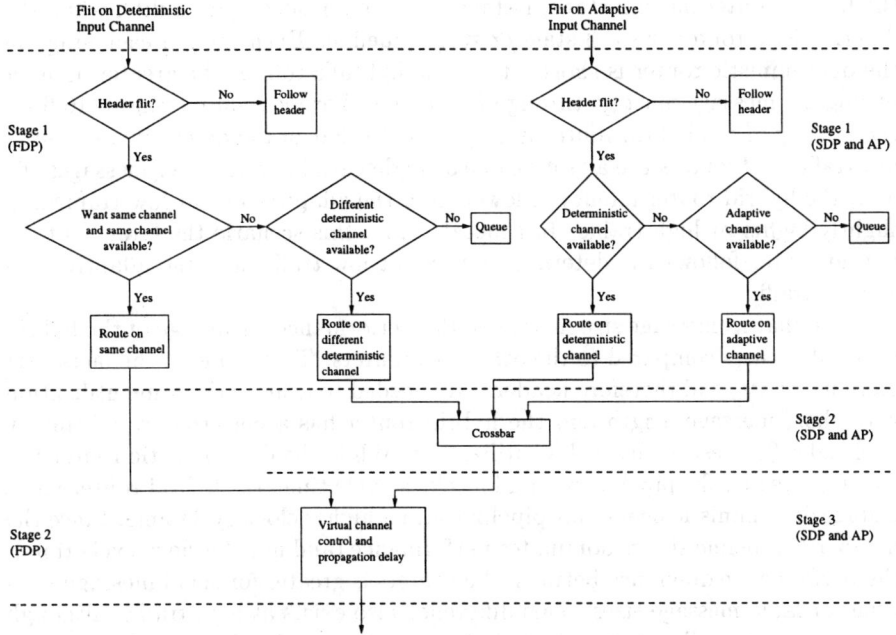

Fig. 4. Flow chart of hybrid routing algorithm

Experimental Results. Simulation of the deterministic, adaptive and hybrid routing schemes were performed using a discrete-time simulator. Simulation results were obtained for various 8-ary 3-cube and 10-ary 3-cube networks. The simulation uses a stabilization threshold of a 0.005 difference between traffic 1000 clock cycles apart to determine steady state. Message sizes varied from 8 to 64 flits and traffic from 0.1 until saturation was reached in 0.1 increments. The buffer sizes used in the simulation are all equal to a single message length. The adaptive router and the adaptive path in the hybrid router use three virtual channels per dimension. The deterministic router and the deterministic path in the hybrid router uses two. The simulator implements a back-pressure mechanism which results in a negative slope of the latency versus accepted traffic plots at higher loads.

The hybrid routing scheme is evaluated using two distinct scenarios for a possible clock cycle time. In the first, the clock cycle time of the hybrid router is equal to that of the adaptive router. In the second, the clock cycle time of the hybrid is equal to the adaptive cycle time plus two gate delays to account for the increased critical path length due to a selector. These two options are referred to as H_{min} and H_{max}, respectively.

The H_{min} Scenario. (Figures 5 and 6). For small messages (8 flits) the latency of the hybrid router is not only lower than the adaptive one but is also lower than the deterministic one at low traffic. This is due to the fact that the hybrid router has a 2-stage/1-stage pipeline for header/data flits, while the deterministic router has a 3-stage/2-stage pipeline. Even though each stage in the deterministic router is shorter than the hybrid's router, the greater number of stages a message must go through dominates. For medium messages (16 flits) the latency of the hybrid router is very close to that of the deterministic one at low traffic and follows the adaptive one at higher traffic. For larger messages (64 flits) the hybrid router latency is lower than the adaptive one at low traffic and slightly higher at high traffic. In general, under this scenario the latency of the hybrid router follows the deterministic one at low traffic and the adaptive one at high traffic.

Note that as message size increases, the performance advantage of the hybrid router decreases compared to the other two routers. This is due to the facts that more messages, and therefore headers, are needed to achieve the same utilization with short message length and the hybrid router has a performance advantage for header flits, especially at low utilization. While the deterministic router has a 3-stage header flit pipeline with a low clock cycle time, the hybrid router has a 2-stage deterministic header flit pipeline with a higher clock cycle time. Since the number of pipeline stages dominates performance (and not the clock cycle time), the performance difference between the routers is greater for small message sizes than for large message sizes. This difference also exists at high traffic, although it's much smaller due to the fact that more message blocking occurs covering up differences in header flit time. This difference is exaggerated in larger sized networks because the average number of hops per message increases, thereby increasing the header flit contribution.

The H_{max} Scenario (Figures 7 and 8). In this scenario the hybrid router clock cycle equals the adaptive router clock cycle plus two gate delays. For small and medium size messages (8 and 16 flits), the latency of the hybrid router is better than the adaptive one at low traffic and in between the deterministic and the adaptive one at medium and high traffic. For a message size of 64 flits, the latency of the hybrid router is always worse than the adaptive but is better than the deterministic at high traffic.

Saturation Point. The saturation point of the hybrid router is, in all cases, much higher than that of the deterministic router. The saturation point of the hybrid router is either equal or lower by at most 3.3% under the H_{min} scenario and by 12.5% to 16.3% under the H_{max} scenario. One reason for the slight decrease in saturation point for the hybrid router, is that the hybrid router routes messages onto the deterministic channels first reducing the number of options available to a message later on. As traffic increases, this less availability cause more blocking and slightly smaller saturation points.

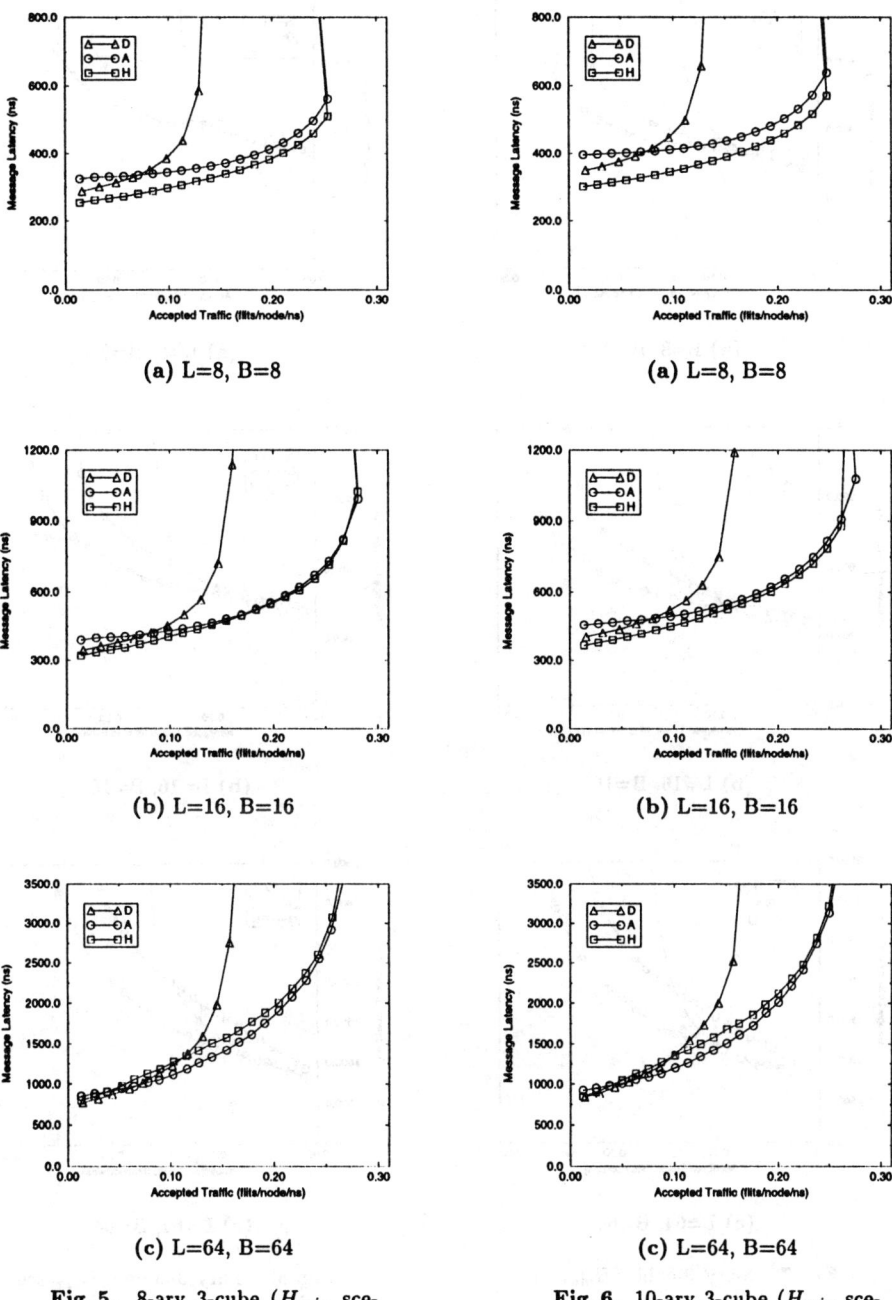

(a) L=8, B=8

(a) L=8, B=8

(b) L=16, B=16

(b) L=16, B=16

(c) L=64, B=64

(c) L=64, B=64

Fig. 5. 8-ary 3-cube (H_{min} scenario)

Fig. 6. 10-ary 3-cube (H_{min} scenario)

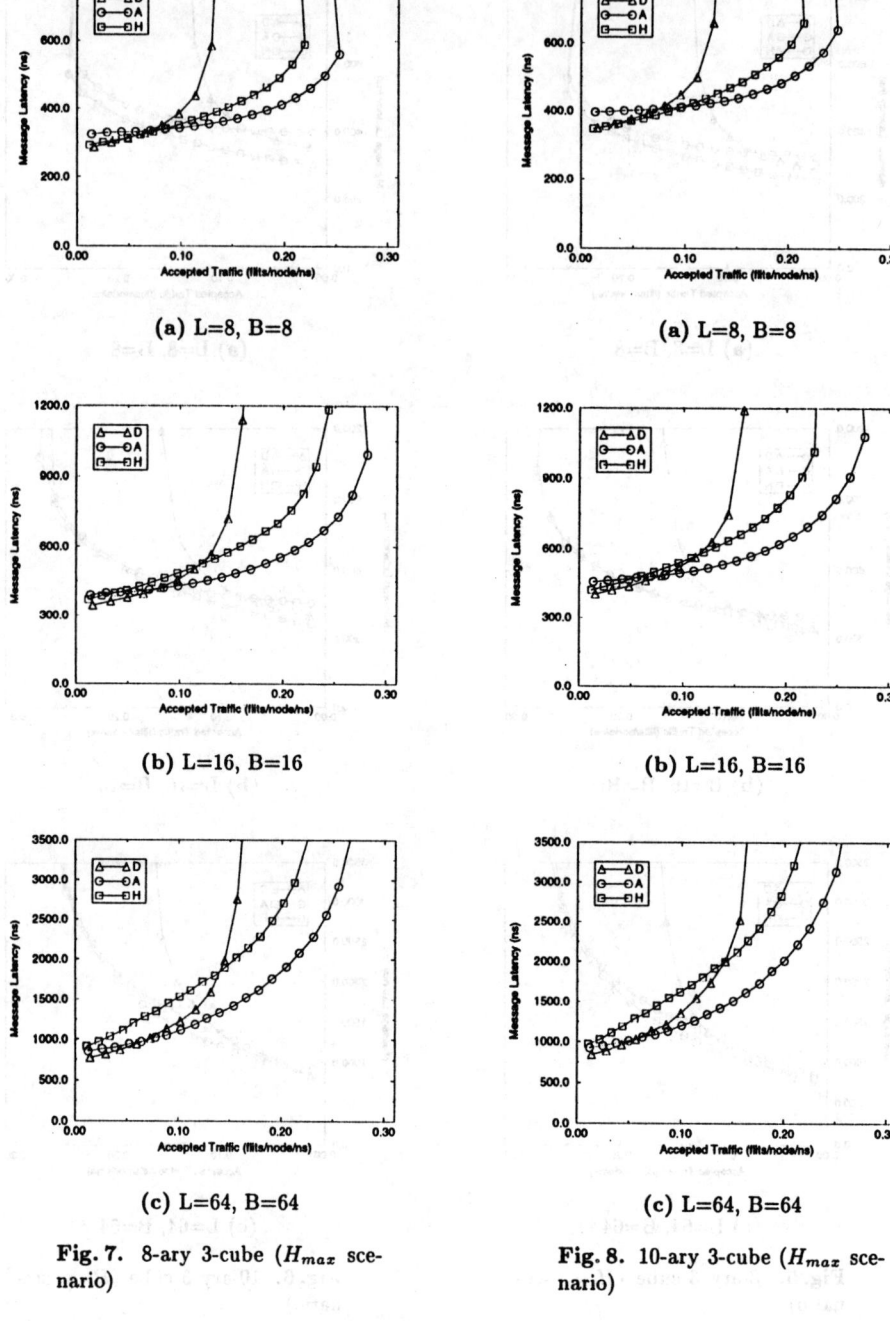

Fig. 7. 8-ary 3-cube (H_{max} scenario)

Fig. 8. 10-ary 3-cube (H_{max} scenario)

Network	L	B	D	A	H_{min}	H_{max}
8by3	8	8	0.139	0.253	0.253	0.219
	16	16	0.169	0.281	0.281	0.244
	64	64	0.175	0.268	0.267	0.234
10by3	8	8	0.142	0.248	0.248	0.215
	16	16	0.170	0.276	0.267	0.231
	64	64	0.173	0.263	0.263	0.230

Table 2. Traffic saturation points (flits/ns/node) for deterministic, adaptive, and hybrid routing

4 Related Work

The architectural support for the reduction of communication overhead is described in [6]. This scheme exploits the communication locality in message passing programs to distinguish between cacheable and non-cacheable virtual channels. Cacheable virtual channels are retained for multiple messages thereby allowing an overlap of communication and computation and eliminating the overhead of multiple message set-up. This mechanism is a hybrid scheme combining circuit and worm-hole switching. The implementation of a router supporting this scheme is described in [10]. Its routing properties are discussed in [11].

Comparisons of adaptive and deterministic router implementations, for worm-hole routing, are described in [1, 3] and [9]. However, the comparison in [1, 3] does not account for the reduced queuing delay in adaptive routing. In [9] the reduction in queuing delay for worm-hole routing is taken into account and the comparison is based on a constant total buffer area.

5 Conclusions

This paper reports on the preliminary evaluation of a hybrid deterministic-adaptive routing scheme. This scheme relies on a pipelined implementation of two routers within each node: a deterministic and an adaptive one. The delay along the deterministic path is one clock cycle shorter than the adaptive one. If the resources are available an arriving message header is routed, by default, on the deterministic path thereby achieving a lower latency per node.

The results from the simulated evaluation of this scheme show that it does achieve its objective: a message latency comparable to that of the deterministic router at low traffic and a saturation point close to that of the adaptive router at high traffic when the hybrid router clock cycle is close to that of the adaptive and for small message sizes when the hybrid router clock cycle is two more gate delays than that of adaptive.

We are currently developing an architecture implementation of the hybrid router in order to evaluate the feasible range of its clock cycle time. We are also evaluating its performance under non-uniform source destination distributions.

References

1. K. Aoyama and A. Chien. The cost of adaptivity and virtual lanes in wormhole router. *J. of VLSI Design*, 2(4), 1995.
2. P. Berman, L. Gravano, G. Pifarre, and J. Sanz. Adaptive deadlock and livelock free routing with all minimal paths in torus networks. In *Proc. of the Symp. on Parallel Algorithms and Architectures*, pages 3–12, 1992.
3. A. Chien. A cost and speed model for k-ary n-cube wormhole routers. In *IEEE Proc. of Hot Interconnects*, Aug. 1993.
4. W. Dally, A. Chien, and et al. The J-Machine: a fine-grain concurrent computer. In *Proc. of the IFIP Congress*, pages 1147–1153, Aug. 1989.
5. W. J. Dally. Virtual-channel flow control. *IEEE Trans. on Computers*, 3(2):194–205, March 1992.
6. B. Dao, S. Yalamanchili, and J. Duato. Architectural support for reducing communication overhead in multiprocessor interconnection networks. In *High Performance Computer Architecture*, pages 343–52, 1997.
7. J. Duato. Deadlock-free adaptive routing algorithms for multicomputers: Evaluation of a new algorithm. In *Proc. of the 3rd IEEE Symp. on Parallel and Distributed Processing*, Dec. 1991.
8. J. Duato. A new theory of deadlock-free adaptive routing in wormhole networks. *IEEE Trans. on Parallel and Distributed Systems*, 4(12):1320–1331, December 1993.
9. J. Duato and P. Lopez. Performance evaluation of adaptive routing algorithms for k-ary n-cubes. In *Parallel Computer Routing and Communication*, pages 45–59, 1994.
10. J. Duato, P. Lopez, F. Silva, and S. Yalamanchili. A high performance router architecture for interconnection networks. In *Int. Conf. on Parallel Processing*, August 1996.
11. J. Duato, P. Lopez, and S. Yalamanchili. Deadlock- and livelock-free routing protocols for wave switching. In *Int. Parallel Processing Symp.*, April 1997.
12. C. L. Glass and L. M. Ni. The turn model for adaptive routing. In *Int. Symp. on Computer Architecture*, pages 278–287, 1992.
13. P. Kermani and L. Kleinrock. Virtual cut-through: a new computer communication switching technique. *Computer Networks*, 3:267 – 286, 1979.
14. Annette Lagman. *Modelling, Analysis and Evaluation of Adaptive Routing Strategies*. PhD thesis, Colorado State University, Computer Science Department, November 1994.
15. L. M. Ni and P. K. McKinley. A survey of wormhole routing techniques in direct networks. *IEEE Computer*, pages 62–76, 1993.

HiPER-P: An Efficient, High-Performance Router for Multicomputer Interconnection Networks[†]

Phil May, Sek M. Chai, D. Scott Wills

PICA Research Group
Georgia Institute of Technology, Atlanta, GA 30332-250

Abstract. As high performance parallel computing architectures make their way into systems with tight size, weight, power, and energy budgets (e.g., portable computing and communications, autonomous vehicles, and space-borne computing), compact and efficient computing and communication mechanisms will be required. To provide such a communication mechanism, the Portable Image Computing Architectures (PICA) group at Georgia Tech is designing the High-Performance Efficient Router (HiPER), a multidimensional router with high-throughput serial channels (1-2 Gbps). Providing high performance for size, weight, power, and energy constrained systems requires careful attention to routing, switching, and error control mechanisms, and the HiPER Prototype (HiPER-P) is a proof-of-concept vehicle that will validate efficient implementations of these mechanisms. The HiPER-P combines mad postman (bit-pipelined) switching with dimension-order routing, producing a router with a very low-latency routing function. To maintain robust communication as link speeds increase and link power budgets decrease, the HiPER-P provides flit-level hop-by-hop retransmission of erroneous flits. This error control mechanism provides built-in error control at the network level. The design of the HiPER-P is presented in this paper as well as results of performance simulations which characterize mad postman switching combined with flit-level error control.

Key Words. networks, router, mad postman, bit-serial, wormhole routing, dimension-order routing, error control, energy efficient, flit-level retransmission

1 Introduction

The performance of the interconnection network in a parallel multiprocessor architecture is critical to the performance of the overall system. The interconnection network must exhibit both low latency and high throughput or the overall performance of the system will suffer. As parallel processing makes its way into systems that require compact designs and power and energy efficient operation (hand-held computing, space-borne computing, autonomous systems), the interconnection network employed will also have to meet these requirements. The High-Performance Efficient Router (HiPER) project at Georgia Tech is focusing on a high-performance network switching element that is being designed with the properties of compactness and power and energy efficiency. These issues are foremost in the design

---

[†] This work is supported by NSF contracts #ECS-9422552, EEC-9402723, and ECS-9058144

requirements for the HiPER-P, a proof-of-concept vehicle for architectural mechanisms that provide high-performance routing in a size, weight, power, and energy constrained system.

HiPER is a router design project that is addressing mechanisms for routing and communications efficiency. HiPER-P is a step in this process which addresses mechanisms for router architecture that will help achieve these goals. Designing a high-performance efficient communication mechanism for a parallel system requires solving problems and addressing issues outside the realm of the router architecture. Such issues include, but are not limited to, transmission media, signal coding, and channel equalization [4]. In addition, for power and energy efficiency, low-power circuit techniques [2, 3] should be employed during the circuit design phase of the project. Since the architecture of the router is the thrust of the HiPER-P design, the aforementioned additional issues will not be directly addressed in this paper. They are, however, being addressed by the HiPER project as a whole.

The HiPER-P employs serial data channels both internal and external to the router. This decision both reduces the router's size and increases its energy and power efficiency. The crossbar physical layout drove the use of serial data channels internally. We have observed, by studying crossbar layouts, that the energy per bit transferred (and therefore the power dissipated at a fixed data rate) increases with the width of the crossbar. This is due to the dominance of interconnect capacitance in switching energy calculations for wide crossbars. Serial data channels are more efficient off-chip as well. Packages and modules are smaller with serial channels and the problem of escape routing [16] is greatly reduced. In addition, serial links are more energy efficient as bit rates increase due to transmission line effects [1 ,14].

As link speeds increase, the network routing function accounts for an increasingly large portion of overall message latency. To address this issue, the switching scheme used in the HiPER-P is mad postman (bit-pipelined) [11] which is an extension of wormhole routing [6, 8] (flit-pipelining), and the routing algorithm is dimension order routing [7]. This combination produces a very low latency routing function ideally suited to serial data channels. As described in the previous paragraph, serial data channels were chosen for the HiPER-P for reasons of efficiency, and the decision to use mad postman switching was based on our desire to maximize the performance of the router using serial links. The HiPER-P will operate in a two-dimensional mesh interconnection topology.

As link speeds increase and power budgets decrease, the operating margin for a router's data channels is reduced. This results in less robust physical links with an increased probability of errors. To address this issue, the HiPER-P supports hop-by-hop flit-level retransmission of data that has encountered errors during transmission. [12] and [13] discuss our work in flit-level error control in multicomputer interconnection networks. The flit-level retransmission capability of the HiPER-P places the responsibility of error control on the network itself, freeing the processor from the additional work required to employ an end-to-end retransmission scheme. Flit-level retransmission is a more efficient mechanism than end-to-end retransmission in terms of both bandwidth and energy, since retransmissions involve small segments of the message (flits) rather than the entire message. The mad postman switching protocol has been extended to support flit-level retransmissions by harnessing the flit-invalidation mechanism required by mad postman switching. Additionally, the HiPER-P utilizes a special set of buffers to store and retransmit erroneous flits. To summarize, the advantages of a flit-level retransmission protocol are:

- Errors are corrected by the network, providing added reliability to data transmissions without processor intervention
- Flit-level retransmission is an efficient protocol since retransmissions involve single flits rather than the entire message
- The flit acknowledgment protocol used in wormhole routing and the flit invalidation scheme used in mad postman switching are easily extended to implement a flit retransmission protocol.
- The potential exists to reduce link power while maintaining a system bit error rate (BER) target (e.g., reducing the driver voltage swing or the light intensity in optoelectronic links)

This paper covers the design of the HiPER-P as well as some preliminary simulations of our unique routing protocol in the presence of flit errors. Section 2 presents an overview of the design, Section 3 covers the use of mad postman switching in the HiPER-P and Section 4 covers the combination of mad postman switching and flit-level retransmission. Section 5 presents the results of some preliminary performance simulations which are designed to both test the validity of the protocol, and identify the characteristics of the protocol in the presence of different link bit error rates. Finally, Section 6 identifies areas we are pursuing to extend this research, including fabricating and testing our router in silicon. The capabilities of the HiPER-P will be extended in subsequent stages of the HiPER project, creating a network switching element that is more capable while retaining the characteristics of efficient operation and compact design.

2 Design Overview

To make the design of the HiPER-P as compact as possible, serial data channels were chosen. To make the router as fast as possible, the results of Chien's analysis for wormhole router performance [5] were applied, and the decision was made to use dimension order routing with no virtual channels. The switching scheme chosen strongly affects the performance of the router, so to maximize the performance of the serial channels, mad postman switching is employed. The advantage of mad postman switching with serial channels manifests itself in message latency. The bit-pipelined nature of mad postman switching produces an end-to-end message latency approaching that of a router with parallel channels equal in width to the size of a flit

[9]. Table 1 identifies these design choices as well as the other design specifications of the HiPER-P.

Table 1, HiPER-P Specifications

Parameter	HiPER-P
Topology	2D Mesh
Channel Width	Bit-Serial
Switching	Mad Postman (bit-pipelined)
Buffering	Multiple Flit Buffering
Error Handling	Basic Parity (flit retransmission)
Routing	Dimension Order, Deterministic
Target Network Size	64 x 64 nodes
Sync/Async	Synchronous

The configuration of the HiPER-P is two unidimensional routers, one for each dimension in the network. This is the same configuration as the canonical dimension-order router presented in [5] (partitioned router), which was based on other routers such as the torus routing chip [6] and the Intel Paragon router [10]. Fig. 1 shows the configuration of the routing node composed of two unidimensional routers.

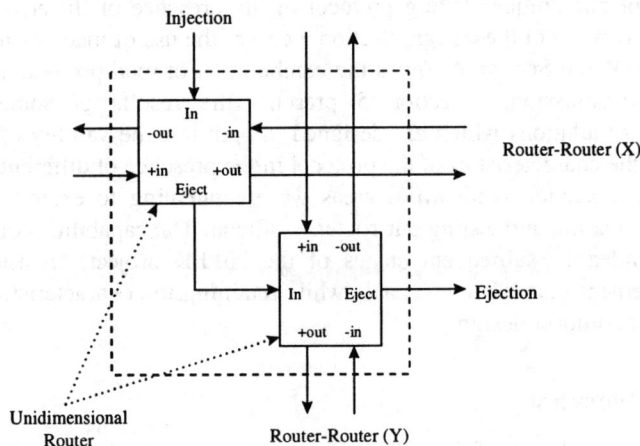

Fig. 1. HiPER-P Node is Composed of Two Unidimensional Routers

2.1 Router Block Diagram

Fig. 2 illustrates the configuration of one unidimensional router showing only one of its inputs and one of its outputs. The routing decision and control is performed by the *Arbiter* block. The switching function is performed by a crossbar that can connect the injection channel to any one of the other three outputs (+, -, eject) and can connect either of the two routing inputs (+ or -) to its corresponding output or to the ejection channel. The error control mechanism for the HiPER-P is single bit parity which is checked in the *Parity* block. The result of this parity calculation is sent back to the transmitting node to initiate a retransmission when an error is detected.

The two elements of the router that support retransmission of flits are the *retransmit buffer* and the *slack buffer*. The *retransmit buffer* is a shift register that samples the output data signal, storing the last two flits sent out over a link. When a retransmission is initiated, the data flits that are retransmitted are taken from the *retransmit buffer*. The *slack buffer* provides storage for input data while a retransmission is under way. This storage prevents the loss of input flits while the output is engaged in retransmission. A more detailed explanation of how the *slack buffer* and *retransmit buffer* support retransmission is presented in Section 4.

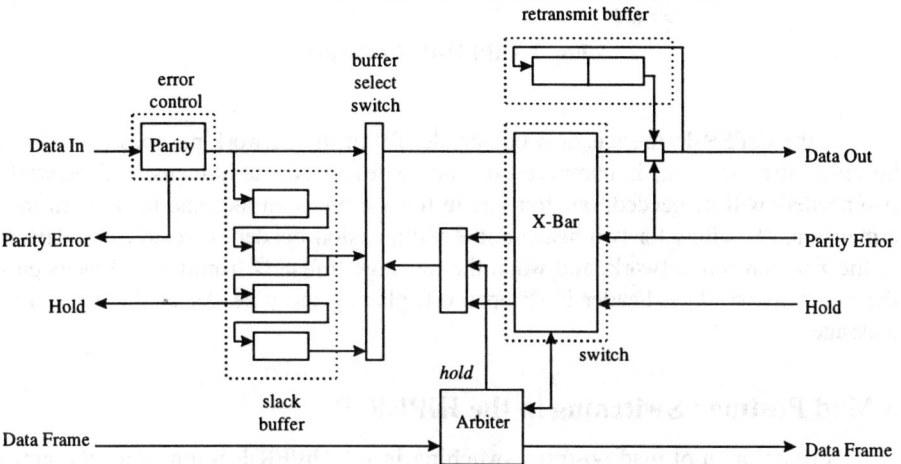

Fig. 2. HiPER-P Unidimensional Router Block Diagram

2.2 Flit Format

The flit format is organized to facilitate serial implementation of the data channels and the channel control hardware, as well as being able to handle incorrect routing speculation and errors in the links. Fig. 3 shows the formats for both header and data flits.

The *Discard* bit serves two purposes. First, it is set if an error is detected in the flit so that the destination node will discard it. The correct flit will be retransmitted following the erroneous flit. Second, when speculative routing fails, the flit that has missed its turn to the ejection channel (the current head flit) is tagged as a discard flit. If this flit blocks in the network, hardware can be put in place to detect the *Discard* bit and eliminate it from the node.

The *Eject* bit is used to speed up routing decisions at the injection channel. The injection channel can make its decision based only on the first two bits of the header (*Sign* and *Eject*). If the *Eject* bit is '1', the ejection channel is the destination, and if the Eject bit is '0', the Sign bit indicates whether the negative or positive direction is to be taken in that dimension. The offset field is represented in magnitude form.

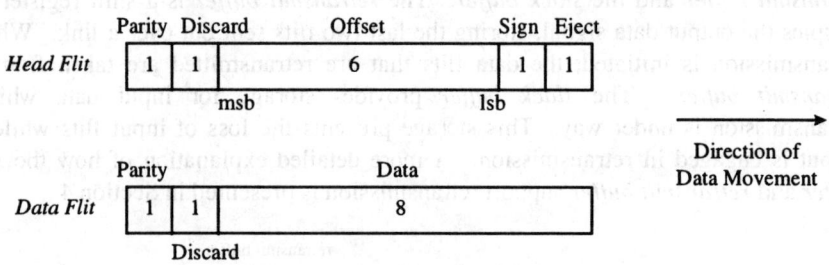

Fig. 3. HiPER-P Flit Format

In the HiPER-P, there is only one header flit in the network per message. Since, however, the 2D mesh is composed of two routes in two unidimensional networks, two headers will be needed; one to route in the x dimension and one to route in the y dimension. To allow for two headers, the y dimension header is treated as a data flit in the x dimension network, and when the message transfers from the x dimension to the y dimension, the x header is stripped off, placing the y header at the head of the message.

3 Mad Postman Switching in the HiPER-P

A description of mad postman switching in the HiPER-P begins with the notion of bit-pipelining. In a system with serial data channels, flits are substantially larger than phits (a bit in the case of serial channels). This size mismatch introduces additional latency for each message by requiring that each flit be completely transferred serially between routing nodes before routing decisions are made. In the case where the phit is equal in size to the flit (when parallel physical channels are used), this additional latency is not present. In order for a router using a serial channel to compete with one using a parallel channel (in the area of latency), the routing decisions must be made at the bit level. This, of course, is not feasible as the number of bits required to make a routing decision and to store the state of the route is greater than one.

In bit pipelining using the mad postman approach, routing decisions are made speculatively (speculative dimension order routing). In a dimension order router, the path from source to destination is chosen such that the distance between source and destination is entirely exhausted in one dimension before routing begins in the next. In a two dimensional mesh (the target configuration for the HiPER-P), for example, all of the *x*-offset between source and destination is completely traversed before the message begins to approach the destination in the *y*-dimension. Because of this regularity of routes, it is easy to speculate which direction is taken at each node. The channel that the flit leaves the node on will be along the same dimension and in the same direction as the one that it entered on. This varies only when the message makes its one turn, and when it is ejected from the network. As explained in [11], this means that only one incorrect decision will be made in each dimension. This incorrect decision must be handled in the network. The HiPER-P handles this incorrect decision by tagging the head flit as invalid by setting its *Discard* bit.

4 Mad Postman Switching and Flit-Level Error Control

The fact that the HiPER-P implements bit-pipelining makes retransmission of erroneous data more complicated. This is because flits are spread across many nodes, each of which holds only two or three bits in its data path. The mechanism used for this retransmission consists of two phases. The first phase is invalidation of the erroneous flit as it leaves the node. The reason that this is required is that the flit has already begun leaving the node before the error is detected and can not be recalled. Instead, the flit is tagged as bad (*Discard* bit set) and handled when it arrives at the destination. The second phase consists of retransmitting a buffered copy of the flit while buffering incoming data in the node's *slack buffer*.

4.1 Retransmit Buffer

Since the error detection and signaling process will take more time than the transmission of a single bit, the *retransmit buffer* holds two flits. This also means that the *Parity Error* signal will arrive at the node responsible for retransmitting sometime during the transmission of the *next* flit (the one following the erroneous flit). We assume that wires hold no more than 4-5 bits in flight. Fig. 4 shows this timing relationship.

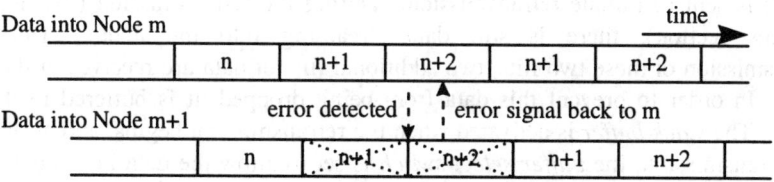

Fig. 4. Error Signal and Flit Timing Relationship

Flit *n+1* contains an error(s) that was accumulated during transmission from node *m* to node *m+1*. This error is detected at node *m+1*, and the *Parity Error* signal is activated after node *m* has begun transmitting flit *n+2*. Because our system guarantees the in-order arrival of flits, both flit *n+1* and *n+2* will be retransmitted.

The time between the arrival of the error signal at node m and the time that node m finishes transmitting flit $n+2$, is the time that node m has to set up for the retransmission. Fig. 4 shows the timeline for this retransmission, including the initial error detection and subsequent error signaling.

In Fig. 4, the flits with the 'x' through them have been marked as "bad" via node $m+1$ setting its *Discard* bit. Actually, in this example, only flit $n+1$ was in error, but both are invalidated due to the in-order delivery requirement. Following the delivery of flit $n+2$, node m retransmits flits $n+1$ and $n+2$. In this example, only flit $n+1$ was erroneous, but both $n+1$ and $n+2$ could have contained errors since both are being retransmitted. In fact, in the HiPER-P, an error indication (*Parity Error*) signal reception during the *retransmission* of flit $n+1$ is ignored. This signal would indicate that flit $n+2$ was received in error, and since this flit is being retransmitted anyway, the *Parity Error* signal may be disregarded for flit $n+2$. Extension of this protocol to handle multiple retransmissions is trivial since the buffering is in place which contains the data to be retransmitted at all times.

4.2 Slack Buffer

The *slack buffer* is required to provide a path for incoming bits that prevents them from colliding with flits being retransmitted. The *slack buffer* is also used to store flits that enter a node while the output path for those flits is being used by another message (head of message blocked). The *slack buffer* for a given node can be activated in one of the three ways:

- Activation of the retransmission process
- Blocking of the current message by another message (crossbar arbitration failure)
- Activation of the Hold line by a downstream node

The following paragraphs explain each of these processes.

If an error is detected in the transmission of a flit, the *Parity Error* signal (see Fig. 4) is sent to initiate retransmission. During the retransmission (detailed in the previous section), there is still data streaming into the node. During the retransmission of these two flits, two additional flits of data are received at the node's input. In order to prevent this data from being dropped, it is buffered in the *slack buffer*. The *slack buffer* is activated when the retransmission begins, and at the end of the retransmission, the *buffer select switch* is set to allow the data in the buffer to be routed to the output (see Fig. 2 and Fig. 5). Retransmission requires that two flit sized registers in the *slack buffer* be allocated to the data path so that no flits are lost. In other words, the slack buffer registers become part of the data-path.

Fig. 5 shows two snapshots of the retransmission process. Fig. 5 (a) shows the router just before flit $n+1$ will be retransmitted in response to the error signal shown in Fig. 4. In Fig. 5 (a), flit $n+2$ has just finished leaving the router, flit $n+3$ is beginning to enter the router, and flit *n+1* is about to be retransmitted. To prevent data collisions, flit *n+3* is being routed to the *slack buffer*. Fig. 5 (b) shows the same router after flits *n+1* and *n+2* have been retransmitted. The first two flit buffers in the *slack buffer* are now part of the datapath. This process, in the presence of an indeterminate number of retransmissions, would require an infinitely large *slack buffer* (a worst case scenario). Since the resources of any one router are finite, another mechanism is required to prevent flit loss. This mechanism is the *Hold* signal.

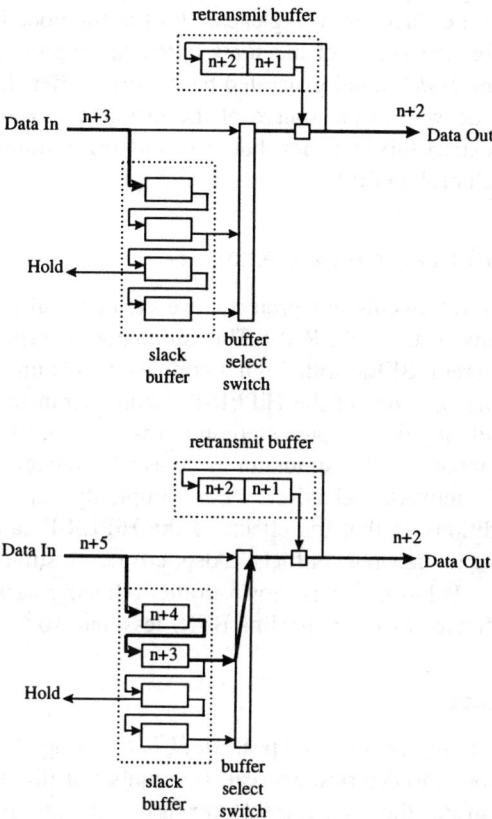

Fig. 5. (a) State of Router Just Prior to Retransmission (b) Slack Buffer Elements Become Part of the Datapath

When multiple retransmissions occur within the same node, the local slack buffer will quickly fill up (this takes ½*n* retransmissions, where *n* is the number of flit sized registers in the *slack buffer*). When this happens, "slack" will be taken up in the pervious node (the upstream node). Another situation where the *slack buffer* fills up is when the head flit blocks and must wait for output resources to free up. If the path through the node were to remain passing through the slack buffer after it has completely filled up, there would be no slack available for future retransmissions. This is the case whenever the *slack buffer* of a node fills up, regardless of the cause (errors, *Hold*, blocked head flit). A mechanism must be put in place to recover this slack so that problems are not created.

The mechanism employed by the HiPER-P requires that the *slack buffer* of the downstream node completely empty before the Hold signal is released to the upstream node. This will reset the slack absorbing capabilities of the node before it accepts any new data. This makes the sizing of the *slack buffer* an important parameter. If the buffer is too small, the *Hold* signal generated by the first buffer that is completely full will ripple back all the way to the source of the message. When the head flit of a message blocks, we expect this behavior, but error induced retransmissions should not cause this (with a high probability).

5 Simulations and Performance Analysis

To validate our retransmission protocol, we created a flit level simulator that mimics the operations of the HiPER-P. This simulator incorporates bit level error manipulation at different BERs with high iterations to obtain realistic data. The simulator captures the behavior of the HiPER-P during retransmission of flits due to erroneous data, and it also captures router resource utilization, and overall performance. The intent of the simulator is to verify logical functionality and to analyze router and network behavior. For simplicity, all simulations assume contention-free conditions so that the effects of the HiPER-P can be studied without message blocking due to resource conflicts. Also, errors are simulated as independent events with $P(0\rightarrow 1) = P(1\rightarrow 0)$. As is shown in the following paragraphs, the HiPER-P is statistically unaffected by errors for link BERs less than 10^{-5}.

5.1 Slack Buffer Usage

Our first simulations analyzed the peak *slack buffer* usage for the HiPER-P. The goal of this simulation is to determine a realistic number of flits for each *slack buffer* to store. Fig. 6 illustrates the peak *slack buffer* usage (in flits) per router for various BERs at conditions of maximum PICA architecture message size (64 flits) and average path length from source to destination (64 router hops).

To prevent all network blockages due to errors (worst case), the number of flits each *slack buffer* must store is equal to the number of flits in a transmitted message. The purpose of the *slack buffer* is to alleviate blocking conditions at the source, and consequently, the worst case condition is the store-and-forward switching case where the entire message is buffered at the intermediate router before transmission. Each additional set of two flit registers in the *slack buffer* allows a retransmission sequence in the HiPER-P to complete without blocking. From our simulations, we determined that the peak *slack buffer* usage at realistic operating conditions of low BER is less than two flits per *slack buffer*. We will implement the HiPER-P with a four flit *slack buffer* to remain robust up to BER of 10^{-5}. This configuration allows each node to experience a single retransmission without blocking its upstream neighbor.

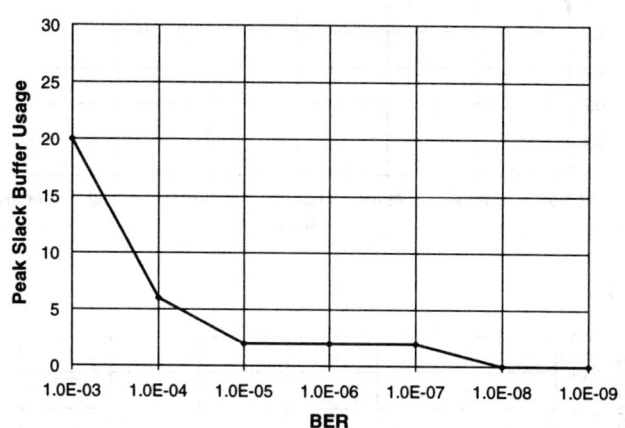

Fig. 6. Peak Slack Buffer Utilization Per Node for Different BERs

5.2 Bandwidth Effects

The effect of bandwidth reduction due to errors manifests itself in two ways. The first is the direct reduction in bandwidth due to invalidated flits which are created by errors. The second is the accumulation of enough errors in the network to block back to the source, preventing the source from injecting new flits and from completing injection of the message. Our simulations gathered data for both of these cases and the results are presented in Fig. 7.

Fig. 7 (a) shows the effective bandwidth in the presence of retransmissions. The region of the plot between BER values of 10^{-3} and 10^{-4} is interesting because it shows an 'avalanching' phenomenon. This results from message dilation brought about by many invalid flits, each of which is subjected to more errors. This effect will effectively stop the network for BERs much greater than 10^{-3}. Also, for BERs less than 10^{-5}, the bandwidth is effectively 100% of available capacity. Fig. 7 (b) shows the normalized number of cycles that the source can not inject due to blocking. This data was gathered at conditions of maximum PICA [15] architecture message size (64 flits) and average path length from source to destination (64 router hops). For BER values less than 10^{-5}, the source is statistically free of blocking.

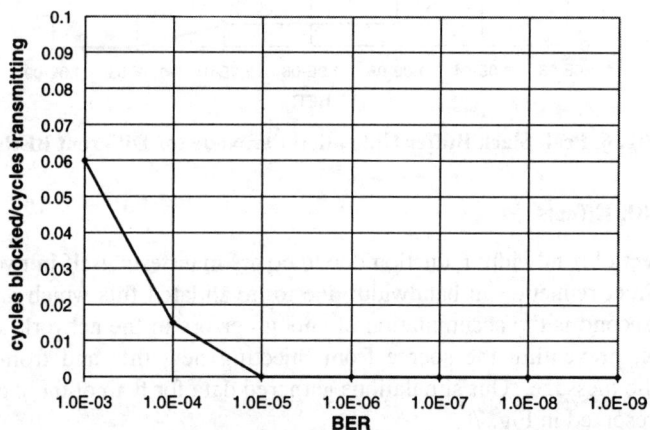

Fig. 7. (a) Effective Bandwidth and (b) Cycles Source is Blocked vs. BER

6 Conclusion and Future Work

The HiPER-P is a compact, efficient router that implements mechanisms to maximize its performance. Dimension order routing is compact, inexpensive to implement, and provides low latency routing. Serial data channels are implemented to further reduce the size of the router. Mad postman switching decreases message latency even further by bit-pipelining flits and making speculative routing decisions. Mad postman switching is also ideally suited to serial data channels in a dimension order router. Flit-level retransmission of erroneous flits is implemented to provide reliable communication and to do so more efficiently than an end-to-end retransmission scheme.

To continue this work, we plan to design and fabricate one of the unidirectional routers using the MOSIS VLSI foundry. We will then be able to construct test networks using these chips as building blocks, as well as having the layouts at our disposal for creating integrated processing nodes with router and processor on the same die. The HiPER-P's capabilities will be extended in future generations of the router, using the HiPER-P as a baseline point of comparison for the performance and efficiency impacts of any additions. The future enhancements planned for study are routing adaptivity, fault tolerance, and real-time guarantees of service.

References

1. H. B. Bakoglu, *Circuits, Interconnections, and Packaging for VLSI*, Addison-Wesley Publishing Company, Reading, MA, 1990.
2. A. Bellaouar and M. Elmasry, *Low-Power Digital VLSI Design: Circuits and Systems*, Kluwer Academic Publishers, Boston, MA, 1995.
3. R. W. Broderson and A. P. Chandrakasan, *Low-Power Digital VLSI Design*, Kluwer Academic Publishers, Boston, MA, 1995.
4. A. B. Carlson, *Communication Systems: An Introduction to Signals and Noise in Electrical Communication*, McGraw Hill, New York, NY, 1986.
5. A. A. Chien, "A Cost and Speed Model for k-ary n-cube Wormhole Routers," *Proceedings of Hot Interconnects '93*, August 1993.
6. W. J. Dally and C. L. Seitz, "The Torus Routing Chip," Journal of Distributed Computing, vol. 1, no. 3. Pp. 187-196, October, 1986.
7. W. J. Dally and C. L. Seitz, "Deadlock-free Message Routing on Multiprocessor Interconnection Networks," *IEEE Transactions on Computing*, Vol. C-36, no. 5, pp. 547-553, May 1987.
8. W. J. Dally, "Performance Analysis of *k*-ary *n*-cube Interconnection Networks," *IEEE Transactions on Computers*, vol. 39, no. 6, pp. 775-785, June 1990.
9. J. Duato, S. Yalamanchili, L. Ni, *Interconnection Networks: An Engineering Approach*, Preliminary Manuscript, 1996.
10. D. Dunning, "Routing Chip Set for the Intel Paragon Supercomputer," *MIT VLSI Seminar Video Tape*, 1992.
11. C. R. Jesshope, P. R. Miller, J. T. Yantchev, "High Performance Communications in Processor Networks," *Proceedings of the 16th International Symposium on Computer Architecture*, pp. 150-157, May-June 1989.
12. P. May, N. M. Jokerst, D. S. Wills, S. Wilkinson, M. Lee, O. Vendier, S. Bond, Z. Hou, G. Dagnall, M. A. Brooke, A. Brown, "Design Issues for Through-Wafer Optoelectronic Multicomputer Interconnects", In *Second International Workshop on Massively Parallel Processing Using Optical Interconnections*, pages 8-15, San Antonio, Texas, 23-24 October 1995.

13. P. May, M. Lee, S. T. Wilkinson, O. Vendier, Z. Ho, S. W. Bond, D. S. Wills, M. Brooke, N. M. Jokerst, and A. Brown, "A 100 Mbps, LED Through-Wafer Optoelectronic Link for Multicomputer Interconnection Networks," To appear in *Journal of Parallel and Distributed Computing*, Special Issue on Parallel Computing with Optical Interconnects, 1996.
14. S. Ramo, J. R. Whinnery, T. VanDuzer, *Fields and Waves in Communications Electronics*, Second Edition, John Wiley and Sons, New York, NY, 1984.
15. D. Scott Wills, W. Stephen Lacy, Huy Cat, Michael A. Hopper, Ashutosh Razdan, and Sek M. Chai, "Pica: An Ultra-Light Processor for High-Throughput Applications," 1993 International Conference on Computer Design, October 3-6, 1993, Cambridge, MA.
16. E. Winkler, "Escape Routing from Chip Scale Packages," *Proceedings of the 1996 IEEE/CPMT International Manufacturing Technology Symposium*, pp. 393-401, 1996.

Session III

ROUTER AND NETWORK ARCHITECTURES II
(Invited Presentations)

Thursday, June 26, 1997
3:00 - 4:30

Session Chair:

D. Panda
Ohio State University

Invited Presentation

ServerNet™ II

David Garcia, William Watson

Tandem Computers Incorporated

19333 Vallco Parkway	14231 Tandem Blvd.
Cupertino, CA 95014	Austin, TX 78278
(408) 285-6116	(512) 432-8470
Fax: 285-7959	Fax: 432-8247
DaveG@snet.tandem.com	watson@austx.tandem.com

Abstract

The second generation of ServerNet expands on the capabilities of the ServerNet I system area network. ServerNet II maintains the scalability and availability features of ServerNet and continues to be a cost effective way to connect large clusters of commodity servers. ServerNet II is a 125MB/s full-duplex, switched, wormhole-routed network, operating over standard 1000BaseX cabling. ServerNet II maintains complete compatibility and interoperability with existing ServerNet I components.

Keywords: ServerNet System Area Network, Gigabit networks, flow control, System Management

1.0 Introduction

In June 1995, Tandem announced a series of new scalable fault-tolerant computers based on the ServerNet System Arean Network (SAN). Since then, Tandem has shipped over one billion dollars of ServerNet equipment to customers around the world. The direct connect ServerNet SAN provides high-bandwidth, low-overhead message passing and IO connectivity. The high bandwidth and low overhead provided by ServerNet allow Tandem to build clusters of commodity processor elements and IO devices with excellent performance and unsurpassed scalability, running the NT, Unix, and NonStop Kernel operating systems.

The ServerNet II SAN improves many features provides by the ServerNet components. The improved protocols and interface chips provide a 150% inprovement in raw link speed, greater than 75% reduction in packet overhead, support for links over 100 times as long, doubled router connectivity, and improved system management performance.

This paper introduces the features of ServerNet II, with a focus on the network and routing attributes. Section 2 reviews the salient points of the ServerNet I SAN, while Section 3 describes the new features in the ServerNet II implementation. Section 4 discusses iteroperability between ServerNet I and ServerNet II components. Section 5 provides a description of the specific features planned for Router II, and Section 6 introduces SAN management protocols.

2.0 ServerNet I Review

ServerNet I is a wormhole-routed network with full duplex links carrying 50MB/s in each direction. Variable sized packets carry a maximum data payload of 64 bytes.

A 6 port crossbar router[†] supports creation of arbitrary network topologies. With more routing elements, the SAN can attach to more processors and IO end nodes. As the SAN grows, so does the total bandwidth for concurrent traffic.

The ServerNet SAN provides memory-like semantics to the end nodes. An end node can create a DMA operation to read or write another memory anywhere in the SAN. IO adapters find the support for read operations particularly useful. It allows the IO adapter to manage all of its own data transfers without involving another processor, whether pushing or pulling data from memory.

Clustered computer availability is paramount. The ServerNet end nodes support two independent interconnect networks. No single failure or service operation, except to an end node itself, can disrupt traffic between end nodes.

3.0 ServerNet II

The second generation of ServerNet components add to the feature set in ServerNet I:

- Higher data rate: 125 MB/s
- Larger Packet Size: up to 512 bytes
- Directly drives standard 8b/10b serializer/Deserializer components.
- New Read and Write packets with a 64 bit ServerNet address.
- Direct support for the Virtual Interface Architecture (VIA)

3.1 Packet Layer

ServerNet II uses the same packet formats defined by ServerNet I, with larger data field sizes and transaction length encodings, and the addition of new transaction types supporting 64-bit ServerNet addressing. The two new Read and Write packet types corresponding to similar ServerNet I packet types, except for the address field size increases.

The ServerNet global address space is defined by the ServerNet ID and an address field (Figure 1). The 20 bit ServerNet ID uniquely identifies an end node and determines the routing of each packet through the ServerNet network. Each Read or Write request packet carries an address field of either 32 or 64 bits. Taken together, the ServerNet ID and Address provide a 52-bit global address space for all ServerNet I end nodes. This is a subset of the 84-bit global Address space for ServerNet II end nodes.

[†]. We use the term "router" to refer to the routing ASIC and "switch" for an assembly containing a router, power supply, cooling, connectors, etc.

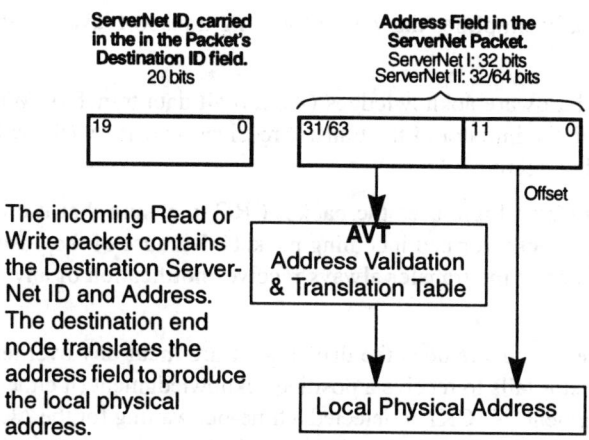

Figure 1. ServerNet Global Address Space

The ServerNet address typically does not directly address the physical memory of an end node. Instead, the end node uses the upper 20/42 bits of the address to index into the Address Validation and Translation (AVT) Table. This allows the end node to confirm that the ServerNet node generating the request has read or write permissions for the specific locations within that page, and also provides a translation to the local physical memory address.

The end nodes translate most ServerNet Write request packets as shown in Figure 1 and write data directly to memory. However, a ServerNet I AVT table entry may indicate that writes to that page should not deposit data directly to memory, but instead put the data into one of four interrupt queues. The ServerNet hardware adds each packet to the circular queue and interrupts the host software. The software then pulls items off the queue and process the interrupt. ServerNet II end nodes also support this feature.

Typically in ServerNet, a write packet is sent to a specific address in the destination memory. The sender must have *a priori* knowledge of where the destination wishes to receive the data. ServerNet II end nodes support a Virtual Interface Architecture (VIA) mode where the sender can blindly post packets with no knowledge of the location of the receive buffer. Hardware in the destination maps the incoming packet to a buffer location specified by the receiver.

While somewhat similar to the ServerNet I method for handling interrupt queues, this approach allows tens of thousands of receive buffer queues. This mode uses packets similar to the normal ServerNet Write packet, but with the logical connection number (queue number) used instead of the address.

ServerNet II maintains the same delivery guarantees and error recovery strategy used in ServerNet I. The low level ServerNet driver software can provide guaranteed delivery of messages as long as a path to the destination exists in either network. (The driver can retry over the original path, then changes to the alternate path if the original path fails again.) This greatly simplifies the work of writing transport layers on top of the ServerNet stack.

The ServerNet hardware acknowledges (ACKs) all data transfers. Whether the data is pushed or pulled, the initiator of the transfer receives a positive acknowledgment that the data transferred correctly.

The end node receive logic uses the packet CRC to ensure that it only processes and acknowledges correctly formed incoming packets. Because of the positive acknowledgments, the initiator of the transfer always receives notification of any data transfer failures.

Only when an error occurs does the driver software incur any overhead for error handling. If a requestor fails to receive a positive acknowledgment (it either received a negative acknowledgment (NACK) or detected a time-out waiting for the ACK), it invokes the driver's error handling. The error handler resends the request packets that failed to complete.

Subsequent data transfers that have a dependency on the transmission with the error halt until error recovery takes place. For example, the completion interrupt message scheduled after a large block write will not start until the entire block correctly transfers.

Error recovery requires idempotent ServerNet read and write operations. Operations such as write packets placed into an interrupt queues require software to maintain a sequence number in the body of the packet data to guard against duplication.

3.2 Link Layer

The ServerNet II link layer protocol performs all the same functions done by the ServerNet I link layer. Specifically, the following features are maintained:

- The link level uses the same flow control scheme. Flow control symbols inserted into the data stream assert backpressure and gate the flow of incoming data. Because of this, the ServerNet SAN is not a lossy network. Barring errors, messages sent into the network will reach their destinations.

- ServerNet II uses the same fault tolerant busy/ready keep alive protocol. To prevent against a failing node causing continuous backpressure, the Busy or Ready flow control symbols must repeat every 2048 clocks. Otherwise, the link receiver reports an error and releases link backpressure.

- The same techniques for isolating a fault to the failing link work in ServerNet II. Each element (router) through which a packet passes checks the CRC. Each element appends the command symbol "This Packet Good" (TPG) to the packet when the CRC check succeeds. A packet with a bad CRC check and a trailing TPG indicates a link failure and gets reported to the SAN management software. The first router that detects a CRC failure on a packet appends a "This Packet Bad" (TPB) command symbol to the packet to indicate that the fault was detected (and reported) earlier.

- Periodic insertion of SKIP symbols into the transmit data stream allow asynchronous operation of senders and receivers while avoiding operating significant portions of the receiver from the received clock. Receivers discard SKIP symbols without losing any data. This prevents link synchronizer overruns caused by differences in the clock rates at the sender and receiver.

ServerNet I encodes link command symbols and data into 9 bits. ServerNet II uses an ordered set of the standard 8B/10B symbols to encode all data, command, and control messages, using a single code for each data byte, and two symbol sequences for link level commands.

3.3 Physical Layer

The 125 MB/s ServerNet II outputs use an 8b/10b encoding scheme compatible with standard low-cost SerDes and optical components intended for the 1000BaseX standard. See Table 1 for a list of the physical interfaces supported.

4.0 Interoperability of ServerNet I & ServerNet II

An installed base of ServerNet I products requires interoperability between the new ServerNet II components and existing ServerNet I end nodes and switches. Interoperability means the user can directly plug together new products and old products and have them work without any modification to the existing application.

Interoperability must work at several levels:

- Physical Interconnect must match.

- Recognition of packet formats between ServerNet I and ServerNet II devices.

- Link Level symbol flow must match the 50 MB/s ServerNet I with the 125 MB/s ServerNet II.

- The packet injection rate should not swamp any slower ServerNet I components.

- ServerNet I and ServerNet II devices must use the same SAN management operations.

Figures 2 through 4 below show different interoperability scenarios.

4.1 Physical Interoperability

Each ServerNet I port on an ASIC has separate 9-bit receive and transmit interfaces. Each can pass 50 million symbols per second. The 9-bit symbols encode either a byte of data or a link control command symbol.

ServerNet II ASICs similarly can pass 125 MB/s on each of their receive or transmit links. They can also use an 8b/10b encoding scheme [5]. The 10-bit inputs and outputs

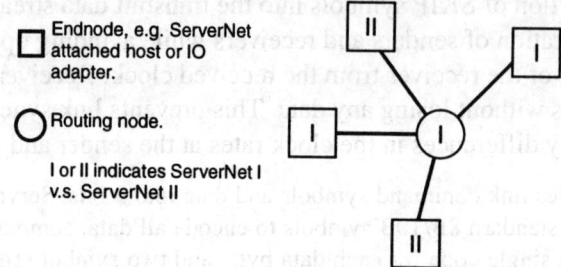

Figure 2. Interoperability, ServerNet I Network

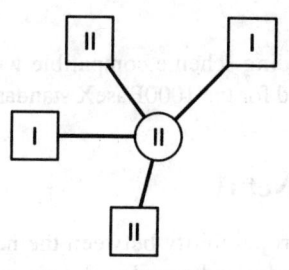

Figure 3. Interoperability, ServerNet II Network

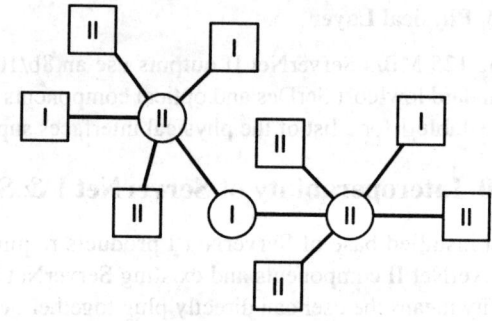

Figure 4. Interoperability, Mixed Network

work compatibly with standard Gigabit Ethernet 802.3z 1000BaseX serializer deserializer (SerDes) components.

ServerNet ASICs installed on the same logic card can directly connect the parallel outputs of one ASIC to the parallel inputs of another ASIC. Longer distance connections require a parallel or serial driver component. Table 1 below lists the physical interfaces supported for ServerNet I and II.

Table 1. ServerNet Physical Interface

Physical Interface	ServerNet	
	I	II
Direct from the ASIC 9b@50MB/s	4	4
Direct from the ASIC 8b/10b @ 125MB/s.		4
Parallel cable with LVDS signaling.	4	
Parallel cable with differential ECL signaling[a].	4	
Copper Serial (1000BaseCX).	4	4
Short haul optical (850nm laser on multi mode fiber, 1000BaseSX).	4	4
Long haul optical (1300nm laser on single mode fiber, 1000BaseLX).	4	4

a. Only Tandem NSK and Integrity Unix products use parallel ECL ServerNet cables.

ServerNet II ASICs have a compatibility mode in which they can communicate at 125MB/s with an 8b/10b encoding or at 50MB/s with a 9-bit output.

A special two port router ASIC allows attachment of ServerNet I end nodes and routing nodes to serial cables. While a router ASIC typically includes a crossbar switch, this two port router serves instead as a bus converter. One side of the two port router operates in ServerNet I compatibility mode. The other side can connect directly to the gigabit SerDes components. This allows ServerNet I devices to use serial links and connect with the ServerNet II components.

The ServerNet I switch uses physical interface drivers and connectors on modular daughter cards. This allows the switch to accommodate the appropriate physical interface. For example, an existing system with parallel LVDS interfaces can add a long haul optical interface to connect with a newer ServerNet II system. See Figure 5 below.

Serial interfaces on the ServerNet I switch use a physical interface daughter card with the two port router and the appropriate serial interface.

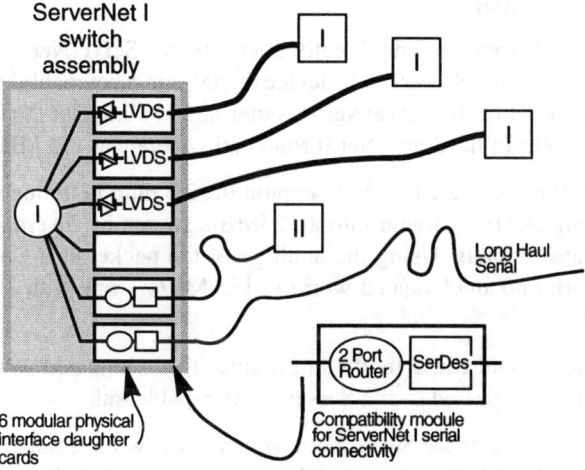

Figure 5. ServerNet I Compatibility with ServerNet II Serial Link

Serial ServerNet connection on ServerNet I and ServerNet II end nodes and switches support a complete "plug and play" model.

4.2 Packet Injection Rate Matching

ServerNet I devices can never process data faster than 50 MB/s. For example, in Figure 4 the ServerNet I router can only pass data at a maximum of 50 MB/s between the two ServerNet II networks.

In this case, if the ServerNet II end nodes were to inject packets at a 125MB/s rate, the relatively lower speed ServerNet I device would form a bottleneck for the high speed packets. This bottleneck would cause backpressure in the network and result in higher network blockage.

To prevent this, the ServerNet II driver software maintains a state bit for each possible destination node indicating whether or not a packet sent to that destination would cross a ServerNet I link. If a ServerNet I link lies anywhere in the path, the driver sets the packet transfer rate such that the ServerNet II device does not generate packets any faster than the ServerNet I rate of 50 MB/s.

At system start-up, SAN management software (see Section 6.0) determines the SAN topology and capabilities of each ServerNet routing node in the system. The driver software uses this information to set the appropriate packet injection rate for each destination on the SAN.

The driver software, when talking to a ServerNet I destination, must also restrict its choice of packet types. ServerNet I end nodes cannot accept the new Read and Write Packets formats with 64 bit addressing.

4.3 Worm Compression

When a ServerNet II routing node directly connects to a ServerNet I device (either end node or routing node), the ServerNet II device operates in a compatibility mode: symbols are clocked in and out of the ServerNet II router at 50 MB/s. But the internal logic and the downstream paths of the ServerNet II router still operate at 125 MB/s.

If the ServerNet II router were to simply exploit the 2:5 ratio in throughput, it could convert the incoming 50MB/s stream into a 125MB/s stream by inserting 3 pad symbols after every 2 data symbols. Using the analogy of the packet as a worm, the 50 MB/s stream would turn into an elongated worm at 125 MB/s -- one with 3 out of 5 symbols simply padding.

Such an approach would cause inefficiency, since the "elongated worm" would waste bandwidth whenever it passed over a ServerNet II-capable link.

To prevent this inefficiency, the ServerNet II router does "worm compression". Whenever it receives a ServerNet I byte stream, it delays forwarding the packet until it has received 60% of the packet. Once 60% of the packet has been received, the ServerNet II router may release the packet and the entire packet will proceed onward at the full 125MB/s bandwidth.

5.0 Router II

The Router II design provides the first implementation of the new ServerNet II protocols. It incorporates 12 full transmit and receive ports into an ASIC of approximately 500k gates. The design provides a good balance between gate count and pin count, while maintaining a relatively modest cost. Twelve ports also provides a good balance between the expansion needs of large systems and the cost limits of smaller systems.

Figure 6 shows a block diagram of Router II. The chip has twelve fully independent input ports, each with its associated output port, a routing control block, a simple packet interface for use with in-band control (IBC) messages as described in Section 6.0, a fully-non-blocking 13x13 crossbar, and interfaces for JTAG test and microcontroller connections.

Each input module contains receive data synchronizers, elastic FIFOs, and flow control logic. The input modules pass the header information to the routing module, which determines the appropriate target port for the packet. Note that the routing module includes a set of "target port disable" bits to prevent routing loops and deadlocks even in the presence of single node faults and packet symbol corruption. The routing module also controls the selection of links in any "fat pipes," as described in Section 5.1 below. Once an input port receives the target port number for a given packet, it contends for the corresponding output port and crossbar resources. The cross-bar arbiters include biasing logic[6], in order to allow for locally *unfair* allocation to reduce the worst-case two-way delivery time of transactions through the network and improve the allocation of bandwidth through the entire system..

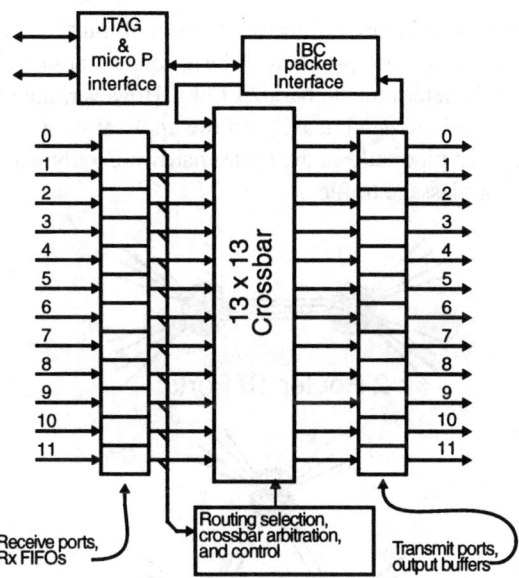

Figure 6. Router Block Diagram

Each transmit port contains symbol encoding, link-level protocol logic, and an output buffer FIFO. This FIFO allows data to flow through the crossbar even when the destination link has received backpressure, or when that link operates at 50 MB/s. Since the crossbar operates at the full speed of 125 MB/s, the presence of the FIFO helps reduce head-of-line blocking when connecting a link that uses the ServerNet I protocols.

The ports can operate at 50 MB/s using the ServerNet I protocols or 125 MB/s using ServerNet II protocols. Each port will automatically configure itself for operation with the appropriate link encoding and at the highest rate supported by both ends of a link.

This allows the exchange of system-level configuration messages without the need of negotiating data rates and encodings in software.

The Router II ASIC also includes a packet interface for communicating IBC messages. This interface connects as a full thirteenth port on the router's crossbar. The microprocessor and JTAG interfaces provide full access to all of the router configuration, status, and performance monitor registers.

5.1 Fat Pipes

The presence of 12 ports allows for a wide variety of topologies with substantial connectivity. However, providing sustained network throughput can present some difficulties. Failure to consider the fan-in to the router-router links within the network could produce system topologies with substantial traffic bottlenecks.

The two topologies shown in Figure 6 illustrate the use of multiple connections between routers as a means to avoiding such problems. These connections could use static routing configurations to provide deterministic parallel links. However, the correct allocation of routing paths to links would depend heavily on the application work-load. Configuring such links to operate as fat pipes allows the router hardware to dynamically select an output port based on recent message traffic.

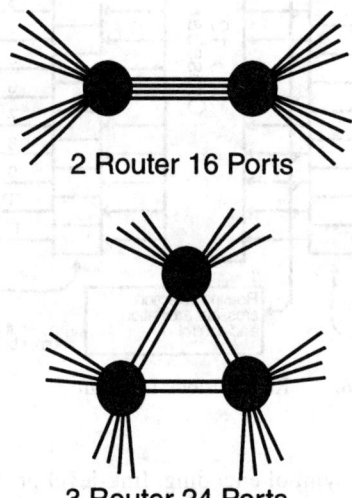

Figure 7. Two Examples of Simple Topologies Using Router II.

The Router II design supports the configuration of up to six fat pipes, or fat pipes containing as many as four links. The former would allow the creation of fractahedral network topologies[7] consisting entirely of fat pipes supporting sustained throughput of 500 MB/s on each of the fat links. Figure 6 shows an example of this usage.

5.2 Design trade-offs

Router II includes no support for virtual channels [1]. The die area required to support a single additional virtual channel on one port nearly equals the logic needed for a complete port. The inclusion of virtual channels would have therefore upset the balance of gate count and pin count, producing a gate-bound chip design with perhaps as few as six ports. Having a large number of real ports allows for very high connectivity per router, or configuration of fat pipes, allowing trade-offs of connectivity and bandwidth at board design and system configuration times.

Router II also uses external SerDes chips. Use of internal serializer/deserializers would also have upset the gate count and pin count balance. No ASIC vendor considered for the Router II supports twelve serializers per chip, even with no other logic included. The inclusion of serial-only ports would also have precluded full flexibility on connection of systems with ServerNet I links, and driven up costs. Further, the jitter obtained by using on-chip phase-locked-loops would have substantially increased the observed bit error rates on the serial links beyond that expected with commodity serializer chips.

5.3 Topology examples

The simplest Router II topology uses a single router chip to provide twelve ServerNet II ports. Such a trivial network has a total bisection bandwidth of 1.5 GB/s (15 Gb/s), with exactly one router hop between end nodes in all cases.

The first example in Figure 6 provides 16 connections, with a maximum of 2 router hops, an average of 1.5 hops, bisection bandwidth of 1.0 GB/s, and a fan-in of 2. Scaling down to three, two, or one link between the routers increases the connectivity (to 18, 20, or 22 ports), but also increases the fan-in and reduces the bisection bandwidth.

The second example of Figure 6 shows how increasing the number of routers can increase the connectivity without sacrificing bisection bandwidth.

Note that any of the ports show in these figures could connect to entire trees of routers, possibly through fat pipes. Such configurations would allow arbitrarily large connectivity, while sacrificing the regularity of the interconnect.

Figure 6 shows a simple network using four Router II chips and fat pipes to connect 12 fat links in a fully non-blocking network with a 1:1 fan-in.

Router II can of course support other fully connected topologies, such as Clos networks. Figure 6 shows an example of a 3x3x2 3D torus network, which illustrates that deadlock-free networks can have substantial capabilities, even without the use of virtual channels. (Shortest-path routing is deadlock free in a 3-ary 1D torus, and simple dimension-ordered or negative-first routing suffices for higher-dimensioned 3-ary tori.) A full 3x3x3 torus could connect to 162 end nodes, with a 1:1 fan-in, a 4.5 GB/s bisection bandwidth and maximum 4 router hops. In the fault-free case, two identical redundant interconnects could absorb 81 GB/s from the directly connected end nodes (810 Gb/s).

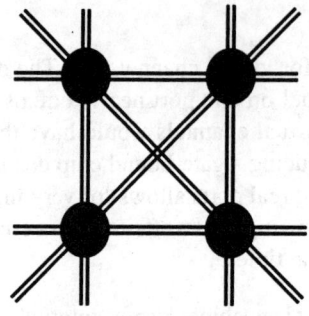

4 Routers 24 Ports

Figure 8.   Tetrahedral Network of Fat Pipes

Note that the 3x3x2 shows a second link in the 3rd dimension which is not required. That link provides extra bandwidth as a fat pipe; removing the link would provide additional connectivity.

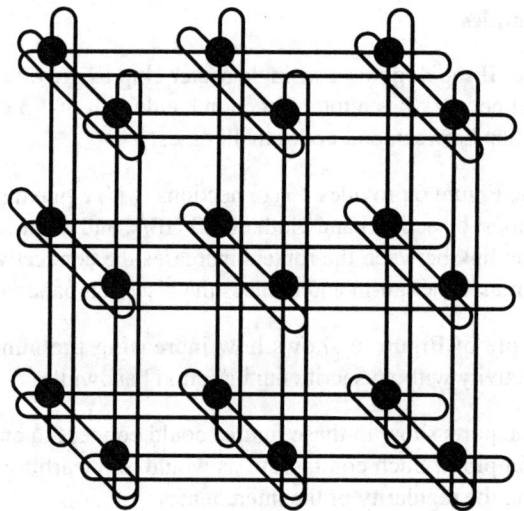

Figure 9.   Example of a 3x3x2 3D Torus Topology

6.0 SAN Management with the IBC Protocol

In a clustered system, a single point must have the capability of management of the different SAN components. Furthermore, the ability to perform system management functions from a single point anywhere in the system but not be constrained to any one hardwired spot simplifies administration. Management provides several necessary functions:

- Discovery of the network topology and end nodes attached to the network.

- Assignment of ServerNet IDs to the end nodes.

- Initialization of the routing tables in each router ASIC.

- Identification and incorporation of new nodes into a cluster as they are added to a running system.

- Collection of error information so as to isolate faults to the link or module on which they occurred.

- Control of LEDs to indicate service operations necessary on a particular cable or assembly.

- Observation and control of performance counters to aid in tuning the system.

Cost goals prevent the addition of any significant processing power or connectivity to the ServerNet routing components for support of these management functions. For example, the ServerNet switch does not have a central processor nor any LAN connection. Adding either would exceed the cost goals for the device.

An "In Band Control" (IBC) mechanism supports a low overhead way of meeting the above manageability functions. The term "in band" indicates that the network management control data travels over the existing ServerNet wire -- with no separate cable or LAN connection.

The IBC mechanism works across both ServerNet I and ServerNet II systems. Section 6.2 below shows that ServerNet I and II use different methods to transport the IBC data, but the same data format.

IBC messages use packets identical to regular ServerNet unacknowledged write requests. As shown below in Figure 10 -- each packet consists of an 8 byte header containing control bits and source/destination IDs, a 4 byte address, variable size data and a 4 byte CRC.

Normally, end nodes generate ServerNet request packets. The network delivers the packets to another end node which, in turn, sends a response or acknowledgment. The routing elements never consume or generate packets, and simply pass the packets from the source end node to the destination end node.

On the other hand, both routing nodes and end nodes generate and consume IBC packets. The IBC packet does not get routed through the ServerNet SAN like normal Read and Write packets. It contains embedded source routing information (see Figure 10). Each router or end node that receives the IBC packet then forwards it to the next destination in the source route list.

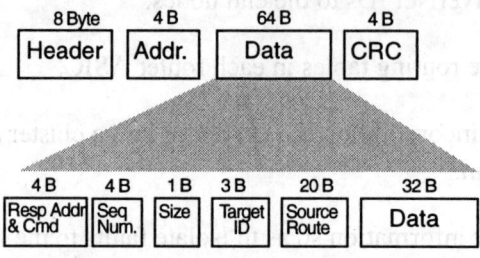

Figure 10. IBC Packet Format

As shown in Figure 10, the data field of a ServerNet unacknowledged write packet carries the IBC control information. These packets only traverse a single link at a time. The receiving nodes do not route them, but instead always consume them. The recipient examines the source route list and forwards the packet along the indicated link to the next node, until the packet reaches its final destination.

The data body of the unacknowledged write packet carries an additional command to do a read or write at the address specified in the overall header field. By convention, each ServerNet routing node and end node supports a standard address space for reading an information and status block. By reading from this space, management SW can determine the type and capabilities of any node attached to the network.

Other write operations specify various management functions (see Table 2 below). A small microcontroller in each switch executes these functions. In host end nodes, an IBC client communicating with the ServerNet driver executes (or generates) IBC requests.

For example, management software can write to RAM resident in the microcontroller, then issue an IBC write to a specific address to cause the RAM contents to be loaded into the Routing table or to update the microcontroller firmware. Table 2 shows the IBC commands supported by the ServerNet I switch.

Table 2. Switch-I IBC Commands

Command	R/W
Read/Write Data RAM	R/W
Read/Write Control & Status Registers	R/W
Update Stored Configuration	W
Update Firmware	W
Read Performance Counters	R
Select/Start Performance Counters	W
JTAG Register Read	R
Read ServerNet Configuration Space	R

The microcontroller in the switch can even access the Router ASIC's internal JTAG registers enabling it to do chip BIST operations†, and examine internal router registers. By reading and writing control registers, management software can control LEDs to direct service operations, query environmental sensors and examine error registers.

We kept the IBC protocol very simple to allow implementation using an inexpensive 8 bit microcontroller. The simple command - response protocol implements commands as basic Read or a Write operations. The protocol places little computational demand on the microcontroller. Keeping the microcontroller simple was key for us to meet switch cost goals.

6.1 IBC Source Routing

Regular ServerNet packets pass through the network using oblivious Markov routing -- the routers only look at the destination ID in order to choose which output port to use. This provides great flexibility, low packet overhead, and allows packets to traverse the network without modification (or recalculation of CRCs). IBC packets have different requirements, in particular, the ability to traverse any path and to do so non-invasively. IBC packets use source routing. The source routing table in the packet allows transmission of IBC commands through 20 levels of routing or end node devices.

The IBC packet always addresses a wildcard node ID accepted by the each node on the selected path. The recipient stores the IBC packet and forwards it as needed towards its final destination. Microcontroller software implements the entire source routing function. IBC packets do not use wormhole routing, they always traverse one link and use the microcontroller store and forward functions.

Source routing has a particular benefit in that it allows transmission of IBC packets along paths that the router might not otherwise support. For example, if deadlock prevention requires disabling a particular path through a router, that router would never pass a packet from that particular input to that particular output. But with store-and-forward source routing, the IBC packets can traverse this otherwise illegal path.

The IBC source routing scheme can also route messages across end nodes. For example, Figure 11 shows a simple redundant ServerNet topology. Collection of error status from the routers in the network allows isolation of a fault. Tracking the error rates on each link can also allow isolation of failing links.

In this example, the SAN management software can direct an IBC packet along a route unusable by normal ServerNet packets. The redundant paths available in the ServerNet network allow access to both sides of a failing link.

Source routing has another benefit: it does not require the configuration or initialization of the routers in a SAN. This allows the management software to discover all the system links, routing and end node devices that make up a ServerNet SAN without changing their state.To discover the topology of the network, management software must do a search of all the ports on the network. By reading the status block of each node in the network, the management software can build a table of devices, their capabilities, and their

---

†. JTAG refers to the IEEE 1149.1 standard test interface for ASICs. This interface allows access to ASIC internal registers and can be used to control test functions such as BIST (Built In Self Test)

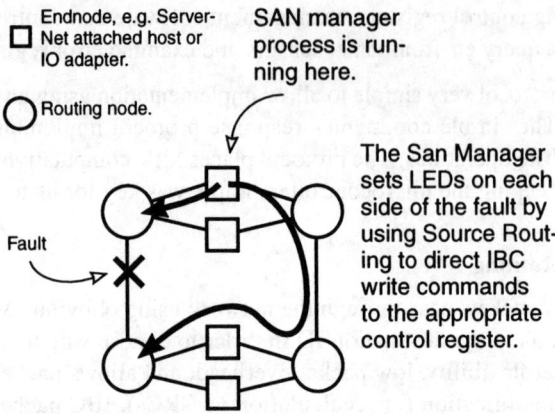

Figure 11. IBC Source Routing Example

connectivity. By continuing this process of examining nodes, all devices attached to ServerNet are eventually discovered.

6.2 IBC In ServerNet I and ServerNet II

ServerNet I and ServerNet II both use the same IBC command packet format. But the means used to transmit the packet over the ServerNet wire differ.

ServerNet I uses a single symbol method to transfer an IBC packet, encoding IBC commands, 4 bits at a time, into non-data symbols and interspersing them into the normal ServerNet Read and Write packet traffic. ServerNet ASICs trap these special symbols and make them available to the local processor, via normal register accesses (end nodes) or special JTAG accesses (Router-I). The processors then build the IBC command 4 bits at a time. This communication method can only transfer about 4K bits/second, adequate for system management use.

ServerNet II accelerates the IBC communication by sending the IBC message (as shown in Figure 10) as a single packet. The ServerNet Router II ASIC dedicates a pair of packet buffers for this purpose. A microcontroller still processes the IBC message and forward it as needed. Moving the IBC command as an entire packet improves throughput of IBC commands to approximately 1 Mbit/sec. The ServerNet II devices use the same IBC command types, and can also support the ServerNet I single symbol method of transmitting IBC commands. This ensures compatibility for IBC between ServerNet I and II.

When network management software first probes a device to read configuration space, it uses the single symbol method, supported by all devices. The configuration space indicates whether the device supports higher speed transfers of ServerNet II.

7.0 Acknowledgments

The second generation of ServerNet owes its development to a great number of people doing chip design and software. In particular David Brown, Bill Bunton, and John Krause led the design of the second generation router. Bill Bruckert, Mike Christensen, Robert Horst, Robert Jardine and Stephen Low contributed throughout the design of ServerNet II. Mel Benedict, Barry Drexler, Dan Fowler, and Mike Knowles contributed to end node design.

8.0 Conclusion

This paper reviews the basic points of the original ServerNet SAN, and describes the improvements provided by the new ServerNet II protocols and ASICs. The ServerNet II components provide improvements in packet overhead, link bandwidth, scalability, link length, and connectivity, without sacrificing interoperability with ServerNet I equipment. ServerNet II preserves the user's investment in ServerNet I hardware and software products and improves throughput considerably. We describe some network topologies supported by the Router II ASIC. The selection of a topology depends on application-specific issues. Router II has sufficient flexibility to support many alternatives.

This paper also describes the ServerNet SAN management functions. It describes the support of those functions on both ServerNet I and II interfaces, showing the substantial performance improvement provided by the new interfaces.

9.0 References

[1]   W. J. Dally and C. L. Seitz, "Deadlock-Free Message Routing in Multi-processor Interconnection Networks". IEEE Transactions on Computers, 36:547-553, May 1987

[2]   R.W. Horst and D.J. Garcia, "ServerNet SAN IO Architecture", Hot Interconnects 1997

[3]   W.E. Baker, R.W. Horst, D.P. Sonnier, and W.J. Watson. "A Flexible ServerNet Based Fault-Tolerant Architecture." In Proc. of the 25th Int. Symp. Fault-Tolerant Computing, pages 2-11, Pasadena, CA, USA, June 1995.

[4]   R.W. Horst, "TNet: A Reliable System Area Network." IEEE Micro, pages 37-45, February 1995.

[5]   A.X. Widmer and P.A. Franzaszek. "A DC Balanced Partitioned Block 8b/10b Transmission Code", IBM Journal of Research and Development, Vol 27, No. 5: 440-451 (September 1983)

[6]   J. Kim, A. Chien, R. W. Horst, J. Krause, D. P. Sonnier, W. J. Watson, "Network Resource Control in the Tandem ServerNet Router, http://www-csag.cs.uiuc.edu/papers/alu.ps

[7]   R. W. Horst, "ServerNet deadlock avoidance and fractahedral topologies," Proceedings of the 10th International Parallel Processing Symposium, Honolulu, Hawaii, pp. 274-280, 1995

Invited Presentation

Embedded Systems Standards

Craig Lund

Mecrcury Computer Systems Inc.

Historically there have been almost as many System Area Network (SAN) designs as there are parallel computing researchers. However, as markets mature, standards evolve. The personal computing industry is working towards a low-level, OS bypass API for leveraging arbitrary SANs from Windows NT. This new API is called the "Virtual Interface Architecture". VI is protocol independent. Extracting optimal performance from VI requires special hardware support at the network interface chip (NIC) level.

Microsoft, Compaq, and Intel, the authors of the VI Architecture specification, do not expect parallel programmers to directly call the VI API. Instead programmers will use layered software products. Software standards that one might layer above VI include MPI (message passing for the scientific niche), MPI-RT (a real-time variant of MPI for signal processing), and High Performance CORBA (a proposed variant of CORBA for parallel programming).

The VI Architecture provides only a programming interface, not a protocol standard. At this writing only the Fibre Channel community has a standards working group focused upon creating a VI layer for the Fibre Channel protocol stack. Thus early VI products that use other popular networks may not interoperate. The VI Architecture specification is very new. Competitive systems based upon other commercial standards currently ship in moderate volume. By shipment volume, today's most popular SAN is the embedded computing community's ANSI RACEway Interlink. RACEway is also used in the I/O subsystems of commercial servers. The RACEway community continues to aggressively evolve its technology.

The IEEE Scalable Coherent Interconnect (SCI) standard has been with us for many years. SCI is used inside commercial servers and inside supercomputers. SCI's biggest advantage is its optional support for coherent shared memory. Although not deployed by any SCI vendor, a shared memory, parallel programming standard exists in Silicon Graphics OpenMP proposal. Silicon Graphics is also working towards ANSI blessing for its unique SAN hardware technology, called HiPPI-6400. The U. S. Department of Energy (DOE), through is ASCI program, is the biggest backer of HiPPI-6400. DOE is paying several other workstation vendors to create HiPPI-6400 interfaces.

With the explosion of both standard and proprietary SANs, the need to interconnect them arises. The TCP/IP protocol is the best option today. Unfortunately, TCP/IP is far from optimal in the SAN environment. Therefore, TCP/IP's parent, the Internet Engineering Task Force (IETF), is developing a SAN internetworking protocol standard called Pkt-Way.

Invited Presentation

Challenges in the Design of Contemporary Routers

Craig B. Stunkel

IBM T. J. Watson Research Center
P.O. Box 218, Yorktown Heights, NY 10598
stunkel@watson.ibm.com

Abstract. The environment and constraints for parallel system interconnection networks have changed dramatically since early research into cut-through routers (switches). In early systems, chip transistors were at a premium. MPP systems were often built using single-chip processor nodes closely packed together, constraining communication bisection area. Unabated increases in VLSI density have led to low-cost high-capacity switch buffering, and complex buffer organizations for maximizing throughput are now possible. In today's parallel systems, the large size of processor nodes effectively eliminates bisection area constraints. Many other network requirements have also arisen within the last few years. We explore these and other challenges that affect design choices and design decisions for contemporary routers.

1 Introduction

The environment and constraints for parallel system interconnection networks have changed dramatically since the Cosmic Cube [28] and other early work that inspired much of the current research into routers, topologies, adaptivity, and deadlock avoidance. In early systems, chip transistors were at a premium, leading to the widespread use of wormhole flow-control [8]. MPP systems were often built using single-chip nodes packed closely together, leading to interconnection schemes that attempted to maximize bisection bandwidth through a constrained area.

Unabated increases in VLSI density have led to low-cost high-capacity switch buffering, and complex buffer organizations for maximizing throughput are now possible. Virtual cut-through switching [15] is now a viable alternative to wormhole flow-control. In most of today's general-purpose parallel systems, the large size of processor nodes effectively eliminates bisection area constraints. Because nodes in these systems are often relatively loosely packed, pipelining along interconnection links is mandatory, and asynchronous clocking is preferred.

Many other network requirements have arisen within the last few years. Irregular networks have become an option for connecting networks of workstations. Distributed shared memory systems present new latency demands and deadlock scenarios. Video servers benefit from quality-of-service guarantees and hardware-supported multicasting. In this paper we explore these and other challenges that affect the design of contemporary routers.

One way to introduce these subjects is to contrast the assumptions often made in contemporary research papers with the actual decisions being made in commercial machines. In doing so, we do not single out specific examples. Rather, Section 2 categorizes and examines common research assumptions that are a poor match to the state of the art. Then, in Section 3, we discuss some of the major problems that we are currently facing in building high-performance switching networks.

2 Some common assumptions versus today's realities

VLSI technological capabilities have progressed enormously since the early days of multicomputer switch (router) design. Despite this fact, much router research proceeds using assumptions targeted at the earlier levels of technology. In this section we examine a few outdated notions that are often used when architecting and evaluating switches.

2.1 Switching and flow-control techniques

Assumptions: One very common assumption is "pure" *wormhole* flow-control. Wormhole is a form of cut-through switching in which flow-control is performed on a sub-packet, or *flit*[1] [8]), basis. By "pure" wormhole we imply that a minimum number of flits—one or two—can be buffered at each input port.

An integral assumption in early wormhole papers and implementations was handshaking flow-control: a flit of a packet could not proceed to the next router until that router had acknowledged acceptance of the previous flit. As a result, link delay was a contributor to the cycle time. This also meant that the cycle time became dependent upon the routing delay, because the time to compute the route would slow down the routing flit, which would in turn gate the progress of every succeeding flit of the packet. This scheme made "pure" wormhole flow-control possible by avoiding any need for pipelining. This assumption also heavily favored short links because they minimized the round-trip transit time of the handshake.

Reality: When wormhole flow-control was first proposed [8, 12], it was difficult to provide input buffers capable of storing an entire packet without relying on off-chip buffers, which increased router cost. But now, VLSI ASICs can easily provide 10s of thousands of bytes of storage in addition to the dataflow logic and buffering. Hence, switches tend to be pin-limited because of bandwidth targets instead of device-limited.

Larger on-chip buffers also allow us to overcome the cycle time limitations of handshaking flow-control. In fact, cycle time can be made independent of link and routing delay. Both link transit and routing logic can be pipelined to

---

[1] In wormhole flow-control, a flow-control digit, or flit, is the smallest unit of a packet that can be accepted or refused by a switch input port. Typically the flit size is equivalent to the internal data path width of the router.

whatever degree is appropriate. In most of today's parallel systems, links are high-speed pipelined transmission lines and can operate with shorter cycle times than today's internal CMOS logic. As an example, current IBM SP switches operate on 13.3ns cycles (75 MHz) using 2-byte-wide internal data paths, but send data at 150 Mb/s per signal over byte-wide links up to 25 meters. The pipelining of data along a link requires a more powerful flow-control than handshaking. One example is the credit-based scheme used in the SP [32].

For wormhole flow-control, the other benefit of increased buffer sizes is that blocked packets hold fewer links. As buffers increase in size, *virtual cut-through* (VCT) [15] becomes a practical alternative. In VCT, flow-control is performed on a *packet* basis, although switching is still cut-through. As a result, blocked packets never hold more than one link in a switching network, improving performance. VCT flow-control requires each buffer to be at least as large as the largest packet. Wormhole (flit-based) flow-control can also be implemented with buffers larger than the largest packet to provide similar blocking characteristics to VCT.

At this point it is worthwhile to survey the types of flow-control selected in recent commercial designs. As Figure 1 shows, most vendors are implementing wormhole flow-control, although some recent designs have chosen virtual cut-through or hybrids of these two methods. However, almost all of the designs

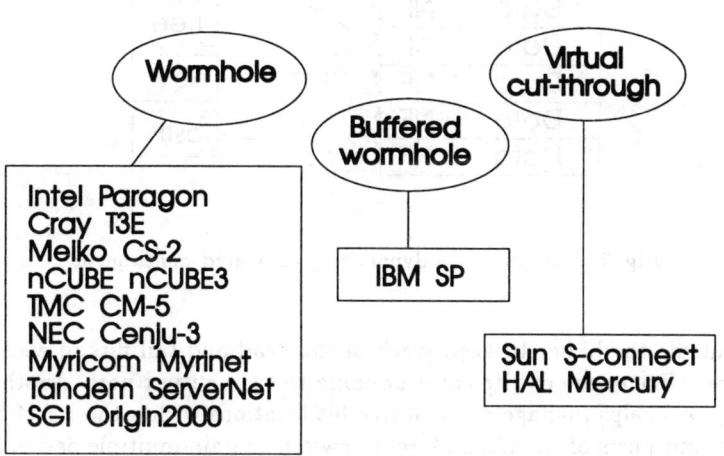

Fig. 1. Cut-through flow-control methods in recent switching networks

listed as wormhole have significant buffering, far more than "pure" wormhole flow-control. For example, all T3E input buffers are larger than the maximum packet size. Thus, even though the T3E flow-control technique is wormhole, the performance of the router will resemble VCT.

2.2 Queuing technique

Assumptions: Another set of common assumptions concerns the queuing technique for buffering packets within switches. Most research studies postulate an *input queuing* approach that relies on fixed-sized input FIFO buffers, and that suffers from head-of-the-line (HOL) blocking. Virtual channels or *lanes* are most often selected as a way to improve utilization through such switches. Each virtual lane shares the bandwidth of the physical link, often interleaving on a flit-by-flit basis over the link. Each lane is associated with a separate input FIFO buffer, and each lane provides an input to the router crossbar.

Reality: In today's systems however, the HOL problem is being attacked in a myriad of ways. For example, at each virtual lane of an input port, the SGI Spider routing chip [10] uses *dynamically-allocated multi-queues* (initially proposed by Tamir and Frazier [34]). Figure 2 shows how a single RAM buffer might be augmented with pointer entries to create multiple packet queues. Pointers are

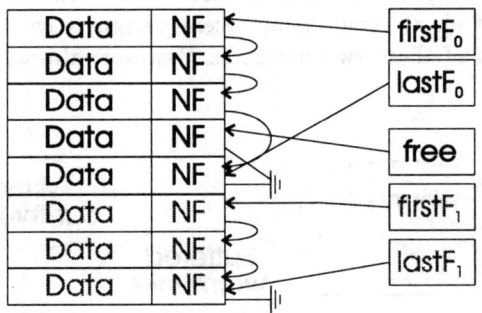

Fig. 2. Structure of a dynamically-allocated multi-queue

added outside the buffer to keep track of the head and tail flits of each queue, and there is one queue of flits corresponding to each output port. Another head pointer (*free*) helps manage a list of free flit locations within the RAM buffer.

The input ports of the HAL Mercury switch contain multiple packet buffers, each of which is connected to a separate input of the internal crossbar [37]. Although this approach has similarities to virtual lanes, the flow-control is packet-based (virtual cut-through), and thus packet flits are not interleaved over the link. This approach was previously used in the MIT Arctic routing chip [4]. It increases utilization by decreasing the probability that a packet will wait behind a blocked packet at the input port.

It is well-known that *output queuing* provides better performance than input queuing [24]. In output queuing, buffers associated with each output port are able to simultaneously accept packet data from all input ports at full bandwidth.

Naturally, this capability is only guaranteed until the buffer fills. Output queuing is more costly to implement, however, due to its requirement for storing multiple flits per cycle (from separate packets) into each output queue. A less costly solution is to provide a "central" buffer space that is shared among all of the input and output ports.

The IBM SP switches [32] implement such an alternative. They rely on a *dynamically-allocated central-buffer* architecture that implements output queuing. Figure 3 illustrates a centrally-buffered switch. This approach is actually

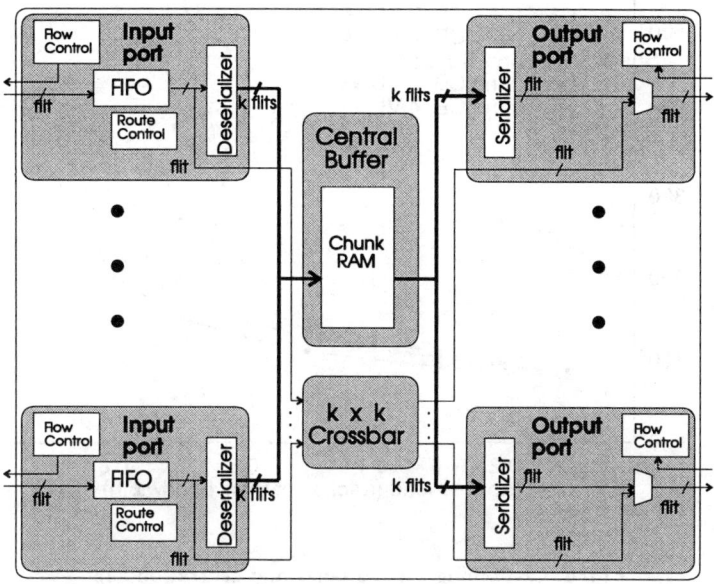

Fig. 3. A centrally-buffered switch

easier to implement than a separate queue buffer at each output port, and it delivers better performance due to the dynamic sharing of buffer space among all ports. A thorough explanation of how output queues are managed in an SP switch's central buffer can be found elsewhere [33].

There are other potential approaches to defeating the HOL blocking problem. Current VLSI technology allows exploration of powerful schemes that were once considered impossible due to limited chip space.

One such area worth exploring is the combining of different techniques for increasing switch utilization. Although it would seem that the combining of two beneficial techniques would increase the overall benefit, this is not always true. For example, both virtual lanes and central buffers are powerful techniques for increasing utilization, and they work in seemingly complementary ways. Several years ago we conducted a study to assess the impact of combining them, and came to the surprising conclusion that combining virtual lanes and central buffering performed worse than central buffering alone.

Figure 4 illustrates one set of simulation experiments conducted for a 16-node SP2 for 64-byte messages. This (original) SP2 network was based upon the

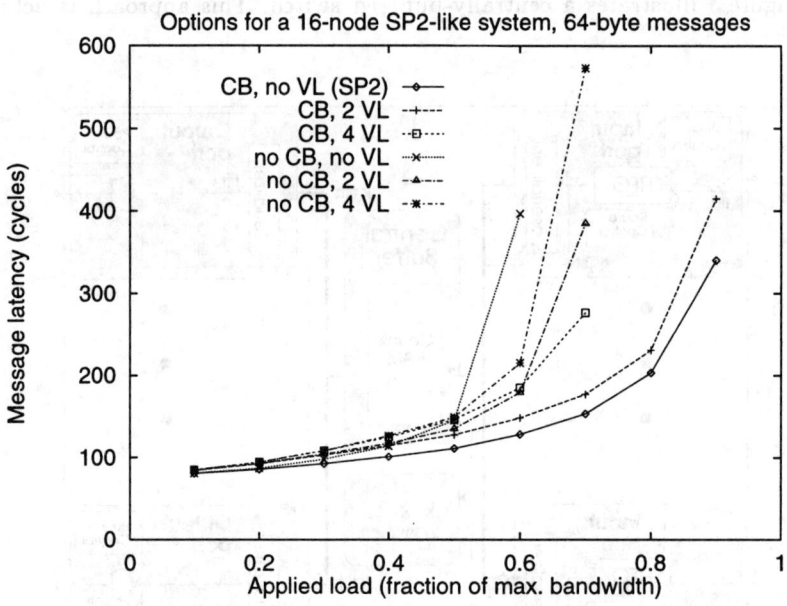

Fig. 4. Combining virtual lanes and central buffers

Vulcan switch, which had byte-wide data paths and the structure shown in Figure 3. A 16-node system contains two stages of bidirectional switching elements, and is equivalent to a 2-stage 4-ary fat-tree. Up to saturation, Figure 4 plots network latency against offered load for a uniform destination distribution. Latency includes injection queuing time, and infinite injection queues are assumed. Several buffer variations were simulated, each with an equivalent amount of total buffering. For instance, the 8-port SP2 switch chips contained a 1024-byte central buffer with 31-byte input FIFOs, for a total of 1272 bytes of storage. Thus for the case of 2 virtual lanes with no central buffer, we assumed $1272/8 = 159$ bytes of storage for each input port. (Adaptivity was not considered, because in fat-tree networks virtual lanes do not increase adaptivity for the case of minimal adaptive routing).

When 2 virtual lanes are combined with central buffering, latency is higher and traffic saturates sooner when compared with central buffering without virtual lanes. Increasing to four virtual lanes decreased performance again. Two observations help explain these results: (1) when the central buffer of a switch is not full, it is able to receive flits from the input ports at full bandwidth, so no alternative approach will perform better until the network nears saturation, and (2) when two virtual lanes share the bandwidth of a single link, each of the packets sharing the link are slowed down by a factor of two. We also tried experiments in which, instead of flit-by-flit multiplexing of link bandwidth between virtual lanes, each packet exclusively holds the link while non-blocked [29]. This increased the performance for virtual lanes. However, we were never able to reach the performance of central buffering alone.

Even without central buffers, increasing the number of virtual lanes (VLs) is not always beneficial, depending on the offered load. For these experiments, systems with two virtual lanes performed better than those with four. For 64-byte packets, the buffers in the 2 VL case were large enough to hold an entire packet, and the 4 VL buffers were not. Thus in the 2 VL case packets were not blocked across multiple links.

This example experiment should *not* be interpreted as an argument against the use of virtual lanes. Instead, the moral is that combining two beneficial techniques is not necessarily more beneficial than the techniques in isolation. Lanes are particularly useful for avoiding deadlock and for increasing the potential adaptivity of direct networks, thereby increasing throughput. They are also useful in creating "virtual networks" for use in avoiding request-reply deadlocks, for instance.

2.3 Topology

Assumptions: Many interconnection network papers tackle the issues and problems relating to 2-dimensional (2-D) meshes or tori. Many more deal with higher-dimensional k-ary n-cubes [7]. A smaller percentage of papers assume other topologies.

Reality: In contrast, current topology choices of commercial machines are quite varied, with only one prominent example of the 2-D mesh: the Intel Paragon [11], which is no more in production. There is also a relatively even mix of direct and indirect networks. Irregular networks [25] are an interesting choice, partly because of the potential power of networks of workstations (NOWs).

Figure 5 illustrates the topology decisions made for many recent parallel systems and network interconnects. As noted, there are many examples of both direct and indirect networks. With respect to direct networks, the hypercube has been given new life with its use in the SGI Origin2000. However, for large systems, the Origin2000 network is actually an indirect network formed by successive stages of hypercube nodes, a "fat" hypercube [10, 17], which is an indirect network related to the fat-tree. This arrangement overcomes the principal disadvantage that first led to the decline of hypercubes: increasing the dimension of the hypercube requires increasing the number of connected ports per router.

On the indirect network side, each of the listed systems is a variation of a multistage interconnection network, or MIN. The IBM SP's BMIN (bidirectional

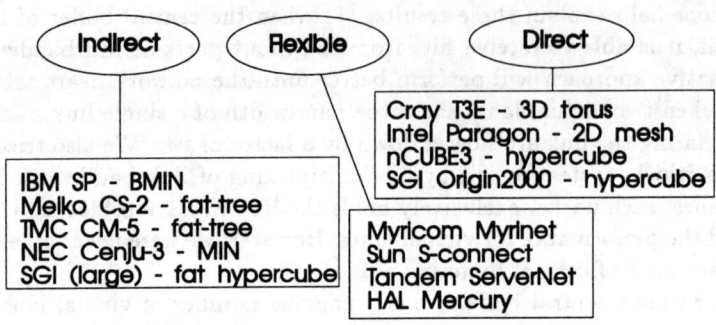

Fig. 5. Topology choices for parallel systems and interconnects

MIN) is closely related to a 4-ary fat-tree, although not every SP configuration fits the standard definition of a fat-tree. As a whole, the indirect network box in Figure 5 shows that bidirectional indirect networks are far more popular than their unidirectional cousins.

A third category is shown in Figure 5: flexible topologies. In each of the examples listed, the network vendor is selling an interconnection network, with or without processing nodes. Each vendor has recognized today's diversity of topology choices, and has thus avoided hard-wiring any topological constraints into their networks. Each of the routers in this category relies on either source routing or table-lookup routing to provide this routing flexibility. Information for this routing is loaded by software whenever the system configuration changes.

The effects of NOWs on topology: Networks of workstations (NOWs) are playing an increasingly important role in high-performance computing, even extending to the MPP arena [2, 31]. Perhaps the most important reason is time-to-market. Every vendor's attention is focused on converting the latest processor technology into workstations or PCs as quickly as possible. The volumes demand and reward this effort. The relatively small volumes of MPPs make it more difficult to "ride the workstation performance curve" unless each MPP node is simply a workstation.

High-performance NOWs benefit from high-performance switching networks. But NOW attributes can also affect the choice of interconnect topology. Off-the-shelf workstations are typically capable of housing a variety of adaptor cards and therefore occupy significant real estate. The space required for communication links within the NOW is therefore likely to be a small fraction of the overall volume of the system. Hence, any assumption of a constrained bisection area [7] that favors 2-dimensional meshes is not applicable. Instead, topologies that are more complex and more richly connected become attractive.

A second effect of NOWs concerns their availability. Nodes are more likely to be added, removed, power cycled, or crashed than in the more controlled environments of MPPs. Thus, any network that connects distributed NOWs must handle node state changes gracefully and without affecting the connectivity of the remaining nodes in the system. Fat-trees are an example of a network that accomplishes this [19]. Irregular networks are another example. It is no accident that networks of workstations are often connected in a hierarchical fashion, and are beginning to employ switches at even the lowest level in the hierarchy. An example of this is the rapid movement toward switched ethernet and ATM LAN technologies.

2.4 Summary of assumptions versus realities

We have looked at three areas of switch design—buffer space and flow control, queuing strategy and buffer organization, and topology—in which common research assumptions do not necessarily match the state of the art. We are not saying that assumptions such as "pure" wormhole flow-control or 2-D mesh are totally irrelevant. We would simply like to see more balance shown in research assumptions. Attempting to use "base cases" that reasonably reflect current networks will improve the chances that one's research will affect future products. In the next section we examine issues that keep switch designers awake at night.

3 Current challenges in router design

In this section we explore several challenges facing router architects and designers of future parallel computer networks. Achieving low latency, high bandwidth, and high reliability at reasonable cost are always primary objectives, and these goals drive many of the challenges. Beyond these goals, maximizing throughput through routers and networks, supporting distributed shared-memory (DSM), providing hardware support for collective communication, and providing quality of service guarantees are other timely issues. The next few subsections elaborate on these goals.

3.1 Low latency and high bandwidth

As processing power continues to grow exponentially, switch bandwidth must grow at a similar rate to scale communication efficiency. Likewise, latency must scale downward at exponential rates. For most message-passing systems to date, the end-to-end latency has been dominated by software. However, lower overhead approaches [22, 36] have made the hardware portion of latency more significant. A trend that accelerates demands for low network latency is DSM.

Distributed shared memory: DSM is now a viable option in the marketplace, as evidenced by recent offerings from SGI/Cray [17], HP/Convex [6], Sequent [20], and others. It is probable that larger and larger DSM systems will be designed, although message-passing architectures will also remain important in the near future. The primary network implication of DSM is the need for dynamic, very low latency routing of packets.

Current link bandwidth and latency: Figure 6 shows approximate latency and bandwidth ranges for current generation interconnects, including LAN, MPP, DSM, and SMP interconnects. As interconnects progress from LAN to

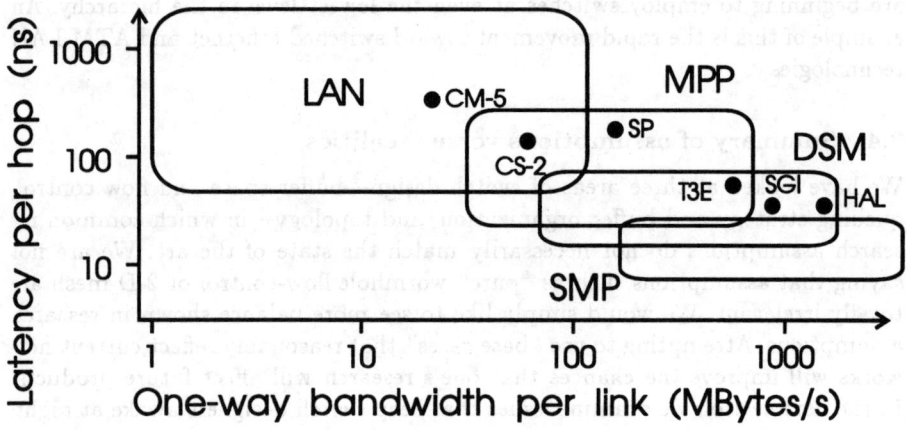

Fig. 6. Link speeds and feeds

MPP to DSM, performance requirements force vendors to provide higher link bandwidth and lower latency. For example, the recently announced SGI Origin 2000 and the HAL Mercury interconnect contain switches with pin-to-pin latencies of 40ns and 42 ns respectively, and are targeted for DSM machines. Other MPP machines shown are the Cray T3E [26], the IBM SP, the Meiko CS-2 [3], and the Thinking Machines CM-5 [18]. The network bandwidth and latency requirements for LAN-connected machines is not as severe, due to high TCP/IP software overheads and due to connection though commodity I/O busses. However, approaches such as U-net [35] are attempting to change this.

However, looking at bandwidth requirements is relatively meaningless without considering the associated link length requirements. Table 1 lists the bandwidth and link length characteristics for many of the interconnects shown in Figure 6 and includes some other LAN and SAN (system area network) technologies. Two trends are evident. The first trend is that the implementations that currently push bandwidth most aggressively have higher per-wire transfer rates, wider data paths, and shorter maximum link lengths. The second trend is technologies that allow links up to 25 meters or so. These technologies currently have a 1-byte link width and lower link transfer rates. The 1-byte link width is a consequence both of cable diameter considerations for long links and of switch chip pin count.

The IBM SP and Myrinet technologies in particular attack a difficult bandwidth versus link-length region for copper. With 25 meter copper links and 150

Table 1. Link speeds and feeds

Interconnect	Per signal (Mb/s)	Link width (Bytes)	Bandwidth (MB/s)	Distance (meters)
Mercury Race [16]	40	4	160	2
Tandem ServerNet [13]	50	1	50	30
IBM SP	150	1	150	25
Myricom Myrinet [27]	160	1	160	10–25
Cray T3E [26]	375	2	600	1
SGI Origin2000 [10]	400	2	800	5
HAL Mercury [37]	400	4	1600	2

Mb/s per signal, skew between the different signals on the parallel link can cause neighboring signal bits to arrive in different clock cycles. It is no coincidence that, of the listed technologies, only the SP and Myrinet implementations perform de-skewing among the bits on the link. As copper implementations become more aggressive, this bit de-skewing will become common, as evidenced by its prominent inclusion in the Super HIPPI physical specification [1]. The smaller skew of optics will be advantageous here.

3.2 Maximizing switch utilization

It is wasteful to make heroic efforts to raise link bandwidth without attempting to achieve high utilization across links. As we argued before, steady VLSI improvements offer switch buffering possibilities for cut-through switches that were unavailable only a few short years ago. Because of this, we are now seeing a proliferation of more complex buffering and queuing schemes to keep interconnection network links as busy as possible. Some of the techniques that have yielded the highest utilization to this point, such as central buffering approaches [14, 32], may prove more difficult to apply as flit sizes increase, because fragmentation will increase for small packet sizes. Alternative organizations of central buffers [9] may extend their usefulness.

3.3 DSM in-order arrival requirements

Network interface units are simpler to design when the network interface is guaranteed to receive packets from a source in order. Allowing adaptive routing or multiple packet routes can improve network utilization and average packet latency, but then packets may arrive out of order.

Many DSM protocols being designed today require in-order arrival, although there are exceptions [17]. Requiring in-order arrival makes the protocol and its verification simpler. ATM networks require in-order arrival, although reordering can take place within a smart network interface. If, because of DSM systems, in-order arrival becomes a common requirement, then much of the timely and important work on adaptive routing will be less applicable. The advantages of in-order arrival should be carefully compared to the advantages of adaptive routing in the context of distributed shared memory systems.

3.4 Multicast and collective communication

Only recently has multicast replication within the network been studied extensively in the context of cut-through routers [5, 21, 23, 33]. For indirect networks, this hardware multicast only becomes a realistic option for virtual cut-through; wormhole methods lead easily to deadlock scenarios that are difficult to solve without severely reducing performance.

However, without means of combining within the network, a multicast may be followed by multiple acknowledgements (acks) back to the source of the multicast to ensure reliability. The source must then serially combine the acks, reducing some of the latency advantages of multicast. Therefore, a network that can combine acks might considerably improve the usefulness of hardware-based multicast. Combining is a difficult problem for switches because each switch must retain state information about each ack-combine in which it participates. If multicast groups are very dynamic—such as are seen in DSM—the state for such record-keeping could grow quite large, requiring a mechanism for handling combine-state overflow.

One related and frequently used collective communication operation is barrier synchronization, which can be implemented with reliability as two multicast-ack-combine phases [30]. Because barrier sync usually involves a relatively static group of processors, it is a much more manageable operation, and containable means for embedding barrier sync support within an existing network have been implemented [26].

4 Conclusion

We noted that a significant portion of router research seems out of step with the needs of designers and with the current state of the art. For instance, while many papers assume "pure" wormhole flow-control and/or 2-D meshes, seldom is either of these used today. Current systems are moving away from these extremes to virtual cut-through flow-control and more richly-connected topologies and more irregular or flexible topologies.

We have also discussed some of the challenges facing today's designers of interconnection network routers (switches). Optimization of latency, bandwidth, and network utilization are always critical. Support of collective communication operations can be improved dramatically. The question of whether or not switching networks should deliver packets in order should be studied further with distributed shared memory systems in mind.

Current VLSI technology allows us to explore architectural and design avenues that were earlier infeasible. Partly because of these new capabilities, router design remains an exciting and challenging research topic.

Acknowledgements

The content and presentation of this paper were improved immensely by the suggestions and comments of Rajeev Sivaram.

References

1. Hippi standards activities. http://www.noc.lanl.gov/~det/.
2. T. E. Anderson, D. E. Culler, and D. A. Patterson. A case for NOW (Networks of Workstations). *IEEE Micro*, 15(1):54–64, Feb. 1995.
3. J. Beecroft, M. Homewood, and M. McLaren. Meiko CS-2 interconnect Elan-Elite design. *Parallel Computing*, 20:1627–1638, Nov. 1994.
4. G. A. Boughton. Arctic routing chip. In *Lecture Notes in Computer Science*, volume 853, pages 310–317. Springer-Verlag, 1994. (Proc. First Int. Workshop on Parallel Computer Routing & Communication, May '94).
5. C.-M. Chiang and L. M. Ni. Deadlock-free multi-head wormhole routing. In *Proc. 1st High Performance Computing-Asia*, 1995.
6. CONVEX Computer Corporation, Richardson, TX. *Exemplar Architectural Manual*, November 1993.
7. W. J. Dally. Performance analysis of k-ary n-cube interconnection networks. *IEEE Trans. on Computers*, 39(6):775–785, June 1990.
8. W. J. Dally and C. L. Seitz. Deadlock-free message routing in multiprocessor interconnection networks. *IEEE Trans. on Computers*, C-36(5):547–553, May 1987.
9. W. E. Denzel, A. P. J. Engbersen, and I. Iliadis. Flexible shared-buffer switch for ATM at Gb/s rates. *Computer Networks and ISDN Systems*, 27(4):611–624, Jan. 1995.
10. M. Galles. Spider: A high-speed network interconnect. *IEEE Micro*, 17(1):34–39, Jan./Feb. 1997.
11. W. Groscup. The Intel Paragon XP/S supercomputer. In *Proc. 5th ECMWF Workshop on Use of Parallel Processors in Meteorology*, pages 23–27, Nov. 1992.
12. A. Hopper and D. J. Wheeler. Binary routing networks. *IEEE Trans. on Computers*, C-28(10):699–703, October 1979.
13. R. W. Horst. TNet: A reliable system area network. *IEEE Micro*, 15(1):37–45, Feb. 1995.
14. M. Katevenis, P. Vatsolaki, and A. Efthymiou. Pipelined memory shared buffer for VLSI switches. In *Proc. ACM SIGCOMM Conference*, pages 39–48, Aug. 1995.
15. P. Kermani and L. Kleinrock. Virtual cut-through: A new computer communications switching technique. *Computer Networks*, 3(4):267–286, Sept. 1979.
16. B. C. Kuszmaul. RACE network architecture. In *Proc. 9th Int. Parallel Processing Symp.*, pages 508–513, April 1995.
17. J. Laudon and D. Lenoski. The SGI Origin: A ccNUMA highly scalable server. In *Proc. 24th Ann. Int. Symp. on Computer Architecture*, pages 241–251, June 1997.
18. C. E. Leiserson et al. The network architecture of the Connection Machine CM-5. In *Proc. 1992 Symp. Parallel Algorithms and Architectures*, pages 272–285. ACM, 1992.
19. Q. Li and D. Gustavson. Fat-tree for local area multiprocessors. In *Proc. 9th Int. Parallel Processing Symp.*, pages 32–36, April 1995.
20. T. Lovett and R. Clapp. STiNG: A CC-NUMA computer system for the commercial marketplace. In *Proc. 23th Ann. Int. Symp. on Computer Architecture*, pages 308–317, May 1996.

21. L. M. Ni. Should scalable parallel computers support efficient hardware multicast? In *Proc. ICPP Workshop on Challenges for Parallel Processing*, pages 2–7, Aug. 1995.
22. S. Pakin, V. Karamcheti, and A. A. Chien. Fast messages: efficient, portable communication for workstation clusters and MPPs. *IEEE Concurrency*, 5(2):60–72, April–June 1997.
23. D. K. Panda, S. Singal, and P. Prabhakaran. Multidestination message passing mechanism conforming to base wormhole routing scheme. In *Proc. of the Parallel Computer Routing and Communication Workshop*, pages 131–145, 1994.
24. C. Partridge. *Gigabit Networking*. Addison-Wesley, Reading, MA, 1994.
25. W. Qiao and L. M. Ni. Adaptive routing in irregular networks using cut-through switches. In *Proc. Int. Conf. on Parallel Processing*, pages I-52–I-60, Aug. 1996.
26. S. L. Scott and G. M. Thorson. The Cray T3E network: Adaptive routing in a high performance 3D torus. In *Hot Interconnects IV*, Aug. 1996.
27. C. Seitz. Myrinet—a gigabit-per-second local-area network. In *Hot Interconnects II*, Aug. 1994. Current information on link bandwidth found at http://www.myri.com/.
28. C. L. Seitz. The Cosmic Cube. *Comm. of the ACM*, 28(1):22–33, Jan. 1985.
29. F. Silla and J. Duato. On the use of virtual channels in networks of workstations with irregular topology. In *Proc. of the Parallel Computer Routing and Communication Workshop*, pages 131–145, June 1997.
30. R. Sivaram, C. B. Stunkel, and D. K. Panda. A reliable hardware barrier synchronization scheme. In *Proc. 11th Int. Parallel Processing Symp.*, pages 274–280, April 1997.
31. C. B. Stunkel. Commercially viable MPP networks. In *Proc. ICPP Workshop on Challenges for Parallel Processing*, pages 52–63, Aug. 1996.
32. C. B. Stunkel, D. G. Shea, B. Abali, et al. The SP2 high-performance switch. *IBM System Journal*, 34(2):185–204, 1995.
33. C. B. Stunkel, R. Sivaram, and D. K. Panda. Implementing multidestination worms in switch based parallel systems: Architectural alternatives and their impact. In *Proc. 24th Ann. Int. Symp. on Computer Architecture*, pages 50–61, June 1997.
34. Y. Tamir and G. L. Frazier. High-performance multi-queue buffers for VLSI communication switches. In *Proc. 15st Ann. Int. Symp. on Computer Architecture*, pages 343–354, May 1988.
35. T. von Eicken, A. Basu, V. Buch, and W. Vogels. U-Net: a user level network interface for parallel and distributed computing. In *Proc. 15th Symp. on Operating Systems Principles*, pages 40–53, Dec. 1995.
36. T. von Eicken et al. Active Messages: A mechanism for integrated communication and computation. In *Proc. 19th Ann. Int. Symp. on Computer Architecture*, pages 256–266, May 1992.
37. W.-D. Weber, S. Gold, P. Helland, T. Shimizu, T. Wicki, and W. Wilcke. The Mercury interconnect architecture: A cost-effective infrastructure for high-performance servers. In *Proc. 24th Ann. Int. Symp. on Computer Architecture*, pages 98–107, June 1997.

Panel Session

Thursday, June 26, 1997
3:00 - 4:30

Moderator:

Dhabaleswar Panda
Ohio State University

Panelists:

Andrew Chien
University of Illinois and Hewlett Packard

Al Davis
University of Utah

Thorsten von Eicken
Cornell University

Dave Garcia
Tandem Computers

Craig Stunkel
IBM T. J. Watson Research Center

Panel Abstract

Designing High-Performance Communication Subsystems: Top Five Problems to Solve and Five Problems Not to Solve During the Next Five Years

In recent years the design of modern parallel systems is changing due to the availability of new interconnection technologies and commodity components (e.g., switches/routers, links, adapters). Should the researchers working in the area of designing high-performance communication subsystems continue to solve the 'traditional' problems? Which of these existing problems continue to merit attention and have the potential to provide substantial performance gains in the context of modern parallel systems? What are the 'new' problems and challenges which the community will be facing in the next five years?

The panelists will provide their view points and debate the above issues. By the end of the panel we hope to shed some light on research and development directions: the top five problems we need to solve and five problems that do not merit continued strong research attention.

Session IV

MESSAGING LAYER SUPPORT

Friday, June 27, 1997
8:30 - 10:00

Session Chair:

D. Schimmel
Georgia Institute of Technology

Evaluation of Communication Mechanisms in Invalidate-Based Shared Memory Multiprocessors

Gregory T. Byrd and Michael J. Flynn

Computer Systems Laboratory
Stanford University, Stanford, CA

Abstract. Producer-initiated mechanisms are added to invalidate-based systems to reduce communication latencies by transferring data as soon as it is produced. This paper compares the performance of three producer-initiated mechanisms: lock, deliver, and StreamLine. All three approaches out-perform invalidate with prefetch in most cases.
Cached-based locks offer 10–20% speedup over prefetch for two of the three benchmarks studies. StreamLine performs well in low-bandwidth environments, but does not improve with increased bandwidth. Deliver is generally competitive with prefetch, but does not offer a significant performance advantage overall.
Keywords: shared memory, lock, deliver, message passing

1 Introduction

Data communication is a critical component of the performance of large-scale multiprocessor systems. All non-trivial parallel applications require the communication of data among the participating processors. The latency of this communication largely determines the performance and scalability of an application on a given parallel platform. For this reason, parallel systems must provide mechanisms for low-latency data communication.

Cache-coherent shared memory systems provide for communication through reading and writing locations in a globally shared address space. The underlying memory system is responsible for transferring data as needed between processors, caches, and memories. Synchronization is separated from data transfer, and typically involves spin-waiting on a shared synchronization variable.

Shared memory communication is inherently consumer-oriented. The producer of the data first writes into its own cache, possibly invalidating the copy contained in the consumer's cache. The consumer must then retrieve the new data from the producer's cache; this is typically done after synchronization, because retrieving the data too early results in increased invalidation traffic.

A more efficient solution is to allow the producer to transfer the new data into the caches of the consumer processors. This makes the data available to the consumers as early as possible and also eliminates the network traffic associated with the consumers' requests for data.

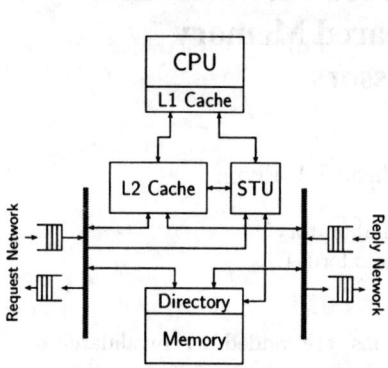

L1 cache size	unlimited
L1 write buffer	8 lines
L2 cache size	unlimited
L2 outstanding accesses	unlimited
L2 line size	8 words (64 bytes)
L2 access	2 cycles
network latency	4 cycles/hop
network bandwidth	4 bytes/cycle
network topology	dual 2D mesh (request + reply)
memory access	6 cycles
memory bandwidth	1 word/cycle
processing nodes	64

Fig. 1. System node architecture and parameters. The simulated system consists of 64 nodes connected via a dual 2D mesh. Other parameters are shown in the table.

This solution only addresses the data transfer portion of data communication. Synchronization is also required, so that the consumer processors know that the data is ready to be consumed. An improved solution couples synchronization with data transfer, as in a message passing system.

In this paper, we study the performance benefits of adding these sorts of producer-initiated mechanisms to an invalidate-based cache-coherent multiprocessor. We investigate three mechanisms: *deliver*, in which a cache line is sent from memory to one or more specified caches; *lock*, which combines synchronization and data transfer by providing atomic access to a cache line; and *StreamLine*, which allows an arbitrary-length message to be sent between caches.

2 Mechanisms

For this study, all mechanisms are implemented in the context of the distributed shared memory architecture shown in Figure 1. Each processing node contains a CPU, a write-through first-level (L1) cache, a write-back lockup-free second-level (L2) cache, and a portion of the global memory with its portion of the cache coherence directory. An eight-entry coalescing write buffer is located between the L1 and L2 caches. The stream transfer unit (STU) is specific to the StreamLine mechanism and is discussed below.

2.1 Invalidate-Based Cache Coherence with Prefetch

We assume a centralized fully-mapped invalidate-based cache coherence protocol, similar to the one used in the Stanford DASH prototype [8]. Centralized means that all information about cached copies of each memory block is stored in the portion of the directory on that block's home node. Fully-mapped means that a directory entry contains enough storage to indicate the presence of a cached copy in every processor in the system.

The base invalidate protocol is enhanced by the addition of non-binding, software-controlled prefetch [9]. Prefetches are issued by the consumer after synchronization, so that only valid data will be prefetched. Prefetching too early causes extra invalidate traffic as the producer stores its data.

2.2 Deliver

Deliver was included in the DASH system [8]. A deliver instruction causes a copy of a cache line to be sent to a list of consumer caches. The consumers are specified through the use of a bit vector. In our experiments, the producer delivers copies of the computed data to consumers before synchronization. The deliver request is sent to the memory which owns the data, and the memory sends copies to all targets that don't already have a copy.

It is not necessary for the processor which issues the deliver to have ownership of the cache line, or even to have a copy in its cache. A deliver request may be issued regardless of the local cache state. If the requesting cache has write ownership at the time of the deliver request, the cache line data is sent to the memory along with the deliver request. If write ownership is pending on the cache line, the processor stalls until write ownership is granted; then the deliver request (with data) is sent to the memory.

If a deliver request arrives at the memory, and the cache line is owned exclusively by another cache, the deliver is ignored. Deliver requests serve as performance hints to the memory system. They can be ignored without affecting the correctness of execution.

Similar mechanisms include PSET_WRITE [11], data forwarding [10], and WriteSend [1]. These mechanisms differ from deliver, in that they combine the writing of data with its delivery to target caches. This can reduce the traffic associated with gaining write ownership of a cache line.

2.3 Cached-Based Locks

Cached-based lock mechanisms [5, 12] have been proposed to integrate synchronization with data transfer. The QOLB (Queue On Lock Bit) mechanism, for instance, is included in the IEEE Scalable Coherent Interface (SCI) standard [2]. This approach adds states to the coherency protocol to provide for atomic access to a cache line. When the owner of the line releases the lock, the data and the lock are transferred to the next waiting processor.

Previous studies [2, 12] have focused on the use of cache-based locks in synchronization primitives, such as mutual exclusion locks and barriers. Our focus is on the use of locks as a producer-consumer data communication mechanism. The producer first locks the cache lines which will contain the data. Consumers request the lock for each line, using a non-blocking request to prefetch the lock. The consumer requests are queued at the memory.

In our implementation, the directory bits used to record cached copies in the cache coherence scheme are also used to record the list of waiting caches. Because a locked cache line can only have one owner, there is no ambiguity between these two uses of the same resource. We do assume that the directory has some means of distinguishing the cache which owns the lock from caches which are waiting.

When the processor unlocks a cache line, it is written back to memory (if dirty), and the memory sends the data, with lock ownership, to the next waiting cache. The centralized scheme described here cannot keep information about the order in which lock requests are received. Instead, lock requests are serviced in ascending order, modulo the number of caches in the system. This guarantees freedom from starvation, since every cache that requests lock ownership will eventually get it.

Note that locks are not strictly a producer-initiated mechanism, since the consumer must ask for the lock before the data is transferred. However, if a consumer is waiting, then it is the producer's unlock operation that initiates the transfer.

2.4 StreamLine

StreamLine [3] is a cache-based message passing mechanism, integrated with a cache-coherent shared memory system. A stream is a region of memory that is managed by the cache hardware as a circular message buffer; a table in the L2 cache contains the current head and tail of the buffer, and the programmer reads and writes data to the stream relative to the head.

A stream-output command causes the data at the head of the stream to be sent as a single message to a target stream, typically on another processor. The message may or may not be removed from the sending stream. The stream transfer unit (STU) (see Figure 1) manages the transfer of data from the cache or memory to the network.

As data arrives at the target cache, the message is written to the destination stream, and the stream's tail pointer is incremented with each write. In this way, the receiving processor can consume data as it arrives. A processor will stall when reading an empty stream.

Stream references bypass the L1 cache. The stream status information (including head and tail pointers) resides with the L2 cache, because it must be accessible to both the processor and the network interface. Stream data is not expected to exhibit much temporal locality, however; a received message will typically be consumed or moved to a local data structure for further processing.

StreamLine is similar to the message passing mechanisms provided by the Alewife architecture [7]. An arriving message on Alewife interrupts the processor, and a user-level message handler is used to remove the message from the network.

3 Methodology

We investigate the performance of the various mechanisms through execution-driven simulation. This section describes the simulation environment, the architecture of the simulated system, and the choice of benchmark programs.

3.1 Simulation Environment

The simulation environment for these experiments is based on the SIMPLE/CARE system [4]. Application programs are compiled and run on the underlying host computer, with explicit calls to increment the simulated processor's clock and to perform operations on shared memory locations.

The architectural parameters used for the base system are shown in Figure 1. We model a load-store limited processor; only accesses to private or shared memory locations cause the processor clock to progress. The L2 cache is lockup-free [13], with an unlimited number of outstanding accesses allowed. An eight-entry coalescing write buffer is placed between the L1 and L2 caches. Because we are interested in the communications aspects of the mechanisms, we use infinite caches to eliminate conflict and capacity misses.

The interprocessor network is a dual two-dimensional mesh, with wormhole routing and separate physical networks for requests and replies to resolve certain types of deadlock. (This could also be accomplished with separate virtual networks.) The network simulation includes contention and buffering at ports and interfaces. The default bandwidth is sufficient to accept or deliver one processor word (64 bits) every two processor cycles, and the default latency is four cycles per hop. At each network port, there is sufficient buffering to absorb the multi-cycle delays, plus an extra eight words. Buffers at the node-to-network interface can hold 32 words.

Benchmark	Description	Comm. Size	Comm. Fanout
PDE1	3D red-black SOR $N \times N \times N$ matrix $M \times M \times M$ pts per processor $(N = 32, M = 8)$	M^2	6×1
Block-LU	LU decomposition, no pivoting $N \times N$ matrix, divided into $M \times M$ blocks $(N = 256, M = 8)$	M^2	$1 \times \sqrt{P}$
Column-LU	LU decomposition, partial pivoting $N \times N$ matrix, divided by column $(N = 256)$	N	$1 \times P$

Table 1. Benchmark kernels. P is the number of processors. *Communication size* is the typical amount of data to be communicated. *Communication fanout* is the typical communication pattern; a fanout of $p \times q$ means that p "messages" are sent to q destinations. Sizes used for this study are shown in parentheses.

3.2 Benchmark Programs

To study the performance of the mechanisms described above, we use three application kernel benchmarks, representing different patterns of interprocessor communication. Characteristics of the benchmarks are shown in Table 1.

PDE1 solves a set of finite difference equations using three-dimensional red-black successive over-relaxation (SOR), with a seven-point stencil. This benchmark is based on the program of the same name from the Genesis[1] benchmark suite. This kernel represents a very regular communication pattern with limited fanout. Each processor communicates with at most six other processors, and the communication pattern and size are fixed for the entire computation.

Block-LU is based on the LU decomposition kernel from the SPLASH-2[2] benchmark suite. A two-dimensional matrix is divided into blocks. After blocks have been processed, they are communicated along the row or column (or both) of the matrix. This represents a computation with moderate fanout.

Column-LU performs LU decomposition with partial pivoting. The matrix is divided into columns, which are assigned to processors in a round-robin fashion. At each step, the column which contains the diagonal element (the pivot column) selects a pivot row and communicates the row index and the column data to all the columns to the right, resulting in a high-fanout communication pattern.

An optimized version of each benchmark program was developed for each communication mechanism. Each benchmark program uses only one producer-initiated mechanism for communication. For example, if deliver is used, then neither lock nor StreamLine is used in that version. Prefetch operations were allowed in all programs, except for the base invalidate-only versions.

4 Simulation Results

Figure 2 shows the execution time of the benchmark codes, relative to the baseline invalidate-only implementation. Execution time has been categorized according to the mean percentage of time spent by a single processor in various stages of execution.

The bottom portion of the bar shows private data references, combined with L1 cache hits. These operations take one processor cycle, so they indicate the "busy" time of the load-store limited processor. L1 stalls are caused either by waiting for access to the write buffer between the L1 and L2 caches, or by cycles in which the L1 cache is busy with cache fills or invalidates initiated by the L2 cache.

L2 read latency involves any shared data read that misses in the L1 cache. Because we're modeling perfect caches, only cold and coherence misses will be present. Also, reads to stream data always go to the L2 cache, so the StreamLine implementations show larger L2 read times than the others. L2 write latency is the delay seen by the processor due to writes, fences, and message sends. The

---
[1] http://www.ccg.ecs.soton.ac.uk/gbis/
[2] http://www-flash.stanford.edu/apps/SPLASH/

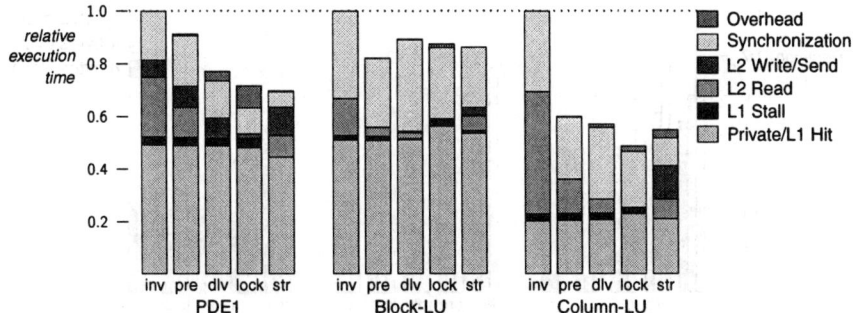

Fig. 2. Relative execution time, using the system parameters shown in Figure 1.

latency of most write operations is hidden by the write buffer, so this time is mostly due to waiting for writes to complete (fences) or for sends to complete.

Synchronization is the time spent spinning on a synchronization variable or waiting for the first word of a stream message to arrive. In the lock and StreamLine implementations, synchronization generally implies data transfer as well.

Finally, overhead is any operation which is not included in one of the above categories. Examples are issuing prefetch, deliver or lock instructions, as well as stream manipulation instructions, such as moving the head or tail pointers.

Lock and StreamLine perform best for PDE1, with execution times around 20% lower than prefetch. Lock is the best performer for Column-LU, again around 20% better than prefetch, while StreamLine outperforms prefetch by only 10%. Deliver is about 5% and 15% better than prefetch on Column-LU and PDE1, respectively. On Block-LU, prefetch holds a slight performance advantage, but all of the mechanisms are within 10% of one another.

Figures 3–5 show the effects of changing network bandwidth, network latency, and cache line size. Again, performance is relative to the invalidate-only implementation. The middle bar in each graph corresponds to the base parameters, as reported in Figure 2.

Most of the mechanisms are sensitive to network bandwidth, but none are very sensitive to latency, except for invalidate. All of the mechanisms are able to hide or reduce latency enough to tolerate a longer effective distance between nodes, at least in the range of tightly-coupled systems that we consider. Limited bandwidth, on the other hand, causes higher network congestion and higher occupancies at the cache and memory, since it takes longer to move data into and out of the network. StreamLine is the least sensitive to decreased bandwidth. Lock is sensitive, but less so than the other shared memory mechanisms.

StreamLine, however, is not able to take advantage of increased bandwidth. For Column-LU, doubling the bandwidth resulted in a 25% improvement in execution time for prefetch, deliver, and lock, but not for StreamLine. For this benchmark, StreamLine is more dependent on the time spent reading, writing, and sending messages than on network performance.

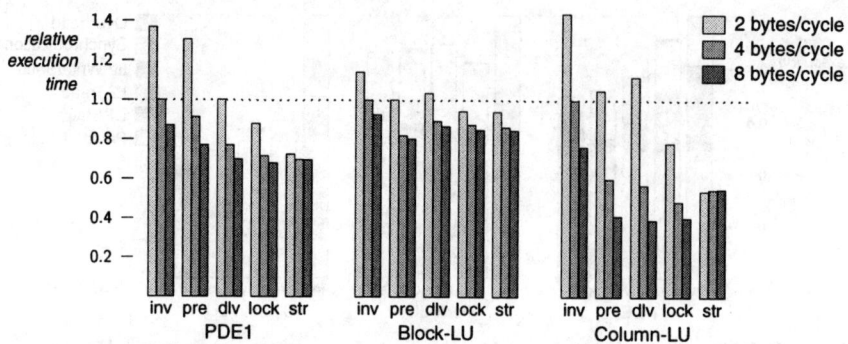

Fig. 3. Sensitivity to network bandwidth. Bandwidth is varied by changing the network cycle time, but latency remains constant at 4 processor cycles per hop.

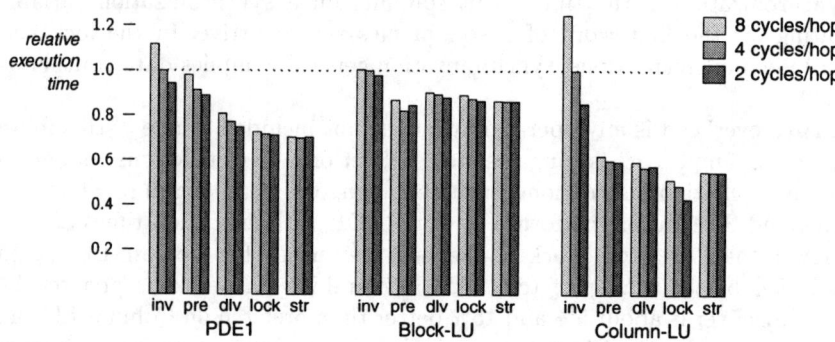

Fig. 4. Sensitivity to network latency. Network bandwidth remains constant at 4 bytes per processor cycle.

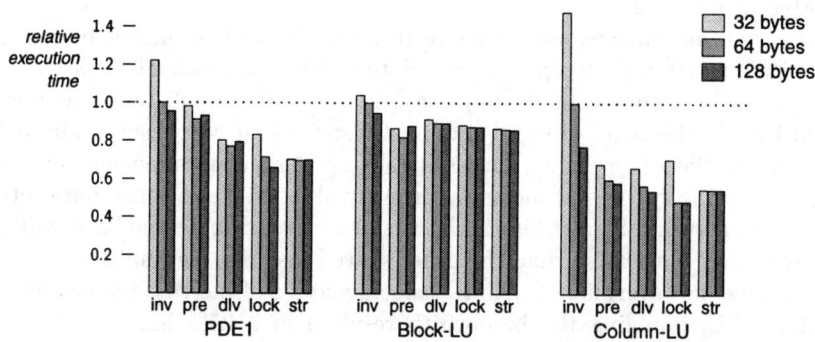

Fig. 5. Sensitivity to cache line size.

Changing the cache line size effects invalidate performance in the expected way: large lines means fewer blocking read misses, which means higher performance. Prefetch and deliver cause lines to be transferred concurrently, before they are read, so they are less sensitive to line size. StreamLine transfers arbitrary-sized messages, so it has very little dependence on line size. Lock, on the other hand, sometimes shows significant degradation for small line sizes, which is discussed in the following section.

5 Further Analysis

5.1 Deliver

As shown in Figure 2, deliver effectively reduces the shared data read time seen by the processor. Time spent writing or synchronizing, however, is not decreased. Synchronization time increases slightly, because we delivers are inserted before the synchronization variable is written; if the consumer is already waiting, this added delay increases the time spent waiting, though it usually decreases the time spent reading the data after synchronization.

One problem with deliver is that the producer first gains write ownership of the line, then delivers it. To hide the cost of write misses, the programmer tends to wait until all writes are complete before delivering the data. The data forwarding approaches mention in Section 2.2 offer an improvement in this area, because the producer need not gain write ownership. Instead, the data is sent to the memory, which updates itself and sends the new data to the consumer. This moves the transfer as close as possible to the time when the data is produced.

Column-LU presents a case for a deliver operation which is separate from writing. In order to reduce contention for the synchronization variable, the consumers use a distributed array for communicating the pivot, rather than a single variable. Each consumer spins on a local copy of the synchronization variable, which is written by the preceding consumer. While this works well for synchronization, using the same approach for communicating the column data involves too much copying and dramatically increases the amount of memory required for the application.

A natural approach to inserting delivers in Column-LU is to have the producer deliver the column data to all consumers (which is usually all of the other processors), before writing the synchronization variable. The results are disastrous, resulting in an execution time nearly three times the invalidate-only case. The network and the memory get swamped with deliver requests, and the pivot column for the next step is delayed in reading the pivot variable and the column data. Reducing the number of target consumers helps, but only offers a small benefit over the prefetch-based implementation.

The optimized approach allows each consumer to deliver the data to the following consumer, just before writing the local synchronization variable. The consumer performing the deliver may not even have its copy of the data yet, but it can deliver a copy to the next consumer anyway. The next consumer also prefetches the data after it reads the synchronization variable.

5.2 Lock

As mentioned earlier, other studies tend to evaluate cache-based locks as a mechanism for speeding up mutex and barrier operations, while we use lock as a producer-consumer communications mechanism. By reducing the grain size of synchronization from a block of data to a cache line, we allow the data to be consumed earlier with little additional overhead. In high-fanout situations, like Column-LU, the lock queue decreases hot spot behavior by sequentializing access to the contentious data.

There are three factors which contribute to lock's sensitivity to line size. First, a smaller line size means more lock and unlock operations. Second, since lines are consumed one processor at a time, the concurrent transfer of lines that is allowed by prefetch and deliver does not occur with lock. Third, performance is sensitive to the order in which locks are granted. Smaller lines means more chances that a processor will have to wait on another processor to release the line.

There are some pitfalls in using locks in this fashion, especially when the non-blocking lock request is used to prefetch the lock and data. The programmer (or compiler) must make sure that locks are acquired and released in a manner which avoids deadlock. Further work is needed to determine whether locks can be inserted by the compiler or encapsulated in runtime libraries.

5.3 StreamLine

StreamLine is expected to perform well, since these benchmarks are well-suited to the message passing style of execution. Each producer knows ahead of time what data should be sent to which consumers. However, StreamLine does not significantly outperform its shared memory counterparts.

StreamLine was designed with fine-grained messages in mind, rather than the medium- to large-grained messages required by these benchmarks. When sending a message, the processor must stall until the previous message has been written to the network interface. This delays the handling of incoming messages by the processor, so the overall rate of computation is decreased. The L2 cache is also kept busy copying the messages to the network interface; in the shared-memory implementations, copies of the data are mostly supplied by the memory, which has a smaller impact on the processor.

Message granularity is directly correlated to synchronization granularity. The good performance of the lock mechanism shows the benefits of smaller-grained synchronization, but StreamLine messages can only be sent once the entire message has been assembled. The StreamLine implementation of Column-LU does use small-grained messages, with no more than eight data words in each message. The program is more complicated than the medium-grained approach, since consumers must deal with interleaved message fragments from different producers, but the resulting code is around 10% faster.

6 Conclusions

Computer system architects generally recognize that there is no single best mechanism to support data communication in scalable multiprocessors. They look for mechanisms which will benefit a large range of applications at a reasonable cost. This limited set of benchmarks would suggest that prefetch and cache-based locks are a good foundation upon which to build large-scale shared memory systems. Both are effective for traditional shared memory applications [6, 9], and this study has shown that locks perform well when producer-initiated communication is desirable.

The L2-oriented implementation of StreamLine used in this study does not seem to offer substantial benefits over shared memory mechanisms, except in low-bandwidth environments. Even then, the system design budget may be better spent on improving bandwidth, which should benefit all applications, rather than on implementing streams.

7 Acknowledgments

The authors thank Prof. Nakamura, Prof. Kobayashi, and the Computer Architecture Laboratory at Tohoku University, who have generously provided computer cycles for the simulations used in this study.

This research was partially supported by ARPA, under the Office of Naval Research (ONR) contract number N00014-93-1-1335.

References

1. Hazim Abdel-Shafi et al. An evaluation of fine-grain producer-initiated communication in cache-coherent multiprocessors. In *3rd Intl. Symp. on High-Perf. Comp. Architecture*, pages 204–215, February 1997.
2. Nagi Aboulenein et al. Hardware support for synchronization in the Scalable Coherent Interface (SCI). In *8th Intl. Parallel Processing Symp.*, pages 141–50, April 1994.
3. Gregory T. Byrd and Bruce A. Delagi. StreamLine: cache-based message passing in scalable multiprocessors. In *1991 Intl. Conf. on Parallel Processing*, volume I, pages 251–254, August 1991.
4. Bruce A. Delagi et al. Instrumented architectural simulation. In *1988 Intl. Conf. on Supercomputing*, volume 1, pages 8–11, May 1988.
5. James R. Goodman et al. Efficient synchronization primitives for large-scale cache-coherent multiprocessors. In *3rd Intl. Conf. on Arch. Support for Prog. Languages and Operating Systems (ASPLOS-III)*, pages 64–75, April 1989.
6. Alain Kägi, Doug Burger, and James R. Goodman. Efficient synchronization: Let them eat QOLB. In *24th Intl. Symp. on Comp. Architecture*, June 1997.
7. John Kubiatowicz and Anant Agarwal. Anatomy of a message in the Alewife multiprocessor. In *7th ACM Intl. Conf. on Supercomputing*, July 1993.
8. Daniel Lenoski et al. The Stanford DASH multiprocessor. *Computer*, 25(3):63–79, March 1992.

9. Todd Mowry and Anoop Gupta. Tolerating latency through software-controlled prefetching in shared-memory multiprocessors. *Journal of Parallel and Distr. Computing*, 12(2):87–106, June 1991.
10. David K. Poulsen and Pen-Chung Yew. Integrating fine-grained message passing in cache coherent shared memory multiprocessors. *Journal of Parallel and Distr. Computing*, 33(2):172–188, March 1996.
11. Umakishore Ramachandran et al. Architectural mechanisms for explicit communication in shared memory multiprocessors. In *Supercomputing '95*, December 1995.
12. Umakishore Ramachandran and Joonwon Lee. Cache-based synchronization in shared memory multiprocessors. *Journal of Parallel and Distr. Computing*, 32(1):11–27, January 1996.
13. C. Scheurich and M. Dubois. Concurrent miss resolution in multiprocessor caches. In *1988 Intl. Conf. on Parallel Processing*, volume 1, pages 118–125, August 1988.

How Can We Design Better Networks for DSM Systems?[*]

Donglai Dai and Dhabaleswar K. Panda

Dept. of Computer and Information Science
The Ohio State University, Columbus, OH 43210-1277
{dai,panda}@cis.ohio-state.edu

Abstract. Most DSM research in current years have ignored the impact of interconnection network altogether. Similarly, most of the interconnection network research have focused on better network designs by using synthetic (uniform/non-uniform) traffic. Both these trends do not lead to any concrete guidelines about designing better networks for the emerging Distributed Shared Memory (DSM) paradigm. In this paper, we address these issues by taking a three-step approach. First, we propose a comprehensive parameterized model to estimate the performance of an application on a DSM system. This model takes into account all key aspects of a DSM system: application, processor, cache/memory hierarchy, coherence protocol, and network. Next, using this model we evaluate the impact of different network design choices (link speed, link width, topology, ratio between router to physical link delay) on the overall performance of DSM applications and establish guidelines for designing better networks for DSM systems. Finally, we use simulations of SPLASH2 benchmark suites to validate our design guidelines. Some of the important design guidelines established in this paper are: 1) better performance is achieved by increasing link speed instead of link width, 2) increasing dimension of a network under constant bisection bandwidth constraint is not at all beneficial, and 3) network contention experienced by short messages is very crucial to the overall performance. These guidelines together with several others lay a good foundation for designing better networks for current and future generation DSM systems.

1 Introduction

Obtaining full potential performance from current generation distributed shared memory (DSM) systems is somewhat limited due to the *high latency* associated with shared memory accesses. Most DSM research in recent years has focused on the design of node architectures, coherence protocols, memory consistency techniques, etc. Many of these studies have either ignored the interconnection network altogether or considered very idealistic model of the network—a model with fixed delay, infinite bandwidth, and no contention. Thus, these models fail to provide any concrete guidelines for designing efficient networks for DSM systems.

---
[*] This research is supported in part by NSF Grant MIP-9309627 and NSF Career Award MIP-9502294.

At the same time, a lot of research in interconnection network [6] has studied the impact of link speed, link width, routing delay, routing adaptivity, or topology on the overall network performance based on synthetic traffic (uniform/non-uniform/hot-spot), arbitrary message length, and message generation intervals following some statistical distributions. These studies typically demonstrate network performance in terms of 'latency vs. throughput' and do not consider many network characteristics specific to a typical DSM system. These characteristics include *cause-effect* relationship between messages (e.g., a remote read/write request message followed by a reply message), *bi-modal* traffic (i.e., short messages reflecting control messages in a cache coherence protocol and long messages reflecting transfer of cache lines), periodic generation of messages by processors based on the computational granularity associated with a thread. Thus, for a DSM system with a given node architecture and cache coherence protocol, the existing network design studies do not provide guidelines on the impact of different network components on the overall performance of the system.

In this paper, we take on such a challenge and solve it in three steps. First, we propose a parameterized performance model for a CC-NUMA architecture, similar to the FLASH [9] using any general network. This model integrates application characteristics (number of threads, number of synchronization points, granularity of computation, and ratio of read/write operation), processor characteristics (*CPI*), cache/memory hierarchy (cache miss rate, access time for cache and memory, protocol overhead, and average number of outstanding memory requests), and network characteristics (message send/receive overhead and bi-modal traffic). To the best of our knowledge, no such comprehensive model exists in the literature before. Next, as an example of using this model, we consider wormhole routed networks and analyze the impact of different network design choices such as link speed, link width, routing delay, and topology on the overall performance of DSMs. Finally, we use an application-driven simulation approach to validate our model and obtain additional insights such as the impact of network contention. The evaluations are based on running four SPLASH2 [10] benchmark applications on a simulated 64 processor system.

From this study, we obtain the following important guidelines for designing better networks for DSM systems: 1) better performance is achieved by increasing link speed instead of link width, 2) increasing dimension of a network under constant link width constraint is somewhat beneficial, 3) increasing dimension of a network under constant bisection bandwidth constraint is not at all beneficial, 4) routing delay plays an important factor in the design choices of other network components, and 5) network contention experienced by short messages is very crucial to the overall performance.

2 Parameterized Model for a Typical DSM System

In this section, we derive a parameterized performance model for a typical DSM system. This model captures three important factors: application behavior on a processor, cache/memory hierarchy, and network.

2.1 Characterizing Application Behavior on a Processor

Conceptually, any shared-memory application can be decomposed into a set of concurrent and coordinated threads as shown in Fig. 1(a). The set size can grow or shrink dynamically during the execution of the application as threads are created or terminated.

Each of these threads carries out a certain amount of computation and communicates with one another by reading from or writing to common memory locations. In order to guarantee the correctness of the application, a subset of these reads/writes must be carried out in a specific order via inserting explicit synchronization primitives, such as barriers and locks. As a general practice to save the high overhead of thread creation and termination, the number of threads are typically kept constant and the same threads are used before and after synchronization points. For the purpose of performance modeling, such a thread exhibits a repeated pattern as follows: executing several register-only instructions successively for computation and then followed by a memory access (load/store) instruction. The short run of the successive register-only instructions is commonly referred to as a computation *grain* of the application. We can call the above description as the *programmer's point of view* of the application. It helps us to understand the essential behavior of an application on a given DSM system. As far as the analysis is concerned, a grain can be extended to contain a sequence of instructions which do not involve any shared memory reference or synchronization operation. Let us denote the average execution duration of a grain as T_{grn}. This can be characterized as follows:

$$T_{grn} = g * CPI * T_{pclk} \tag{1}$$

where g is the number of instructions in a grain, known as *grain size*, CPI is the average number of cycles per instruction of the processor, and T_{pclk} is the processor's clock cycle time. In essence, the value of g represents the inherent computation to communication ratio of an application.

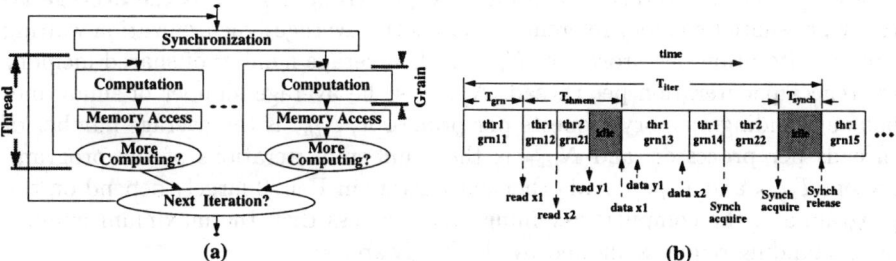

Fig. 1. Time decomposition of a typical DSM application: (a) a programmer's point of view and (b) a processor's point of view.

As an alternative to the programmer's point of view, a *processor's point of view* can be established to provide us additional insights into the execution time of an entire application. This alternate view describes the behavior of an individual processor when running its portion of the application. Let us assume that the processor in our modeled system supports multithreading and multiple outstanding requests. Such a processor model is powerful enough to capture almost all the characteristics introduced by existing latency reduction or latency tolerance techniques, such as lockup-free caches [13], relaxed memory consistency [11], hardware and software data prefetching, speculative load and execution [14], and multithreading.

As an example, let us consider the behavior of a typical application on a processor for a short duration, as depicted in Fig. 1(b). Assume two threads, $thr1$ and $thr2$ are mapped onto this processor. At the beginning of the observed duration, which is also assumed as the beginning of one iteration, thread $thr1$ executes a grain $grn11$ and issues a nonblocking read from location $x1$. The thread continues to execute its next grain $grn12$, then issues another nonblocking read from $x2$ at the end of $grn12$ and is suspended because of data dependency. Instead of waiting for either x's data to be available, a thread context switch takes place. The processor starts running a grain $grn21$ from the second thread $thr2$. At the end of $grn21$, a blocking read from $y1$ is issued. At the moment, the processor becomes idle until one of the data items is available. As soon as the earliest item, say $x1$, is available, thread $thr1$ resumes to execute the next grain $grn13$. Assume the data items $y1$ and $x2$ become available during the execution of $grn13$. This allows thread $thr1$ to continue to execute another grain $grn14$, which waits for $x2$. Finally, thread $thr1$ issues a synchronization acquire signal and is blocked. Immediately, thread $thr2$ starts running its next grain $grn22$ and is suspended after finishing $grn22$ and issuing its synchronization acquire signal. Again, the processor is left idle until a synchronization release signal comes back. Once the expected synchronization release signal arrives, the next iteration starts.

Based on above observation, in general, the overall execution time of an application can be expressed as below assuming a perfect load balancing algorithm. For simplicity and clarity, we ignore the overheads for context switching and scheduling.

$$T_{exec} = (((T_{grn} + T_{shmem}) * N_{ref}/N_{pend}) * N_{thr} + T_{sync}) * N_{iter} \quad (2)$$

where T_{grn} is the average execution time per grain, T_{shmem} is the average latency per shared memory reference, T_{sync} is the average synchronization waiting time per iteration per processor, N_{ref} is the average number of shared memory references per iteration per thread, N_{pend} is the average number of simultaneous outstanding memory requests per processor, N_{thr} is the average number of threads per processor, and N_{iter} is the number of iterations of the program. Except T_{sync} and T_{shmem}, all other parameters in Eqn. 2 largely depend on the program and the compiler, assuming N_{pend} is less than the maximum number of outstanding requests allowed by the hardware.

Conceptually, the synchronization waiting time contains the time processors wait for one another to reach the same synchronization point and the pure time of a synchronization operation which the last participating processor executes. A synchronization operation is usually a special variant of shared memory reference, such as Fetch&Inc instruction, memory fence instruction, or QOLB scheme [8] supported in typical DSM systems. Thus, we can rewrite T_{sync} as follows:

$$T_{sync} = N_{bal} * T_{grn} + T_{shmem} \quad (3)$$

where N_{bal} is a load balance parameter. It depends on both the application and load balancing algorithm. Since the number of processors in a DSM system is often not a divisor of the total number of grains in an iteration, the difference of workload per processor is typically one grain unit ($N_{bal} = 1$) in the optimal scenario. In next section, we estimate the value of T_{shmem}.

2.2 Characterizing Cache and Memory Hierarchy

It is not very difficult to characterize the effect of caching on T_{shmem}. For simplicity, we focus on a single level cache. However, it can be very easily extended to multi-level cache hierarchy. The parameter T_{shmem} can be expressed as follows:

$$T_{shmem} = R_{read} * T_{read} + R_{write} * T_{write} \qquad (4)$$

$$T_{read} = R_{rhit} * T_{hit} + R_{rmiss} * T_{r,mem} \qquad (5)$$

$$T_{write} = R_{whit} * T_{hit} + R_{wmiss} * T_{w,mem} \qquad (6)$$

where R_{read} (or R_{write}) is the rate of reads (or writes) out of total shared memory references, T_{read} (or T_{write}) is the average latency per shared read (or write), R_{rhit} (or R_{whit}) and R_{rmiss} (or R_{wmiss}) are the hit and miss ratios for shared reads (or writes), $T_{r,mem}$ (or $T_{w,mem}$) is the latency of a shared read (or write) miss reference, and T_{hit} is the latency for a cache hit reference.

The values of $T_{r,mem}$ and $T_{w,mem}$ depend on the design of memory subsystem in the DSM system. More specifically, they depend on two factors: a) cache coherence protocol being used and b) memory access latency. The overhead of a cache coherence protocol can be further broken down into two components: delays incurred at a node controller and the average number of messages generated for each read or write operation.

In this paper, we assume directory-based protocols. Let us assume that the node controller incurs a fixed delay T_{prot} for handling each message and manipulating the directory. In a situation where data must be retrieved from the main memory, the access is assumed to proceed in parallel with the node controller operation. In a scenario where the processor of a node has a load/store miss to a clean block whose home node is the node itself, we assume the access to the memory module can be pipelined with the cache. In other words, the retrieval of the block, the filling of the cache line, and the manipulation of the directory information are all overlapped. Such overlapping is common in modern DSM systems. Under these assumptions, $T_{r,mem}$ and $T_{w,mem}$ can be estimated as follows:

$$T_{r,mem} = T_{prot} + T_{mmod} + N_{r,s} * T_{smsg} + N_{r,l} * T_{lmsg} \qquad (7)$$

$$T_{w,mem} = T_{prot} + T_{mmod} + N_{w,s} * T_{smsg} + N_{w,l} * T_{lmsg} \qquad (8)$$

where T_{mmod} denotes the memory module access time, $N_{r,s}$ and $N_{r,l}$ denote the average number of short and long messages generated by the coherence protocol which fall on the critical path of the program's execution per read operation. Similarly, $N_{w,s}$ and $N_{w,l}$ are those numbers per write. It is worth noting that such a bimodal distribution of the message length has very important implications on the overall performance of a DSM system and especially on the design of better networks for a DSM system. We study these implications in Section 3 in detail.

2.3 Characterizing Interconnection Network

In this section, we examine the components of communication latencies for short (T_{smsg}) and long (T_{lmsg}) messages in a general network. Both latencies contain certain amount of header processing overhead at sender (T_{snd}) and receiver sides (T_{rcv}). Each of them also contains the network delay, T_{snet} or T_{lnet}, respectively. Thus, we have:

$$T_{smsg} = T_{snd} + T_{snet} + T_{rcv} \tag{9}$$
$$T_{lmsg} = T_{snd} + T_{mmod} + T_{lnet} + T_{rcv} \tag{10}$$

The term T_{mmod} in Eqn. 10 is required for long messages (e.g., reply messages containing data) because the cache/memory block must be copied before the message is sent into the network.

2.4 Putting All Components Together

Now, let us put all components together by substituting and merging Equations 2-10 and rename some of the coefficients as below,

$$R_{hit} = R_{read} * R_{rhit} + R_{write} * R_{whit} \tag{11}$$
$$R_{miss} = R_{read} * R_{rmiss} + R_{write} * R_{wmiss} \tag{12}$$
$$N_{short} = R_{read} * R_{rmiss} * N_{r,s} + R_{write} * R_{wmiss} * N_{w,s} \tag{13}$$
$$N_{long} = R_{read} * R_{rmiss} * N_{r,l} + R_{write} * R_{wmiss} * N_{w,l} \tag{14}$$

where R_{hit} and R_{miss} reflect the overall cache hit/miss ratio of all shared memory references, N_{short} and N_{long} mean the average number of short and long messages generated by the cache coherence protocol for each shared memory reference and which fall on the critical path of the program's execution. Using these compressed notations, the overall execution time can be re-expressed as follows:

$$\begin{aligned} T_{exec} = & [T_{grn} * (N_{ref}/N_{pend} * N_{thr} + N_{bal}) + [R_{hit} * T_{hit} \\ & + R_{miss} * (T_{prot} + T_{mmod}) + (N_{short} + N_{long}) * (T_{snd} + T_{rcv}) \\ & + N_{long} * T_{mmod} + N_{short} * T_{snet} + N_{long} * T_{lnet}] \\ & * (N_{ref}/N_{pend} * N_{thr} + 1)] * N_{iter} \end{aligned} \tag{15}$$

The above equation is quite general. It incorporates the key factors related to the performance of a DSM system with no restrictions to the memory consistency model, cache coherence protocol, or type of network being used. Once a set of values are given to the above parameters/terms, this equation can predict the execution time of any given application. It can also identify the bottlenecks associated with different components of the system.

From the recent literature [1, 10], the current generation DSM systems and applications exhibit the following range of values for the parameters used in our model: T_{grn} from 2 to 500 processor cycles, R_{hit} from 0.90 to 0.99, R_{miss} from 0.01 to 0.10, T_{hit} from 0 to 2 processor cycles, T_{mmod} from 10 to 50 processor cycles, $T_{prot} + T_{mmod}$ from 20 to 55 processor cycles (with partial overlapping), N_{short} from 0.10 to 0.30, N_{long} from 0.02 to 0.10, $T_{snd} + T_{rcv}$ from 10 to 30 processor cycles, N_{ref} from 2 to 100, N_{pend} from 1 to 8, N_{thr} from 1 to 4, and N_{bal} being either 0 or 1.

In the following section, in order to focus on the impact of different components of a network, we use the following representative set of values: $R_{hit} = 0.97$, $T_{hit} = 0$, $R_{miss} = 0.03$, $T_{mmod} = 24$, $T_{prot} = 2$, $T_{snd} = 15$, $T_{rcv} = 5$, $N_{short} = 0.10$, $N_{long} = 0.02$, $N_{ref} = 20$, $N_{pend} = 1$, $N_{thr} = 1$, and $N_{bal} = 1$. The timing values are expressed in terms of numbers of processor clock cycles. For convenience in the following discussion, let us denote $T_{iter} = T_{exec}/N_{iter}$ as the average execution time of an application per iteration per grain.

We consider three different computational granularities to represent three different application types: $Type1$ ($T_{grn} = 80$), $Type2$ ($T_{grn} = 40$), and $Type3$ ($T_{grn} = 5$). These represent medium coarse-grain to fine-grain applications. After substituting the parameters in Eqn. 15 with all these values, the value of T_{iter} for each type of applications can be written as follows:

$$T_{iter,type1} = 1756.86 + 2.10 * T_{snet} + 0.42 * T_{lnet} \qquad (16)$$

$$T_{iter,type2} = 916.86 + 2.10 * T_{snet} + 0.42 * T_{lnet} \qquad (17)$$

$$T_{iter,type3} = 181.86 + 2.10 * T_{snet} + 0.42 * T_{lnet} \qquad (18)$$

3 Impact of Network Components

In this section we study the impact of different network components on the overall performance of DSM systems based on the general model from last section. We consider the k-ary n-cube wormhole interconnection, a popular choice among the current generation DSM systems, and focus on four major components of a network design: link speed, link width, routing delay, and topology.

It is well known that the average message latency in such a network contains two components: no-contention latency and contention delays. Since it is difficult to model network contention analytically [6], we consider no-contention latencies only in this section. In the simulation section, we measure message latencies with and without contention and compare them with one another. For more detailed research result on the performance impact of *network contention* under various processor speed, cache/memory hierarchy, and network design choices in current generation DSMs, readers are requested to refer to [4].

Now let us consider the average message latencies for short and long messages, as indicated in Eqns. 9 and 10, respectively. Based on the wormhole-routing principles [5], the no-contention network latencies (i.e., T_{snet} and T_{lnet}) can be further estimated as follows:

$$T_{snet} = D * (T_{rout} + T_{phy}) + (\lceil L_{short}/W \rceil - 1) * (T_{sw} + T_{phy}) \qquad (19)$$

$$T_{lnet} = D * (T_{rout} + T_{phy}) + (\lceil L_{long}/W \rceil - 1) * (T_{sw} + T_{phy}) \qquad (20)$$

where D is the average distance (number of hops) traveled by a message, L_{short} is the length of a short message, L_{long} is the length of a long message, W is the width of a link (flit) in the network, T_{rout} and T_{sw} are the routing and switching delays at each router/switch for a message, T_{phy} is the propagation delay of a flit along a single link.

The short messages in a DSM system are due to control messages resulted from cache coherency. The length of such messages are determined by the number of message types used in a cache coherency protocol, the total number of cache

Table 1. Predicted performance of three different application types under different network design choices using Eqns. 16-20.

Network Design Choices			T_{snet} (pcyc.)	T_{lnet} (pcyc.)	Type 1 Estim.	Type 1 Relat.	Type 2 Estim.	Type 2 Relat.	Type 3 Estim.	Type 3 Relat.
Link Speed (MHz)	T_{rout}: 1 ncyc.	100	40	168	1911.42	100.0%	1071.42	100.0%	336.42	100.0%
		200	20	84	1834.14	96.0%	994.14	92.8%	259.14	77.0%
		400	10	42	1795.50	93.9%	955.50	89.2%	220.50	65.5%
	T_{rout}: 4 ncyc.	100	88	216	2032.38	100.0%	1192.38	100.0%	457.38	100.0%
		200	44	108	1894.62	93.2%	1054.62	88.4%	319.62	69.9%
		400	22	54	1825.74	89.9%	985.74	82.7%	250.74	54.8%
Link Width (bytes)	T_{rout}: 1 ncyc.	1	26	154	1876.14	100.0%	1036.14	100.0%	301.14	100.0%
		2	20	84	1834.14	97.8%	994.14	95.9%	259.14	86.1%
		4	18	50	1815.66	96.8%	975.66	94.2%	240.66	79.9%
	T_{rout}: 4 ncyc.	1	50	178	1936.62	100.0%	1096.62	100.0%	361.62	100.0%
		2	44	108	1894.62	97.8%	1054.62	96.2%	319.62	88.4%
		4	42	74	1876.14	96.9%	1036.14	94.5%	301.14	83.3%
Topol. (dim, width (bytes))	const. link width	2, 2	20	84	1834.14	100.0%	994.14	100.0%	259.14	100.0%
		3, 2	16	80	1824.06	99.5%	984.06	99.0%	249.06	96.1%
		6, 2	16	80	1824.06	99.5%	984.06	99.0%	249.06	96.1%
	const. bisec. width	2, 4	18	50	1815.66	100.0%	975.66	100.0%	240.66	100.0%
		3, 2	16	80	1824.06	100.5%	984.06	100.9%	249.06	103.6%
		6, 1	22	150	1866.06	102.8%	1026.06	105.2%	291.06	120.9%

blocks, and data protection information in the system. The length of a long message depends on the above factors as well as the cache line size. In this paper, we assume a directory-based cache coherency protocol with 32 different message types, 64 processing nodes, 512 MBytes of globally shared memory, and cache line size of 64 bytes. These lead to the following message lengths: $L_{short} = 6$ bytes and $L_{long} = 70$ bytes. These values are also used in the simulation experiments for easy comparison. The sizes of memory, message header and cache are small by the current standard in real DSM systems. However, these carefully selected values are large enough to run the SPLASH2 benchmark applications using the recommended input sizes from [10] and to keep the simulation time reasonable.

3.1 Impact of Link Speed

Let us study the impact of link/router speed on the overall performance of DSM systems. Consider an 8 × 8 mesh with 16-bit wide links as our network. This leads to $D = 8$ and $W = 2$. Let us examine three values of speed: 100 MHz, 200 MHz, and 400 MHz, corresponding to link bandwidths of 200, 400, and 800 MBytes, respectively. In this paper, we have assumed default processor speed to be 200 MHz. For a 100 MHz link, we have $T_{phy} = T_{sw} = 1$ *ncycle* (network cycle), which is equal to 2 *pcycles* (processor cycles). Depending on the current trends in router design, let us consider two different representative values for routing delays (T_{rout}): 1 and 4 ncycles.

By using the above values in Eqns. 16-20, the overall execution times are computed and shown in the top section of Table 1. It can be observed that as the granularity of an application decreases, increasing link speed has a substantial benefit on the overall execution time. These benefits can vary from 6.1% for a medium coarse-grain application to 35.5% for a fine-grain application. These benefits are more for networks with higher routing delays, ranging from 10.2% to 45.2%.

3.2 Impact of Link Width

Next, let us consider the impact of increasing network link width. Assume the same network with 200 MHz link speed and consider link widths of 1 byte, 2 bytes, and 4 bytes. The estimated execution times are shown in the middle section of Table 1. Clearly, the message latencies do not reduce linearly as seen with link speed. This is because only a portion of the message latency is affected by the link width, as shown in Eqns. 19-20. Increasing link width can benefit in reduction of execution time by 3.2% to 21.1% for lower routing delay and 3.1% to 16.7% for higher routing delay. Comparing these benefits with those of increasing link speed, it can be observed that increasing link speed is more beneficial than increasing link width.

3.3 Impact of Topology

Finally, we consider the impact of changes in topology. For a fair comparison, we consider two different strategies for varying topologies: *under constant link width constraint* and *under constant bisection bandwidth constraint* [5]. Under the former constraint, link width is kept constant as the dimension of the network changes. Under the second constraint, link width is changed so as to maintain constant bisection bandwidth.

Let us consider three different topologies: 2d (8^2), 3d (4^3), and 6d (2^6) mesh. Under constant link width constraint, let us assume the link width to be kept constant at 2 bytes. The link speed is kept constant at 200 MHz (400 MBytes/sec bandwidth). Changes in topology lead to a change in the average distance traveled by the messages ($D = 8$, 6, and 6 for the above topologies, respectively). The corresponding execution times are shown in the bottom section of Table 1. The latencies for 4d and 6d systems are identical because the average distances traveled in both (given) topologies happen to be identical. With respect to the overall execution time, increasing the degree of network dimension provides very little benefit (0.5% to 3.9% only).

Under constant bisection bandwidth constraint, the link width for hypercube topology is assumed as 1 byte. This indicates that the link width of 4d and 2d systems needs to be 2 and 4 bytes, respectively. The latencies for short and long messages under this constraint show interesting trends. As the degree of dimension changes from 2 to 4 to 6, the average latency for small messages first reduces and then increases. The reduction is due to lowering the average distance traveled. However, it is quickly overpowered by reduction in link width. The average latency for long messages continue to rise with increase in dimension because of reduction in link width. These changes show increasing effect on the overall execution time for the three representative applications. The increase is quite substantial for fine-grain applications, indicating that higher dimension networks under constant bisection bandwidth constraint are not suitable for designing DSM systems.

The guidelines derived in this section are based on only no-contention message latency. In the following section, we present detailed execution-driven simulation results to validate these guidelines and study the possible changes caused by network contention.

4 Simulation Results

In order to validate the analytical model and the guidelines derived in the last section, we simulated a DSM system similar to the FLASH machine [9]. Before presenting and discussing the simulation results, we first describe the basic architectural features assumed, the applications and their input sizes, and the performance metrics used in our experiments.

4.1 Simulation Environment

We simulated a 64-node DSM system with a default interconnection as an 8×8 mesh. The processor in each processing node was assumed to be a 200 MHz single-issue microprocessor with a perfect instruction cache and a 128 KBytes 2-way set associative data cache with a line size of 64 bytes. The cache was assumed to operate in dual-port mode using write-back and write-allocate policies. The instruction latencies, issue rules, and memory interface were modeled based on the DLX design [12]. The memory bus was assumed to be 8 bytes wide. On a memory block access, the first word of the block was returned in 30 pcycles (150 ns). The successive words in the block followed in a pipelined fashion. The machine was assumed to be using a full-mapped, invalidation-based, three-state directory coherence protocol [2, 4, 7, 9]. The node controller took 3 pcycles to forward a message and 14 pcycles to manipulate the directory. The network interface took 15 pcycles to construct a message and 8 pcycles to dispatch it. The synchronization protocol assumed in the system was the QOLB protocol similar to the one used in DASH [8]. The node simulator modeled the internal structures, as well as the queuing and contention at the node controller, main memory, and cache. For more information about the simulation setup, please refer to [3].

The major difference between our simulated architecture and the FLASH was as follow: sequential memory consistency, instead of the release memory consistency, was enforced by the coherence protocol. A load/store miss stalled the processor until the first word of data was returned. Therefore, at most one outstanding request could be pending in a processor.

We used four SPLASH2 [10] applications—Barnes, LU, Radix, and Water in our simulation experiments. Problem sizes for these applications were as follows: Barnes ($8K$ particles, $\theta = 1.0$, 4 time steps), LU (512×512 doubles, 8×8 blocks), Radix ($1M$ keys, $1K$ radix, max $1M$), and Water (512 molecules, 4 time steps). These sizes were recommended in [10] to keep the important behaviors of the applications to be the same as in a full fledged system.

4.2 Performance Metrics

We present all our simulation results in two sets: execution time and network latency. This helps us to correlate the behavior of underlying network with the overall DSM system performance and provide important insights into the network design issues. The overall execution time is broken down into four components: computation (C), memory read waiting (R), memory write waiting (W), and synchronization waiting (S) from bottom to top shown in Fig. 2. All times are normalized to that of the left most system configuration in the figures for each application.

The network latencies of two types (short and long) of messages are presented separately in absolute time (microseconds). Furthermore, we present the average latencies of short and long messages in three different ways: *estimated, ideal, and real*. The *estimated latency* was calculated according to Eqn. 19-20, where D is taken as half of the network diameter, i.e., the average distance traveled per message under uniform traffic. The *ideal latency* presented in this section (shown with a legend 'w/o contention') is the average per message among all the messages of the same type. The ideal latency for short and long messages were computed dynamically during the simulation execution by accumulating the essential delays (such as T_{rout}, T_{phy}, and T_{sw}) along the actual traversal path of the messages. In other words, this should be the measured value of average latency per message if there exists no contention in the network. Lastly, the *real latency* (shown with a legend '/w contention') is the average of network latencies across all messages of the same type. The network latency for a message was measured from the start of its injection at the sender until the completion of its consumption at the receiver. This latency includes contention at injection channel, consumption channel, and communication links. It is to be noted that the difference between the values of ideal latency and estimated latency of a message type tells us how close is the traffic of that message type to the 'uniform' traffic. Similarly, the difference between the values of ideal latency and real latency of a type tells us the effect of network contention.

4.3 Impact of Network Speed

Figures 2(a) and 2(b) show the impact of network speed on the overall execution time. The network speed was changed from 100 MHz to 400 MHz (200 MBytes/sec to 800 MBytes/sec bandwidth). These results refer to two different routing delays ($T_{rout} = 1$ and 4 ncycles), as discussed in Section 3. As predicted in section 3.1, the overall execution time reduces as the speed of the network increases. The reduction in execution time varies across applications, ranging from 7.3% in Water to 54.6% in Radix. From the timing breakdowns, Water appears to be the most computation intensive whereas Radix is communication intensive. In other words, the average grain size in Water is quite large compare to that in Radix. The reduction in execution time is higher for networks with higher routing delay, as predicted in section 3.1.

Figures 2(g) and 2(h) show the average message latencies for the same set of simulation experiments. Several important observations can be drawn from these data. First of all, the curves of the estimated latency are slightly above to the curves of ideal latency (no-contention) for both short and long messages. The two set of curves follow exactly the same trend and their difference margin is very small. This reveals the fact that the traffic of both message types (short and long) in a typical DSM system is close to 'uniform' traffic with a somewhat smaller average distance per message because of locality. Similar trends can also be observed from the remaining subsections.

Second, the real (with contention) latency might be much higher than the ideal latency under certain network designs. In such scenarios, contention inside the network becomes the dominant factor for network latency. Since both types of messages share the same network, the link contention between short and long messages causes the delay for short messages to be disproportionately greater. Increasing network speed causes contention to be reduced substantially for short messages, leading to overall reduction in execution time (up to 40%). Similar trends can also be observed from the remaining subsections.

4.4 Impact of Link Width

Figures 2(c) and 2(i) show the execution time and average latencies for the applications running under the default system configuration with varying link widths, (8, 16, or 32 bits each). These results are for routing delay of 1 ncycle. Figures 2(d) and 2(j) show the trend for routing delay of 4 ncycles. As expected from the analysis in section 3.2, it can be observed that wider links help reducing the overall execution time. The reduction varies from 5.3% in Water to 51.7% in Radix. The reduction is smaller for higher routing delay. The performance improvements are also smaller compared to the respective improvements obtained by increasing link speed.

4.5 Impact of Topology

We examine the impact of different topologies by comparing the results for 2d (8×8), 3d (4^3), and 6d (2^6) meshes under two different constraints: constant link width and constant bisection bandwidth. The data presented here were for routing delay of 1 ncycle. Other results of different topologies can be found in [3].

Under Constant Link Width Constraint: Figures 2(e) and 2(k) show the execution time and average message latencies of each application running under various topologies. The link width was kept at 16 bits for all experiments. As predicted in Section 3, increasing the dimension of the network helps in reducing the execution time. However, the relative improvement is very small.

Under Constant Bisection Bandwidth Constraint: Figures 2(f) and 2(l) show the execution time and average message latencies of each application running under various topologies. The link width was varied to maintain constant bisection bandwidth. As predicted in Section 3, increasing the dimension of the network has negative impact on the overall execution time. With increase in network dimension, both short and long messages undergo increasing contention, leading to increase in overall execution time. Thus, 2D systems are shown to be the best for a 64 processor system under this constraint. More generally, a low dimension k-ary n-cube is a more preferable topology to a high dimension k-ary n-cube for medium or large scale DSM systems under this constraint.

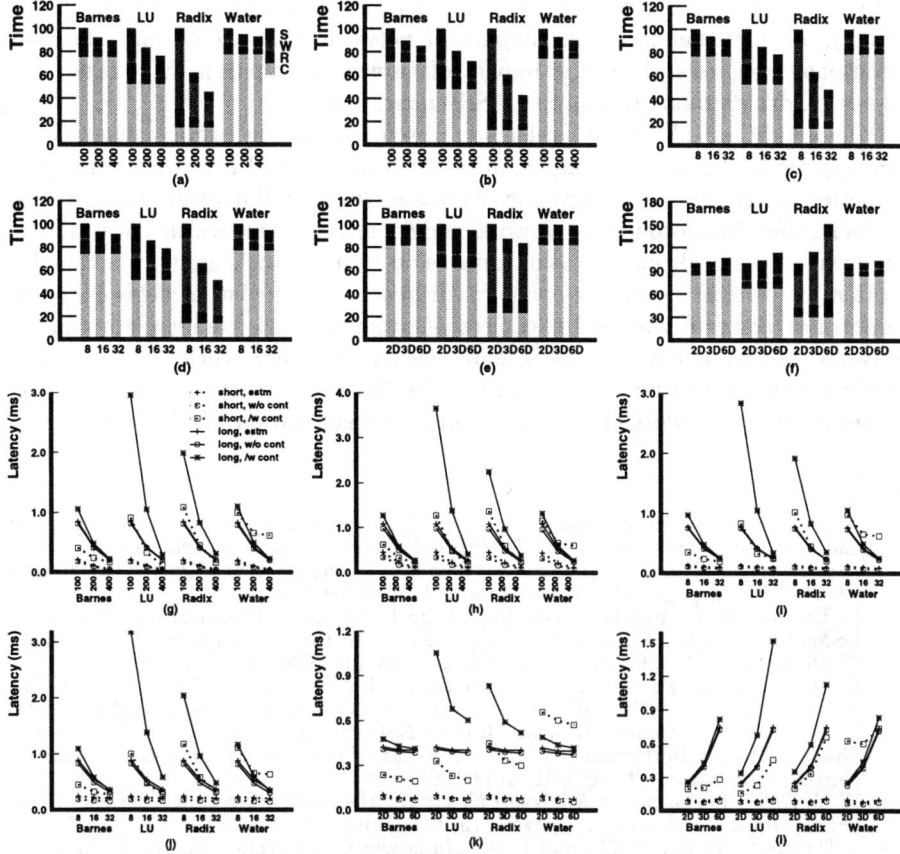

Fig. 2. Impact of different network components on the overall execution time of benchmark applications and on the message latencies under the bi-modal network traffic.

5 Conclusion

Advances in processor technology is making network latency an increasingly important architectural bottleneck in DSM systems. In addition to the continued research efforts in developing latency reduction and latency tolerance techniques, a better understanding of the basic communication characteristics of DSM systems/applications and a set of concrete guidelines for designing more efficient networks targeted specifically for DSM systems are very desirable. In this paper, we have developed a comprehensive parameterized model to estimate the performance of a CC-NUMA multiprocessor system using k-ary n-cube wormhole interconnection. This model integrates all the key aspects of a DSM system: application characteristics (number of threads, number of synchronization points, and granularity of computation), components of the node architecture (access time for cache and memory, protocol overhead, and number of outstanding memory requests allowed), and network components (link speed, link width, router delay, and topology). Based on this model we have studied the impact of different network components on the overall performance of DSM systems/applications. Finally, we have validated the impact of network components and obtained additional insights such as the impact of network contention by results from execution-driven simulation of SPLASH2 benchmarks.

Our study establishes several guidelines for designing better networks for DSM systems. Some of the important guidelines obtained from this study are: a) better performance is achieved by increasing link speed instead of link width, b) increasing dimension of a network under constant link width constraint is somewhat beneficial, c) increasing dimension of a network under constant bisection bandwidth constraint is not at all beneficial, d) routing delay plays an important factor in the design choices of other network components, and e) network contention experienced by short messages is very crucial to the overall performance. These guidelines can be used by the architects as a good foundation to design better networks for current and future generation DSM systems.

References

1. S. Chandra, J. R. Larus, and A. Rogers. Where is time spent in message-passing and shared-memory programs? In *Proceedings of the sixth International Conference on Architectural Support for Programming Languages and Operating Systems (ASPLOS-VI)*, pages 61–73, San Jose, CA, October 1994.
2. D. Dai and D. K. Panda. Reducing Cache Invalidation Overheads in Wormhole DSMs Using Multidestination Message Passing. In *Proceedings of the International Conference on Parallel Processing*, pages I:138–145, Chicago, IL, Aug 1996.
3. D. Dai and D. K. Panda. How Can We Design Better Networks for DSM Systems? Technical Report OSU-CISRC-3/97-TR19, The Ohio State University, March 1997.
4. D. Dai and D. K. Panda. How Much Does Network Contention Affect Distributed Shared Memory Performance? In *Proceedings of the International Conference on Parallel Processing*, Chicago, IL, Aug 1997.
5. W. J. Dally. Performance Analysis of k-ary n-cube Interconnection Network. *IEEE Transactions on Computers*, pages 775–785, June 1990.
6. J. Duato, S. Yalamanchili, and L. Ni. *Interconnection Networks: An Engineering Approach*. The IEEE Computer Society Press, 1997.
7. D. Lenoski et al. The Directory-Based Cache Coherence Protocol for the DASH Multiprocessor. In *Proceedings of the 17th Annual International Symposium on Computer Architecture*, pages 148–159, May 1990.
8. D. Lenoski et al. The Stanford DASH Multiprocessor. *IEEE Computer*, pages 63–79, March 1992.
9. J. Kuskin et al. The Stanford FLASH Multiprocessor. In *Proceedings of the 21st Annual International Symposium on Computer Architecture*, pages 302–313, 1994.
10. S. C. Woo et al. The SPLASH-2 Programs: Characterization and Methodological Considerations. In *Proceedings of the 22nd Annual International Symposium on Computer Architecture*, pages 24–36, 1995.
11. K. Gharachorloo et al. Memory Consistency and Event Ordering in Scalable Shared-memory Multiprocessors. In *Proceedings of the 17th Annual International Symposium on Computer Architecture*, pages 15–26, May 1990.
12. J. L. Hennessy and D. Patterson. *Computer Architecture: A Quantitative Approach*. Morgan Kaufmann, 1990.
13. D. Kroft. Lockup-free instruction fetch/prefetch cache organization. In *Proceedings of the 8th Annual International Symposium on Computer Architecture*, pages 81–85, 1981.
14. A. Rogers and Kai Li. Software support for speculative loads. In *The Fifth International Symposium on Architectural Support for Programming Languages and Operating Systems (ASPLOS-V)*, pages 38–50, October 1992.

Invited Presentation

Integration of U-Net into Windows/NT

Thorsten von Eicken

Department of Computer Science
Cornell University
Ithaca, N.Y. 14853

U-Net provides user-level network access such that applications can send and receive messages without operating system intervention on every send and receive. The network is exposed to applications as a pair of transmit and receive buffer queues. Depending on the sophistication of the network interface hardware, these queues are serviced directly in hardware or via interrupt handlers and fast traps. A number of implementations of U-Net exist for Unix workstations connected to ATM and Fast Ethernet networks. This talk will present our experience in moving U-Net from Unix to Windows/NT and in allowing the operating system to demand-page network buffers.

Session V

ROUTING II

Friday, June 27, 1997
10:30 - 12:00

Session Chair:

T. Pinkston
University of Southern California

Distance-Based Flow Control in Wormhole Networks

A-H Smai   L-E Thorelli

Department of Teleinformatics, Royal Institute of Technology
Electrum 204, 164 40 Kista, Sweden

Abstract. The introduction of wormhole routing over a decade ago enabled the use of networks with large diameter, such as the 2-D and 3-D meshes. In direct networks with possibly large diameters, the distances between nodes vary significantly. This will affect communication latencies especially with varying traffic loads. In this paper, we propose a new, low-cost *distance-based flow control* for wormhole networks. Conventional virtual channel flow control does not take into account distances and the physical channel is scheduled in a strict round-robin manner. The proposed flow control is achieved through two mechanisms, a distance-based message priority mapping and an efficient deadlock-free prioritized physical link allocation strategy. This paper presents the motivation behind the proposed flow control, a description of the mechanisms, and its implementation. The distance-based flow control is evaluated and compared against conventional virtual channel flow control for a wide range of system parameters. Results based on thorough simulation show that the performance of local and long-distance communication can be significantly improved, latency can be improved by up to 45%. The results demonstrate significant potential for designing high performance highly parallel wormhole systems.

1 Introduction

The interconnection network is a critical component of a parallel system. In recent years, parallel computers with more than a thousand computation nodes have been developed. The most expensive resources in the interconnection network are physical bandwidth associated with communication links and buffer space associated with routers. Over the years, new switching technologies are being developed to utilize these network resources in the best possible manner. Current generation parallel systems use wormhole switching technique [5, 12]. This switching technique allows low message latency while using very little amount of buffer space at the routers. Over the recent years, a large number of research directions have emphasized designing efficient k-ary n-cube wormhole networks. These include the virtual channel flow control scheme [4], developing adaptive routing algorithms [2, 7, 15, 16, 17, 22], algorithms for collective communication [3, 12, 18], and designing efficient router architecture and network interface support [1, 6, 13], and flow control schemes under real-time traffic [11, 13].

With the store-and-forward switching technique, the communication latencies are linear in the distance travelled by a packet. The introduction of wormhole routing over a decade ago enabled the use of networks with large diameter, such as the 2-D or 3-D meshes. These networks are favourable from a technical point of view, and 2-D meshes in particular are suitable for multiple processors on a single chip or wafer. Being direct networks with possibly large diameters, the distances between nodes vary significantly. This will affect communication latencies especially when traffic load is high. It then becomes important to study the impact of distances on the network performance. The goal of this work is to investigate this issue and to provide low-cost architectural support to provide different services based on distances.

Demand multiplexing is the method of choice today for wormhole networks. It considers only those virtual channels which have an available transferable flit, when allocating the physical link bandwidth. Access to the link is performed in a strict round-robin manner. However, demand multiplexing does not take into account priorities in general, and status information such as the distance between the source and destination of messages in particular. In this paper, we propose a new distance-based flow control approach to provide specific support for short- and long-distance communication in wormhole networks. This flow control is achieved through two mechanisms, a distance-based message priority mapping and an efficient prioritized physical link allocation. Each flit that has acquired a virtual channel is tagged with high or low priority, according to the message priority carried in the header flit. The message priority is a function of the distance between source and destination (static priority mapping), and is determined prior to message injection into the network. The priority tag of a flit is used in the arbitration process between ready flits awaiting access to the physical link.

This simple change in the flow control scheme promises reduced latency for either short- or long-distance communication traffic. The method can benefit many other switching techniques and can be used with many deterministic and minimal adaptive routing methods. It can as well benefit specific applications such as those which exhibit locality or applications with more uniform traffic pattern. The flow control scheme can be integrated into existing router architectures with little additional logic. It does not require any virtual channel assignments based on priorities. Results based on exhaustive simulation show that the performance of local and long-distance communication can be significantly improved, latency can be reduced by up to 45%.

The rest of the paper is organized as follows. In Section 2, we present the motivation behind the proposed flow control, and describe the priority mapping strategy based on distances. In Section 3, we review conventional demand multiplexing and discuss some limitations, and describe the prioritized flit selection and discuss some implementation issues. In Section 4, the performance of the distance-based flow control is evaluated and compared against the conventional virtual channel flow control. Related work and a discussion are presented in Section 5. Finally, conclusions are drawn in Section 6.

2 Multihop Network Communication

2.1 Impact of Locality and Long-Distance Communication on Performance

One goal in the execution of parallel programs is to take full advantage of locality information while keeping all processors busy. However, locality and load balancing are contending goals. Many approaches were proposed to manage long latency operations. Multithreading and data prefetching were proposed to tolerate long latency, whereas exploiting temporal and physical locality are approaches to avoid and reduce long latency communications. In this paper, we are most interested in physical locality.

Figure 1 shows that the message latency increases with the distance between the source and the destination of messages. The variation in latency is sublinear in distances, but still significant. In figure 1 (b), we observe that with large message size, the latency is well distance-insensitive at very low load (2% circa). Roughly, beyond a few percent applied load the latency becomes distance-dependent, with both small and large message sizes.

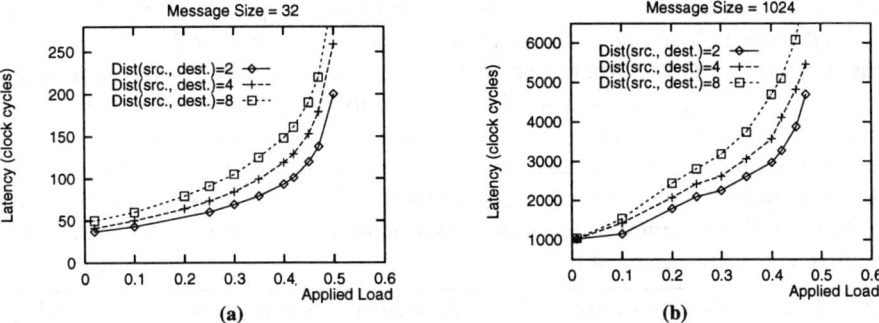

Fig. 1. Latency versus distances. (8x8 2-D mesh, 4 virtual channels). Message Size: (a) 32 flits (b) 1024 flits

Flow control in the interconnection network should exploit short-distance communication and provide support for long-distance communication. Reducing long latency communication can provide more flexibility to load balancing, and hence can relax the necessity to rely on locality only for maximizing performance. This paper proposes schemes to complement the benefits of locality and reduce long latency communication, through distance-based message priority mapping and efficient prioritized physical link allocation. The schemes can be applied with applications that exhibit locality. However, even when locality is important but difficult to achieve, the schemes provide support for improved low-latency communication.

2.2 Distance-Based Priority Mapping

The interconnection network in a parallel system carries traffic created by application and runtime systems. In particular, the traffic is characterised by the traffic pattern including the distribution of sources and destinations. In this section, we present the message priority mapping strategy based on distances. The strategy promotes messages through priority assignments according to distances.

We distinguish two types of distance based priorities: fixed and dynamic. Fixed distance priorities are defined by the distance between the message source and destination. Dynamic distance priorities are defined by the distance between the current position of the head flit and the destination of the message. There are two approaches which can be applied with both fixed and dynamic distances. Both approaches use a threshold distance to make a decision on whether a message should be assigned high priority or not. This threshold distance can be expressed in terms of the network diameter. In the first approach, only messages whose distances to the destination are *less* than the threshold distance are given high priority. In the second approach, only those messages whose distances are *larger* than the threshold are given high priority. This strategy can separate short-distance and long-distance communications. It can speed up long-distance communication and can complement the benefits of locality of computation. Fixed distance priorities are simple to use and implement. To assign a priority, we need to check the distances only once and only at the source. A simple calculation and comparison are sufficient. It should be noted that it is required that the routing algorithm must be deterministic or minimal adaptive routing. With non-minimal routing algorithm, packets can be routed away from their destination, which makes it difficult to use distance-based priority assignments. With dynamic distance priorities, all messages are assigned the same priority initially. Every time the head flit reaches a new node, the switch must check the distance left to destination in order to decide about the priority. This task can be similar to testing and updating ΔX and ΔY in the XY routing algorithm. In summary we distinguish the following approaches based on distance: fixed shortest distance first, fixed longest distance first, shortest distance left first, longest distance left first.

Threshold is the threshold distance. Dist($n1$, $n2$) = Number of hops between nodes $n1$ and $n2$

For each message do

Prior to injection, read source address *src.* and destination address *dest.*

if Dist(*src.*, *dest.*) >= *Threshold*   /* use <= instead of >= to promote short-distances */

      then assign *high priority*

      else *assign low priority*

endif

Fig. 2. Outline of the distance-based priority mapping scheme

Some first experiments with the dynamic type approach show that using dynamic distances is not very rewarding. One of the main reasons we found out is that in the case of longest-distance-left-first, the priority of a message can change from high to low, and in the case of shortest-distance-left-first, each message will ultimately be promoted to high priority since the distance left will decrease at each hop. In the remaining of the paper, we will consider the fixed type approach only. Figure 2 outlines the priority mapping scheme.

3 Prioritized Demand-Driven Physical Link Scheduling

The selection of ready flits is the procedure by which a single flit is selected amongst several ready flits in order to acquire and use the physical link during the next cycle. This task of selecting a flit is done prior to the actual physical link allocation. In this section, we first point out some limitations of conventional demand multiplexing and then present the prioritized flit selection to support the distance-based scheduling.

3.1 Limitations of Conventional Demand Multiplexing

The physical link is the ultimate resource a flit must acquire to complete a hop, that is to initiate the flit transfer from one router to one of its neighbours. Physical link multiplexing can be done in a fixed way or on demand. In the fixed physical link multiplexing, each virtual channel is assigned a time slot. In each time slot, the channel arbitrator picks up the flit from the corresponding virtual channel and assigns it to the physical link. If no flits are available or it is not possible to send a flit because there is no space available at the receiving end, then the time slot is not used for transmission and the bandwidth is therefore wasted.

Demand multiplexing uses round-robin scheduling as well. In the context of interconnection networks for multiprocessors, round-robin has been introduced in virtual channel flow control [4]. Demand multiplexing is the method of choice in today's wormhole systems. It considers only those virtual channels which have a ready flit to send. In the presence of several virtual channels with eligible flits, each channel must wait its turn to use the link in a round-robin manner. Each channel uses the link for one clock cycle only. To use the link for one more clock cycle, a virtual channel must wait for its turn. In the worst case, a channel has to wait for all other virtual channels associated with the output link to finish accessing it.

As long as all the messages in the network have the same characteristics and requirements, flit-level demand multiplexing is fair, simple and efficient. However, when the network traffic is composed of messages with different types and requirements it is more appropriate to favour messages according to priorities.

Hence, conventional round-robin becomes insufficient since it does not allow flexibility for prioritized flit transmissions. Consequently, in order to speed up transmission of high priority messages, we should adopt an approach different from the classical round-robin. The proposed prioritized flit selection approach uses both round-robin and priority scheduling.

3.2 Prioritized Ready Flit Selection

A flit has a priority. Flits from the same message have the same priority. The priority of a flit is inherited from a tag associated to each virtual channel. The tag is set to high or low depending on the priority of the message or its head flit to which it has been assigned. The tag is updated each time a new head flit is assigned the virtual channel.

The flit selection task has to keep track of the priority tag of every ready flit, prior to a flit selection. One additional bit is associated with each virtual channel, to hold the virtual channel tag. The bit is set according to the priority in the head flit which has acquired the virtual channel. All the subsequent body flit will inherit the priority of the head flit. The bit is not altered until the tail flit has left the router and the path is torn down. When a new head flit acquires the virtual channel, the bit is updated, i.e. set to high or low according to the priority in the header flit. It is important to note that the virtual channel allocation to head flits is not based on priorities, the priority bit associated with each virtual channel is set *after* the virtual channel allocation. However, the bit is used to select the next flit to use the physical channel.

The basic idea in the prioritized ready flit selection is to allocate the physical link to flits with high priority tags only, *as long as* there is at least one *ready* flit with *high priority* tag. In the presence of several ready high priority flits, round robin is applied. Similarly, in the presence of only low priority flits, round-robin is applied.

Virtual channel allocation is done on FCFS basis, that is a free virtual channel may be used by any message, or head flit, requesting it, irrespective of message priorities. Maintaining an FCFS output queue ensures a *starvation-free* prioritized link allocation, provided that new low priority messages will continue to arrive.

It should be noted that only ready flits are considered in the selection process. For instance, if two flits with high and low priority respectively are contending for the physical channel and the high priority flit cannot move because there is no available space at the receiving end, then the low priority flit can proceed and use the physical channel. Hence a flit is blocked only when there is no available space at the receiving end, otherwise it will at most take a finite number of clock cycles to get the chance to use the link. A flit does not "hold and wait" a physical channel. Consequently, the inter-node flit transmission is *deadlock-free*.

The proposed flow control provides support for prioritized traffic but requires additional hardware support. It can be integrated with little additional logic to existing router designs, in the virtual channel arbitration unit. The selection of flits, or virtual channel arbitration, can incur extra overhead and extra synchronization with the physical link and other flow control tasks in the router, which can affect the switch and the utilization of the physical link. However, one can advocate that using overlapping techniques between the flit transmission and other flow control tasks can hide this extra overhead. For instance, assuming that there are two or more ready flits, while a flit is using the link the next flit can be selected, and so on. A detailed description of the implementation is beyond the scope of this paper.

As shown by experiments reported below, this additional priority scheduling to the conventional round-robin achieves reduced latency for high priority messages with relatively little or no increase in latency for low priority messages. It should be noted that promoting high priority traffic is achieved through allocation of physical link only.

4 Simulation Experiments and Results

In this section we present simulation results evaluating and comparing the distance-based flow control against conventional virtual channel flow control for a wide range of system sizes, message sizes, number of virtual channels, and priority assignment schemes for messages.

4.1 System Model and Methodology

The evaluation was done through simulation experiments. We have developed a time-driven simulator to model cut-through or wormhole routing in a two-dimensional mesh network, at the flit level. We assumed that routing and transmission of a head flit take two clock cycles whereas moving a body flit from one router to another takes one cycle. The header flit can hold all the routing information. Deterministic dimension-order routing was used with neighbour nodes connected by unidirectional links. The traffic was modelled by generating messages using a Poisson process at each node. Applied load was normalized to the maximum network capacity which is the load when all links in the network are transmitting at the same time. Applied load was derived using the mean value of message inter-arrival time. Prior to injection, each message is stored in an infinite injection queue in the source node. When a message is generated but cannot be injected because of lack of free channels, it gets queued at the source in the injection queue until a channel becomes available. Source queuing time is therefore included in the message delay. We assumed multiple injection/consumption channels per router, hence internal channels do not constitute bottlenecks. We modelled an output (centralized) queue for each output link. We considered uniform traffic load, that is each node sending messages to all other nodes in the network with equal probability. We ran each simulation experiment for 200000 clock cycles and statistics were collected after the first 100000 cycles. In all experiments, we assumed the following parameters except where it is stated otherwise. The system size was fixed to 8x8. The number of virtual channels per physical link was set to 4. The message size was fixed to 32 flits (we assume a physical link can send a whole flit in one clock cycle). The size of the flit-buffer of a virtual channel was fixed to 2, that is when a packet blocks it is compressed to have a maximum of two flits in each router.

We compared the *conventional* (i.e. the virtual channel flow control using conventional demand multiplexing) and the *distance-based* flow control approaches, for various network and system parameters settings. We carried out several experiments to study the variation of the threshold distance on short- and long-distance communications, the impact of the message size, the system size, and the number of virtual channels. In the evaluation, the main performance metric is the message delay. In fact, the throughput (defined as the amount of traffic received per clock cycle) is essentially unchanged in all the experiments. So, we do not show results on throughput versus applied load.

4.2 Promoting Long-Distance Communication

In this section, we evaluate the longest-distance-first strategy. In this strategy, any message whose distance between source and destination is larger than a predefined threshold is assigned high priority. We assumed the default system size 8x8 (thus the network diameter is 14) and performed experiments with threshold values of 8, 10 and 12. Figures 3(a)-(b) and 4(a)-(b) show the results. All cases yield significant improvement in latency performance. For example, assuming a 35% load, the improvement obtained with the distance-based flow control compared to the conventional flow control for high priority traffic is 36%, 41% and 43% when the threshold value is 8, 10 and 12 respectively. The improvement is better with higher threshold values, which is due to the fact that when the threshold is increased less messages are qualified and therefore there is less competition between high priority messages to access the physical link.

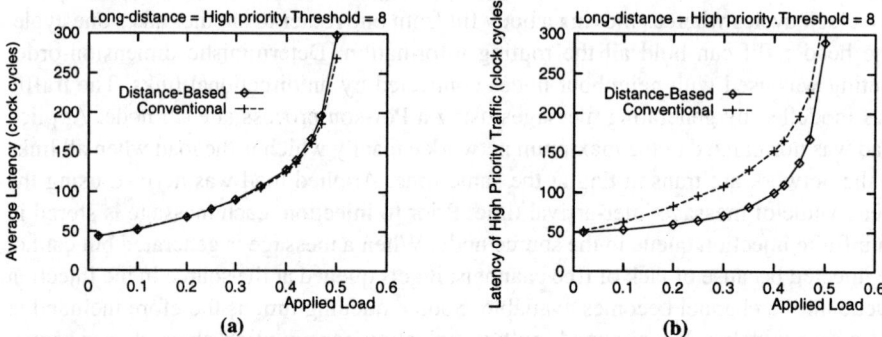

Fig. 3. Promoting long-distance messages. Threshold=8. Latency (a) Average (b) High priority traffic

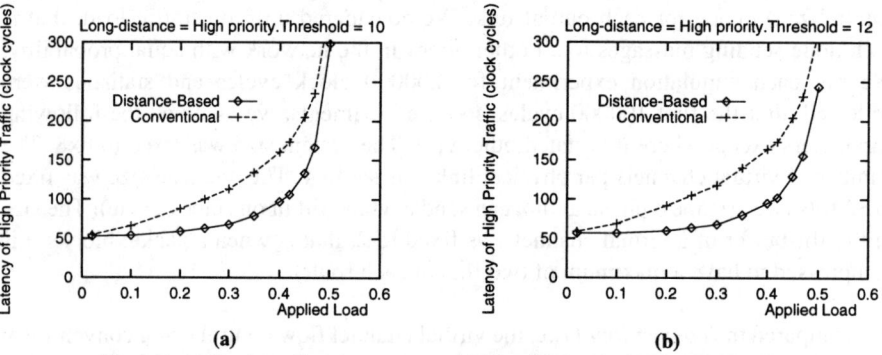

Fig.4. Promoting long-distance messages. (a) Threshold = 10. (b) Threshold = 12.

We measured the amount of accepted high priority traffic and we found that it roughly represents 20% of the total traffic when the threshold is 8, 7% when the threshold is 10, and 2% when the threshold is 12. The performance of the low priority traffic is altered most when the threshold is 8, the delay is increased by 12% when the load is 35%. This delay is altered by only 4% with threshold of 10, and it is unchanged with threshold of 12. The average latency (in the paper, average latency means latency of both high and low priority traffic together) is unchanged in all cases. Overall, performance of long-distance communication is improved with relatively negligible performance cost.

4.3 Promoting Local Communication

We assumed that in a local communication the distance between the source and destination of messages does not exceed 2. Hence, high priority is assigned to messages that travel through at most one intermediate router. Figures 5(a)-(b) show the latency of high priority traffic and the average latency. With the distance-based flow control, the performance of local communication is improved by 10% when the applied load is high (close to saturation) and by 13% to 16% when the load is from low to medium.

We measured the proportion of local communication messages and found that it represents about 15% of the total traffic. When the distance threshold is increased from 2 to for example 4, the distance-based flow control still benefits the short-distance communication, but at some little cost of low priority and average traffic.

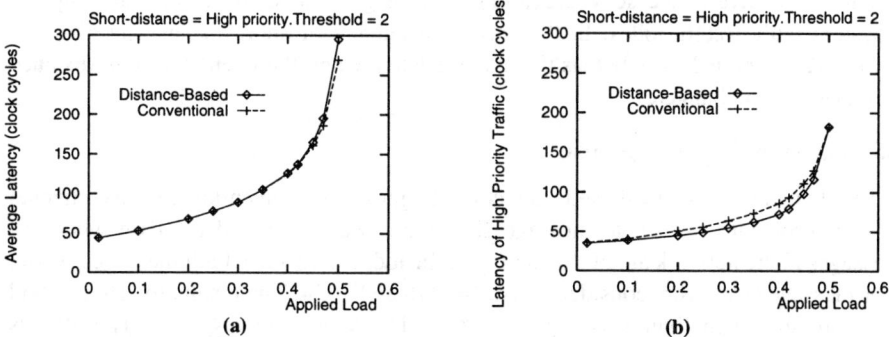

Fig.5. Promoting short-distance messages. (a) Average latency (b) Latency of high priority traffic

In summary, the experiments in this subsection and in the preceding one show that the distance-based flow control can benefit both long- and short-distance communication, with relatively no performance cost of the low priority or the average traffic. In the following subsections, we studied the impact of the system size, the message size and the number of virtual channels on the performance of the distance-based flow control. We considered that long-distance messages have high priority and that the threshold is 2/3 of the network diameter. When the threshold value is 2/3 of the network diameter, the high priority traffic is expected to be between 10% and 15% of the total traffic.

4.4 Impact of the System Size

We studied the impact of the system size on the performance of the distance-based flow control. In addition to the default system size 8x8, two more sizes were considered: 16x16 and 32x32. Figures 6(a)-(b) show the latency of the high priority traffic with 16x16 and 32x32 system sizes respectively. For a 35% load, the improvement is 37%

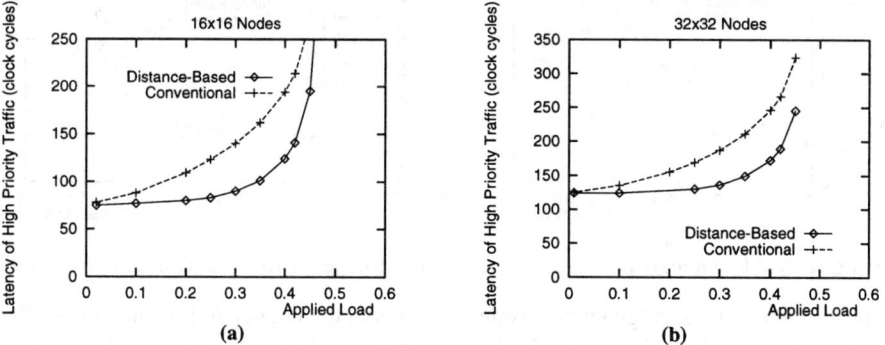

Fig. 6. Latency of long-distance messages (high priority). (a) 16x16 nodes. (b) 32x32 nodes.

and 30% respectively. The average latency in both cases (not shown) is unchanged. The performance of the low priority traffic is practically unchanged too.

With 8x8, we obtained similar results, at 35% load, the improvement for high priority traffic is 38%. Hence, the improvement is at least 30% in all three cases. Nevertheless, it is slightly less with larger system sizes. This difference is probably due to the fact that as system size increases, a message encounters more blocked messages and busy links. We also considered the case where high priority is given to short-distance messages in a system with 16x16 nodes. In this case, the latency of short-distance messages is improved by about 17% whereas the average latency and the latency of long-distance messages are unchanged.

4.5 Impact of the Message Size

We evaluated the distance-based flow control against the conventional virtual channel flow control with respect to message size. First, we considered the case where all messages in the network are of the same size. In addition to the default message size 32, four message sizes were considered: 16, 64, 256 and 1024. The results for 16, 256 and 1024 are shown in figures 7(a)-(b) and 8(a). The latency of high priority traffic is

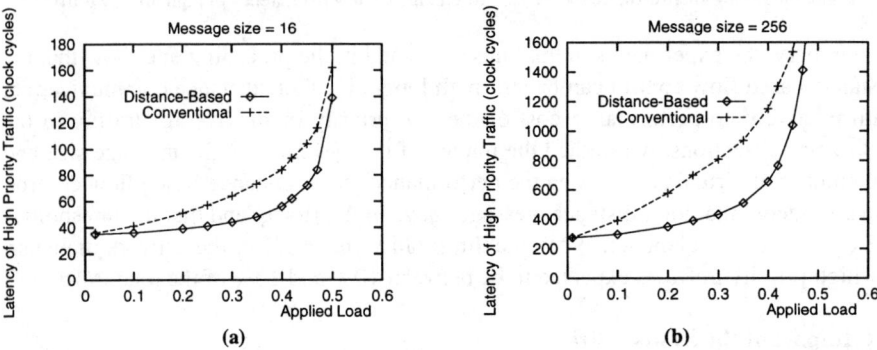

Fig.7. Latency of long-distance messages (high priority). (a) Message size=16. (b) Message size=256

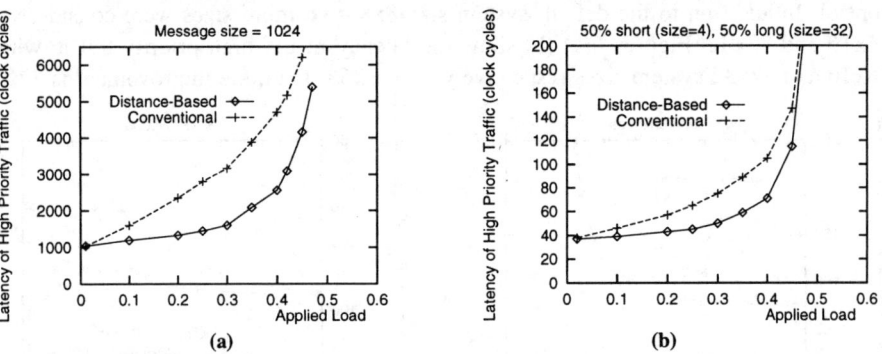

Fig. 8. Latency of long-distance messages (high priority). (a) Message size=16. (b) Hybrid traffic. 50% short.

improved while the average latency is unchanged and the latency of low priority traffic is about the same. For a 35% load, the improvement for the high priority traffic is 35%, 43%, 46% and 47% for message sizes 16, 32, 256 and 1024 respectively. We observe that the improvement in latency for high priority traffic increases with the message size and gradually becomes stable from message size 32.

The system size in these experiments is 8x8, which can explain why the increase becomes stable when the message size is around 32. With 8x8 system size and for message sizes around 32 and up, the tail flit of a message is still in the source when the head flit and many following body flits have been consumed at the destination. In summary, most of the performance gain is obtained when the message size is relatively small (with respect to the system size), after that the gain is about the same or increases relatively little as the message size increases. Figure 8(b) shows results with hybrid traffic conditions. The message sizes are 4 and 32. The performance is comparable to the case of traffic with messages of the same size.

4.6 Impact of Number of Virtual Channels

Finally, we studied the impact of the number of virtual channels. We assumed a fixed amount of buffer space, thus the depth of the flit-buffers decreases when the number of virtual channels increases. Figures 9(a)-(b) show the performance of the distance-based flow control compared to the conventional flow control. The performance is much better with higher number of virtual channels. For instance, for a 35% load, the improvement is 17% and 49% with two and eight virtual channels respectively.

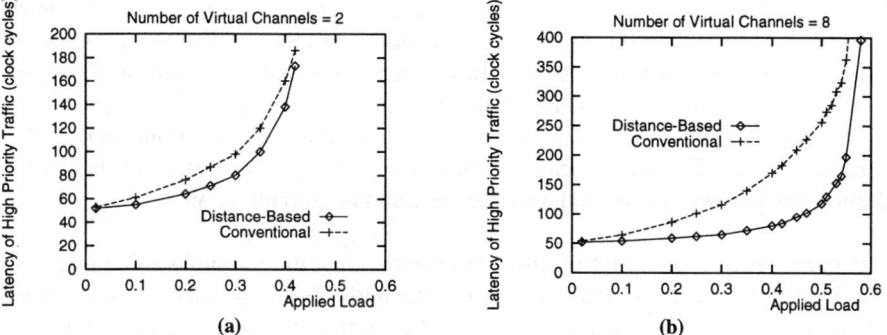

Fig. 9. Latency of long-distance messages (high priority). (a) 2 virtual channels. (b) 8 virtual channels.

5 Related Work and Discussion

Some related work presented in the literature are: description of virtual channel flow control [4], a discussion on advantages and disadvantages of virtual channel utilization [8], the use of virtual channel flow control in real-time systems [11], and prioritized demand multiplexing [14]. Other related work includes studies on computer networks and real-time systems [6, 9, 12, 19, 20, 21]. None of these contributions take advantage of the concept of distances in direct networks to improve performance of classes of messages.

The proposed distance-based flow control is supported by means of a message priority mapping scheme and a prioritized physical link scheduling. The distance-based flow control can benefit networks using different switching techniques and routing algorithms. It can be used in combination with many of the mechanisms and techniques in the mentioned related work. It is particularly relevant for systems built of processors with hardware support for efficient message handling.

To the best of our knowledge, we know of no published work where the concept of distances has been used to define the priority of messages in the interconnection. In [21], the authors point out the effect of distances on short messages in distributed shared-memory multiprocessors, and compare the hypercube topologies against the 2D-mesh. Physical link allocation based on priority has been cited in [4, 11]. Nevertheless, except in [14], no specific algorithm description, implementation or evaluation has been reported, in particular for general purpose networks using cut-through routing. Prioritized demand multiplexing is a framework for prioritized traffic, the study was conducted with various types of message priorities [14]. In the conventional virtual channel flow control [4], the physical link scheduling is done using round-robin scheduling, other types of scheduling such as random, priority, and deadline scheduling like earliest deadline or oldest first are cited. In [8], time-dependent selection functions are added to the routing selection. Real-time virtual channel flow control [11] is a study which performs priority mapping and adjustment based on real-time constraints. The main performance is the ratio of missed deadlines. Many efforts have been devoted to explore hybrid switching mechanisms [6, 13] and different queue management strategies to support integrated network services [10].

In the mentioned related work, message priority or type is taken into account in the allocation of network resources. However, in most cases the physical link arbitration is done in a strict round-robin manner. In the distance-based flow control, the output queue and the virtual channels associated to a physical channel are all scheduled on FCFS basis. The physical link is the only network resource the distance-based flow control manages. Further, the calculation of the priority as a function of the source-destination distance is done in the source node and is straightforward.

The proportion of high priority traffic decreases when the threshold value increases. The higher the threshold value, the lower the performance penalty for low priority traffic. The study shows that a good value of the distance threshold is 2/3 of the network diameter. For such a value, the proportion of the high priority traffic is around 15% which is suitable to reduce the delay of high priority traffic with almost no change in the delay of low priority traffic.

The distance-based flow control is starvation-free, assuming that new low priority messages will continue to arrive. For instance, assuming 20% high priority traffic and uniform traffic distribution, starvation will not occur. With non-uniform traffic patterns, starvation can be a problem for individual messages. However, because blocking is inherent in wormhole networks, it is very likely that high priority flits will block, which will allow low priority flits to proceed. In this respect, an interesting metric is a histogram of latencies observed.

A message aging mechanism can also be used to even out the message latency. However, there is a difference. When distances are used, only a small proportion of the traffic benefits from the scheme, whereas when aging mechanisms are used, all messages are eligible and ultimately the mechanism will speed up any message.

6 Conclusion

In this paper, we have presented a new flow control scheme based on the concept of distances in multihop networks. Conventional demand multiplexing does not distinguish between different groups of messages while allocating a physical channel to virtual channels. Thus, it does not allow flexibility for prioritized traffic. We have proposed a simple and low-cost extension to this scheme to implement the distance-based flow control. The proposed flow control consists in a priority mapping scheme based on distances and a prioritized physical link scheduling.

With the distance-based flow control the latency of long-distance communication is reduced and brought closer to the latency of short-distance communication. On the other hand, the flow control can be applied to promote close-distance communication. Hence, it can benefit applications with different degree of load balancing. When the software overhead for message passing is reduced, the hardware latency in nearest-neighbour or close-distance communication becomes important and the distance-based flow control will be more relevant and rewarding.

The distance-based flow control has been evaluated and compared against the conventional virtual channel flow control for a wide range of system parameters and distance-based priority assignment schemes for messages. Thorough simulation studies show that latency of both long- and short-distance communication can be significantly reduced. Furthermore, while the performance of one group is improved, the performance of the other group and the performance of the total traffic are almost unchanged. The study indicates that a suitable value of the distance threshold is 2/3 of the network diameter. The examination of the implementation issues shows that the prioritized physical link scheduling can be integrated into existing router architectures.

The study shows that using distances is quite promising for providing low communication latency in highly parallel computers. It equips network designers with a new framework for low-latency flow control. The flow control scheme can be extended so that both short and long-distance communication are simultaneously promoted as high priority traffic. But, only very short and very long distances should be considered, to keep the proportion of high priority traffic close to between 10% and 20% of the total traffic. Also, even though we considered the 2D-mesh topology and strict wormhole routing with e-cube routing, using distances is a very general concept and can be used for other types of k-ary n-cube topologies, switching techniques and routing schemes.

References

1. D. Basak and D. K. Panda, Alleviating Consumption Channel Bottleneck in Wormhole-Routed k-ary n-cube Systems. Technical Report OSU-CISRC-09/95-TR36. The Ohio State University, 1995.
2. R. V. Boppana and S. Chalasani. A Comparison of Adaptive Wormhole Routing Algorithms. In Proceedings of the International Symposium on Computer Architecture, 1993

3. R. V. Boppana and S. Chalasani and C. S. Raghavendra. On Multicast Wormhole Routing in Multicomputer Networks. In Proceedings of the IEEE Symposium on Parallel and Distributed Processing, 1994, pp. 722-729.
4. W. J. Dally. Virtual Channel Flow Control. IEEE Trans. on Parallel and Distributed Systems, 3(2):194-205, 1992.
5. W. J. Dally and C. Seitz. Deadlock-Free Message Routing in Multiprocessor Interconnection Networks. IEEE Trans. on Computing. C-36(5), pp. 547-553, May 1987.
6. J. Duato, P. Lopez, F. Silla and S. Yalamanchili. A High Performance Router Architecture for Interconnection Networks. In Proc. of the Int. Conference on Parallel Processing, 1996.
7. J. Duato and P. Lopez. Performance Evaluation of Adaptive Routing Algorithms for k-ary n-cubes. In Proc. of Parallel Computer Routing and Communication Workshop, 1994.
8. J. Duato. Improving the Efficiency of Virtual Channels with Time-Dependent Selection Functions. In Proceedings of Parallel Architectures and Languages Europe, 1992.
9. P. Kermani and L. Kleinrock. Virtual Cut-Through: A New Computer Communication Switching Technique. In Computer Networks, 3(4):267--86, 1979.
10. J. H. Kim and A. Chien. Rotating Combined Queueing (RCQ): Bandwidth and Latency Guarantees in Low-Cost, High-Performance Networks. In Proceedings of the International Symposium on Computer Architecture, 1996.
11. J-P. Li and M. W. Mutka. Real-Time Virtual Channel Flow Control. In Journal of Parallel and Distributed Compting 32, 49-65, 1996.
12. Lionel Ni and Philip McKinley. A Survey of Wormhole Routing Techniques in Direct Networks. IEEE Computer, February 1993.
13. J. Rexford, J. Hall and K. G. Shin. A Router Architecture for Real-Time Point-to-Point Networks. In Proceedings of the International Symposium on Computer Architecture, 1996.
14. A-H Smai, D. K. Panda and L-E Thorelli. Prioritized Demand Multiplexing (PDM): A Virtual Channel Flow Control Framework for Prioritized Traffic. Submitted for Publication
15. A. A. Chien and J. H. Kim. Planar-Adaptive Routing: Low-Cost Adaptive Networks for Multiprocessors. In Proc. of the International Symposium on Computer Architecture, 1992.
16. C. J. Glass and L. Ni. The Turn Model for Adaptive Routing. In Proceedings of the International Symposium on Computer Architecture, 1992.
17. Z. Liu and A. A. Chien. Hierarchical Adaptive Routing: A Framework for Fully Adaptive and Deadlock-Free Wormhole Routing. In Proceedings of the IEEE Symposium on Parallel and Distributed Processing, 1994.
18. D. K. Panda. Issues in Designing Efficient and Practical Algorithms for Collective Communication in Wormhole-Routed Systems. 1995 Workshop on Challenges for Parallel Processing.
19. A. Chien and S. Konstantinidou. Workloads and Performance Metrics for Evaluating Parallel Interconnects. Special issue of IEEE TCCA Newsletter on Interconnection Networks for High Performance Computing Systems, Winter 1995.
20. .S. Konstantinidou and L. Snyder. The Chaos Router. IEEE Trans. on Computers, 43(12):1386-97, Dec. 1994.
21. J. Duato and M.P. Malumbres. Optimal Topology for Distributed Shared-Memory Multiprocessors: Hypercubes Again?. In Proceedings of European Conference on Parallel Processing Vol. I. 1996.
22. J. Duato. A New Theory of Deadlock-Free Adaptive Routing in Wormhole Networks. IEEE Trans. on Parallel and Distributed Systems, 1993.

On the Use of Virtual Channels in Networks of Workstations with Irregular Topology *

F. Silla and J. Duato

Facultad de Informática
Universidad Politécnica de Valencia
Camino de Vera s/n.
46071 - Valencia, SPAIN
E-mail: {fsilla,jduato}@gap.upv.es

Abstract. Networks of workstations are becoming increasingly popular as a cost-effective alternative to parallel computers. Typically, these networks connect processors using irregular topologies, providing the wiring flexibility, scalability and incremental expansion capability required in this environment. Recently, we proposed a design methodology as well as fully adaptive routing algorithms for irregular topologies. These algorithms increase throughput considerably with respect to previously existing ones but require the use of virtual channels.
In this paper we propose a very efficient flow control mechanism to support virtual channels when link wires are very long, and/or have different lengths. This flow control mechanism relies on the use of channel pipelining and control flits. Control traffic is minimized by assigning physical bandwidth to virtual channels until the corresponding message blocks or it is completely transmitted. Simulations show that the resulting flow control protocol performs almost as efficiently as an ideal network with short wires and flit-by-flit multiplexing.

Keywords Networks of workstations, irregular topologies, wormhole switching, adaptive routing, virtual channels, channel pipelining, flow control.

1 Introduction

Research in parallel computing has traditionally focused on multicomputers and shared-memory multiprocessors. One of the most important components of these machines is the interconnection network, since it allows processors to communicate with each other. In the first generation of multicomputers, the interconnection network inherited the flow control technique used in computer networks. The research effort made on these machines led to improved routing mechanisms and better switching techniques, like wormhole [5, 15].

Currently, networks of workstations are being considered as a cost-effective alternative to parallel computers. Recent proposals, like Autonet [17], Myrinet [2], or ServerNet [11], use point-to-point links between switching elements instead of the traditional bus used in computer networks. These networks, unlike the regular interconnection networks used in multicomputers and multiprocessors, present an irregular topology as a consequence of the needs in a local area network. Such irregularity provides the wiring flexibility,

---
* This work was supported by the Spanish CICYT under Grant TIC94–0510–C02–01

scalability, and incremental expansion capability required in this environment. Moreover, instead of being a direct network, irregular networks are often arranged as switch-based interconnects.

Multicomputers and networks of workstations share many features but also have some different characteristics. Mainly, distances between routers are relatively small in multicomputers because, usually, several routing elements are arranged in the same printed circuit board and boards are close to each other. However, distances between switches are usually much longer in networks of workstations. Additionally, different links may have very different lengths. As a consequence of this different length, clock frequency must be reduced in order to transmit information properly through long wires. This lower frequency reduces the maximum bandwidth and throughput also increasing message latency. In order to avoid the negative effects of long wires, a technique named channel pipelining was studied in [18]. This technique is very common in computer networks. It makes clock frequency completely independent of wire length. Therefore, current switches use channel pipelining [2] to increase throughput.

Another important difference between multicomputers and networks of workstations is that, due to the long wires in the latter, channel width is usually smaller. Multicomputers with 8-bit or 16-bit channels are not rare. Moreover, each channel has several control lines that signal the presence or lack of free buffers, and also the virtual channel that is currently owning the physical channel [6]. Such amount of wires is not feasible in long channels. Therefore, either the amount of data lines or control lines, or both, should be reduced in order to implement efficiently the long connections in irregular networks. In case that the number of control lines is reduced, it is no longer possible to use dedicated lines for flow control signals.

Routing algorithms in irregular networks are inherently different from those in regular networks, mainly due to the irregular connection patterns between switches. Several deadlock-free routing algorithms have been proposed for irregular topologies, like the up-down routing scheme [17] or the adaptive-trail routing algorithm [16]. A general methodology for the design of adaptive routing algorithms for irregular networks has also been proposed [19, 20]. Routing algorithms designed according to this methodology improve the network throughput considerably and also reduce message latency. This methodology makes use of two virtual channels connecting each pair of switches. Furthermore, the use of virtual channels, by itself, can increase throughput by dynamically sharing the physical bandwidth among several messages [6]. However, as mentioned above, the use of long and narrow links makes the implementation of virtual channels and the associated flow control mechanism quite complex. As far as we know, there is no switch for networks of workstations that implements wormhole switching with virtual channels. Therefore, a virtual channel flow-control mechanism that fits the needs of networks of workstations must be designed.

One can see how the results obtained for regular networks are now migrating to networks of workstations. Wormhole switching has been introduced in irregular networks like Myrinet [2] or ServerNet [11]. Also, the methodology proposed in [19, 20] is based on results initialy developed for regular topologies [8, 9]. However, the use of virtual channels has not been proposed yet for networks of workstations.

In this paper, we propose an implementation of virtual channels in irregular networks that takes into account real aspects of this environment, like the very different length of the links. In Section 2, networks of workstations are introduced. Section 3 proposes an efficient implementation of virtual channels in a network with irregular topology. In

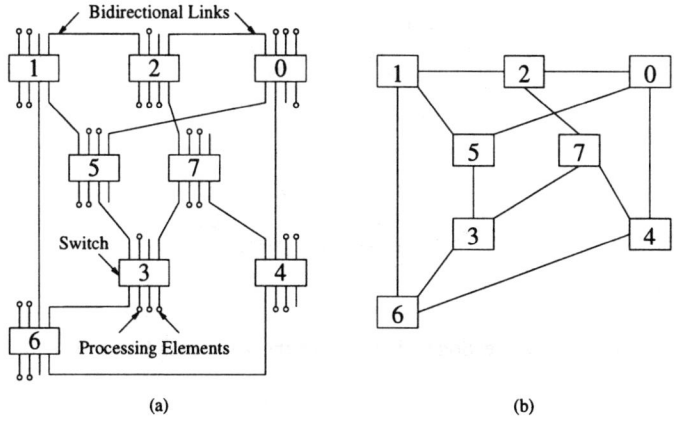

Fig. 1. (a) A network with switch-based interconnect and irregular topology; (b) the corresponding graph G.

Section 4, the performance of the mechanism proposed in Section 3 is evaluated. Finally, in Section 5 some conclusions are drawn.

2 Networks of Workstations

Networks of workstations are usually arranged as a switch-based network with irregular topology. In a switch-based network each switch is shared by several processing elements, which are connected to it through some of the switch ports. The remaining ports are either left open or connected to ports of other switches to provide connectivity between the processing elements. Such connectivity is usually irregular, but guarantees that the network is connected. Typically, all links are bidirectional full-duplex, and multiple links between two switches are allowed. Figure 1(a) shows a typical network of workstations using a switch-based interconnect with irregular topology. In this figure, it is assumed that switches have eight ports and each processor has a single port. The interconnection network I can be modeled by a multigraph $I = G(N, C)$, where N is the set of switches and C is the set of bidirectional links between the switches. Figure 1(b) shows the graph for the irregular network in Figure 1(a).

The switch may implement different switching techniques, like wormhole, virtual cut-through, or ATM. Since recently proposed networks like Myrinet or Servernet use wormhole switching [5], we will restrict ourselves to wormhole switching in this paper.

Routing decisions in irregular networks can be based on source routing or on distributed routing. In the former, the message header contains the sequence of ports to be crossed along the path between the source and the destination [2]. On the other hand, in distributed routing each switch has a routing table that indicates which output port must be taken by the incoming message. Independently of the place where decisions are taken, a routing algorithm must determine the path to be followed. Several deadlock-free routing schemes have been proposed for irregular networks [17, 2, 11, 16]. Moreover,

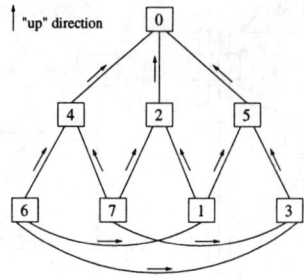

Fig. 2. Link direction assignment for the network in Figure 1(a).

a general methodology for the design of adaptive routing algorithms for irregular networks has been recently proposed [19, 20]. In order to make this paper self-contained, we briefly present the routing algorithm used in the simulations carried out in the performance evaluation section.

2.1 Up/Down Routing

The up/down routing algorithm is the scheme used in Autonet networks [17]. It is a distributed deadlock-free routing scheme that provides partially adaptive communication between the nodes of an irregular network. When a message arrives at a switch, the destination address stored in its header is used, concatenated with the incoming port number, to address the routing table of the switch. As a result, the outgoing port number is returned. In case that there are several suitable outgoing ports, the routing table returns all of them, and the routing scheme selects one port randomly.

Before the routing table in each switch can be used, it must be filled. Routing is based on an assignment of direction to the operational links. To do so, a breadth-first spanning tree is computed and then, the "up" end of each link is defined as: (1) the end whose switch is closer to the root in the spanning tree; (2) the end whose switch has the lower ID, if both ends are at switches at the same tree level (see Figure 2). The result of this assignment is that each cycle in the network has at least one link in the "up" direction and one link in the "down" direction. To eliminate deadlocks while still allowing all links to be used, this routing uses the following up/down rule: a legal route must traverse zero or more links in the "up" direction followed by zero or more links in the "down" direction. Thus, cyclic dependencies between channels are avoided because a message cannot traverse a link along the "up" direction after having traversed one in the "down" direction. Such routing not only prevents deadlock but also provides partial adaptivity.

Up/down routing is not always able to provide a minimal path between some pairs of nodes, as shown in the following example. In Figure 2, a message transmitted from switch 4 to switch 1 cannot go through any minimal path. The shortest path (through switch 6) is not allowed since the message should traverse a link in the "up" direction after one in the "down" direction. All the allowed paths (through switches 0, 2, and through switches 0, 5) are nonminimal. The amount of forbidden minimal paths increases as the network becomes larger.

2.2 Adaptive Routing

Recently, a general methodology for the design of adaptive routing algorithms for irregular topologies has been proposed in [19, 20]. The aim of this methodology is providing minimal routing between all pairs of nodes, as well as increasing adaptivity. In summary, this methodology starts from a deadlock-free routing function defined on an interconnection network, and splits all the physical channels into two virtual channels: *original* channels and *new* channels. Then, the routing function is extended so that newly injected messages can only leave the source switch using new channels belonging to minimal paths, and never using original channels. When a message arrives at a switch from another switch through a new channel, the routing function gives a higher priority to the new channels belonging to minimal paths. If all of them are busy, then the routing algorithm selects an original channel belonging to a minimal path (if any). To ensure that the new routing function is deadlock-free, if none of the original channels provides minimal routing, then the original channel that provides the shortest path will be used. In case that several outgoing original channels belong to shortest paths, only one of them will be provided. This channel will serve as escape path to avoid deadlock [8, 9]. Once a message reserves an original channel, it will be routed using this kind of channels according to the original routing function until it is delivered.

The new routing algorithm is deadlock-free. It can be informally proved by taking into account that when a message cannot make progress by using new channels, it is routed using the original channels and the original routing algorithm, which is deadlock-free. New channels cannot produce deadlock because messages using original channels cannot use new channels again. A formal proof can be given using the theory proposed in [9].

This methodology can be applied to any deadlock-free routing scheme. In particular, the routing algorithm used in this paper is the result of applying this methodology to the routing scheme described in Section 2.1. As a result, a minimal adaptive routing algorithm is obtained. The new routing function is a direct application of the design methodology revisited above.

The routing algorithm presented above tries to minimize the transition from new channels to original channels, at the same time that routes messages through minimal paths whenever possible. A variation of this routing algorithm could be as follows. Instead of routing through an original channel once all of the new channels belonging to minimal paths are busy, it could be worth to reduce even more the use of original channels by routing the message through a nonminimal new channel that conforms to the up/down rule. If this new channel is also busy, then try the original channel (escape path). However, this routing algorithm increments the complexity of the selection function, while the increment in performance obtained by simulation (assuming the same routing time) is negligible. This is due to the use of nonminimal paths.

3 Flow Control

In the previous section, the fully adaptive routing algorithm proposed by us for irregular networks has been described. This algorithm makes use of two virtual channels per physical channel, considerably increasing the maximum achievable throughput, as well as reducing message latency [19, 20]. However, the implementation of virtual channels when physical channel wires are long has not been analyzed yet. There are several issues

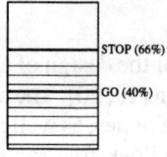

Fig. 3. Minimum and maximum watermarks.

that must be considered. In this section we present an efficient flow control mechanism to be used when links are long.

3.1 Channel Pipelining

The physical layout of a network of workstations usually leads to long links that may differ in their length. These characteristics have two consequences. First, differences in length cause that propagation time is not the same for all the links in the network. Therefore, clock frequency must be reduced in order to transmit information properly through all the links. This lower frequency reduces the maximum achievable bandwidth in short connections, and reduces throughput at the same time that increases message latency. A solution to this problem consists of allowing different channel lengths and using a technique named channel pipelining [18]. This technique makes clock frequency completely independent of wire length by allowing multiple bits to be simultaneously in flight on a wire. Pipelining the information through the links matches the requirements of networks of workstations, supporting long wires as well as wires with different lengths.

The second consequence is that links are, in general, narrow. For cost reasons, it is not feasible using wide links when wires are very long. Thus, adding several lines per link to manage virtual channels and flow control is not a good decision. Instead of dedicating some wires to flow control tasks, it is preferable to use control flits. However, these flits will consume channel bandwidth, increasing message latency. In order to reduce the negative effects of control flits, their usage must be minimized. One way of reducing the flow of control flits is using a "Stop & Go" protocol, as the one implemented in Myrinet [2]. This protocol works as follows: Input buffers have two watermarks, "Stop" and "Go" (see Figure 3), so that when the buffer fills over the "Stop" mark, the switch sends a "Stop" control flit to the previous node. When that switch receives the control flit, it stops sending more flits. As the input buffer empties, when the number of stored flits is below the "Go" mark, the switch sends a "Go" control flit to the previous node so that it restarts sending flits again.

Buffer size is an important issue, since it must be calculated in order to avoid buffer overflow and underflow. Buffer overflow produces the loss of some flits. Buffer underflow introduces bubbles in the message pipeline. In Figure 3 it can be seen that input buffers are divided into three parts. The part above the "Stop" mark must be able to store incoming flits that are in flight since the receiving switch sends the "Stop" control flit until the previous switch stops sending more flits. This period of time is twice the propagation delay through the link plus the time required to process the control flit. Taking into account that channels are pipelined, the amount of flits that can arrive in this time interval is considerable. Following this reasoning, the part below the "Go" mark must be, at least, as large as the part above the "Stop" mark, in order to avoid that the input buffer empties completely before the flit flow is resumed after sending the "Go" control flit. If this part is slightly larger, we ensure that the input buffer will not empty unnecessarily. The part between the "Go" and the "Stop" marks must be large enough to allow some histeresys, avoiding sending control flits continuously. Therefore, assuming that input buffers have capacity for all the flits arriving during a time period equal to three times the maximum round trip delay, each buffer can be split as shown in Figure 3.

It is important to note that when using pipelined channels in a wormhole network, input buffer size is larger than in a non-pipelined channel network. However, with the current integration scale this is not a problem. Also, although links with different lengths are supported, the maximum link length is bounded by buffer size.

3.2 Virtual Channels

One of the main constraints for using virtual channels in wormhole networks has been their cost in silicon area. As the number of virtual channels increases or buffer size grows, the chip area dedicated to temporal storage also enlarges. At present, this is not a constraint because technology allows very high scales of integration. Therefore, designing a switch with several large input buffers is not an unaffordable issue nowadays.

The routing algorithm proposed in Section 2.2 makes use of two virtual channels per physical channel. Traditionally, the virtual channel flow control has been implemented on a flit-by-flit basis [6]. When a physical channel is multiplexed, flits from the different virtual channels are transmitted alternatively one after another, and several control lines signal which virtual channel is owning the physical link during each transmission cycle. However, it has been indicated in Section 3.1 that channels in irregular networks are usually narrow, and therefore, it is not recommendable to use dedicated lines to signal the virtual channel number. As an alternative, we can use control flits to indicate which virtual channel owns the link. In this case, before transmitting a data flit, a control flit must be sent in order to specify which virtual channel this data flit belongs to. This flow control strategy wastes the network bandwidth because half of the bandwidth is consumed by control information. Instead of using flit-by-flit multiplexing, a better mechanism that minimizes the use of control flits consists of transmitting several data flits every time a virtual channel gets the physical channel. In this way, a virtual channel will transmit its identifier, and then it will send flits until, for some reason, it cannot continue sending more flits. At this time, the next ready virtual channel will transmit its identifier followed by data flits, and so on.

Besides reducing the traffic of control flits, transmitting blocks of flits instead of multiplexing on a flit-by-flit basis has another advantage. Consider two messages, message A and message B, that share a physical channel. If both messages have the same length, and both of them reserved a virtual channel in the same physical link at the same time, Figure 4 shows the advance of those messages across the physical link. In Figure 4 (a), a flit-by-flit flow control mechanism is used to transfer these two messages from one switch to another. If message length is n flits, then the average latency is approximately $2n$. However, Figure 4 (b) shows that transferring blocks of flits reduces the average latency down to $1.5n$. This is because when two messages share a channel, with a flit-by-flit multiplexing mechanism both messages are delayed, while with a block mechanism only one of them is delayed. The reduction in latency is more important as messages are longer.

Message Size: n flits

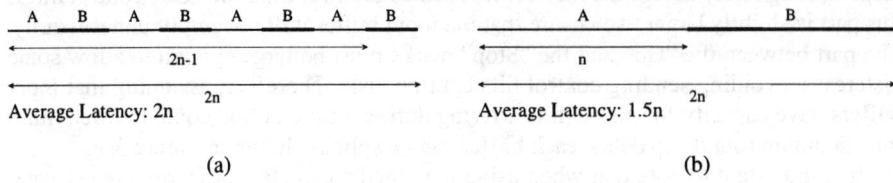

Fig. 4. Flit-by-flit transfer versus block transfer.

In summary, the flow control mechanism can be stated as follows: Physical channels are multiplexed into two virtual channels. The sending switch, before transferring data flits through one of the virtual channels, sends a control flit ("Select 0" or "Select 1", depending on the virtual channel) and then starts sending data flits until the message has been completely transferred or it blocks. If the input buffer at the receiving node fills over the "Stop" mark, then the receiving switch sends a "Stop n" control flit to the previous node, where n is the virtual channel identifier (0 or 1), but continues receiving and storing the incoming flits on the same virtual channel (due to the use of channel pipelining, flits will keep arriving during a period of time equal to twice the propagation time). Once the sending switch receives the "Stop" control flit, it stops the transmission on this virtual channel and switches to the other virtual channel (if ready), sending a "Select n" control flit followed by data flits. While sending flits on a virtual channel, a "Go n" control flit on the other virtual channel may arrive. In this case, the sending node does not switch to that virtual channel (unless priorities are used), but records this change of status. It is important to remark that the receiving node cannot decide by itself to switch from a virtual channel to another, since flits on the wire would not be received on the correct buffer. Also, this flow control protocol can be easily generalized for more than two virtual channels.

4 Performance Evaluation

In this section, we evaluate the performance of the flow control protocol described in Section 3. We will refer to this protocol as PB (Pipelined channels with Block multiplexing). Depending on the fly time (time required to transmit a flit across a link, measured in clock cycles) considered, the names PB4 and PB8 will be used. PB4 will refer to a network where the propagation time along the physical link is four times the internal crossbar delay. In the same way, PB8 will refer to networks where the propagation time along the wire is eight times the crossbar delay. We have assumed that it takes one clock cycle to transmit one flit across a crossbar, and one clock cycle to compute the routing algorithm. Independently of the propagation time along the wire, data is injected into the physical channel at a rate of one flit per cycle. According to Section 3, buffer size will be 27 flits for PB4 and 51 flits for PB8. In these sizes we have considered that the switch needs one clock cycle to decode the "Stop" or "Go" control flit. Therefore, when the fly time is 4 cycles (8 cycles), buffer size should be three times the round trip delay (which is twice the fly time) plus the decoding delay, therefore being 27 flits (51 flits). With respect to the output buffer size, we have fixed it to be 4 flits, independently of the wire length.

In order to evaluate the performance achieved by the proposed flow control protocol, we have compared it with the traditional flow control protocol. This protocol uses a flit-by-flit multiplexing mechanism where channels are not pipelined, that is, when multiple virtual channels in the same physical channel have flits to transmit, one of them sends one flit, and then yields the channel to the next ready virtual channel, which transmits one flit and switches to the next ready virtual channel, and so on. Moreover, since physical channels are not pipelined, before sending a new flit, virtual channels must wait until the current flit has arrived at the next switch. We will refer to this flow control mechanism as FT4 when fly time is 4 cycles, and will be compared with PB4. In the same manner, PB8 will be compared with FT8. Obviously, PB4 and PB8 will achieve higher performance than FT4 and FT8. So, we have also included the results for this flow control protocol (FT) when fly time is one cycle. The reason for this is to compare the performance of the proposed mechanism with an ideal network, in which long links do not have long propagation delays, and flit-by-flit multiplexing does not produce any overhead. We have named this protocol FT1. Note that this protocol assumes a fly time equal to one clock cycle independently of wire length. We have also included the PB1 plots, that display the performance of a system similar to FT1 but instead of a flit-by-flit multiplexing, it implements a block multiplexing mechanism. This plots are intended to compare the behavior of the traditional virtual channel multiplexing versus the one proposed without taking into account other considerations like the link lengths.

We analyzed the impact of using priorities when multiplexing virtual channels onto a physical channel. However, when using priorities on new channels or in original channels performance did not increase. On the contrary, the best results were obtained when virtual channel multiplexing was performed with no priority. Therefore, only these results are shown in this section.

Instead of analytic modeling, simulation was used to evaluate the routing algorithms. Our simulator models the network at the flit level. The evaluation methodology used is based on the one proposed in [9]. The most important performance measures are latency and throughput. The message latency lasts since the message is introduced in the network until the last flit is received at the destination node. Latency is measured in clock cycles. Traffic is the flit reception rate, measured in flits per node per cycle. Throughput is the maximum amount of information delivered per time unit (maximum traffic accepted by the network).

Message latency should also include software overhead at source and destination processors (system call, buffer allocation, buffer-to-buffer copies, etc.). This overhead traditionally accounted for a high percentage of message latency [14, 12]. However, we did not considered such an overhead because some recent proposals reduce and/or hide that overhead, thus exposing hardware latency [10, 1, 13, 7]. So, we only considered network hardware latency in this study.

4.1 Network Model

The network is composed of a set of switches. Network topology is completely irregular and has been generated randomly. However, for the sake of simplicity, we imposed three restrictions to the topologies that can be generated. First, we assumed that there are exactly 4 nodes (processors) connected to each switch. Also, two neighboring switches are connected by a single link. Finally, all the switches in the network have the same size. We assumed 8-port switches, thus leaving 4 ports available to connect to other switches.

Each switch has a routing control unit that selects the output channel for a message as a function of its destination node, the input channel and the output channel status. Table look-up routing is used. The routing scheme is the one described in Section 2.2. The routing control unit can only process one message header at a time. It is assigned to waiting messages in a demand-slotted round-robin fashion. When a message gets the routing control unit but it cannot be routed because all the alternative output channels are busy, it must wait in the input buffer until its next turn. A crossbar inside the switch allows multiple messages traversing it simultaneously without interference. It is configured by the routing control unit each time a successful routing is made.

4.2 Message Generation

Message traffic and message length depend on the applications. For each simulation run, we considered that message generation rate is constant and the same for all the nodes. We have evaluated the full range of traffic, from low load to saturation. On the other hand, we have considered that message destination is randomly chosen among all the nodes in the network. This pattern has been widely used in other performance evaluation studies [6, 4, 3]. For message length, 16-flit, 64-flit and 128-flit messages were considered, and also a mixture of short and long messages (50% 32-flit messages, 50% 128-flit messages).

4.3 Simulation Results

Figure 5 shows the average message latency versus traffic for each of the flow control protocols on a 16-switch (64 nodes) irregular network. Note that traffic has not been normalized because the bisection bandwidth varies from an irregular network to another even when they have the same size. Message length is 16 flits. As can be seen, PB4 achieves a considerably higher throughput and lower latency that FT4. This result indicates that by using pipelined channels and the proposed flow control mechanism for virtual channels, performance increases drastically when channel wires are long. This result was expected because channels are pipelined in PB4 and therefore wire length does not affect its performance significantly. However, when PB4 is compared with FT1, it can be seen that differences in latency and throughput are very small. This effect is more visible in Figure 6, where messages are longer (64 and 128 flits). This figure shows that for long messages, the PB4 protocol achieves performance similar to that of FT1. PB4 achieves almost the same latency as FT1 when messages are long, except when the network is heavily loaded, where the effect of control flits is more important. These results are very important. It means that the proposed flow control mechanism for virtual channels achieves almost the same performance as an ideal multiplexing mechanism on an ideal network with short wires. It also means that performance only decreases by a small amount when wire length increases, provided that the flow control mechanism proposed in this paper is used. Note that the FT1 protocol is a non-implementable protocol, since wire propagation delay has been considered constant, regardless of wire length. Besides, it assumes that flow control and virtual channel management is carried out by using several dedicated control wires, and this is not possible with long links. The effect of block

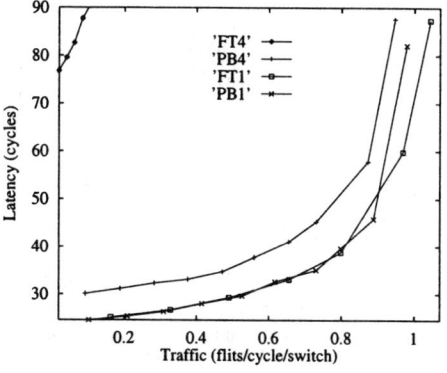
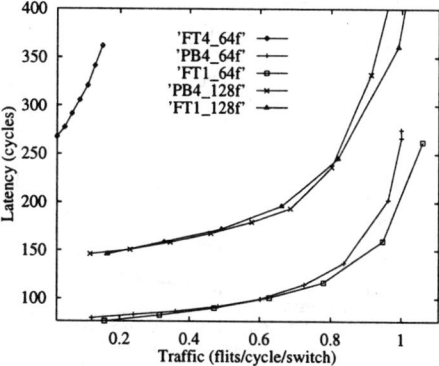

Fig. 5. Average message latency versus traffic for an irregular network with 16 switches. Message length is 16 flits. Fly time is 4 cycles.

Fig. 6. Average message latency versus traffic for a network with 16 switches. Message length is 64 and 128 flits. Fly time is 4 cycles.

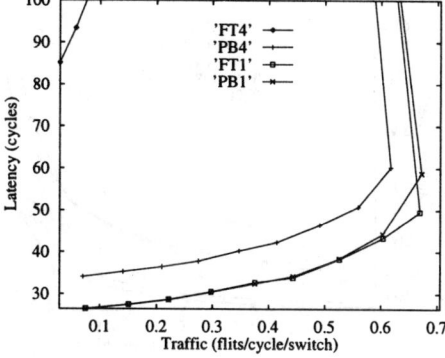
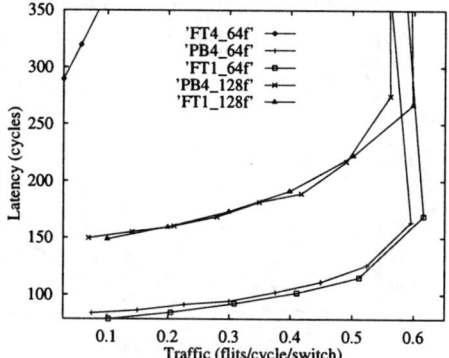

Fig. 7. Average message latency versus traffic for an irregular network with 32 switches. Message length is 16 flits. Fly time is 4 cycles.

Fig. 8. Average message latency versus traffic for a network with 32 switches. Message length is 64 and 128 flits. Fly time is 4 cycles.

multiplexing versus flit-by-flit multiplexing has also been measured. In Figure 5, PB1 shows the performance achieved by a system with short wires that does not use channel pipelining but uses the proposed flow control mechanism. It can be seen that the use of control flits does not increment the latency because the way messages are multiplexed balances this overhead. Only with high loads, the effect of control flits is noticeable.

As network size increases, the relative behavior of the new flow control mechanism remains the same. Figures 7, 8, 9 and 10 show the average message latency versus traffic for 32-switch (128 nodes) and 64-switch (256 nodes) irregular networks. It can be seen that for medium and long messages, when the network is close to saturation, the

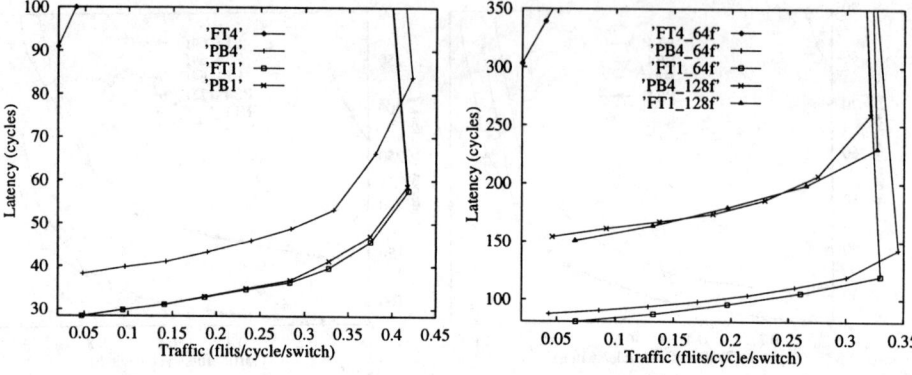

Fig. 9. Average message latency versus traffic for an irregular network with 64 switches. Message length is 16 flits. Fly time is 4 cycles.

Fig. 10. Average message latency versus traffic for a network with 64 switches. Message length is 64 and 128 flits. Fly time is 4 cycles.

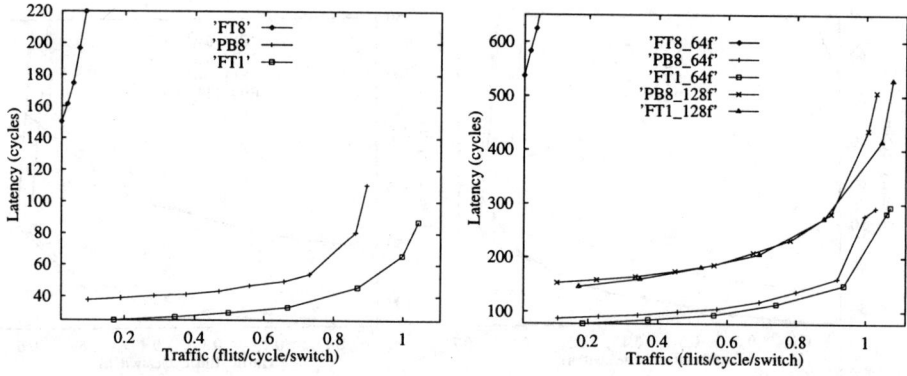

Fig. 11. Average message latency versus traffic for an irregular network with 16 switches. Message length is 16 flits. Fly time is 8 cycles.

Fig. 12. Average message latency versus traffic for a network with 16 switches. Message length is 64 and 128 flits. Fly time is 8 cycles.

use of control flits slightly reduces the maximum achievable throughput with respect to the ideal network. However, when the network is moderately loaded, the use of the new flow control mechanism provides even a lower latency than the ideal flow control mechanism for all the considered network sizes when messages are long (128-flit messages). This result confirms the improvement expected in section 3.2 when discussing about transferring blocks of flits instead multiplexing flit by flit.

In Figures 11 and 12 the average message latency when wire delay is eight times the crossbar delay is shown for a network with 16 switches. It can be seen, comparing with Figures 5 and 6, that the FT8 strategy doubles latency, as expected, with respect to FT4, and drastically reduces the maximum achievable throughput. However, the PB8 protocol slightly increases latency and reduces throughput with respect to the ideal network. With respect to PB4 we can see that pipelining channels makes message latency and network throughput largely insensitive to implementation details like wire length.

Results for the different network sizes when message length is a mixture of short and long messages (not shown in order to save space), are similar to those presented.

5 Conclusions

Networks of workstations are becoming increasingly popular as a cost-effective alternative to parallel computers. Typically, these networks connect processors using irregular topologies [2, 11]. Irregularity provides the wiring flexibility, scalability and incremental expansion capability required in this environment. Recently, we proposed a design methodology as well as fully adaptive routing algorithms for irregular topologies. These algorithms increase throughput considerably with respect to previously existing ones but require the use of virtual channels [19, 20].

In this paper we have proposed a flow control mechanism to support virtual channels when link wires have different lengths, and/or can be very long. These requirements are typical in networks of workstations with irregular topologies.

Propagation delay is proportional to wire length. Also, when links are long, they use to be narrow to keep cost at an affordable level. Hence, the use of control signals to implement flow control protocols should be limited. The proposed flow control mechanism relies on the use of channel pipelining and control flits. Channel pipelining makes clock cycle and channel bandwidth independent of wire length. Control traffic is minimized by assigning physical bandwidth to virtual channels until the corresponding message blocks or is completely transmitted. The sequence of control flits required to implement the protocol has been described in the paper.

The resulting flow control protocol has been evaluated by simulation on networks with irregular topology, using the fully adaptive routing algorithm previously developed by us. The proposed flow control protocol considerably increases performance over non-pipelined channels, as expected. Moreover, the proposed protocol performs almost as efficiently as an ideal network with short wires and flit-by-flit multiplexing. In particular, throughput is almost the same when messages are long enough (64 flits or longer). This is an important result. It means that the overhead of channel multiplexing can be kept small, therefore allowing the implementation of networks of workstations with virtual channels and fully adaptive routing. It also means that performance is not very sensitive to wire length, allowing the use of links with varying lengths.

As for future work, we plan to study the effect of adding more virtual channels per physical channel. We also plan to analyze the design of the internal crossbar, in order to adapt it to the new flow control mechanism and reduce the complexity and delay of the crossbar (results presented in this paper assume the same crossbar for both flit-by-flit transfer and block transfer). Finally, we plan to analyze the behavior of irregular networks by using traces from real applications.

References

1. M. A. Blumrich, K. Li, R. Alpert, C. Dubnicki, E. W. Felten and J. Sandberg, "Virtual memory mapped network interface for the SHRIMP multicomputer," *Proceedings of the 21st International Symposium on Computer Architecture*, pp. 142–153, April 1994.
2. N. J. Boden, D. Cohen, R. E. Felderman, A. E. Kulawik, C. L. Seitz, J. Seizovic and W. Su, "Myrinet - A gigabit per second local area network," *IEEE Micro*, pp. 29–36, February 1995.
3. R. V. Boppana and S. Chalasani, "A comparison of adaptive wormhole routing algorithms," in *Proceedings of the 20th International Symposium on Computer Architecture*, May 1993.
4. A. A. Chien and J. H. Kim, "Planar-adaptive routing: Low-cost adaptive networks for multiprocessors," in *Proc. of the 19th International Symposium on Computer Architecture*, May 1992.
5. W. J. Dally and C. L. Seitz, "Deadlock-free message routing in multiprocessor interconnection networks," *IEEE Transactions on Computers*, vol. C–36, no. 5, pp. 547–553, May 1987.
6. W. J. Dally, "Virtual-channel flow control," *IEEE Transactions on Parallel and Distributed Systems*, vol. 3, no. 2, pp. 194–205, March 1992.
7. B. V. Dao, S. Yalamanchili and J. Duato, "Architectural support for reducing communication overhead in pipelined networks," *Third International Symposium on High Performance Computer Architecture*, February 1997.
8. J. Duato, "On the design of deadlock-free adaptive routing algorithms for multicomputers: Design methodologies," in *Proceedings of Parallel Architectures and Languages Europe 91*, June 1991.
9. J. Duato, "A new theory of deadlock-free adaptive routing in wormhole networks," *IEEE Transactions on Parallel and Distributed Systems*, vol. 4, no. 12, pp. 1320–1331, December 1993.
10. T. von Eicken, D. E. Culler, S. C. Goldstein and K. E. Schauser, "Active messages: A mechanism for integrated communication and computation," in *Proceedings of the 19th International Symposium on Computer Architecture*, June 1992.
11. R. Horst, "ServerNet deadlock avoidance and fractahedral topologies," in *Proceedings of the International Parallel Processing Symposium*, pp. 274–280, April 1996.
12. J.-M. Hsu and P. Banerjee, "Performance measurement and trace driven simulation of parallel CAD and numeric applications on a hypercube multicomputer," *IEEE Transactions on Parallel and Distributed Systems*, vol. 3, no. 4, pp. 451–464, July 1992.
13. V. Karamcheti and A. A. Chien, "Do faster routers imply faster communication?," in *Proceedings of the Workshop on Parallel Computer Routing and Communication*, May 1994.
14. R. J. Littlefield, "Characterizing and tuning communications performance for real applications," in *Proceedings of the First Intel DELTA Applications Workshop*, February 1992.
15. L. M. Ni and P. K. McKinley, "A survey of wormhole routing techniques in direct networks," *IEEE Computer*, vol. 26, no. 2, pp. 62–76, February 1993.
16. W. Qiao and L. M. Ni, "Adaptive routing in irregular networks using cut-through switches," in *Proceedings of the 1996 International Conference on Parallel Processing*, August 1996.
17. M. D. Schroeder et al., "Autonet: A high-speed, self-configuring local area network using point-to-point links," Technical Report SRC research report 59, DEC, April 1990.
18. S. L. Scott and J. R. Goodman, "The Impact of Pipelined Channels on k-ary n-Cube Networks," in *IEEE Transactions on Parallel and Distributed Systems*, vol. 5, no. 1, pp. 2–16, January 1994.
19. F. Silla, M. P. Malumbres, A. Robles, P. López and J. Duato, "Efficient Adaptive Routing in Networks of Workstations with Irregular Topology," in *Proceedings of the Workshop on Communications and Architectural Support for Network-based Parallel Computing*, February 1997.
20. F. Silla and J. Duato, "Improving the Efficiency of Adaptive Routing in Networks with Irregular Topology," in *Proceedings of the 1997 Int. Conference on High Performance Computing*, December 1997.

Multicasting on Switch-Based Irregular Networks Using Multi-drop Path-Based Multidestination Worms*

Ram Kesavan and Dhabaleswar K. Panda

Dept. of Computer and Information Science
The Ohio State University, Columbus, OH 43210-1277
E-mail: {kesavan,panda}@cis.ohio-state.edu

Abstract. This paper presents a novel concept of *multi-drop path-based* multidestination message passing on switch-based irregular networks. First, the multi-drop mechanism is defined with an associated header encoding scheme, and this mechanism is used to develop path-based multidestination worms. Next, a method is proposed to identify valid multidestination paths on arbitrary irregular networks with a typical deadlock-free routing. Then, the deadlock-free property of multi-drop path-based worms is emphasized. Using the above concepts, three multicast algorithms are proposed: multi-drop path-based greedy (MDP-G), multi-drop path-based less-greedy (MDP-LG), and multi-drop path-based binomial (MDP-B). The proposed algorithms are compared with each other and with the best unicast based algorithm, the CCO [5], for a range of system and technological parameters. The MDP-LG scheme is shown to be the best to implement multicast with reduced latency.

1 Introduction

The cut-through/wormhole-routing switching technique is becoming the trend in building future parallel systems due to its inherent advantages like low-latency communication and reduced communication hardware overhead [8]. Intel Paragon, Cray T3D, Ncube, J-Machine, and Stanford DASH are systems using this switching technique. These systems have regular network topologies with various deadlock-free routing schemes. More recently, this switching technique is being applied to switch-based interconnects like Myrinet [1] and ServerNet [4] to build networks of workstations for cost-effective parallel computing. Such networks typically have irregular topology which provides flexibility to design scalable systems with incremental expansion capability. The irregularity also makes the routing on such systems quite complicated. Typically deadlock-free adaptive routing schemes [12, 13] are supported on such systems to achieve low-latency and high-bandwidth communication.

In order to to support the paradigms of distributed memory or distributed-shared memory, these systems need fast implementation of collective communi-

---

* This research is supported in part by NSF Grant MIP-9309627 and NSF Career Award MIP-9502294.

cation operations (*broadcast, multicast, global combine,* and *barrier synchronization*) [10]. Traditionally, wormhole-routed systems support only *point-to-point* (unicast) message passing. This mechanism allows a message to have exactly one destination. This leads to collective communication operations being implemented as *multiple phases* of unicast message exchange.

In order to reduce the number of phases to implement collective communication operations, a Hamiltonian Path-based scheme was proposed on MPP networks [7]. This scheme uses a modified router organization to support propagation of multidestination messages (a message with multiple destinations) and allows a message to be consumed at a destination node while being forwarded to the next node concurrently. Such an approach demonstrated that collective communication operations can be implemented on MPP networks with reduced latency. This concept was futher extended to allow multidestination worms to take row-column paths [2] and all paths conforming to the base routing using the *Base Routing Conformed Path* (BRCP) model [11].

Modern cut-through switches possess the capability of simultaneous replication of an incoming worm to multiple output ports [13]. Although this facility has been exploited for implementing broadcast by flooding the network, there has been little prior work on using this capability for arbitrary multicast. Recently, a multiport encoding scheme has been proposed to construct multidestination worms in multistage interconnection networks [14]. Similarily, a bit-string encoding scheme and the associate architectural issues in supporting multidestination worms have been discussed in [16]. However, these schemes use the tree-based mechanism. This leads to a challenge of designing an efficient path-based multidestination message passing mechanism on irregular networks. This challenge includes design of an efficient header encoding scheme, a scheme for constructing such worms, determining valid paths in the system, and designing efficient multicast algorithms.

In this paper we take on the above challenges. First, the multi-drop mechanism with an associated header encoding is proposed. Next, the path-based multidestination message passing mechanism is developed on switch-based irregular networks. A method to identify valid multi-drop paths with respect to the Autonet routing is proposed and proved to be deadlock-free. Then, we propose three new multicast algorithms using the proposed path-based multidestination message passing mechanism: a) Multi-drop Path-based Greedy (MDP-G) algorithm, b) Multi-drop Path-based Less-Greedy (MDP-LG) algorithm, and c) Multi-drop Path-based Binomial (MDP-B) algorithm. These algorithms are evaluated over a range of system parameters and compared with the best unicast-based multicast algorithm, the CCO algorithm [5]. The MDP-LG algorithm shows benefits of 50%, 40%, and 20% for multicast latency when compared to the CCO, MDP-G, MDP-B algorithms, respectively. These results clearly demonstrate that the multi-drop path-based multidestination mechanism promises significant potential to implement fast and efficient collective communication operations in future switch-based irregular systems.

The rest of the paper is organized as follows. Section 2 provides an overview of switch-based irregular networks and deadlock-free routing on such networks. Section 3 describes the basic concepts of multidestination message passing. Section 4 presents the multi-drop path-based multidestination mechanism. A method of creating valid multi-drop worms on irregular networks is described in Section 5. Section 6 discusses three new multicast algorithms. Performance evaluation results of these algorithms are presented and compared with those of the CCO algorithm in Section 7. Finally, concluding remarks are made in Section 8.

2 Switch-Based Irregular Networks

In this section we provide a brief overview of switch-based irregular networks and focus on a typical deadlock-free routing on such networks.

2.1 Irregular Interconnection

Figure 1(a) shows a typical parallel system using switch-based interconnect with irregular topology. Such a network consists of a set of switches where each switch can have a set of bidirectional ports. The system in the figure consists of eight switches with eight ports per switch. Some of the ports in each switch are connected to processors, some ports are connected to ports of other switches to provide connectivity between the processors, and some ports are left open for further connections. The topology of the network is typically irregular and can be represented by a graph $G = (V,E)$ where V is the set of switches, and E is the set of bidirectional links between the switches. Figure 1(b) shows the interconnection graph for the irregular network in Fig. 1(a). The switches can implement different types of switching techniques: wormhole, virtual cut-through, or ATM. These switches can also implement different routing schemes [1, 4, 12, 13]. In this paper we focus on wormhole switches and assume the Autonet [13] routing scheme due to its simplicity and its commercial implementation. The scheme is briefly described below.

2.2 The Autonet Routing

In the Autonet routing scheme [13], a breadth-first spanning tree (BFS) on G is first computed using a distributed algorithm. The edges of G can be partitioned into *tree edges* and *cross edges*. According to the property of BFS trees, a cross edge does not connect two switches which are at a difference of more than one level in the tree. Deadlock-free routing is based on a loop-free assignment of direction to the operational links. In particular, the "up" end of each link is defined as: 1) the end whose switch is closer to the root in the spanning tree; or 2) the end whose switch has the lower UID, if both ends are at switches at the same tree level. Figure 1(c) shows the BFS spanning tree embedded on graph G shown in Fig. 1(b). The assignment of the "up" direction to the links on this network is illustrated. The "down" direction is along the reverse direction of the link.

To eliminate deadlocks while still allowing all links to be used, this routing uses the following up/down rule: a legal route must traverse zero or more links in the "up" direction followed by zero or more links in the "down" direction. In other words, a packet may never traverse a link along the "up" direction

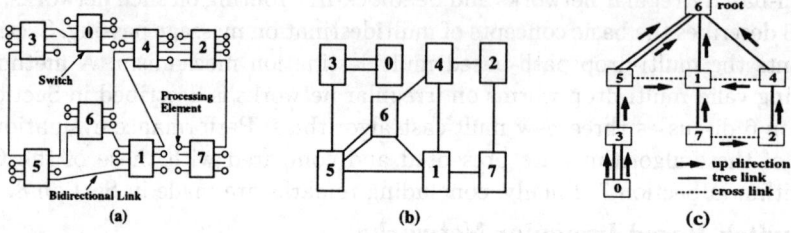

Fig. 1. (a) An example system with switch-based interconnect and irregular topology, (b) the corresponding interconnection graph G, and (c) the BFS spanning tree rooted at node 6 of G.

after having traversed one in the "down" direction. Therefore, this routing is also called *up*/down** routing. In order to implement the above routing, each switch has an indexed forwarding table. When a worm reaches a switch, the destination address is captured from the header flit of the incoming worm. This address is concatenated with the incoming port number and the result is used to index the switch's forwarding table. The table lookup returns the outgoing port number that the worm should be routed through. The forwarding tables can be constructed to support both minimal and non-minimal adaptive routing. During configuration the current implementation of Autonet switches constructs tables to support minimal adaptive routing [13]. In this paper, we assume that the forwarding tables allow only legal routes with the minimum hop count.

3 Multidestination Message Passing

In this section, we describe the basic concepts of multidestination message passing and path-based multidestination worms. Next, we discuss tree-based multidestination worms on switch-based irregular networks and show the motivation for path-based multidestination worms on such networks.

3.1 Multidestination Message Passing and Path-Based Worms

The concept of wormhole message passing with multiple destinations was first introduced by Lin and Ni for [7] Hamiltonian meshes. Then, multidestination message passing was introduced [11] for k-ary n-cube networks with different base routing schemes. These schemes were proposed for regular direct networks typical of MPPs. In such networks each node consists of a router and a processor. The processor is connected to the router through a set of injection and consumption channels. The routers are connected in some given topology. A path-based multidestination worm in such networks carries the *ids* of multiple destinations in its header. After being injected into the network by the source, the worm is routed based on the first destination in the header. When the worm reaches the router of an intermediate destination, the address of the destination is removed from the header, and the next destination is used to route the worm onwards. As the data flits pass through routers corresponding to intermediate destinations, they are forwarded to the next router and absorbed to the processor. The final destination absorbs the complete worm.

3.2 Tree-Based Multidestination Worms

The above path-based multidestination mechanism (with a header of destination ids) cannot be directly applied to switch-based networks because there is no one-to-one correspondence between switches/routers and processors on such networks. Thus, a tree-based mechanism [3, 9, 14, 16] has been proposed which allows a multidestination worm to replicate at switches with multiple replicas of the worm following different paths in the network. In this approach, the switches possess the capability to replicate flits of an arriving multidestination worm to multiple output ports. The issues of synchronous and asynchronous replication of flits in a deadlock-free manner within the switch have been discussed in detail in [14, 16]. Figure 2 shows an example of a tree-based multidestination worm for MINs using the *multiport encoding scheme* [14]. It must be noted that such a worm branches out in a symmetric fashion. For example, switches s_1 and s_2 replicate to output ports 0, 2, and 3, and switches s_3, s_4, s_5, and s_6 replicate to output ports 0 and 2. The symmetry is required because all replicas of a multiport encoded multidestination worm created at a switch must possess the same header information.

It can be easily observed that it is difficult to create such multiport encoded worms for irregular networks. In [16] the authors show how precomputed *reachability information* at switches can be used to generate asymmetric multidestination worms with *bit-string encoded* headers. The authors have also extended this bit-string encoded mechanism to irregular switch-based networks [15]. However, computation of reachability information at each switch for an arbitrary switch-based irregular network may be quite a non-trivial task. Therefore, the question arises whether path-based multidestination mechanism can be adapted to switch-based irregular networks using the replication capability at the switches. The challenges to doing this are in deriving solutions to the following problems: a) the concept of path-based worms on a switch-based network, b) a suitable header encoding scheme, c) defining valid paths on a given base routing scheme, d) prevention of deadlock due to coexistence of such worms with unicast worms, and e) developing multicast algorithms. In the next sections we look at these problems, and propose solutions.

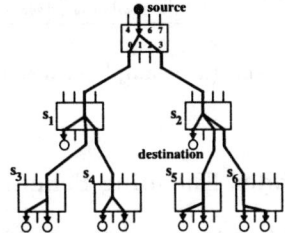

Fig. 2. Example of tree-based multidestination worm for MINs using the multiport encoding mechanism [14].

4 Multi-drop Path-Based Multidestination Worms

In this section, we describe the concept of multi-drop path-based multidestination worms and a new header encoding scheme for such worms.

4.1 The Multi-drop Mechanism

In this mechanism, the capability at switches to replicate incoming worms and to forward the copies to several output ports simultaneously is used, but the replication is restricted. The multi-drop mechanism is defined as follows.

Definition 1 *A multidestination worm is defined as a multi-drop worm if a) it can replicate to multiple outgoing ports on a traversed switch, b) no more than one of these ports is connected to another switch, and c) the remaining are connected to processors (destinations).*

Such a mechanism allows easy construction of paths (of switches) in an irregular network. It simplifies handling of deadlock problems because a worm does not get replicated into several worms, branched over multiple paths. It also allows simplified header encoding by using a variation of the all-destination encoding [7, 11] where 'destination' ids are replaced by 'switch' ids and ids of 'destinations connected to a switch'. Figure 3(a) shows an example of a multi-drop path-based multidestination worm. If we abstract a switch-based irregular network to the interconnection graph G, then multi-drop worms can be abstracted to strict path-based multidestination worms on G. The path of a multi-drop worm is defined by the set of inter-switch links taken by the worm. From this point on, we refer to a path as a sequence of inter-switch links. Although the number of destinations covered in a single step by such a multi-drop multidestination worm can be less than that covered by a worm using the tree-based mechanism, this scheme is much simpler. It also requires minimal modification to the switch and results in low complexity for creation of multidestination worms.

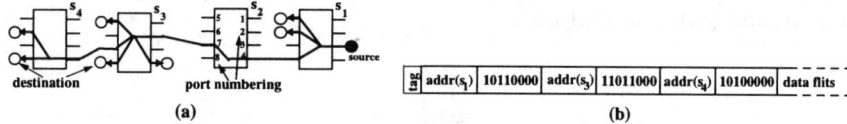

Fig. 3. The Multi-drop mechanism: (a) example of a multidestination worm and (b) the header encoding.

4.2 The Multi-drop Header Encoding Scheme

This new scheme is a hybrid of the *all-destination* [7, 11] and *multiport* [14] encoding schemes. It makes use of the fact that switches too have unique addresses in a typical switch-based irregular network like Autonet [13]. The current implementation of the Autonet switch can route messages addressed to a particular switch. The multi-drop worm header encoding for each set of destinations on a switch contains the switch address followed by the multiport encoding of destinations for that switch. A tag bit can distinguish whether it is a unicast or multidestination worm. Figure 3(b) shows the multi-drop scheme encoded header of the worm shown in Fig. 3(a). Since switch s_1 is the first switch with destinations on it, the header encoding begins with the address of s_1. The following 8 bits encode the information about which output ports the worm replicates to. The bits correspond to output ports 1 to 8 from right to left. In the first switch, the worm is intended to be replicated to two destinations and one outgoing link to switch s_2. Similarly, information about switches s_3 and s_4 is encoded in the header.

In this scheme, the source does not have to completely specify the route taken by the worm - intermediate switches with no destinations can be excluded. Since the routing tables at the switches are used to route a worm, any adaptivity provided by the underlying routing scheme is fully utilized between any two consecutive participating switches. The length of the header of a worm only increases linearly with the number of participating switches in the worm, and not the number of hops traversed by the worm or the number of destinations. Also, this new scheme requires only a minor change in the routing logic of a switch which already provides the replication facility, like the Autonet switch.

Now, the challenge is in defining valid paths on a given base routing scheme, and prevention of deadlock due to coexistence of such worms with unicast worms. In the next section we solve this problem in the context of Autonet routing.

5 Creation of Multi-drop Worms on Irregular Networks

A multi-drop path-based multidestination worm needs to get routed in a *piece-wise* manner from the source switch to the final switch. This raises the following fundamental problems at any intermediate switch: a) it should be feasible for the multidestination worm to find a path leading to the next switch in its list and b) the piece-wise routing of a multidestination worm should not violate the routing scheme to prevent deadlock. In this section, we first propose a method to identify valid multi-drop multidestination paths which conform to the base Autonet routing on an arbitrary irregular graph. Then, we discuss the requirements for deadlock-freedom.

5.1 Valid Multidestination Paths with the Autonet Routing

Let us define the list of participating switches, $L_{sw}(w)$, of a multi-drop multidestination worm w as follows. $L_{sw}(w)$ consists of switches directly connected to the destinations of w, in the order in which the corresponding destinations will be covered. Let us denote the jth processor on the ith switch as $p_{i,j}$. If w starts from source processor $p_{s,1}$ and covers the processors $p_{1,1}, p_{1,2}, \ldots, p_{2,1}, p_{2,2}, \ldots, p_{n,m}$, in that order, then $L_{sw}(w)$ is given by the switches $< s_s, s_1, s_2, \ldots, s_n >$. Therefore, generating a valid multi-drop multidestination path for a worm w on an arbitrary switch-based irregular network N is equivalent to generating a valid path which covers the switches in $L_{sw}(w)$, in that order, on the interconnection graph G of that network.

In our recent work [5], we have defined the concept of a partial ordered chain (POC) with the specific purpose of constructing an ordering among switches in an irregular network to reduce link contention between two messages of the same multicast using *unicast* message passing. In this paper, we use this concept to construct valid multi-drop multidestination paths. The POC is defined as follows:

Definition 2 *A partial ordered chain (POC) is any ordered list of switches $< s_1, s_2, \ldots, s_n >$, where s_i is connected to s_{i+1} by a "down" tree link (from the BFS spanning tree) or a "down" cross link connecting switches at different levels of the BFS spanning tree [5].*

It can be easily observed that the path of a multi-drop multidestination worm can possibly lie on some POC. Since up*/down* routing is deadlock-free, such multi-drop multidestination worms can also implement deadlock-free multicast. This leads to:

Theorem 1 *A multi-drop path-based multidestination worm w, where $L_{sw}(w) = < s_s, s_1, s_2, \ldots, s_n >$ and the switches $s_1, s_2, \ldots, s_n$ lie on some POC, in that particular order, always follows a valid up*/down* path and introduces no deadlocks.*

Due to lack of space, we are not able to present the proof of this Theorem here. Interested readers are requested to read [6] for the detailed proof.

It must be noted that the concept of valid multi-drop multidestination worms using POCs on Autonet routing can also be extended to the case when the routing tables support non-minimal paths. In this case, multi-drop multidestination worms are not routed using the routing tables at intermediate switches, instead the source specifies the exact route (all switches in a path) in the header encoding of the worm. Such a header encoding for the sample multi-drop worm in Fig. 3(a) is shown in Fig 4(a) (it includes the address of s_2 with a single port replication). It can be easily observed that the switch addresses in this encoding is redundant information, and the header encoding can be further simplified by dropping the switch addresses completely, and retaining only the multiport encoding, as shown in Fig. 4(b).

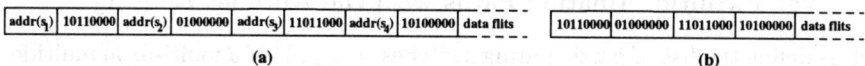

Fig. 4. Header encoding of the multi-drop worm of Fig. 3(a) for routing tables supporting nonminimal routing: (a) each switch in the route is specified with its multiport encoding and (b) an enhanced encoding by eliminating the switch addresses.

5.2 Deadlock-Freedom

It is shown in [14] that asynchronous replication with buffers at least as large as the largest multidestination worm ensures deadlock freedom on multistage interconnection networks for tree-based multidestination worms. The Autonet switch provides similar guarantee with input buffer size of 4096 bytes [13]. (This feature is provided to prevent deadlock that arises in the case of broadcast worms which use the replication mechanism at the switches to flood the network.) Since multi-drop worms form a subset of all tree-based worms, addition of multi-drop worms cannot cause deadlock in an Autonet switch-based network provided the message length is less than the given buffer size.

Interestingly, the buffer requirement for deadlock-freedom with multi-drop worms can be actually lowered depending on the scheduling policy used at the switch. It can be shown that for the *centralized* scheduling policy of the Autonet switch, multi-drop path based multidestination worms using the valid paths as defined in Section 5.1 is deadlock-free with even single flit buffers at each input port of a switch. Due to lack of space, we are not able to present this proof here. Interested readers are requested to read [6] for the detailed proof.

6 Multicast Algorithms

In this section we propose three multicast algorithms using the multi-drop path-based mechanism. All these algorithms use the POC concept to construct as many longest POCs as possible from the participating switches and group these POCs in some hierarchy to implement multicast. Let us first look at how the POCs are constructed.

6.1 Construction of POCs

In [5], we described a method to construct as many longest POCs as possible from the participating switches of a multicast. We explain the method using an example multicast. Interested readers can refer to [5] for details.

Figure 5(a) shows the BFS graph of a sample irregular network. Let us assume that there are two processors connected to each switch of the irregular graph and let the processors on the switch numbered i be labelled as $p_{i,1}$ and $p_{i,2}$. Let us consider a multicast with the source as $p_{10,1}$ and two destinations on each switch except switches 10 and 6. In the first step, a depth-first search (DFS) is applied on the BFS spanning tree, starting with the root node r and considering only the down links specified in Definition 2. This is to facilitate the construction of the longest POCs. Figure 5(b) shows the DFS tree, T, on the sample irregular network. A participating switch is one with at least one participating processor connected to it. The resultant DAG, T, from the DFS can be reduced to a DAG, T', which contains only the participating switches. Fig. 5(c) shows the reduced DAG T'. Each switch is given a weight equal to the number of participating processors connected to it and to all its descendent switches. Subsequently, chains of switches are stripped off from T' according to their weights. In other words, the heaviest chain gets stripped first from T', and the lightest the last. Figure 5(d) shows the obtained set of chains, C. In all these figures, the participating switches are highlighted.

6.2 The Multi-drop Path-Based Greedy (MDP-G) Algorithm

This algorithm uses a greedy approach on the set of POCs generated by the above steps, to implement multicast. First, the source node covers the destination

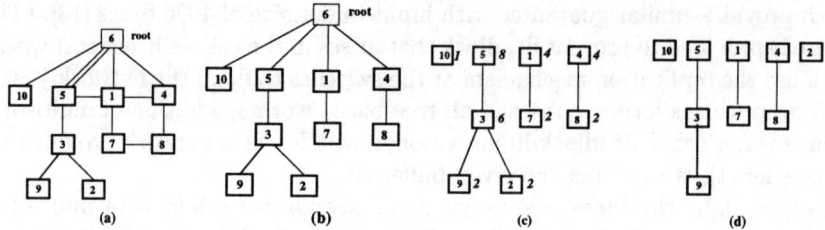

Fig. 5. Illustrating steps for construction of POCs: a) sample BFS graph of an irregular network, b) DFS tree T, c) DAG T' and the associated switch weights, and (d) the set C of chains.

processors on the switches of the heaviest chain with a single multi-drop worm. Then, in each successive step, the destinations that have been covered in previous steps cover destinations on chains that have not been covered yet (in C) using multi-drop worms. Figure 6(a) shows these steps for the example multicast: $p_{10,1}$ covers all the destinations on switches 5, 3, and 9 with a single multi-drop worm in the first step. In the second step, $p_{10,1}$ covers all destinations on switches 1 and 7 using a multidestination worm, $p_{5,1}$ covers all destinations on switches 4 and 8, and $p_{5,2}$ covers all destinations on switch 2. Therefore, the multicast completes in two steps.

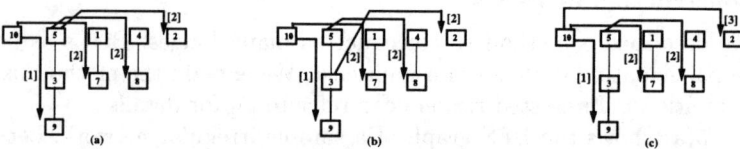

Fig. 6. Illustrating the multicast algorithms for the sample multicast of Fig. 5: a) the MDP-G algorithm, b) the MDP-LG algorithm, and c) the MDP-B algorithm. The numbers in brackets denote communication step numbers.

Since at each step maximum possible destinations are being covered using multi-drop worms constructed with longest possible POCs, this algorithm takes minimum number of steps to execute. However, it has the drawback that the number of multi-drop worms starting from a single switch might be large leading to link contention.

6.3 The Multi-drop Path-Based Less Greedy (MDP-LG) Algorithm

We propose the MDP-LG algorithm to address the above drawback. This algorithm also uses the output from the POC construction method, like the MDP-G algorithm. Following the first step, only one destination from each switch that has been covered chooses chains that have not been covered yet (in C), and covers them using multidestination worms. Since all destinations covered in the particular step do not send out worms, this scheme is given the name Less Greedy. As shown in Fig. 6(b), $p_{10,1}$ covers all the destination on switches 5, 3, and 9 with a multi-drop worm in the first step. In the second step, $p_{10,1}$ covers all destinations on switches 1 and 7, $p_{5,1}$ covers all destinations on switches 4 and 8, and $p_{3,1}$ covers all destinations on switch 2. This algorithm may take more steps to complete, but it reduces link contention by making sure that only one multi-drop worm starts from a switch during one step.

6.4 The Multi-drop Path-Based Binomial (MDP-B) Algorithm

We propose the MDP-B algorithm to further reduce link contention in the MDP-LG algorithm. Again, the MDP-B algorithm starts the same way as the MDP-G algorithm with the construction of the POCs. Following the first step, only the source processor and the leader processor of each chain are involved in sending worms. The leader processor is chosen as a destination processor on the first switch of the chain. The source covers all destinations on one chain in the first step using a multi-drop worm. In the second step, the source and the leader of the covered chain cover all destinations on two other chains using multi-drop worms, and so on. As shown in Fig. 6(c), $p_{10,1}$ covers all the destination on switches 5, 3, and 9 with a multi-drop worm in the first step. In the second step, $p_{10,1}$ covers all destinations on switches 1 and 7 with a single worm, and $p_{5,1}$ covers all destinations on switches 4 and 8 using a single worm. In the third step, $p_{10,1}$ covers all destinations on switch 2. Therefore, this algorithm requires $\lceil log_2|C| \rceil$ steps, where C is the set of POCs constructed at the start of this algorithm. But, the link contention as compared to the MDP-G and MDP-LG algorithms is reduced, since there are no two destinations on the same chain trying to send out worms at the same time.

The proposed algorithms can be implemented either at the library routines on host processor or at the network interface card of the source node of the multicast using software. In either case, information about the topology of the network is available to the communication layer, like in the IBM SP amd Myrinet.

7 Simulation Experiments and Results

We performed simulation experiments to evaluate and compare performance of the MDP-G, MDP-LG, MDP-B, and CCO [5] algorithms for single multicast. A flit-level wormhole-routed simulator WORMULSim was used to model the irregular network. For all simulation experiments, we assumed system and technological parameters representing the current trend in technology. The following default parameters were used: t_s (communication start-up time) = 10 microseconds, t_{phy} (link propagation time) = 10 nanoseconds, t_{route} (routing delay at switch) = 40 ns, t_{sw} (switching time across the router crossbar for a flit) = 10 ns, t_{sched} (time for scheduler to process a request) = 20 ns, t_{inj} (time to inject a flit into network) = 10 ns, and t_{cons} (time to consume a flit from network) = 10 ns. For all experiments (unless otherwise stated) we assumed the following default system configuration: a 256 processor system interconnected by 64 eight-port switches and network having 75% connectivity, as defined in [5]. The default message length was assumed to be 128 flits.

We performed several experiments to study the impact of system size, message length, communication start-up time, switch size, and degree of connectivity on single multicast latency for varying sizes of destination sets. The destinations and network topologies were generated randomly. For each data point, the multicast latency was averaged over 30 different sets of destinations for each of 10 different network configurations. The 95% confidence intervals generated for the data points were observed to be extremely narrow.

7.1 Effect of System Size

We simulated the four multicast algorithms on four different system configurations with 64, 128, 256 and 512 processors, respectively. Figure 7 shows these results. It can be observed that the MDP-LG algorithm performs the best for almost all system sizes and destinations. As system size increases, the MDP-LG algorithm shows steady benefits compared to the CCO algorithm. For example, on a 512 processor system with 256 destinations, the reduction in multicast latency achieved by the MPD-LG algorithm is around 50%, 40%, and 20% compared to the CCO, MPD-G, and MDP-B algorithms, respectively.

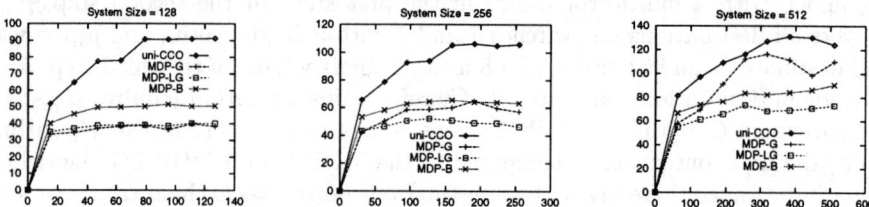

Fig. 7. Multicast latency (in microseconds) vs. number of destinations for three different system configurations: 128, 256, and 512 processors.

As expected, the multi-drop algorithms outperform the CCO algorithm. Since the number of destinations covered in one step is increased by using multidestination worms, the total number of steps for the completion of the multicast algorithm is reduced. As discussed in Section 6, the MDP-G suffers from link contention at higher destination set sizes since multiple destinations on the same switch send worms simultaneously, and this leads to severe link contention. The MDP-B algorithm incurs less link contention, but undergoes more number of steps, and hence it is outperformed by the MDP-LG which strikes a balance between the number of steps and link contention. It can also be observed that as the number of destinations increase, the latency for some multi-drop algorithms reduces. This is because with increase in multicast set size more destinations can be grouped along each multi-drop path. This results in fewer and longer POCs being constructed which leads to fewer communication steps. Such a property is inherent to multidestination based schemes [11].

7.2 Effect of Message Length

We studied the impact of message length on the four algorithms. Four different message lengths - 128, 256, 512, and 1024 flits, on a 256 processor system with default parameters were considered. Figure 8 shows the respective results. It can be easily observed that as message length increases the link contention effect dominates the results, and the MDP-B algorithm outperforms the remaining algorithms although it requires more steps.

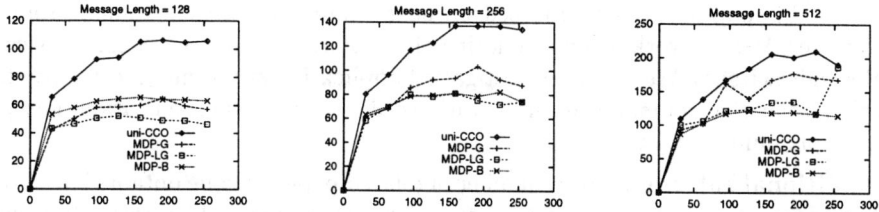

Fig. 8. Multicast latency (in microseconds) vs. number of destinations for three different message lengths: 128, 256, and 512 flits.

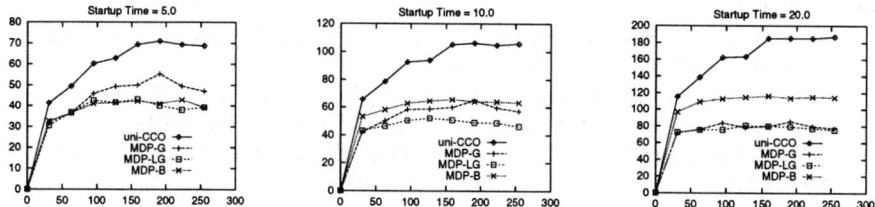

Fig. 9. Multicast latency (in microseconds) vs. number of destinations for three different communication start-up times: 5.0, 10.0, and 20.0 microseconds.

7.3 Effect of Communication Start-Up Time

We studied the effect of communication start-up time on the performance of the four algorithms. The default 256 processor system configuration was used with three different communication start-up times: 5.0, 10.0, and 20.0 microseconds. Figure 9 shows the respective multicast latencies. It can be observed that with higher communication start-up time, the MDP-G and MDP-LG algorithms outperform the other two algorithms. This is expected, because for a given message length, higher start-up times reduce the effect of link contention, and the MDP-G and MDP-LG algorithms take the minimum steps.

Due to lack of space, we are not able to present the results of variation in switch size and connectivity. Similar benefits were observed by the multi-drop algorithms in these experiments too. Interested readers are requested to refer to [6] for these results.

8 Conclusions

In this paper we have proposed a new multi-drop path-based multidestination message passing mechanism on switch-based irregular networks. A method to identify valid multi-drop paths with respect to a typical deadlock-free routing on arbitrary irregular networks has been proposed. Using this new mechanism three multicast algorithms, MDP-G, MDP-LG, and MDP-B, have been developed. These algorithms have been simulated and compared with each other and the best unicast-based multicast algorithm, the CCO algorithm. Compared to the CCO algorithm, the MDP-LG algorithm shows an improvement in multicast latency up to a factor of 60%. These results demonstrate significant potential for the multi-drop multidestination mechanism to be applied to current and future switch-based irregular networks.

In this paper, we have focused on single multicast with wormhole routed switches. We are working on evaluating the performance of our schemes for cut-through switches. We are also investigating application of this new mechanism for other collective communication operations like barrier synchronization, gather, multiple multicast, etc.

Additional Information: A number of related papers can be obtained from the homepage of *Parallel Architecture and Communication* (PAC) research group. The URL is http://www.cis.ohio-state.edu/~panda/pac.html.

References

1. N. J. Boden, D. Cohen, and et al. Myrinet: A Gigabit-per-Second Local Area Network. *IEEE Micro*, pp 29–35, Feb 1995.
2. R. V. Boppana, S. Chalasani, and C. S. Raghavendra. On Multicast Wormhole Routing in Multicomputer Networks. In *SPDP*, pp 722–729, 1994.
3. C. M. Chiang and L. M. Ni. Deadlock-Free Multi-Head Wormhole Routing. In *First High Performance Computing-Asia*, 1995.
4. R. Horst. ServerNet Deadlock Avoidance and Fractahedral Topologies. In *IPPS*, pp 274–280, 1996.
5. R. Kesavan, K. Bondalapati, and D. K. Panda. Multicast on Irregular Switch-based Networks with Wormhole Routing. In *HPCA-3*, pp 48–57, 1997.
6. R. Kesavan and D. K. Panda. Multicasting on Switch-based Irregular Networks using Multi-drop Path-based Multidestination Worms. Technical Report OSU-CISRC-4/97-TR21, Mar 1997.
7. X. Lin and L. M. Ni. Deadlock-free Multicast Wormhole Routing in Multicomputer Networks. In *ISCA*, pp 116–124, 1991.
8. L. Ni and P. K. McKinley. A Survey of Wormhole Routing Techniques in Direct Networks. *IEEE Computer*, pp 62–76, Feb 1993.
9. Lionel Ni. Should Scalable Parallel Computers Support Efficient Hardware Multicasting? In *ICPP Workshop on Challenges for Parallel Processing*, pp 2–7, 1995.
10. D. K. Panda. Issues in Designing Efficient and Practical Algorithms for Collective Communication in Wormhole-Routed Systems. In *ICPP Workshop on Challenges for Parallel Processing*, pp 8–15, 1995.
11. D. K. Panda, S. Singal, and R. Kesavan. Multidestination Message Passing in Wormhole k-ary n-cube Networks with Base Routing Conformed Paths. Technical Report OSU-CISRC-12/95-TR54, Dec 1995. *IEEE TPDS*, to appear.
12. W. Qiao and L. M. Ni. Adaptive Routing in Irregular Networks Using Cut-Through Switches. In *ICPP*, pp I:52–60, 1996.
13. M. D. Schroeder et al. Autonet: A High-speed, Self-configuring Local Area Network Using Point-to-point Links. SRC research report 59, DEC, Apr 1990.
14. R. Sivaram, D. K. Panda, and C. B. Stunkel. Efficient Broadcast and Multicast on Multistage Interconnection Networks using Multiport Encoding. In *SPDP*, pp 36–45, 1996.
15. R. Sivaram, D. K. Panda, and C. B. Stunkel. Multicasting in Irregular Networks with Cut-Through Switches using Tree-Based Multidestination Worms. In *PCRCW '97*, 1997.
16. C. B. Stunkel, R. Sivaram, and D. K. Panda. Implementing Multidestination Worms in Switch-Based Parallel Systems: Architectural Alternatives and their Impact. In *ISCA-24*, pp 50–61, 1997.

Power/Performance Trade-offs for Direct Networks[†]

Chirag S. Patel, Sek M. Chai, Sudhakar Yalamanchili and David E. Schimmel

School of Electrical and Computer Engineering
Georgia Institute of Technology
Atlanta, Georgia 30332-0250
e-mail: sudha@ece.gatech.edu
Fax: (404) 894-9959

Abstract

High performance portable and space-borne systems continue to demand increasing computation speeds while concurrently attempting to satisfy size, weight, and power constraints. As multiprocessor systems become necessary to satisfy the computational requirements, interconnection network design will become subject to similar constraints. This paper focuses on the design of multiprocessor interconnection networks under power constraints. We analyze and study the relationship between the no-load message latency and system parameters such as network dimension, channel width, distance, and available power to determine guidelines for multiprocessor interconnection network designs. This study is an extension and application of the model developed in [8], and provides a number of interesting results: i) we have observed that under a fixed power constraint, the network dimension which achieves minimal latency is a slowly growing function of system size, ii) as we increase the available power per node for a fixed system size, the dimension at which message latency is minimized increases, iii) the overall message latency is very sensitive to the distribution of power between driving inter-router channels and switching data through the intra-router datapaths. The paper concludes with a summary of trade-offs predicted by the model and proposals for validating the model.

Keywords: multiprocessor interconnection network, power constraint modeling, low power embedded systems, spaceborne systems.

1.0 Introduction

The design of modern high performance multiprocessor interconnection networks is a process of optimizing the performance of the network in the presence of implementation constraints. Past analysis has focused on constraints such as wiring area [3], pin out [9], wire delays [6], and switching speeds [1]. This paper focuses on a similar analysis in the presence of a constraint on the available power.

The motivation for this research came from an analysis of the computational requirements of future deep space missions. Unoptimized designs have power dissipations

---

[†]. This research was partially supported by the NASA Jet Propulsion Laboratory under contract 960586.

reported in the tens of watts. This is clearly infeasible for on-board computing in deep space missions where power budgets for computations are on the order of several watts. We need a comprehensive approach to system design that involves low power technologies, compatible system level design, and algorithms that support activity minimization. The explosive growth of telecommunications applications and portable computing has also produced a need for minimizing the consumption of limited available power. As the computational requirements of space and portable systems grow, we will begin to see architectures that employ multiple processors. The interconnection network is a major consumer of power in these systems and must come under the same scrutiny as the rest of the system if we are to be able to design networks that can be efficient consumers of power. This study focuses on the low power optimizations that can be achieved by varying the topology and channel widths of the network. We wish to study the sensitivities to application characteristics such as message injection rates, and communication/computation ratios.

The following section describes concepts for discussing the relationships between application characteristics, network topologies, physical implementation parameters, and available power. This model is used to study the trade-offs between the no-load message latency and available power in Section 4.0. The paper concludes with a summary of trade-offs and our future research directions.

2.0 Power Dissipation in Pipelined Networks

The class of networks considered in this paper are the torus connected, bidirectional, k-ary n-cubes. A k-ary n-cube is a network with n dimensions and k processors in each dimension. In torus connected k-ary n-cubes, each processor is connected to its immediate neighbors modulo k in every dimension. Routing within each dimension is orthogonal to routing in other dimensions. The mesh networks differ from tori in that there are no wrap around links in each dimension. Most contemporary parallel machines utilizes such networks or variants including the Intel Paragon [12], Cray T3 models D [10] and E [11], and Ametek 2010.

Power is the rate of energy dissipation in a system. In a typical VLSI CMOS circuit, this energy is consumed in switching transistors, in leakage due to circuit device structures, and in holding the logic state of a circuit. The rate at which this energy is used by a system determines its power dissipation. We assume that a network consumes approximately the same quantity of energy to transport a message to its destination independent of the switching technique used (i.e. either packet switching or virtual cut-through switching may be employed). This analysis assumes no contention in the network. A model of contention is necessary to accurately reflect power consumption in active networks. However, as a first step we study the basic relationships between topology, power and physical constraints. We will then seek to extend this model to incorporate the effects of contention within the network.

The latency of message delivery and the dissipated power are related by the architecture of the network. For example, a network architecture with wide channel widths can transport data packets in less time compared to a network architecture with smaller channel

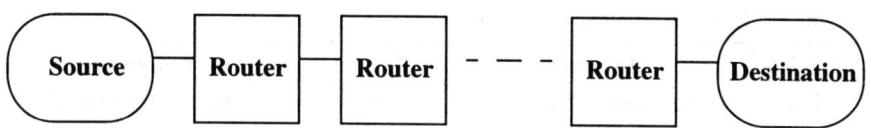

Figure 1. Interconnected Sequence of Routers in a Network

widths. However, the wider channel network will consume energy at a higher rate because of the larger data buffers and wider buses. For example, consider the pipelined transmission of a single message across multiple routers as illustrated in Figure 1. Since our power model relies on switching transistors, we can model the network routers with a certain number of transistors, with a distinct transistor count for the routing/arbitration, switching unit, and line drivers. To find the peak power consumed during the pipelined transmission of a message, we can visualize a sequence of network nodes from the source to destination. Peak power dissipation occurs when the largest number of transistors switch, and this event might be expected to occur when the pipelined message is spread across the maximum number of routers. We use this view of power dissipation in the pipelined network to model the peak power dissipation during a message transmission. This view of power consumption is a *message-centered* view. The total available power is regarded as being distributed to each transmitted message, and each such message has a certain available power to navigate through the network towards the destination.

Another view of power dissipation involves a *router-centered* view. For each router in the system, a subset of the total available power is allocated for routing and arbitration, switching, and driving inter-router channels. From this perspective, each router is allocated a power budget to locally switch messages.

3.0 Power and Latency Models

From a system performance point of view messages encounter three distinct delays: routing delay, switching delay, and inter-router channel or wire delay. Routing delay is the time it takes for the routing and arbitration unit (RAU) to make a decision in routing the incoming messages. The switching delay is the time it takes to transport a flow control unit through the crossbar; and the wire delay is the time it takes for the message to be transferred across the channel between routers. To route a message from one router to the next, all of the units — RAU, switch, and channel — dissipate power. Therefore, in our model the critical path for a message involves the routing & arbitration unit, switching logic and inter-router wire delays. We will examine the power and time delays associated with each component. The parameters used in the model section are defined in Table 1. The following assumptions are made in the derivation of the model.

1. Wormhole switching for message transmission

2. The total power dissipated in the node is a function of power dissipation in the routing and arbitration unit, internal switch, and the intra-router wire. Note that in this model any power dissipation in writing and reading buffers is included in the switching power.

Table 1. List of symbols and their definitions.

Symbol	Description	Symbol	Description
C_{in}	Input gate capacitance	P_r	Power dissipated in the RAU
C_o	Output capacitance of minimum transistor in the cascaded drivers	P_s	Power dissipated in the switch
C_{ox}	Gate oxide capacitance	P_{sc}	Short circuit power consumption
C_p	Next stage capacitance in the driver chain	P_s	Power dissipated in the wire
C_{pad}	Output pad capacitance	P_t	Total power dissipated in the system
C_t	Total capacitance of the node	R_o	Output resistance of minimum transistor in cascaded drivers
C_w	Total wiring capacitance	R_w	Wiring resistance
D	Average distance or hops	S_n	Delay constant of nFET transistor
f_i	Frequency of the driver	T_{clk}	Period of the clock in the driver chain
f_s	Frequency of the switch	T_{chain}	Time delay in the driver chain
f_w	Frequency of the wire	T_{line}	Time delay in the wire or the line
G_m	Messages injected into network	T_{tof}	Time of flight
G_n	Messages handled per node	t_r	RAU delay
K_1	Duty cycle	t_s	Switch delay
K_m	Number of messages injected by the system	t_w	Wire delay
K_n	Number of messages injected by the system	V_{dd}	Supply voltage
K_r	RAU to switch transistor ratio	V_t	Threshold voltage
K_s	Fraction of active gates during switching	v_p	Propagation velocity of a signal
L	Message bit length	W	Message channel width
l_2	Base latency	W_1/L_1	The size of the minimum transistor in the driver chain
M_r	Number of transistors in the RAU	w_{avg}	Average wire length between processors
M_s	Number of transistors in the switch	X	Number of inverters in cascaded driver chain
N	Number of nodes	α	Driver scaling factor
n	Network dimension	β	Minimum size transistor transconductance
P_{cap}	Capacitive power consumption	Γ	Total power constant coefficient
P_{msg}	Power dissipation per message	μ	Mobility of electrons
P_{node}	Power dissipation per router	τ	Rise time of the input clock pulse to the driver

3. Power dissipated in the RAU is related to the power dissipated in the switch. We use a simple model where this relationship is given by the ratio of number of transistors in the RAU to that in the switch.

4. The inter-router wire delay is given by the time of flight and the RC delay of the wire.

5. Driver chains are used to drive the off-chip physical channel and the delay through the driver chain is included in the total wire delay.

6. The RAU delay is equal to the switching delay. This is generally the case in most modern high speed routers.

3.1 Model Development

The time delay through the switch is referred to as the switching delay and is characterized by t_s. The delay through the RAU is denoted by t_r. The time to transfer a flow control unit of the message across a physical channel on the wire is denoted by t_w. Using a wormhole switching implementation, the overall routing delay is given by,

$$t_{wormhole} = D(t_r + t_s + t_w) + max(t_s, t_w) \left\lceil \frac{L}{W} \right\rceil \qquad (1)$$

where D is the average number of links traversed by a message through the network, L is the length of the message in bits and W is the channel width of the physical channel [4]. We proceed to determine expressions for t_s and t_w constrained by the available power, which also constrains message latency. For a fixed number of nodes, the choice of topology also affects D, W, t_s and t_w (assuming t_r is constant). We can now establish a relationship between available power and message latency as a function of topology. We first develop power dissipation models for the network components and couple these with models of the three network delays: routing, switch, and wire.

3.2 Power Dissipation Models

The available power can be obtained from the available energy used in a finite amount of time. The total power available for the network is assumed to be equally divided among all of the nodes, and can be expressed in terms of the power per node or power per message. The power per node, P_{node}, is simply the sum of the power dissipated in the RAU, switch, and the wire connecting two adjacent nodes and can be written as:

$$P_{node} = (P_r/D) + P_s + P_w \qquad (2)$$

The power per message P_{msg}, can be expressed as:

$$P_{msg} = P_r + (P_s + P_w)D \qquad (3)$$

where P_r, P_s and P_w are respectively, the power per bit dissipated in the RAU, switch, and the wire between routers, and D is the average number of links traversed by a message. It is important to note that (2) and (3) simply represent two different interpretations of the distribution of the total available power in the network and they are not independent equations. P_{node} and P_{msg} are related to the total power available to the network as follows:

$$P_t = NG_nP_{node} = G_mP_{msg} \tag{4}$$

where G_m and G_n represent two ways to capture the demand on network activity. G_m represents the number of messages injected into the network by all of the processing nodes and therefore captures the total demand on the network. A model for G_m can found in [7] where the effect of processor and interconnect speed is taken into account. The model of [7] is not constrained by the total power available to the network and therefore has to be modified. The total number of messages injected into the network, G_m, under a fixed power constraint can be expressed as

$$G_m = (S_p t_w N)/(rL) \tag{5}$$

where S_p is the processor speed in (MFLOPS/sec) and r is the computation to communication ratio in (MFLOPS/bit), t_w is the time it takes to transfer a bit between routers and it is constrained by the amount of power available to do so. G_n is the number of messages handled by the processing nodes of the network. It is obtained by noting the fact that a message has to traverse D number of hops and therefore G_n is simply DG_m. It is now seen that P_{node} and P_{msg} are equivalent.

The power dissipation in the RAU and switch is governed by the mechanism of charging and discharging the total capacitance. Therefore in our analysis of the router we assume that the power dissipated in the RAU is related to the power dissipated in the switch as follows:

$$P_r = \frac{M_r}{M_s}P_s = K_rP_s \tag{6}$$

Substitution of (4) and (6) into (2) yields the following expression for the total power dissipated in the network:

$$P_t = NG_n\left[\left(\frac{K_r}{D}+1\right)P_s + P_w\right] \tag{7}$$

This equation expresses the distribution of total power in the network from a system perspective and it is constrained by various system parameters such as the average distance between communicating nodes, the number of nodes, and the number of messages handled by a node. It is an equation with two unknowns P_s and P_w. We leave them as free variables to study the effect of distribution of power between the switch and inter-router channels (wire) on network performance. Now (7) can be rearranged to provide an expression for P_s

$$P_s = \frac{D(P_{node} - P_w)}{K_r + D} \qquad (8)$$

This expression permits us to study the distribution of power between the wire and through the switches. Note that under a fixed constraint on total power, minimum wire power corresponds to maximum switch power dissipation and vice versa.

The preceding equations were derived from a system architecture stand point. In order to relate the system architecture parameters to device and technology parameters, we must develop models in terms of power dissipation within the switches and physical channel interface drivers. We follow the same modeling technique of viewing power dissipation as simply charging and discharging of the total capacitance. In doing so we arrive at the following equations.

$$P_s = \frac{1}{2} K_s M_s C_t V_{dd}^2 f_s \qquad (9)$$

$$P_w = K_1 C_w V_{dd}^2 f_w w_{avg} W \qquad (10)$$

Here, $M_s = n^2 W$ is the number of transistors in the switch assuming a full physical crossbar connecting all input ports and output ports, and W is the channel width.

For the purpose of analyzing the effect of wire length we can determine this increase in wire length as [8]

$$w_{avg} = 2l_2(\sqrt{N} - 1)/(nk) \qquad (11)$$

following the approach in [1] where N is number of nodes, n is the dimension of the network, and l_2 is the physical distance between adjacent nodes. Thus the expression is normalized to the distance between two routers in a two dimensional torus. In this manner the analysis is relative to the best that can be achieved for 2-D tori in any given technology. The above expression in based on a linear wire delay model, and is therefore conservative.

3.3 Time Delay Models

The delay through the switch can simply be found by rearranging (9) ($t_s = 1/f_s$) to obtain,

$$t_s = \frac{0.5 K_s n^2 W C_t V_{dd}^2}{P_s} \qquad (12)$$

Substitution of W from (10) into (12) yields,

$$t_s = \left(\frac{P_w}{P_s}\right)\frac{0.5 K_s C_t V_{dd}^2 n^2 t_w}{K_l C_w V_{dd}^2 w_{avg}} \tag{13}$$

Normally the connection between two routers are off-chip signal paths and we have to treat this interconnect as a transmission line rather than as an RC line. The geometry of these off-chip wires is assumed to be "fat" to reduce resistance. However, the inductance will dominate the signal propagation and it must be taken into consideration. The scaling of the drivers in the cascaded chain is traditionally derived under the assumption that we have enough power to use the optimum number of drivers to realize minimum latency. This is unlikely to be the case under stringent power constraints, reducing the maximum number of drivers permitted. From our model captured in (7), the total power is distributed between the switch and the wire. An important question is the nature of this power distribution. What is the desired ratio? *Should we build faster drivers or should we design faster switches? What are the trade-offs on power distribution?* These are very important questions and must be addressed for future low power network designs. Therefore, in our analysis of low power network designs, we have to constrain the drivers by the maximum allowable power to the network. Under such constraint the maximum allowable drivers can be given by [8]

$$X = \frac{\ln(1 + (\alpha-1)P_w/\Gamma)}{\ln(\alpha)} \tag{14}$$

where $\Gamma = (Vdd^2 f(\alpha C_{in} + C_p)) + ((\beta/12)(Vdd - 2Vt)^3(\tau/T_{clk}))$ is the coefficient of the total power term. From (14), X is a function of both the scaling factor, α, the maximum available power, and the power dissipated in the wire, P_w. The motivation for this simplification is that for a given power budget, we can distribute the power in several ways: a) completely within the switch, b) completely within the wire c) across the switch and the wire. By leaving P_w as a free variable, we can study all three cases with the number of drivers be limited by the power allocated to driving the wires.

The delay through the wire is modeled as the sum of the delay through the driver chain, the RC line, the time of flight and can be derived [8] to give

$$t_w = 3\alpha(X-1)R_o C_o + S_n\left(\frac{R_o}{\alpha^X - 1}\right)(2C_{pad} + C_w + (\alpha^X - 1)C_o) + \frac{w_{avg}}{v_p} \tag{15}$$

The delay through the RAU will be assumed to be equal to the delay through the switch ($t_r = t_s$). This is reasonable since modern routers attempt to perform routing decisions in the time it takes to drive a flit through the switch. We are now equipped with all of the necessary models to be substituted in (1) to study the overall latency through the router as a function of network topology and power distribution under a maximum allowable power constraint. Thus, the complete expression for the no load latency of a message through a k-ary n-cube network under a power constraint given as

$$t_{wormhole} = D(t_r + t_s + t_w) + \max(t_s, t_w)\left\lceil \frac{L}{W} \right\rceil \qquad (16)$$

where t_s is defined in (13), t_w is defined in (15), W is defined in (10), and $D = (nN^{1/n})/4$ [1,4].

4.0 Performance Analysis

The goal of our analysis is to understand the relationship between the topology of the interconnect, message latency, and workload parameters under a fixed power budget. The preceding analysis has identified the relationships between power and features of the topology such as switching speeds, channel delays, and channel widths, in addition to numerous physical parameters. These relationships are complex, and their impact in determining the choice of topology is not obvious. We utilized the Maple V symbolic computational package to study these relationships [2]. Fixed power budgets are represented by total power in watts. This study focuses on the relationship between three variables: i) message latency, ii) distribution of power between the switches and wire (channels), and iii) network dimension. We are interested in the network dimension that minimizes message latency. In this section the preceding relationship is examined for small (16 nodes) and medium (256 nodes) systems. The section concludes with some observations about the behavior of the bisection bandwidth under a fixed power constraint.

4.1 Power Constrained Analysis of Small Systems

We studied the effect of a fixed power budget on the topology of small systems. The total power dissipation was initially fixed at two watts. In our model the total power budget is distributed equally among all of the nodes in the network, i.e., each node has a maximum dissipation of P_t/N watts. The simulations were carried out for a 16 node system and the overall latency as a function of network dimension and power dissipated in the wire is illustrated in Figure 2. *Note that the vertical axis corresponds to decreasing latency. Thus a maximum on the surface corresponds to minimum latency.* When power dissipated in the wire is a small (10-20%) fraction of the total power allocated per node, the latency is very high and is very sensitive to the network dimension. Low dimensional network are clearly preferred at any power distribution as seen in the figure. As we increase the power allocated to the wire, the latency starts to decrease until we reach a certain threshold in the value of P_w after which there is no significant change in the value of overall latency. In this regime, the overall delay is also insensitive to the network dimension. For a 16 node system, the threshold point occurs when power dissipated in the wire is approximately 40% of the total power allocated per node. When P_w is small, relatively more power is being dissipated in the switch and therefore the wire delay will be dominant; the converse is true at high values of P_w as is apparent from the figure.

From (5), it is clear that a change in r is inversely related to a change in S_p, the processor speed. Normally, improvement in the processor speed leads to lower latencies since we are able to process more messages in a given time cycle. This is not necessarily true when a system is constrained by power. Higher processor speed results in a higher mes-

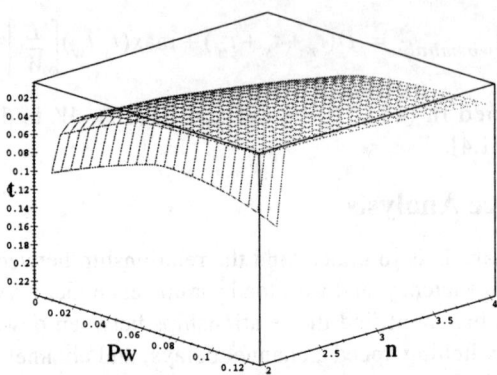

Figure 2. Message latency (in μ sec) as a function of network dimension and power distribution for 16 nodes system

sage injection rate, yet the total available power is fixed. This will require the network to handle a larger number of messages with the same amount of power. If the power budget is very tight, the increased number of messages in the network will cause an increase in the overall latency. Note that as we increase processor speed, larger systems tend to favor slightly higher dimensions and smaller systems favor lower (generally two) dimensions.

Finally, the system was analyzed under various power budgets. We decreased the available power from two to one watt and observed the effect on network performance. The shape of the surface of the graph remained qualitatively the same as in Figure 2 except that the overall latency became larger. The system also became more sensitive to dimension at low values of P_w as discussed above.

4.2 Power Constrained Analysis of Medium Systems

With a power budget of two watts, we analyzed the network performance of a system of 256 nodes. In trying to simulate this system, we encountered impractical solutions for the overall latency of the network. Subsequent analysis produced the following constraint on minimum power dissipation. Consider a network of 256 nodes which admits approximately 10^3 more injected messages per unit time than a network of 16 nodes. The delivery of these messages requires a specific minimum amount of energy in order to ensure that messages are delivered at the same rate that they are injected. Maintaining this injection rate necessitates a minimum power budget for network operation to be feasible. For a given power budget per node, the number of messages switched through the node must "share" this power dissipation capacity. The profile is given in Figure 3 for a total power of 100 watts. The power, P_{node} is further allocated between driving flits through the switch and across the wire. The condition for maximum wire power dissipation is the point at which P_{node} equals P_w which is infeasible as switching power is zero.

We increased the total power to ten watts. Even though the maximum power per node is approximately 40 mwatts, we found that wire power dissipation must be in the vicinity of 0.1 mwatt to yield minimum latency. This observation is shown in Figure 4(a). In contrast to a 16 node system, it is preferable to operate in a regime where P_w is very small.

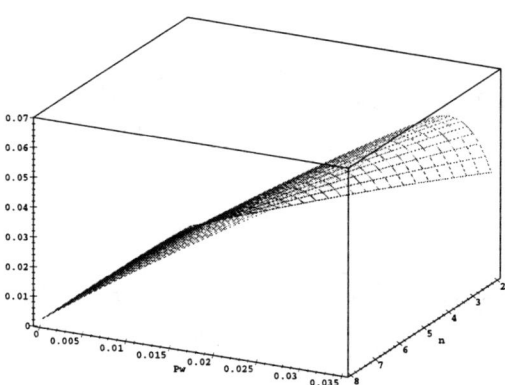

Figure 3. Power per node profile for a 256 nodes system

As increased power is dissipated in driving the physical channel, the system becomes more sensitive to the network dimension. As we increase the available power dissipation to 100 watts, the maximum power dissipated in the wire depends on the choice for the network dimension. This budget is approximately 0.3 watts per node. However, the optimum value clearly depends on the choice of network design. If we wanted to build low dimensional networks we have to sacrifice latency and power as seen in Figure 4(b). A three dimensional system can be built at the expense of using small amount of power in the wire (i.e. using 0.035 watts instead of 0.3 watts) and therefore penalizing the overall latency. Another interesting feature of the analysis is the response of latency to power distribution. As more power becomes available (10 to 100 watts), the latency exhibits the same response to the fraction of power spent in the wire as it does in the 16 node system (i.e. above a threshold there is insignificant change in latency). This design enables the consideration of a system with three dimensions. On the other hand, if the dimension is not a crucial factor in the design, and latency is the primary concern, then we can build the network by permitting higher power dissipation in the wire and achieving smaller latencies as seen in Figure 4(c). Note that the optimal dimension in this graph is strictly a function of power dissipated in the wire. If P_w is less than 0.05 watts, the optimal dimension is four with a latency of 2.8 μ sec. The optimal P_w is approximately 0.1 watts giving latency of 0.8 μ sec at (n=4). Note that this value of the wire power correlates to the optimal value found for 16 node system (~40% of maximum power).

A preference for higher dimensional network for large systems can be explained as follows. Higher dimensional networks embedded in the plane lead to longer wire lengths for the inter-router physical channels. As available power is increased with larger system size, the negative effect (larger power consumption) of these longer wires is reduced with smaller number of switches to traverse. Moreover, the smaller number of switches that are traversed reduces the power consumption in the switches. The net effect is to favor low dimensional networks in low power applications (minimize wire power dissipation) and higher dimensional networks when power is not so constrained.

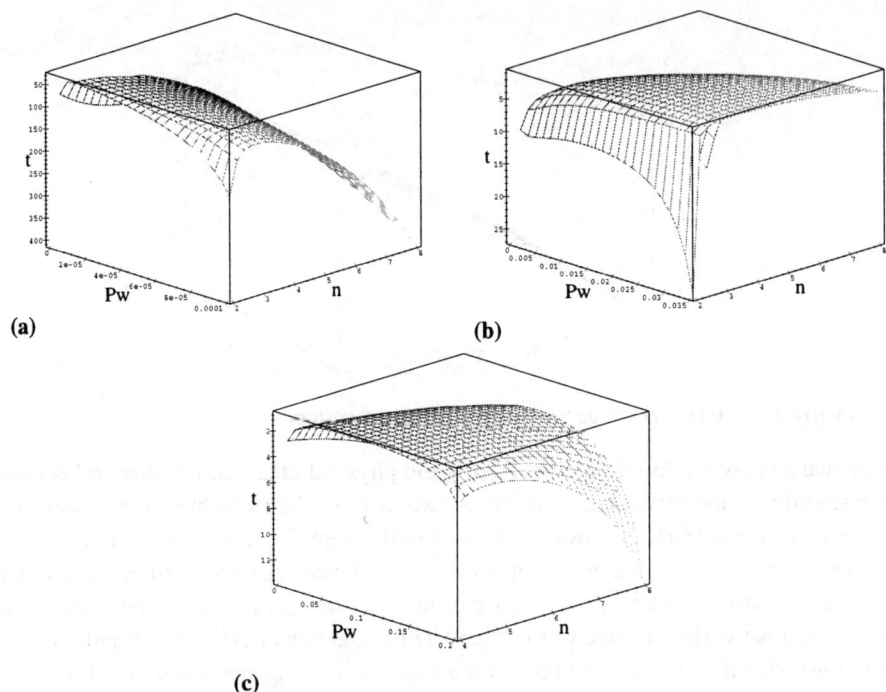

Figure 4. Message latency for various total power budget and power distribution (a) 10 watts (b) 100 watts using small fraction of maximum available power (c) 100 watts with larger fraction of maximum power

This paper analyzes network performance under a fixed power budget permitting the bisection bandwidth to vary with changes in dimension and power distribution. The total number of messages in the network and the bisection bandwidth for a 256 node system is shown in Figure 5.

5.0 Concluding Remarks and Directions for Future Research

This paper has reported our study of the relationships between a fixed power budget and the network topology from the point of view of message latency. Under a fixed total power constraint, the network performance is mainly a function of system size, network dimension, and the power distribution.

- For a small system size (16 nodes), the optimum latency is achieved at low dimensions (2-3) with at least 40% of total power dissipated in the wire.

- As we increase the size of the network, a "minimum power dissipation" is required to satisfy the traffic requirements. Power budgets that are close to the minimum value result in relatively high latency and very high dimensional networks (7-8).

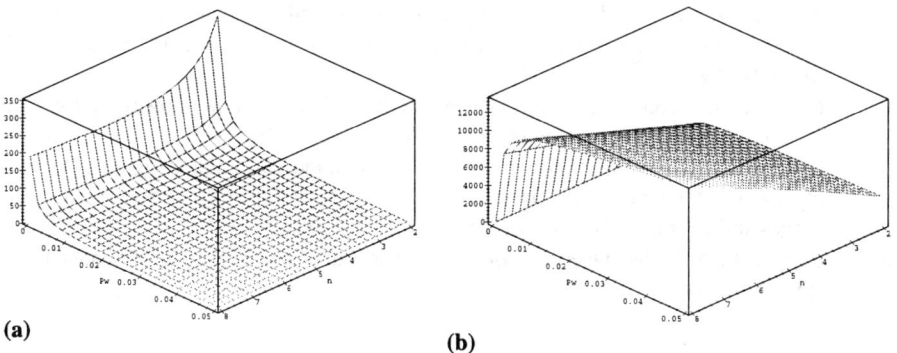

Figure 5. (a) Number of messages, and (b) bisection bandwidth of a network with 256 nodes.

- Power budgets in excess of minimum result in lower latency, however, the networks only exhibit the optimum performance at medium dimensions (3-4).

- Power distribution between the switch and the wire in the network provide various trade-offs between the hardware and system design.

These models only begin to address the major issues in the power constrained design of multiprocessor interconnection networks. The expectation is that these models can aid the designers of embedded multiprocessor systems in which power is at a premium.

6.0 References

[1] A. Agarwal, "Limits on interconnection network performance," *IEEE Transactions on Parallel and Distributed Systems,* October 1991.

[2] B. W. Char, K. O. Geddes, G. H. Gonnet, B. L. Leong, M. B. Monagan, S. M. Watt, *Maple V,* Waterloo Maple Publishing, Virginia, 1991.

[3] W. J. Dally, "Performance Analysis of k-ary n-cube interconnection networks," *IEEE Transactions on Computers*, June 1990.

[4] J. Duato, S. Yalamanchili, and L. Ni, *Interconnection Networks, An Engineering Approach*, IEEE Press, 1997.

[5] S. L. Scott and G. M Thorson, ``The Cray T3E networks: adaptive routing in a high performance 3D torus", Proceedings of Hot Interconnects, August 1996.

[6] S. L. Scott and J. R. Goodman, "The Impact of Pipelined Channels on k-ary n-cube networks", IEEE Transactions on Parallel and Distributed Systems, vol. 5, no. 1, pp. 2-16, January 1994.

[7] D. Basak and D. K. Panda, "Designing Clustered Multiprocessor Systems under Packaging and Technological Advancements," *IEEE Transactions on Parallel and Distributed Systems,* vol. 7, no. 9, pp. 962-978, Sep. 1996.

[8] C. S. Patel, S. M. Chai, S. Yalamanchili and D. E. Schimmel, "Power Constrained Design of Multiprocessor Interconnection Networks", Proceedings of International Conference on Computer Design, October 1997.

[9] S. Abraham and K. Padmanabhan, "Performance of Multicomputer networks under pin-out constraints", Journal of Parallel and Distributed Computing, vol. 12, no. 3, pp. 237-248, July 1991.

[10] R. E. Kessler and J. L. Schwarzmeier, "CRAY T3D: A new dimension for Cray Research", Proceedings of Compcon, pp. 176-182, Spring 1993.

[11] S. L. Scott, "Synchronization and communication in the T3E multiprocessor", Proceedings of the 7th International Conference on Architectural Support for Programming Languages and Operating Systems, pp. 26-36, October 1996.

[12] Paragon XP/S Product Overview, Beaverton, OR, Intel Corporation, Supercomputer Systems Division, 1991.

Session VI

ROUTER AND NETWORK ARCHITECTURES III

Friday, June 27, 1997
1:00 - 2:30

Session Chair:

J. Duato
Universidad Politécnica de Valencia

ChaosLAN: Design and Implementation of a Gigabit LAN Using Chaotic Routing

Neil R. McKenzie[1], Kevin Bolding[2], Carl Ebeling[3] and Lawrence Snyder[3]

[1] MERL - A Mitsubishi Electric Research Laboratory,
201 Broadway, Cambridge MA 02139
mckenzie@merl.com
[2] Seattle Pacific University, 3307 3rd Ave. W, Seattle WA 98119
bolding@spu.edu
[3] Department of Computer Science and Engineering, Box 352350,
University of Washington, Seattle WA 98195
{ebeling,snyder}@cs.washington.edu

Abstract. In recent years, the Chaos Project at the University of Washington has analyzed and simulated a dozen routing algorithms. Three new routing algorithms have been invented; of these, the chaotic routing algorithm (a.k.a. Chaos) has been the most successful. Although the Chaos router was developed for multicomputer routing, the project has recently directed its attention towards the application of Chaos technology to LAN switching. The present task is to implement a gigabit LAN called ChaosLAN, based on a centralized switch (hub) and high speed serial links to workstations. The switch itself is a fully-populated two-dimensional torus network of Chaos routers. The host adapter is Digital's PCI Pamette card. To evaluate the performance of ChaosLAN, we are supporting the Global Memory System (GMS), a type of distributed virtual memory also developed at UW. We also describe an application involving real-time haptic rendering used in a surgical simulator.

Key words: gigabit LAN, Chaos router, Cranium network interface architecture, PCI Pamette, Fibre Channel, Global Memory System, haptic user interface, surgical simulator.

1 Introduction

The case for a high-performance local area network for the construction of a parallel computer using a network of workstations (NOW) is well understood [1]. One goal is to provide a scalable platform for parallel programs using low-cost workstations or PCs, comparable in performance to that of a multiprocessor system but at far lower cost. Another goal is to provide a high-performance distributed computing environment that is typical in robotics, medical simulators and virtual reality systems, where real-time performance is critical to achieving a high quality experience. Standard LAN technology such as Ethernet, initially developed for less demanding applications such as e-mail or file transfer, does not provide the performance necessary for these kinds of distributed real-time applications. Faster versions of Ethernet provide higher network throughput but generally do not significantly improve the underlying latency, which is on the order of a millisecond. Low latency communication, on the order of a few tens of microseconds or less, is critical for providing both a high-performance cluster computing environment for parallel execution of scientific codes and for real-time response in distributed systems running complex applications.

Since the early 1990's the Chaos Project at the University of Washington [2] has studied network communications and routing algorithms, in the context of multicomputer routing. The group has analyzed and simulated dozens of routing algorithms and also studied approaches to fault tolerance and constructing network interfaces. Three new routing algorithms have been invented: chaotic, zenith, and triplex. Of these, the chaotic routing algorithm [3] (a.k.a. Chaos) has been the most successful. The Chaos router has been extensively simulated on several topologies under a variety of work loads. Generally, it delivers higher throughput than its competitors with similarly low latency. In fact, the Chaos router delivers better than 95% of the theoretical maximum bandwidth for random traffic on a 256-node torus. The results for Chaos are consistent across traffic patterns and on other topologies using a variety of performance metrics (e.g. throughput, latency and network saturation level). Additionally, the Chaos router is logically simple in structure, so that it can be readily implemented in silicon inexpensively.

Chaos is characterized as an *adaptive, non-minimal* algorithm for fixed-length (or bounded-length) packets. Long messages are segmented into packets at the sender and re-assembled at the receiver. Adaptivity increases the number of paths between sender and receiver, so that more of the network can be active at once and help distribute the work load evenly compared with an *oblivious* algorithm in which there is only one possible path from sender to receiver. Adaptivity also complicates the re-assembly of packets at the receiver, because packets can overtake one another due to internal congestion, and cause packets to arrive in a different order than they were injected into the network. Hardware assistance for re-assembly of non-ordered packets has been studied extensively [4] and an inexpensive, streamlined host adapter to interface with an adaptive network has been proposed by McKenzie [5].

Although the Chaos router was developed for multicomputer routing, the project has recently directed its attention towards applying Chaos technology to LAN switching. This move is similar to Myricom's use of the Caltech Mosaic router in a gigabit LAN [6]. The Mosaic router, based on the oblivious dimension-order routing algorithm, was also developed initially for multicomputers. Since the underlying performance potential of Chaos is greater than that of Mosaic for similar cost, there is an opportunity for LAN technology based on Chaos to become adopted on a wide scale. The first step in making the research contribution of Chaos widely available is the development of a prototype system called ChaosLAN.

The remainder of this paper is organized as follows. Section 2 presents an overview of the ChaosLAN switch. Section 3 discusses the approach to constructing the host adapter that provides the interface between the network and an attached workstation. Two software environments are described: Section 4 introduces the Global Memory System and Section 5 discusses the use of ChaosLAN in a real-time distributed system for use in surgical simulation.

2 ChaosLAN Switch

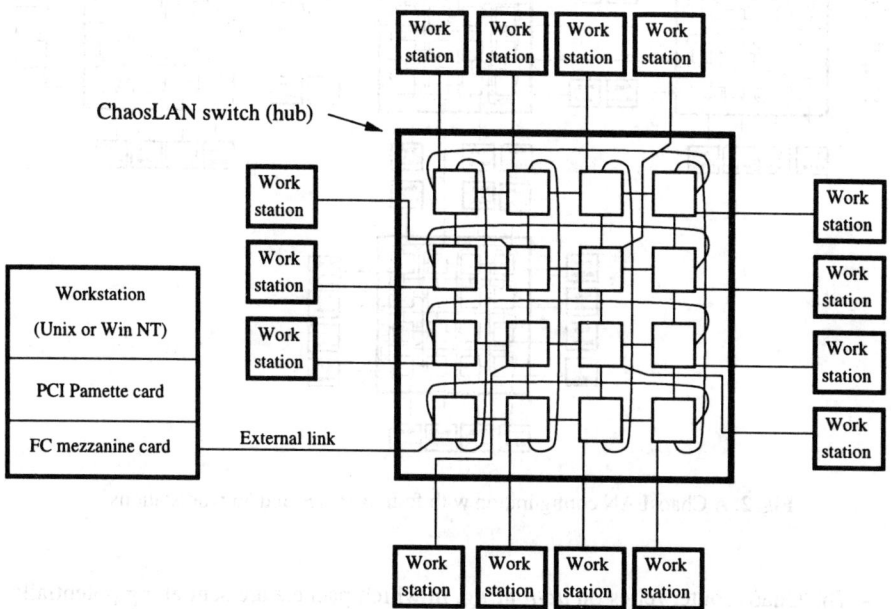

Fig. 1. Overview of the implementation of ChaosLAN

The idea of using a network of multicomputer routers to form a LAN switch is very natural. The essential idea is to take a multicomputer system (e.g. a massively parallel processor or MPP system) and replace the directly attached processing nodes with remote workstations, as illustrated in Figure 1. In this example, sixteen network router chips organized as a torus are contained within the switch. Since each router chip can be linked to a workstation via its processor port, such a network can interconnect up to sixteen workstations. It is also possible to form larger networks by connecting multiple switches together through their processor ports. There are a large number of possible network configurations using multiple switches. As an example, Figure 2 demonstrates a configuration using four switches to connect 56 workstations. Note that redundant connections between pairs of switches may be used to increase the inter-switch bandwidth.

Although the conceptual transformation of a multicomputer network into a LAN switch is straightforward, there are some complicating issues. Three issues that arise when using Chaos networks are described below:

- The Chaos router expects the network to be a fully-populated regular mesh or torus. LANs usually have irregularly-shaped networks.
- The Chaos router relies on network nodes being physically close together (i.e. within 10cm of each other) so that transmission-line delays between nodes are negligible. LANs usually allow workstations to be at least 30-50 meters apart.

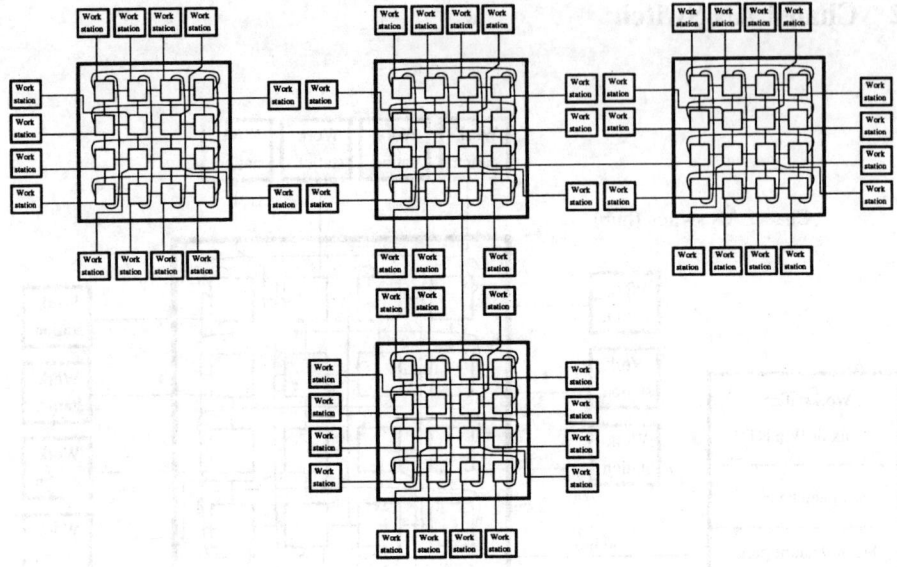

Fig. 2. A ChaosLAN configuration with four switches and 56 workstations

- The Chaos router relies on *de-routing*, in which packets are sent along potentially non-minimal paths to route around congestion. De-routing provides deadlock freedom and performance benefits. For de-routing to be beneficial, the cost of an extra network hop must be small. This is not the case in a LAN environment, where an extra hop may cause a large amount of additional latency.

All of these issues arise from the fact that the Chaos router is designed to take advantage of the special constraints provided by a multicomputer environment. To allow the Chaos router to work in the more general LAN environment, the ChaosLAN isolates the Chaos router inside of the switch by designating *internal* and *external* links. Internal links connect routers within a switch, providing a closely controlled environment that meets all of the needs of the Chaos router: a regular network, short internal links, and small delays per-hop. External links are used to connect workstations to the switch and to connect switches to other switches.

The interface between internal and external links is the processor port of each router. Specifically, each Chaos router chip has an extra port reserved for communication between the router and a host processor. The protocol for this port is allowed to be different from the protocol used for router-to-router communication. Because the processor port is not constrained to use the same transmission protocol as the regular router ports, it can be designed to tolerate the distances and irregularity found in LANs. Furthermore, once packets have been transmitted out of a switch and into the processor port, they are considered to be outside the Chaos router network and are no longer subject to its deadlock prevention protocol or de-routing. Thus, internal links use the Chaos protocol, while external links use a protocol designed specifically for the longer distances found in a LAN.

2.1 External Links

The linkage between the switch and a workstation (or from switch to switch) is serial and simultaneously bi-directional. The physical link protocol is based on the Fibre Channel physical interface (FC-PH), an ANSI standard for gigabit serial interconnection [8]. While the physical transfer protocols are the same as specified in the Fibre Channel standard, a custom protocol is used for higher levels. The specification of FC-PH describes three different layers, called FC-0, FC-1 and FC-2, representing the physical medium, the parallel-to-serial conversion and packet framing, respectively. Only FC-0 and FC-1 are used in ChaosLAN. Variants of FC-0 use either copper wire or optical fiber. The link length of low cost copper media can be up to 25 meters and the more expensive media allow link lengths to be up to several kilometers. The serial bit rates are specified at 1062.5 Mbit/s, 531.25 Mbit/s and 265.625 Mbit/s. FC-1, the protocol for parallel to serial encode and decode, is based on an 8b/10b coding scheme patented by IBM [9]. Eight bits of message data are converted into 10 bits of serial data using multiple codings. To improve the reliability of the link, the encoder chooses an encoding on a byte-by-byte basis over long byte strings that best equalizes the total number of high and low bits sent. The 8b/10b encoding provides redundancy; if the decoder detects an illegal serial bit sequence, it asserts that the corresponding byte has been corrupted and causes the packet containing this byte to be discarded. The encoding scheme also allows the transmission of control rather than data values, such as an acknowledgment character or the start or end of a data block. FC-1 is simple to implement: the encoder and decoder require only about 100-200 gates each, so that high-speed versions can be readily constructed.

2.2 The ChaosLAN Router Chip

Once we have made the separation of links into internal and external switch links, the job of modifying the Chaos router chip for LAN operation is much simpler. Most of the modification is concentrated on the external (processor) port, although some modifications must also be made to the internal ports as well. To facilitate the transfer of data from the external ports to internal ports, we use a common packet size and format throughout the entire network. Specifically, we use a packet with a 64-byte payload and a 12-byte header, requiring a total of 76 bytes in the packet, as opposed to the original Chaos router chip's 40-byte packets. Also, since the chosen external channel interfaces are effectively 8-bit uni-directional channels, the internal channels have been changed to reflect 8-bit words instead of the original 16-bit words.

The external link port has been modified extensively since it now must communicate over a relatively long wire length using a bit-serial protocol. The original router was able to function with single-packet input/output buffers because the short links between routers allowed for very fast transmission of flow control information. To support the relatively long length of the links on ChaosLAN's ports, more buffering has been added. A credit-based scheme provides the flow control. This scheme is implemented by providing buffering for four packets on the input side of each link. The sender keeps a count of the number of free buffers at the receiver and decrements the counter each time it sends a packet. When the receiver frees up a buffer (by forwarding the packet) an acknowledgment is sent to the sender, causing the sender to increment its count of free buffers at the receiver. Full-speed transmission can proceed as long as the round-trip time across a link is shorter than the time to send four packets. With a packet size of 76 bytes, this amount of buffering allows links of over 300 meters in length to run at full rate.

Finally, in order to allow packets to follow routes through networks with more than one switch, the ChaosLAN router must support some sort of source-based routing. Our implementation allows each packet to specify up to four packet headers. Each header is used to route a packet from a source link to a destination link in a single switch, allowing packets to cross a maximum of four switches in their route from source to destination. Each header consists of one byte, thereby allowing a maximum switch size of 256 routing nodes. In all there are four bytes needed to specify the route through four switches. Each router byte is subdivided further into two four-bit fields to represent the X and Y displacement within a single switch. An internal router-to-router hop causes either the X or the Y displacement to be incremented or decremented by one. When the header becomes zero then the whole packet is ejected from the internal network and out of the switch along an external link. Each time a packet leaves a switch, the set of four headers is rotated to place the next routing byte at the front of the packet.

3 Host Adapter

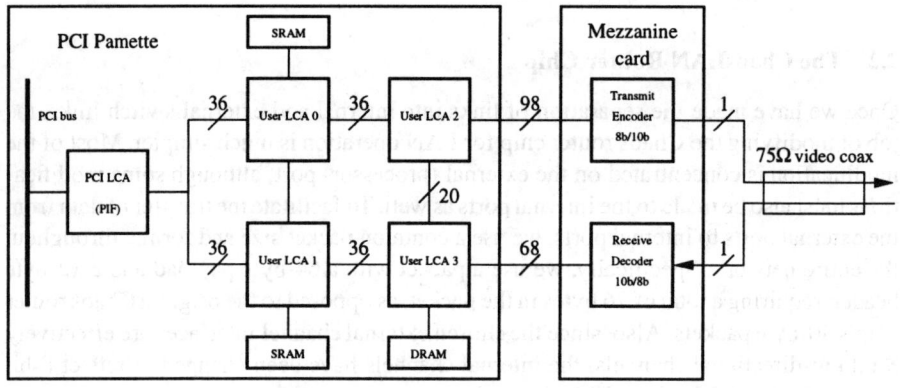

Fig. 3. Organization of the Pamette card and the Fibre Channel mezzanine card

The host adapter provides an interface between the peripheral bus in the workstation host and the serial link to the ChaosLAN switch. We chose PCI as the peripheral bus standard due to its wide availability across IBM PC compatibles, Power Macintoshes and Unix-based workstations. To expedite the construction of the host adapter card, we are basing it on Digital Equipment Corporation's PCI Pamette card [7]. Figure 3 shows an overview of the Pamette. It contains five Xilinx logic cell arrays or LCAs, more generically known as field programmable gate arrays (FPGAs). One FPGA, called the PCILCA or PIF, provides an interface with the PCI bus. The other four FPGAs are the user programmable LCAs that contain the network interface circuit. The development environment for the Pamette includes a compiler and simulator for the Verilog hardware description language and the Xilinx logic synthesis tools. Interaction with the serial link requires a mezzanine card to perform the 8b/10b encode on the transmit side and the 10b/8b decode on the receive side, along with the voltage level conversion required for the physical medium.

To be successful, the network interface circuit in the host adapter must provide user programs with low latency access. The implementation of the Pamette network interface circuit is based on the Cranium network interface architecture [4, 5], a low latency interface framework that also provides compatibility with adaptive routers such as Chaos. Providing a low latency, low overhead solution requires two important features. The first requirement is to bypass the operating system and provide direct application program access to the network wherever possible. The second requirement is for the host adapter to perform bus-master direct memory access (DMA) to the host's system DRAM over the PCI bus. The idea is to transfer data to and from the network at the full rate of the PCI bus. There should be no intervention from the host processor in the common case. DMA channels at the sender automatically segment the message into packets and inject them one-by-one into the network without host intervention. Likewise, the DMA channels at the receiver perform automatic re-assembly of incoming packets. The host adapter notifies the host processor when all packets for a given DMA channel have arrived.

The following is a brief overview of how direct application access is implemented in the host adapter. (Also see the documents on Cranium [4, 5] for a more detailed description.) The host adapter must act on behalf of the operating system to check arguments in message commands coming from the application program, to prevent buggy or malicious user programs from crashing the operating system, for instance. In a send command, the user program selects the ID of the destination workstation, a reference to a local message buffer containing the message to be sent, and a DMA channel to execute the command. All message buffers are the size of an MMU page; a single send command results in the sending of a message up to the size of a page. In order to use a particular message buffer, the user program must register it with the operating system in advance so that the OS can pin it into memory. The OS passes back a *handle* (a small integer) to the user program to represent this message buffer. Under direct application access, the user program executes a send command by passing the buffer handle directly to the host adapter instead of sending the address of the buffer. Mapping tables in the network interface are used to translate the handle into the physical address of the message buffer. Unmapped handles are rejected; if the entry in the table indexed by the buffer handle contains a null value, then the message command is cancelled. A receive command works the same way: it specifies the ID of the workstation representing the source of the message, the handle of a local buffer to place the incoming data and a DMA channel. Note that a receive DMA channel must be activated before any packets regarding that channel are sent.

The user can specify two different ways for each receive DMA channel to be managed by the network interface. For small messages, the receive DMA channel is managed as a ring-queue; the memory location assigned to an incoming packet is determined by the receiver's queue pointers that index into the message buffer. For large messages, the locations of incoming packets are determined by using the sequence number in the packet header as an offset from the physical address of the message buffer. The effect is that packets are re-ordered in the message buffer automatically regardless of what their arrival order is. A hardware packet counter determines when all the packets in the message have arrived. The host processor can poll a status register to test for the arrival of a complete message. An alternative approach is for the network interface to notify the host using an interrupt.

Figure 4 describes the packet format used in ChaosLAN. The routing information is contained in of the first four bytes of the packet and is manipulated by the switches directly. The next eight bytes contain the network interface header. The send channel and receive channel fields are both single byte fields, meaning that each field can address up to 256 DMA channels. The packet payload contains up to 64 bytes worth of application data; the payload length is specified in the flags field in the header. Assuming that the page size is 8K bytes, a single DMA transfer contains up to 128 packets. The sequence number field (also a single byte) represents the cache-line offset into the memory page. For most processor architectures, a single full length packet represents two or four cache lines worth of data. The last two bytes in the network interface header are reserved for future expansion.

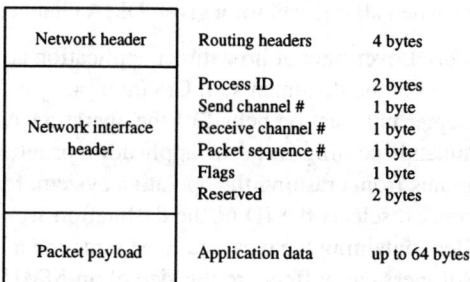

Fig. 4. Packet format

4 Application: Global Memory System

To evaluate the effectiveness of ChaosLAN and the Pamette-based network interface, we plan to run a software environment called the Global Memory System (GMS) [10, 11]. GMS is based on the idea of paging over the network to idle workstations instead of to local disk. As network bandwidth approaches the bandwidth of a locally attached disk, paging over the network becomes the faster solution once the communication latency becomes sufficiently low.

Here is a brief introduction to GMS. Under standard virtual memory, recently accessed pages remain in main memory while inactive pages must be read from disk. GMS introduces a new class of page called a *global page*. A local page is a recently accessed page, currently available in main memory. A global page is one that was accessed some time ago but not recently enough to keep it in main memory. A page is demoted from local to global when the user program runs out of page frames. The user program makes room by selecting the least recently used local page and moves it onto another workstation (hence making it a global page). The global page is promoted to local when the user program faults it back into memory. In many cases, a single page fault results in an exchange of pages between two workstations: first a page is pushed out, then another page is pulled in.

The requirements of GMS are a natural fit with the Cranium network interface architecture because both are page-oriented. One simplification is that all network activity is the side effect of taking a page fault, rather than being activated explicitly by the underlying user program built on top of GMS. Therefore the capability of direct application access is not strictly necessary. The primary benefit of Cranium is the use of bus-master DMA to move pages at the full rate of the hardware without host processor intervention on a packet-by-packet basis.

An extension to the simple page-oriented technique is to use sub-page transfers. In this way the application program that executes the page fault can start operating immediately after the particular cache line containing the data element that was requested in the page is brought in. The remainder of the page is sent shortly afterward. Since Cranium is cache-line oriented, there is a natural fit with the sub-page extension to the basic GMS framework.

5 Application: Surgical Simulation

The idea behind a surgical simulator is to model a surgical instrument (such as a scalpel or forceps) and allow the user to perform simulated surgery on a computer model of the human anatomy by manipulating a simulation of the instrument. It is very important for the simulation to be as realistic as possible, by displaying visual changes to the anatomical model in real time with no perceived lag. The most effective surgical simulators also provide force feedback, also known as *haptic* (touch) rendering. Thus, the computer system must provide haptic rendering as well as graphics rendering.

Computational approaches for surgical simulation include finite element modeling, volume rendering and other compute-intensive techniques. In most cases, single processor systems are not adequate to provide enough realism to make the system usable. Currently it is necessary to use large multiprocessor compute servers. The electrical and environmental requirements of these compute servers are more substantial than those of ordinary workstations and personal computers; it is common for medium to large compute servers to be placed in a dedicated machine room containing additional cooling capability and high-wattage electrical power distribution. Thus, the compute servers are usually located remotely from the laboratory where the user interacts with the simulator. The effect is that the haptic input device cannot plug directly into the compute server

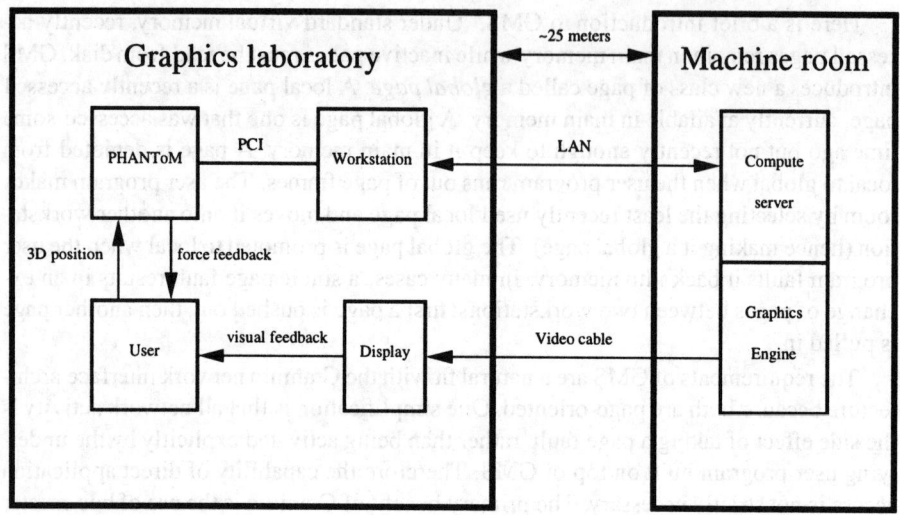

Fig. 5. Schematic diagram of the surgical simulation demonstration system at MERL

due to cable length limitations. The solution is to drive the haptic device off a local workstation and communicate with the compute server over a LAN.

Figure 5 describes the environment for a surgical simulation demonstration system that has been constructed at MERL – A Mitsubishi Electric Research Laboratory [12]. The haptic input device is the PHANToM from SensAble Devices. The position of the PHANToM stylus in 3-space is captured by a local workstation. The local workstation performs haptic rendering and a remote compute server performs graphics rendering. Position information from the PHANToM is transferred over the LAN to the compute server, an SGI Onyx SMP system containing eight R10000 processors and an Infinite-Reality graphics accelerator. The Onyx performs the graphical rendering in real time. The graphics output is delivered from the Onyx back to the room with the PHANToM over video cable and then displayed on a monitor.

Currently, the haptic model is contained entirely within the workstation attached to the PHANToM. Eventually we would like to perform haptic rendering on the compute server. The advantages are that the larger computational capability of the Onyx will allow us to model deformable tissues and simulate cutting, tearing and squishing. Currently, this capability is defeated by the large latencies of the Ethernet-based LAN. Haptic forces must be re-calculated and refreshed a rate of at least 1000 Hz and ideally 5000 Hz or greater. With standard LAN technology a round trip takes 2 to 5 milliseconds. Therefore it is impossible to sustain a 1000 Hz refresh rate. By contrast, the human visual system tolerates a much slower refresh rate, on the order of 20-25 Hz (40-50 milliseconds per video frame), so the latency of standard LANs is not detrimental to the visual quality.

A high-performance LAN such as ChaosLAN with a low latency network interface provides a solution to the problem of locating the haptic model remotely on the compute server. If the round-trip latency due to the network and host adapter can be reduced to 50 to 100 microseconds instead of 2 to 5 milliseconds, then the haptic refresh rate can be improved to an acceptable level. Unlike the case of GMS, this application requires direct access from the user level on the sender to the user level on the receiver to bypass the operating system entirely. The amount of information in each message is small (on the order of three to eight floating point values) and can be contained in a single packet. Therefore, the application can manage the receive DMA channels as ring-queues. A credit-based protocol can be used to prevent overflow: the workstation sends one packet (containing position information) and waits for a response from the compute server (containing force information) before it sends its next packet.

6 Project Status

The implementation is divided into several tasks: the router chip, the circuit board containing the router chips to implement the switch, the mezzanine circuit board to extend the PCI Pamette to provide a Fibre Channel physical interface, and programming the Pamette's FPGAs to implement the host interface circuitry. The ChaosLAN router chip is expected to be completed and fabricated in the summer of 1997. Using an 0.8 micron process and 8-bit ports, it should be easy to achieve the 125 MHz operating speed necessary to provide the 1 Gbit/s transmission rate per link. Likewise, the printed circuit boards are expected to be fabricated during the summer of 1997. If all goes well, we expect to have an operational system by the end of the year.

At time of publication we do not have any performance measurements available for ChaosLAN. Results of simulation studies are available on the Chaos routing algorithm [3] and the Cranium network interface [5]. Some variables not captured by prior simulation studies on chaotic routing are the effects of the PCI bus implementation and the operating system on overall system performance. Both factors are expected to have a significant impact on the performance of ChaosLAN. Moll and Shand [13] measured the PCI bandwidths and interrupt response times for a number of different workstations and PCs, under both the Digital Unix and the Microsoft Windows NT operating systems. Their measurements demonstrate that PCI performance results vary considerably across different implementations. Interrupt response times for a *single* implementation vary widely, from a few microseconds to a few hundreds of microseconds, and under rare circumstances are over a millisecond. Since the interrupt response time profile is difficult to model analytically, the best simulation is provided by a physical implementation.

7 Related Work

Recent work on networks and network interface designs that we find intriguing includes the U-Net user level network interface software architecture from Cornell [14] and the ServerNet II network from Tandem (now a division of Compaq) [15]. U-Net has been ported to several combinations of operating system (Linux, Windows NT and Solaris), processor architecture (x86 and Sparc) and network interface circuit (FORE Systems ATM interface and DECchip 21140 fast Ethernet interface). U-Net succeeds at bringing the software latency below 100 microseconds on these commodity systems.

ServerNet II is a cluster interconnect for Windows NT and Unix based workstations. Like ChaosLAN, it uses Fibre Channel bit-serial links running at gigabit rates. An important difference in approach between ServerNet II and ChaosLAN is the complexity of the routing chip. In ChaosLAN, a collection of sixteen simple routing chips configured as a torus implements a 16-port switch. In ServerNet II, a single ASIC implements a 12-port switch. This ASIC is relatively complex as it requires 750,000 gates.

8 Summary

We describe ChaosLAN, a high-performance local area network based on the Chaos router, originally used in multicomputer routing. The network consists of a hub (switch) containing 16 Chaos routers; the switch is able to connect up to 16 workstations over serial links. Some changes to the Chaos chip are needed to address the problems of the long wire length from the switch to the workstation. The serial link is based on the Fibre Channel physical layer. We are using the PCI Pamette card to implement the host adapter. A subset of the Cranium network interface architecture is executed by the Pamette's FPGAs to provide a low latency interface with the network. Two software environments with latency-critical properties are under consideration to test and exercise ChaosLAN: the Global Memory System (GMS) and an environment tailored for haptic rendering and surgical simulation.

Acknowledgments

We appreciate the contribution of UW undergraduate students Ville Aikas, Jason Murray and Kevin Taylor to the development of ChaosLAN. We also acknowledge the assistance of Mark Shand at Digital's System Research Center.

References

1. Thomas E. Anderson, David E. Culler and David A. Patterson. A case for networks of workstations (NOW). *IEEE Micro*, Feb. 1995.
2. Lawrence Snyder et al. The World Wide Web home page for the Chaos research group at the University of Washington. URL: http://www.cs.washington.edu/research-/projects/lis/chaos/www/chaos.html.
3. Kevin Bolding. *Chaotic routing: design and implementation of an adaptive multicomputer network router*. PhD dissertation, University of Washington, Dept. of CSE, Seattle WA, July 1993.
4. Neil R. McKenzie, Kevin Bolding, Carl Ebeling and Lawrence Snyder. Cranium: an interface for message passing on adaptive packet routing networks. *Proceedings of the 1994 Parallel Computer Routing and Communication Workshop*, Seattle WA, May 1994, pp. 266-280.
5. Neil R. McKenzie. *The Cranium network interface architecture: support for message passing on adaptive packet routing networks*. PhD dissertation, University of Washington, January 1997.

6. Nanette J. Boden et al. Myrinet: a gigabit-per-second local area network. *IEEE Micro*, February 1995. Also available on the World Wide Web through http://www.myri.com/research/index.html.
7. Mark Shand et al. The PCI Pamette V1. World Wide Web site, http://www.research.digital.com:80/SRC/pamette/.
8. Fibre Channel – Physical and Signaling Interface (FC-PH). ANSI document X3.230-1994.
9. A. X. Widmer and P. A. Franaszek. A DC-balanced, partitioned-block, 8b/10b transmission code. *IBM Journal of Research and Development* 27(5), September 1983, pages 440-451.
10. M. J. Feeley, W. E. Morgan, F. H. Pighin, A. R. Karlin, H. M. Levy, and C. A. Thekkath. Implementing global memory management in a workstation cluster. *Proceedings of the 15th ACM Symposium on Operating Systems Principles*, December 1995.
11. H. A. Jamrozik, M. J. Feeley, G. M. Voelker, J. Evans II, A. R. Karlin, H. M. Levy, and M. K. Vernon. Reducing network latency using subpages in a global memory environment. *Proceedings of the Seventh ACM Conference on Architectural Support for Programming Languages and Operating Systems (ASPLOS VII)*, October 1996.
12. Sarah Gibson, Joseph Samosky, Andrew Mor, Christina Fyock, Eric Grimson, Takeo Kanade, Ron Kikinis, Hugh Lauer, Neil R. McKenzie, Shin Nakajima, Hide Ohkami, Randy Osborne and Akira Sawada. Simulating arthroscopic knee surgery using volumetric object representations, real-time volume rendering and haptic feedback. *Proc. of the Joint Conference on Computer Vision and Virtual Reality in Medicine and Medical Robotics and Computer Assisted Surgery*, Grenoble, France, March 1997.
13. Laurent Moll and Mark Shand. Systems performance measurement on PCI Pamette. *Proc. of FCCM'97 Symposium on Field-Programmable Custom Computing Machines*, Napa CA, April 1997.
14. Matt Welsh, Anindya Basu, and Thorsten von Eicken. ATM and Fast Ethernet network interfaces for user-level communication. *Proceedings of the Third International Symposium on High Performance Computer Architecture* (HPCA), San Antonio, Texas, February 1-5, 1997.
15. David Garcia and William Watson. ServerNet II. *Proceedings of the 1997 Parallel Computer Routing and Communication Workshop*, Atlanta GA, June 1997, pp. 266-280.

Does Time-Division Multiplexing Close the Gap Between Memory and Optical Communication Speeds?

X. Yuan, R. Gupta and R. Melhem

The University of Pittsburgh, Pittsburgh, PA 15260

Abstract. Optical interconnection networks have the potential of transmitting data much faster than the speed at which this data can be generated at the transmitting nodes or consumed at the receiving nodes. Even when the communication protocols are simplified and most of the protocol signaling at the end nodes is done in hardware, the data cannot be processed at the end nodes at a rate faster than the rate of memory operations. We study the effect of multiplexing the network on both its throughput and latency for different ratios of memory to link transmission speeds. We found that multiplexing reduces the impact of the gap between data transmission and data generation/consumption speeds.

1 Introduction

Optical interconnection networks have the potential of offering bandwidths that are orders of magnitude larger than those of electronic interconnection networks. However, packet switching techniques, which are usually used in electronic interconnection networks are not quite suitable when optical transmission is used. The absence of appropriate photonic logic devices makes it extremely impractical to process packet routing information in the photonic domain. Moreover, conversion of this information into the electronic domain increases the latency at intermediate nodes relative to the internode propagation delay, especially in multiprocessor networks where the internode propagation delays are very small. Hence, to take full advantage of optical transmission, all-optical paths should be established between the communicating nodes before data is transmitted.

In order to exploit the large bandwidth of all-optical networks in massively parallel systems, the speed mismatch between the components of the communication system must be resolved. An imminent speed mismatch in systems involving all-optical networks is the gap between the fast transmission of signals in the optical domain and the slow network control, which is usually performed in the electronic domain. Another gap is between the high optical data transmission rate and the relatively slow data generation/consumption rate at the source and destination nodes.

Time-Division-Multiplexing (TDM) techniques [3, 4] have been proposed to resolve the speed mismatch between the fast optical data network and slow

---

* This work was supported in part by NSF awards MIP-9633729 and CCR-9157371.

network control. However, to our knowledge, no previous work has considered the impact of the speed mismatch between the fast data transmission and the slow data generation/consumption, which is bounded by the electronic speed. Specifically, the bandwidth of optical links may not be fully utilized if the data generation/consumption rate at the end points of a connection cannot match the transmission speed. In this paper, we present a study of the effect of this mismatch. First, however, we briefly describe *Time Division Multiplexing* (TDM) as applied to interconnection networks.

2 Time division multiplexing (TDM)

We consider switching networks in which the set of connections that can be established simultaneously may be changed by changing the state of the network. A set of connections that can be supported simultaneously will be called a *configuration*. In a TDM system, each link is multiplexed in the time domain to support multiple virtual channels. Hence, multiple connections can co-exist on a link, and thus, multiple configurations can co-exist in the network.

Figure 1 (a) shows an example of such a system. In this example, each processor has an input and an output connection to a 3×3 switch. Each link is multiplexed with degree 2 by dividing the time domain into 2 time slots, and using alternating time slots for supporting two channels, $c0$ and $c1$. Four connections, $(0,2)$, $(2,1)$, $(2,4)$ and $(3,2)$, are established with connections $(0,2)$ and $(2,1)$ using channel $c0$, and connections $(2,4)$ and $(3,2)$ using channel $c1$. The switches are globally synchronized at timeslot boundaries, and each switch is set to alternate between the two states that are needed to realize the connections. For example, Figure 1 (b) shows the two states that the 3×3 switch attached to processor 2 must realize for the establishment of the connections shown in Figure 1 (a). Note that each switch is an electro-optical switch ($Ti : LiNbO_3$ switch, for example [1]) which connects optical inputs to optical outputs without optical/electronic conversion. The state of the switch is controlled by an electronic signal.

There are two main advantages for optical TDM networks. First, multiplexing increases the number of connections that can co-exist in the network, thus, increasing the chance of successfully establishing a connection. The cost of control is amortized over the number of co-existing connections, thus reducing the control overhead. This effect was studied in [4], where TDM was shown to reduce the impact of the gap between data transmission and control network speeds.

The second advantage of TDM is that it can reduce the impact of the speed mismatch between the large bandwidth of optical transmission rate and the low data generation rate at each node, especially when transmitted data is to be fetched from (or stored into) memory. In other words, if data cannot be fetched from (or stored into) memory fast enough to match the optical transmission bandwidth, the extra bandwidth in the path will be wasted. In such cases, multiplexing allows the large optical bandwidth to be shared among multiple connections. Notice that under current technology, assuming that 64 bits

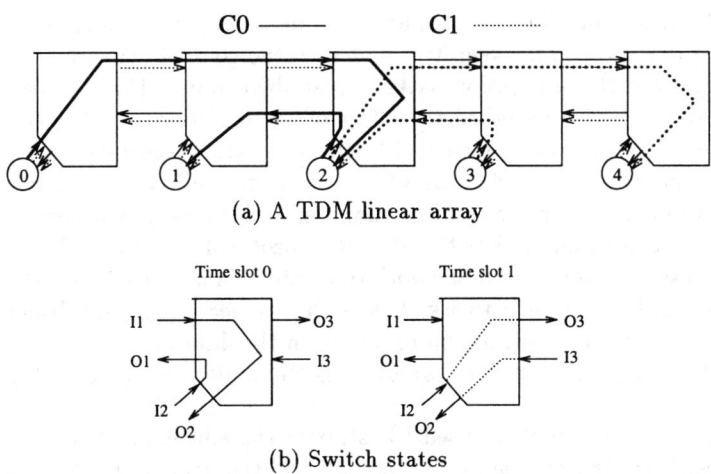

Fig. 1. Time division multiplexing

can be fetched from (or stored into) memory in 40ns, the end nodes can have 1.6Gb/s data generation/consumption rate, while optical network with bandwidth of 250Gb/s have been demonstrated [2]. We focus on the impact of this gap on TDM systems.

3 Effect of memory speed on network performance

Let's define the *memory/link bandwidth ratio* to be the ratio between the time it takes to transmit a data packet between two nodes on an already established all-optical connection to the time it takes to fetch/store a data packet from memory. Time will be measured in terms of time slots, where a time slot is large enough to transmit a packet between two nodes on an optical connection. In a multiprocessing environment, where nodes are at most a few feet apart, it is reasonable to assume that the time for packet transmission is independent of the length of the optical connection (light signals travel at a speed of about one foot per nano-second).

We conducted extensive simulations to study the effect of the memory speed on the communication performance of TDM systems. This section presents some sample results of our study. We simulated random communications on a 16×16 torus network which uses the *conservative backward reservation protocol* [4] for the dynamic reservation of all-optical paths. To support this protocol, a shadow control network, which has the same topology as the optical data network, is needed. The control network, is an electronic network which operates in a packet switching fashion, and in which control packets are processed at each intermediate node to execute a distributed protocol for the establishment of optical data paths. The speed of the control network is characterized by the control packet processing time, which is the time required at each intermediate node to process a control packet, and the control packet propagation time, which is the time to transmit the packet to between two nodes on the control network.

We modified the simulation package described in detail in [4] to account for memory speed, and we studied the effect of the memory to link speed ratio on the efficiency of the communication. In the simulation, during each time slot, a message is generated at each node with a fixed probability, r. Each message has a fixed size measured in terms of the number of data packets it contains. When a message is generated, a distributed control protocol is executed by exchanging control packets on the control network to establish a connection for the message on the multiplexed data network. When the connection is established using a given TDM channel, transmission proceeds on the data network at a rate of one data packet every K time slots, where K is the multiplexing degree of the data network.

The performance metrics used to estimate the efficiency of the communication network are the *maximum throughput*, and the *average message delay*. The maximum throughput is defined as the number of packets delivered to their destinations per time slot when the network is saturated. The message delay is the length of the period, in time slots, between the time a message is submitted to the network to the time at which the first packet in the message is received at the destination. Message delay is measured at low traffic conditions. Specifically, we will measure the delay when, r, the message generation rate at each node, is much smaller than the rate at which the network saturates.

3.1 Effect of memory speed on throughput

Figure 2 shows the maximum throughput that the network can achieve with different multiplexing degrees and different memory/link bandwidth ratios. In this experiment, we set the message size to be 8 packets, the control packet processing time to be 1 time slot and the control packet propagation time to be 1 time slot. It is clear from Figure 2 that for any memory/link bandwidth ratio, the throughput increases when the multiplexing degree increases. This is due to the decrease in the connection establishment time.

For a given multiplexing degree, K, the data generation/consumption at the end nodes is not a bottleneck when the memory speed is the same as the network speed (memory/link bandwidth ratio equal to 1). For slower memory speeds, the network throughput does not decrease as long as data can be fetched from (or stored into) memory faster that the speed at which it can be transmitted on the network. That is, as long as one packet is ready for transmission on each established connection every K time slots. However, for each multiplexing degree, there exists a memory/link bandwidth ratio, called *the throughput critical ratio*, CR_t, after which data are not available when it can be transmitted. In other words, when the memory/link bandwidth ratio is larger than CR_t, the memory speed does not affect the network throughput and when the memory/link bandwidth ratio is smaller than CR_t, the throughput decreases (almost linearly) with the decrease in memory speed.

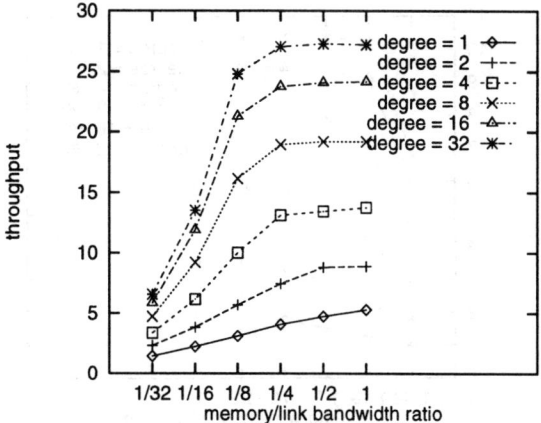

Fig. 2. Effect of memory speed on the maximum throughput (message size = 8)

As shown in Figure 2, CR_t in a multiplexed network is smaller than CR_t in a non-multiplexed network (degree = 1). For example, CR_t for non-multiplexed network is 1, while CR_t for networks with multiplexing degree 16 is between $\frac{1}{4}$ and $\frac{1}{8}$ in this experiment. In other words, for non–multiplexed networks, any mismatch between the memory and the transmission speed will reduce the network throughput, while when the multiplexing degree is 16, slowing down the memory speed up to $\frac{1}{8}$ of the optical transmission speed does not degrade the throughput. This indicates that TDM results in less memory pressure on the source nodes to achieve its maximum throughput. Hence TDM bridges the gap between the data transmission speed and the memory speed.

It is possible to approximate CR_t for a given multiplexing degree, K. Specifically, if C is the average number of connections that originate or terminate at a node at any given time, then in order not to reduce the throughput, the memory should be fast enough to fetch (or store) C packets every K time slots. This will allow one packet to be sent over each connection every K time slots, thus fully utilizing the bandwidth available on the K-way multiplexed connections. This gives:

$$CR_t = \frac{C}{K}.$$

Clearly, the value of C is between 0 and K since at most K channels can be established at any source or destination. Moreover, C should increase when K increases since multiplexing increases the number of connections that can co-exist at the source or destination nodes. In fact, in an ideal network in which network control is very fast and efficient, it is reasonable to assume that doubling K will double C, thus making CR_t unaffected by the multiplexing degree. However, as can be seen from Figure 2, CR_t decreases with K, which means that C is a sublinear function of K. The decrease in CR_t is not linearly proportional to K since C increases with K.

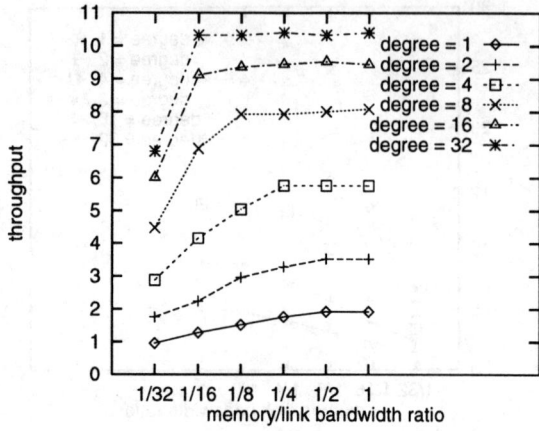

Fig. 3. Throughput when control network is slow (message size = 8)

The above argument can be further validated by considering the effect of the control network speed. Figure 3 shows the communication performance with a slow control network speed. This experiment has the same setting as in Figure 2 except that the control network speed is 4 times slower. We observe that, for a given multiplexing degree, slowing down the control network results in a smaller CR_t (in addition to reducing the network's throughput). This can be explained by noting that a slower control network reduces the number of established connections, and thus reduces C. Moreover, notice that the decrease in CR_t with K is closer to linear than the case of the faster control network. Again, this is because, with a slow control network, the communication bottleneck is shifted from the data network to the control network, and thus C does not increase as much with K.

The number of connections C is also affected by the message size. Specifically, long messages will result in long connections, which will tend to increase the number of connections established in the network, thus increasing C. Figure 4 shows the effect of the message size, measured in terms of the number of data packets, on the maximum throughput. In this experiment, we set the multiplexing degree to be 16 and set all other parameters to be the same as in Figure 2. We can see from this figure that, for message size 2, CR_t is $\frac{1}{16}$, while for message size 32, CR_t is between $\frac{1}{2}$ and $\frac{1}{4}$. Hence, TDM is more effective in bridging the gap between memory and data transmission speeds when the message size is small.

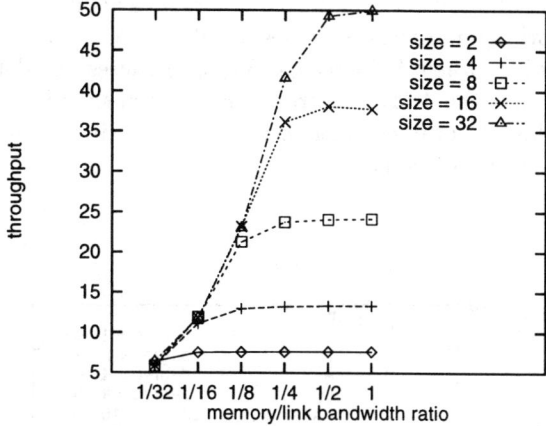

Fig. 4. Effect of message size on CR_t (degree = 16)

3.2 Effect of memory speed on communication delay

The communication delay is defined in this section as the average delay between the time a connection request is generated to the time at which the first packet of the data is received at the destination node. The delay in establishing a data communication path can be due to conflict induced by the control network or due to conflict induced by the data network. The former conflict results from control packets contending for the same buffers in the packet-switched control network, while the latter conflict results from the unavailability of data channels. Either conflicts causes the control packets to be blocked waiting for resources to be released (buffers in the former case and data channels in the latter case). In order to avoid deadlock, we use "packet dropping" in our simulation; a control packet is dropped as soon as it is blocked and a "fail" message is sent to the sending node, which re-starts the path reservation phase after a random waiting period.

In this section, the communication delay will be estimated at low traffic compared to the saturation traffic considered in the last section. Given than the throughput is equal to the number of packets delivered per time slot, it is also equal to the number of packets generated per time slot. For instance a throughput of 24 packets per time slot in Figure 2 corresponds to a generation rate $r = \frac{24}{8*256}$ = 0.0117 messages per node per time slot. In Figure 5, we show the delay for $r = 0.0005$ and 0.0015 in a 256 node network as a function of the memory/link bandwidth ratio, assuming 8-packet messages and different multiplexing degrees.

The multiplexing degree affects the delay in establishing a connection in two opposing manners. On the one hand, a larger multiplexing degree means that there is more data channels available for establishing the connection, thus reducing the delay. We will refer to this effect by $E_{channel}$. On the other hand, with a multiplexing degree of K, one packet of a given message is sent on an established connection every K time slots, which means that connections are held longer when the multiplexing degree is larger. This in turns increases the probability of blocking and thus increases the delay. We will refer to this effect by $E_{duration}$. That is, when K increases, $E_{channel}$ causes the delay to decrease while $E_{duration}$ causes the delay to increase. Because of the two opposing effects, the minimum delay is obtained at a certain multiplexing degree, K_{opt}, which depends on many factors (see [4]).

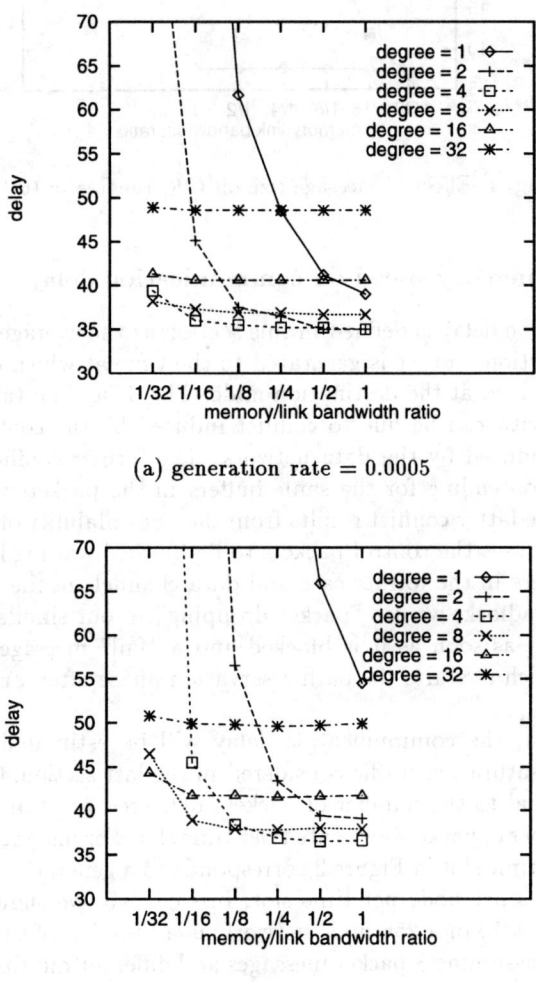

Fig. 5. Effect of memory speed on the delay (message size = 8)

Although we will not study the effect of $E_{channel}$ and $E_{duration}$ on the optimum multiplexing degree, we will use $E_{duration}$ to clarify the effect of the memory/link bandwidth ratio on the delay. Specifically, as we did in the last section for the throughput, we define *the delay critical ratio*, CR_d, as the memory/link bandwidth ratio below which the delay increases. That is, slowing down the memory up to CR_d does not affect the delay. For very low generation rates (as is the case for Figure 5(a)), the probability of having more than one connection established per node is very low, and thus slowing down the memory speed by a factor of up to the multiplexing degree K does not affect the delay. However, when the memory speed is slowed down by a factor larger than K, the duration of each connection is increased since data will not be available for transmission when needed. This will cause the delay to increase due to the $E_{duration}$ effect. Hence, $CR_d = \frac{1}{K}$. When the generation rate, r, increases (as is the case for Figure 5(b)), the number of connections established per node increases, thus causing CR_d to be larger than $\frac{1}{K}$. Hence, in general,

$$CR_d = \frac{C}{K}.$$

where C is the average number of connections established per node.

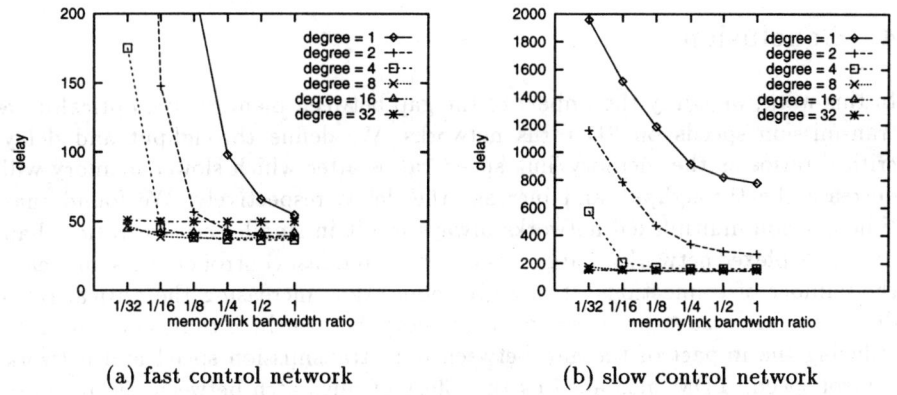

(a) fast control network (b) slow control network

Fig. 6. Effect of control network speed on the delay (message size = 8, $r = 0.0015$)

In Figure 6, we show the effect of the control network speed where Figure 6(a) is a re-drawing of Figure 5(b) using a different scale, and Figure 6(b) is the delay for the case when the control network is slowed down by a factor of four. Clearly, slowing down the control network increases the delay, but the value of CR_d seems to be relatively unaffected since the value of C is more affected by the generation rate, r, rather than by the control speed.

Finally, we show in Figure 7 the effect of the message size on the delay. For a given memory/link bandwidth ratio, longer messages lead to increased delay due

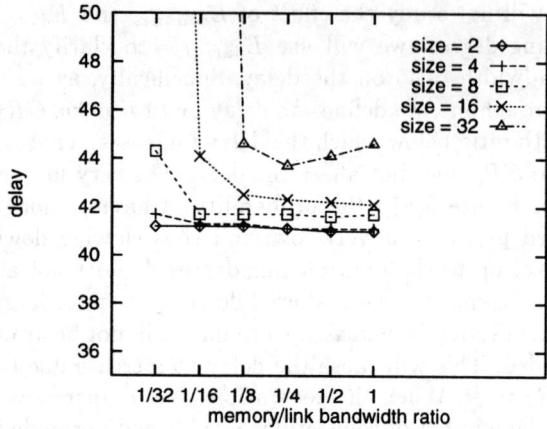

Fig. 7. Effect of message size on the delay (degree = 16, $r = 0.0015$)

to the $E_{duration}$ effect. Also, longer messages means larger traffic on the network (message generation rate is fixed at $r = 0.0015$), which in turns increases CR_d as discussed earlier.

4 Conclusion

In this work, we study the impact of the gap between memory and optical data transmission speeds on 2D torus networks. We define throughput and delay critical ratios as the memory/link speed ratios after which slower memory will decrease the throughput and increase the delay, respectively. We found that time-division multiplexed networks always result in smaller critical ratios than non-multiplexed networks. Large message sizes and fast control networks increase the number of connections at any give node, thus increasing the critical ratio due to the increase in pressure on the memory. We conclude that, in addition to reducing the impact of the gap between data transmission speed and network control speed, TDM also absorbs the effect of mismatch between the memory speed and the optical communication speed, especially for small message sizes or slow network control. That is, TDM leads to the efficient utilization of the large optical bandwidth.

References

1. H. Scott Hinton, "Photonic Switching Using Directional Couplers," *IEEE Communication Magazine*, Vol. 25, No. 5, pp 16-26, 1987.
2. P.R. Prucnal, I. Glesk and J.P. Sokoloff, "Demonstration of All–Optical Self–Clocked Demultiplexing of TDM Data at 250Gb/s", In *Proceedings of the first international workshop on massively parallel processing using optical interconnections*. Pages 106–117, Cancun, Mexico, April 1994.

3. C. Qiao and R. Melhem, "Reconfiguration with Time Division Multiplexed MIN's for Multiprocessor Communication." *IEEE Trans. on Parallel and Distributed Systems*, Vol. 5, N0. 4, April 1994.
4. X. Yuan, R. Melhem and R. Gupta, "Distributed path reservation algorithms for multiplexed all–optical interconnection networks." *Int. Symp. on High Performance Computer Architecture - HPCA-3*, 1997.

Session VII

DEADLOCK ISSUES

Friday, June 27, 1997
3:00 - 4:00

Session Chair:

S. Yalamanchili
Georgia Institute of Technology

Modeling Message Blocking and Deadlock in Interconnection Networks

Sugath Warnakulasuriya and Timothy Mark Pinkston

SMART Interconnects Group
Electrical Engineering - Systems Department, University of Southern California
3740 McClintock Avenue, EEB-208, Los Angeles, CA 90089-2562
{sugath@scf, tpink@charity}.usc.edu;
http://www.usc.edu/dept/ceng/pinkston/SMART.html

Abstract. This paper presents an approach to modeling resource allocations and dependencies within cut-through and wormhole interconnection networks. This model allows various types of message blocking to be represented precisely, including deadlock. Our model of deadlock distinguishes between messages involved in deadlock and those simply dependent on deadlock, thus providing specification criteria for precise deadlock detection and recovery. The model and its implementation in a network simulator are described. Time and space complexity of the implementation is also discussed.

1 Introduction

The performance of an interconnection network depends critically on its ability to minimize message blocking. Designing high-performance interconnection networks requires a thorough understanding of various types of message blocking phenomena that can occur and the network's susceptibility to experiencing these phenomena. Although a large number of interconnection networks and routing algorithms with various performance and message blocking attributes have been proposed in the past [3, 4, 5, 6, 7, 8, 9, 10], few studies have provided insight into the characteristics of various types of message blocking. While some studies (i.e., [9]) have noted the consequences of certain types of correlated message blocking as they relate to performance degradation, to our knowledge, no previous attempt has been made to precisely describe these types of blocking phenomena. Other work (i.e., [11]) has provided descriptions of blocking related to deadlock and its overall effects on the network but has not provided precise characterization of message blocking useful for distinguishing between the causes and consequences of deadlock.

A practical approach to better understanding message blocking is through modeling and simulation. In this paper, we develop and present an approach to modeling network resource allocation and contention and various types of message blocking, including deadlock. The model allows the precise description of blocking behavior in a wide range of network classes including wormhole and cut-through switched k-ary n-cubes which support deadlock avoidance and deadlock recovery routing. Our model precisely describes deadlock as well as other "non-deadlock" correlated blocking phenomena. The precise definition of deadlock included in the model allows distinguishing between causes and consequences of deadlock, thus providing guidelines and an evaluation critera for accurate detection of and recovery from deadlock. We have incorporated this model in an implementation of an interconnection network simulator. We use this simulator to perform detailed characterization of various types of message blocking and deadlock. Results of deadlock characterization performed using this simulator are presented in [1, 2]. Other potential applications of our model include its use to characterize message blocking and deadlock in irregular networks, to evaluate recovery-based routing algorithms, to evaluate mechanisms for minizing correlated message blocking and deadlocks when unrestricted routing is allowed, and to devise efficient mechanisms for the detection of and recovery from deadlock. The message blocking framework described in this paper is implemented in a network simulator for characterization purposes and is not intended to be a technique that should be implemented in network routers. though aspects of it could be.

The outline of this paper is as follows. Section 2 presents, through example, our network resource model used for representing allocation and contention of network resources by messages. Section 3 presents our message blocking model used to describe message blocking and deadlock. Section 4 describes our implementation of the mesage blocking and deadlock model in a network simulator. Related work is discussed in Section 5, and we summarize and conclude the paper in Section 6.

2 Network Resource Model

We present here through example our approach to modeling resource dependencies, message blocking, and deadlock within interconnection networks. Our model encompasses maximally adaptive routing, and thus accommodates both restricted (deadlock avoidance-based [7, 8, 9]) and unrestricted (deadlock recovery-based [4, 5, 6]) routing algorithms. It uses *channel wait-for graphs* (CWGs) to represent resource allocations and requests *existing within the network at a given point in time*. The CWGs consist of a set of vertices $vc_1 \ldots vc_n$, each representing an independently allocatable virtual channel resource in the network. The messages in the network at a given time are uniquely identified as $m_1 \ldots m_k$. We assume a fixed number of reusable virtual channels and a dynamically variable number of messages which can be in the network at any time for a given network configuration. A formal version of this model is presented in [12].

2.1 Virtual Channel Allocation and Requests

Here we describe how vertices in the CWG are connected to reflect resource allocations to and requests by messages. When a message progresses through the network, it acquires exclusive ownership of a new virtual channel (VC) prior

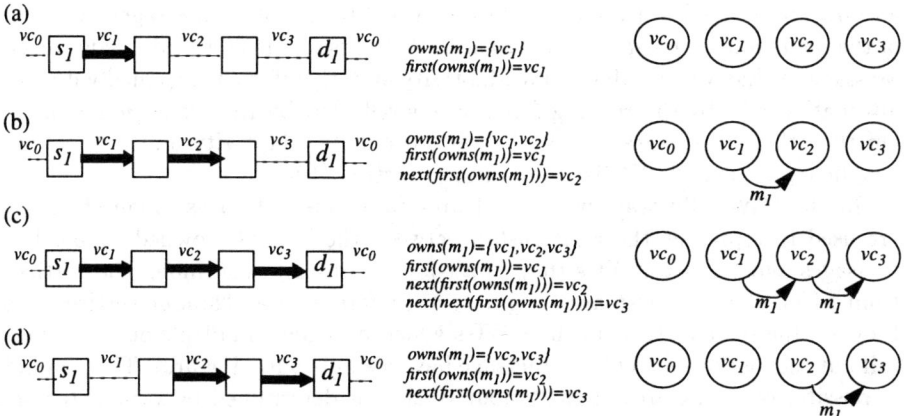

Fig. 1. Network and CWG states for message m_1 being routed from source s_1 to destination d_1 in a unidirectional ring network with one VC per physical channel.

to each hop. If the message header blocks, it waits to obtain exclusive use of one of possibly many alternative VCs in order to progress to the next hop. A blocked message can resume once a new VC is acquired. As the tail of a message moves through the network, it releases (in the order of acquisition) previously acquired VCs which are no longer needed, and these VCs then become available for other messages to acquire.

We represent VCs owned by message m_i as the set $owns(m_i)$ and the order in which the VCs are acquired using the functions $first$ and $next$. As an example, Figure 1 shows the network and CWG states for a message m_1 being routed from its source node s_1 to its destination d_1 in a unidirectional ring network (4-ary 1-cube) with one VC per physical channel. Figures 1 (a), (b), and (c) show the network and CWG states as the message header moves towards and reaches its destination (assuming a message length > 3 flits). The order in which this message acquired the VCs it owns at a given time can be expressed by $first(owns(m_1))$, $next(first(owns(m_1)))$, $next(next(first(owns(m_1))))$, etc. Figure 1 (d) shows the state after the tail of the message has left the source node and has released the first VC it acquired.

The routing function determines the alternative VCs a message may use to reach the next node for a given current node and destination node pair. When none of the VCs supplied by the routing function are available (due to those VCs being owned by other messages), the message becomes blocked. For a blocked message m_i, the set $requests(m_i)$ represents the set of alternative VCs it may use to resume, thus reflecting the set of VCs supplied by the routing function. As an example, Figure 2 shows four messages $m_1 \ldots m4$ within a 4x2 unidirectional torus network with one VC per physical channel and which uses minimal adaptive routing. In this example, messages m_2 and m_4 have acquired all of the VCs needed to reach their respective destinations, while message m_1

and m_3 are blocked waiting for resources owned by the other messages (a listing of the *owns* and *requests* sets for each of the messages is included in Figure 2). Message m_1 has yet to exhaust its adaptivity and, therefore, is supplied with two alternative VCs by the routing function (as reflected by the set $requests(m_1)$). On the other hand, message m_1 has exhausted its adaptivity and is therefore supplied only a single VC by the routing function [10].

In the CWG illustrations, dashed arcs (also referred to as "request arcs") are used to represent the relationship between the last VCs owned by blocked messages and the set of VCs they "wait-for" in order to continue. The vertices from which these request arcs originate are referred to as "fanout vertices", as they are the only vertices in the CWGs which may have multiple outgoing arcs (all but the last owned VC of a message have a single outgoing arc). The number of possible outgoing arcs at the fanout vertices is determined by various factors including the number of physical and virtual channel resources in the network and the amount of routing freedom allowed in the use of these resources by the routing algorithm.

In order for a blocked message m_i to resume, it must acquire any one of the VCs in the set $requests(m_i)$ after it is released by its previous owner. Continuing the example in Figure 2, when message m_4 releases vc_3 (after its tail flit has traversed this channel), the VC can be acquired by message m_3. The CWG state resulting from this along with the updated *owns* and *requests* sets are shown in Figure 3a. Subsequently, message m_2 may release vc_{13}, thus allowing message m_1 to continue. The CWG depicting this is shown in Figure 3b. In such cases where a blocked message resumes, its *requests* set becomes empty as any one of its members is acquired and becomes a member of the *owns* set. In essence, a message has dashed arcs (in the CWG illustrations) to *all* of its alternative VCs when it is blocked, and these dashed arcs are replaced with a *single* solid arc to the newly acquired VC upon resumption. We discuss exceptions to this for supporting VC queue (buffer) sharing in Section 2.2.

In these illustrations, the VC labeling is done only to facilitate explanation and is not intended to convey information regarding the relative positions of VCs within the network. Also, to facilitate explanation, we label the outgoing arc(s) at each CWG vertex with the message which currently owns that VC. As described above, a *path* formed by a series of solid arcs with the same label implies the temporal order in which the VCs represented by the vertices in the path were acquired and continues to be owned by a particular message. Given exclusive ownership of VC resources, there can be at most a single outgoing solid arc at any given node. At any vertex, the labels of incoming dashed arcs represent the group of messages that desire to use that VC at this instant in time. While we showed all of the vertices of the CWGs in Figures 1, 2, and 3, from now on we will show only those connected components of the CWGs useful for illustrative purposes.

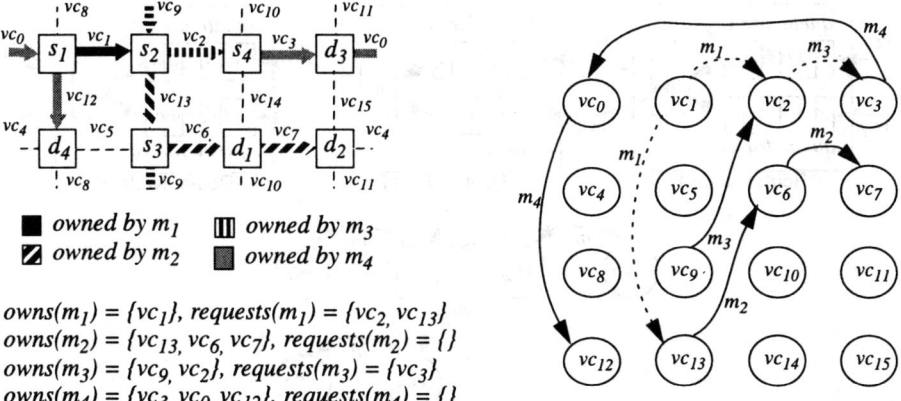

Fig. 2. Network and CWG state for messages $m_1 \ldots m_4$ being routed within a 2x4 unidirectional network.

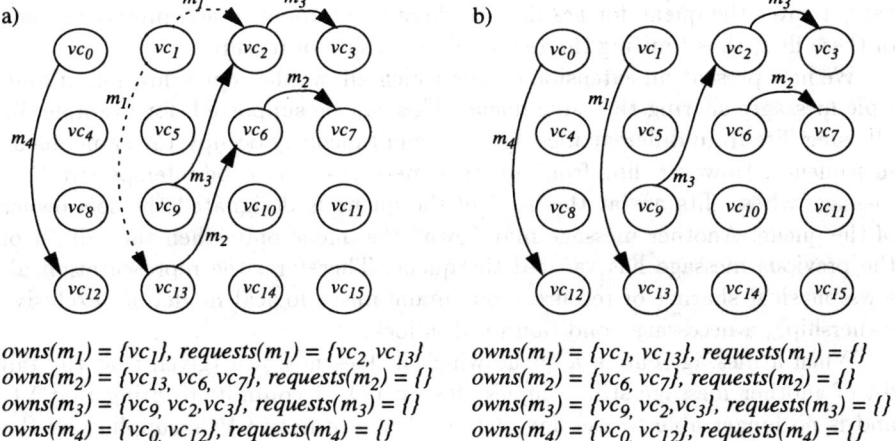

Fig. 3. a) CWG state when message m_3 acquires vc_3 and (b) CWG state when message m_1 acquires vc_{13}.

2.2 Sharing Virtual Channel Queues

In our basic model, we assume that each channel is exclusively owned by a single message, and therefore, each channel queue is occupied exclusively by flits belonging to that message. For example, Figure 4 shows the routers and their VC queues for a portion of a unidirectional ring network with two VCs per physical channel (along with CWG) for a network based on this assumption. In the networks, flits h_i, d_i, and t_i correspond to the header, data, and tail flits of message m_i. This figure shows that with restrictions on the simultaneous use of a channel queue by more than one message, the leading flits of message m_3

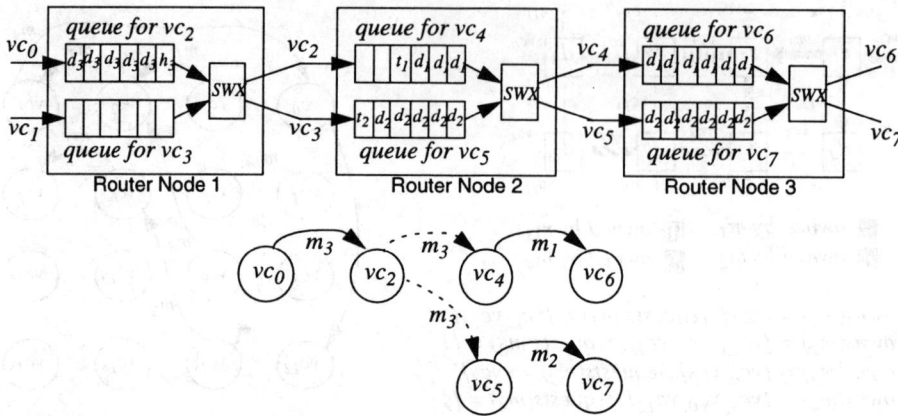

Fig. 4. Internal state of network routers and the corresponding CWG state when sharing of queues is not allowed.

cannot enter the queue for vc_4 despite there being room to accommodate some of these flits, thus limiting the maximal utilization of resources.

We now present an extension of this which allows the representation of multiple messages sharing the same queue. This can be supported, for example, by allowing flits from different messages to simultaneously occupy the same queue in sequence. However, flits from different messages cannot be interspersed. The message whose flits are at the head of the queue is designated the sole owner of the queue. Another message may "own" the queue only when the tail flit of the previous message has vacated the queue. Therefore, the representation allows physical sharing of resources but maintains a logical model of "exclusive ownership", a necessary condition for deadlock.

When a message enters a queue which it does not own (given that the tail flit of another message still occupies this queue), it commits to using that VC and is no longer able to use any of the other alternative VCs supplied by the routing function. To reflect this in the resource model, all request arcs (dashed arcs) in the CWG are removed except for the one representing the VC being allocated to the message. This single dashed arc becomes a solid arc only when the message acquires ownership of the VC (when the tail flits of other messages in the queue have vacated the queue).

Figure 5 gives an example which illustrates shared queue representation. Here, the leading flits of message m_3 have entered the queue for vc_4 and, thus, is committed to using vc_4. By committing early to using vc_4, m_3 is no longer able to use vc_5 (as reflected by the lack of a dashed arc to vc_5 in the CWG) even though the queue for vc_5 may become available for ownership sooner than vc_4. Empirical results suggest that reducing "fanout" as is done here by committing to VCs early may increase the probability of deadlocks forming as routing freedom is reduced [1, 2].

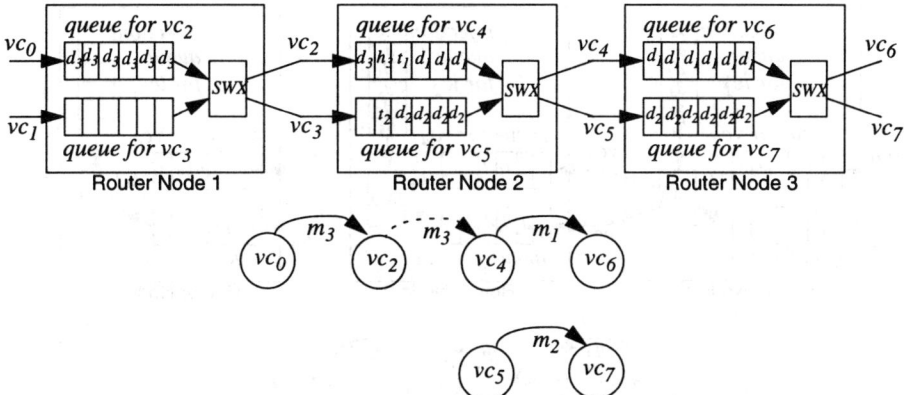

Fig. 5. Internal state of network routers and the corresponding CWG state when sharing of queues is allowed.

2.3 Injection and Reception Channels

Our basic resource dependency model takes into account only those messages which have already entered the network and, therefore, have already acquired at least one resource (i.e., $|owns(m_i)| > 0$ for all messages m_i). So far, it does not take into account those messages which are waiting in injection queues (from the processor) trying to acquire the first VC. Since message blocking and deadlock within the network can also impact these messages, it is useful to expand the model to include these resources.

In the expanded model ownership rules for injection channels remain the same as for VCs. The representation of wait-for relationships between messages in injection channels and VCs owned by other messages is similar as well. Figure 6 shows an example of this where messages m_4 and m_5 in injection channels ic_1 and ic_2 (respectively) are waiting for channels owned by messages m_1 and m_2. Dependence on reception channels (to the processor) can also be modeled in a similar fashion.

3 Message Blocking Model

3.1 Acyclic Paths, Cycles, and Reachable Sets

Paths in CWGs are formed when two or more vertices are connected by a series of arcs. For example, in the CWG in Figure 2 a path exists from vc_{13} to vc_6, from vc_6 to vc_7, and from vc_{13} to vc_7 (through vc_6), etc. A path can be represented using an ordered list, and it may contain VCs owned by different messages as in the path from vc_1 to vc_{12} in Figure 2. Here, the path is represented by the ordered list $(vc_1, vc_2, vc_3, vc_0, vc_{12})$ and contains VCs owned by messages m_1, m_3 and m_4. When all of the vertices in a path are unique, an *acyclic path* is said to exist. All of the paths in Figures 1, 2 and 3 are acyclic.

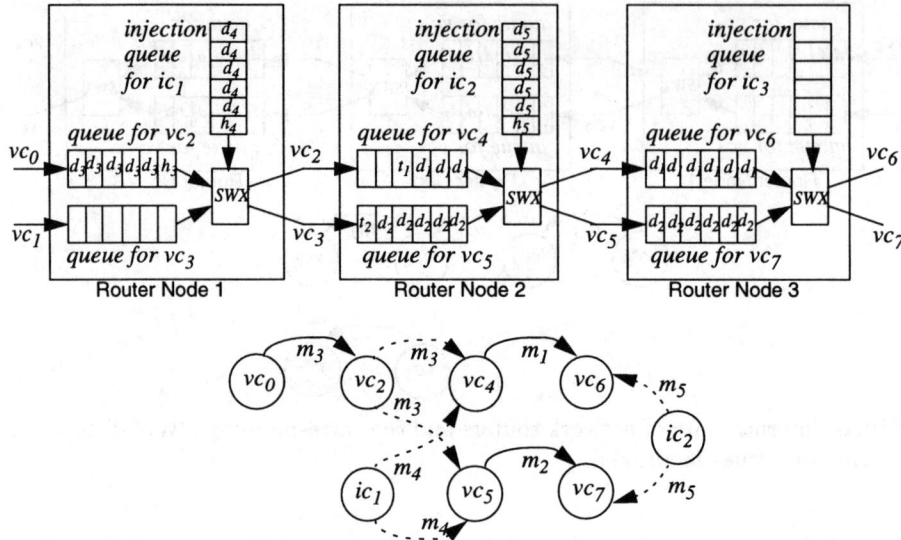

Fig. 6. Internal state of network routers and the corresponding CWG state when including injection channels in the resource model.

Figure 7 shows an example of a *cycle* within a CWG for a 2x4 unidirectional torus network with minimal adaptive routing. In general, a cycle in a CWG can be viewed as being composed of an acyclic path and an additional edge from the end of the path to the beginning of the path. The only cycle in the CWG depicted in Figure 7 consists of the set of vertices $\{vc_4, vc_5, vc_6, vc_7\}$ and can be viewed as being composed of the acyclic path (vc_4, vc_5, vc_6, vc_7) and the edge (vc_7, vc_4). Alternatively, it can be viewed as being composed of the acyclic path (vc_5, vc_6, vc_7, vc_4) and the edge (vc_4, vc_5), among other variations. All of these variations represent a unique cycle in that they all refer to the same set of vertices and edges. Note that another unique cycle involving the set of vertices $\{vc_4, vc_5, vc_6, vc_7\}$ can exist if, for instance, edges (vc_7, vc_6), (vc_6, vc_5), (vc_5, vc_4), and (vc_4, vc_7) also exist in the CWG. However, since there can be at most a single edge *in a given direction* between any two vertices, we can refer to a unique cycle by an ordered list of vertices.

A *reachable set* of a vertex in a CWG is the set of vertices comprising all acyclic paths and cycles starting from that vertex. In Figure 7, the reachable set for vertex vc_{14} is $\{vc_3, vc_0\}$; for vc_3 is $\{vc_0\}$; for vc_0 is $\{\}$; and for vertices vc_4, vc_5, vc_6 and vc_7 is $\{vc_4, vc_5, vc_6, vc_7, vc_{14}, vc_3, vc_0\}$.

3.2 Deadlocks and Cyclic Non-deadlocks

Figure 8 shows six messages being routed within a 4-ary 2-cube unidirectional network with one VC per physical channel and which allows minimal adaptive routing. Here, message m_1 has acquired vc_1 and vc_2, message m_2 has acquired

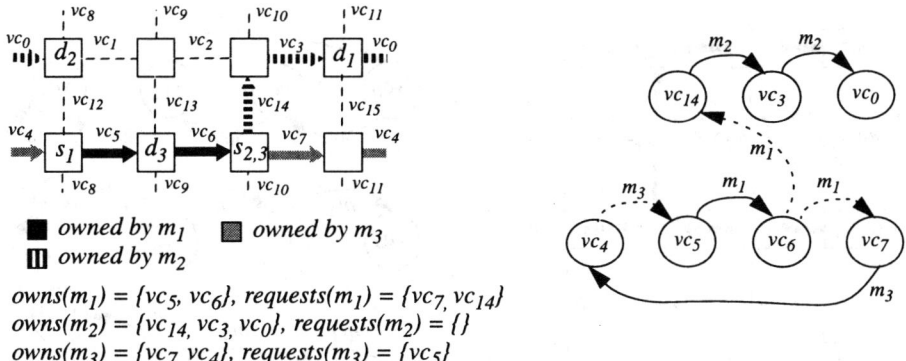

owns(m_1) = {vc_5, vc_6}, requests(m_1) = {vc_7, vc_{14}}
owns(m_2) = {vc_{14}, vc_3, vc_0}, requests(m_2) = {}
owns(m_3) = {vc_7, vc_4}, requests(m_3) = {vc_5}

Fig. 7. Network and CWG state for messages m_1, m_2, and m_3 being routed within a 2x4 unidirectional network. There is a cycle in the CWG.

vc_3 and vc_0. Each of these two messages are waiting to acquire an additional VC in order to reach their respective destinations. In the accompanying CWG, there is a cycle containing the set of vertices {vc_0, vc_1, vc_2, vc_3}. The set of vertices in this cycle has the property that the reachable set of each of its members is the set itself. A set of vertices which has this property is referred to as a *knot*. A network whose CWG contains a knot is said to contain a deadlock because none of the messages which own the vertices in the knot are able to advance. We show that a knot is a necessary and sufficient condition for deadlock in [12]. So here we will use the terms knot and deadlock interchangeably. In a deadlocked state, for example, messages m_1 and m_2 in Figure 8 will wait for the other to release the required VC, thus waiting indefinitely assuming that this deadlock is not properly resolved. We also show that removing one or more messages in the knot is sufficient to resolve deadlock in [12]. Messages not directly involved in a knot but whose progress also depends upon the resolution of the deadlock are discussed in the next subsection.

From the description of a knot, it is implied that a cycle is necessary for a knot since a cycle must exist in order for a vertex to be in its reachable set. However, a cycle is not sufficient for a knot or deadlock [10]. For example, the CWG in Figure 7 contains a cycle with vertices {vc_4, vc_5, vc_6, vc_7}, and the reachable set of all of its members is {$vc_4, vc_5, vc_6, vc_7, vc_{14}, vc_3, vc_0$}. However, notice that this set contains members which have different reachable sets than the set itself (i.e., vc_{14}, vc_3, and vc_0 have different reachable sets), thus violating the requirements for a knot. Such network configurations which contain one or more unique cycles, but no knot (deadlock) are said to contain what are referred to as *cyclic non-deadlocks*. Although cyclic non-deadlocks do not cause messages to block indefinitely, the "drainage dependencies" caused by large cyclic non-deadlocks can lead to substantial performance degradation [1, 2, 9]. Both deadlock avoidance and recovery based routing algorithms are susceptible to the formation of cyclic non-deadlocks.

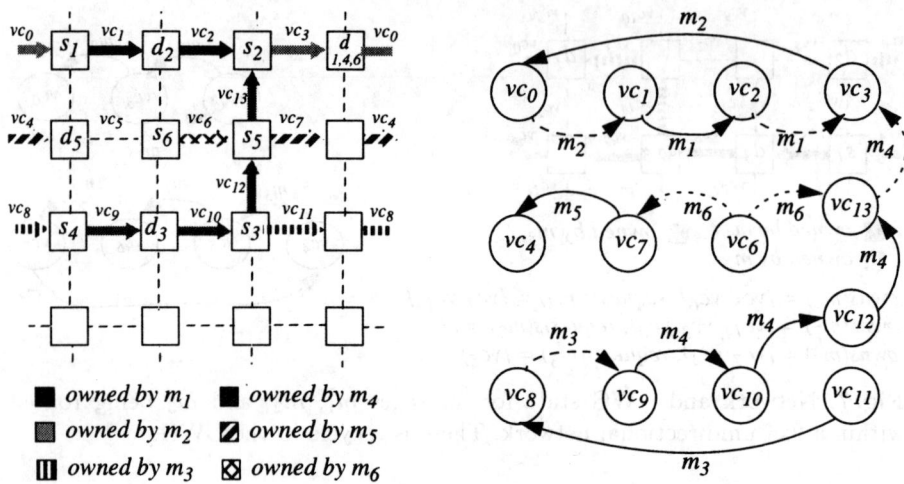

Fig. 8. Network and CWG state for messages $m_1 \ldots m_4$ being routed within a 4-ary 2-cube unidirectional network. There is a knot (deadlock), and message m_4 is fully directly deadlock dependent, message m_3 is fully indirectly deadlock dependent, and message m_6 is partially deadlock dependent.

The deadlock depicted in Figure 8 is what is referred to as a *single-cycle deadlock* (the knot is composed of a single unique cycle). The number of unique cycles in a knot, referred to as *knot cycle density*, is a measure of deadlock complexity. All single-cycle deadlocks have a knot cycle density of one. Knots which involve multiple cycles are referred to as *multi-cycle deadlocks*. The *deadlock set* represents the set of messages which own the VCs represented by the vertices in the knot (the set $\{m_1, m_2\}$ in this example). Once a deadlock forms, it must be resolved by either removing [3, 4] or routing using some additional resources [5, 6, 8] one of the messages in the deadlock set. Finally, the *resource set* of a deadlock represents the set of all resources owned by members of the deadlock set (the set $\{vc_0, vc_1, vc_2, vc_3\}$ in this example). All these attributes are useful for characterizing deadlocks.

3.3 Deadlock Dependent Messages

In addition to affecting those messages in the knot, an unresolved deadlock may also force other messages not in the deadlock set to wait, indefinitely in some cases. Such messages are referred to as *deadlock dependent messages*. For example, in Figure 8, the progress of messages m_3, m_4, and m_6 is affected by the deadlock. These messages are distinguished from those properly in the deadlock set since removing these deadlock dependent messages will not resolve the deadlock [12].

Deadlock dependent messages can be further categorize into *directly* and *indirectly* deadlock dependent as well as *partially* and *fully* deadlock dependent.

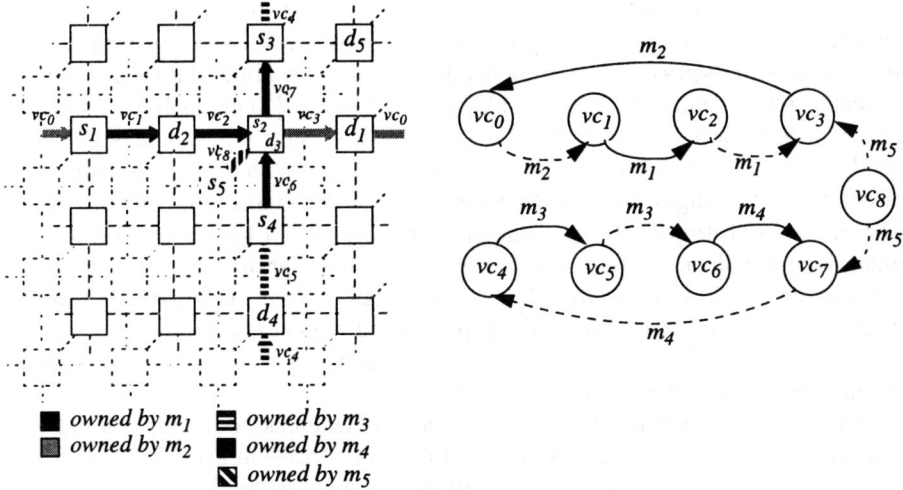

Fig. 9. Network and CWG state for messages $m_1 \ldots m_5$ being routed within a $3D$ unidirectional network. There are two independent knots (deadlocks) and message m_5 is fully directly dependent upon the two deadlocks.

In the example shown in Figure 8, message m_4 is fully and directly deadlock dependent as each and every member of $requests(m_4)$ is owned by a message in the deadlock set. Message m_3 is fully and indirectly deadlock dependent because at least some members of $requests(m_3)$ are owned by other fully directly or fully indirectly deadlock dependent messages and all remaining members are owned by messages in the deadlock set. Both fully directly and fully indirectly deadlock dependent messages are referred to simply as "fully deadlock dependent messages." Partially deadlock dependent messages are those messages whose *requests* sets contain VCs which are owned by non-blocked and/or blocked but non-fully deadlock dependent messages. These messages may resume even if the deadlock is not resolved. Message m_6 in Figure 8 is an example of a partially dependent message; it may resume when message m_5 relinquishes vc_7 despite the deadlock remaining unresolved.

Fully deadlock dependent messages do not necessarily have to be dependent upon a single deadlock. For example, Figure 9 shows a $3D$-torus network with unidirectional channels and a single VC which contains two distinct deadlocks: knots $\{vc_0, vc_1, vc_2, vc_3\}$ and $\{vc_4, vc_5, vc_6, vc_7\}$. Here, message m_5 is fully directly deadlock dependent since all vertices in $requests(m_5)$ are owned by members of the deadlock sets, although different deadlock sets. Although both deadlocks need to be resolved, the resolution of only one of the two will allow m_5 to resume. This example also points out that multiple deadlocks each requiring an independent resolution may exist simultaneously within a network.

Classifying dependent messages provides a basis for evaluating the accuracy of deadlock detection and recovery mechanisms. It also allows us to precisely describe and differentiate between previous notions of deadlock. For instance, "deadlocked configurations" in [11] encompass not only messages in deadlock sets, but also all types of deadlock dependent messages and non-blocked messages as well. "Canonical deadlocked configurations" in [11] include both messages in deadlock sets and fully deadlock dependent messages but excludes partially deadlock dependent and non-blocked messages. Also, neither of these definitions of deadlocked configurations distinguish between single and multiple deadlocks and, more importantly, they do not distinguish between the causes and consequences of deadlock. In contrast, our model allows identification of each independent deadlock and distinguishes between causes (messages participating in knots) and consequences (indefinitely postponed dependent messages) of deadlock, thus enabling us to identify more fundamental components (knots) which require resolution for deadlock recovery.

Further, in measuring the total impact of deadlock, not only should the resources held by the deadlock set be taken into consideration, but also the resources held by deadlock dependent messages. We put forth the notion of *extended resource sets* when describing all of the resources indefinitely occupied by both members of the deadlock set and fully deadlock dependent messages. When a deadlock is allowed to persist, the number of deadlock dependent messages will grow to eventually encompass all of the messages within the network, and the extended resource set of the deadlock will grow to include most, if not all, channel resources in the network. Therefore, the number of deadlock dependent messages and the size of extended resource sets are *time-dependent*, just as the canonical deadlocked configurations in [11]. This time-dependence can also be a useful attribute used in evaluating the performance of various deadlock detection and recovery mechanisms which should quickly resolve impending deadlocks well before the network comes to a halt.

3.4 Fault-Dependent Messages

While unresolved deadlocks can lead to permanent blocking of messages, there are non-deadlock related occurrences which can also cause this type of permanent blocking. Specifically, faults which disconnect the routing function can cause messages to block indefinitely and can eventually lead to all messages in the network blocking permanently. To illustrate, Figure 10 shows four messages being routed within a 4x2 unidirectional network with one VC per physical channel and minimal adaptive routing. In the example, the link for vc_2 has failed causing the routing function to be disconnected (i.e., at the node marked 'd_4', the routing function cannot supply a usable VC for message m_1 which is destined for node d_1). In spite of the fact that no knot exists in the CWG, messages $m_1 \ldots m_4$ still will wait indefinitely or until the failed link is functioning once again. Hence, allowing such faults to persist can also result in the eventual blocking of all messages in the network—the same consequence as allowing deadlock to remain unresolved.

Despite the similarity in consequence, this scenario is not considered to be a deadlock since 1) it does not meet the necessary conditions for deadlock as there

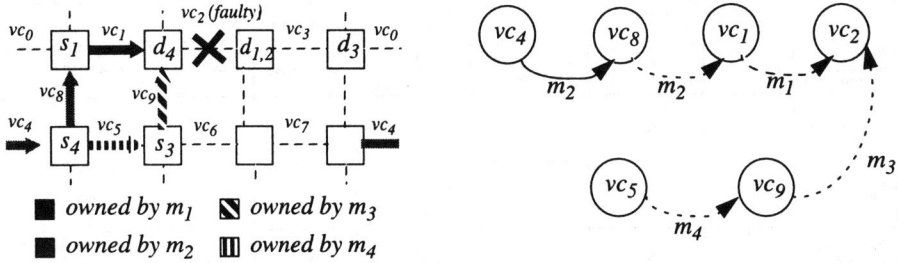

Fig. 10. Network and CWG state for messages $m_1 \ldots m_4$ being routed within a 2x4 unidirectional network containing a faulty link (vc_2). Messages m_1 and m_3 are fully directly fault dependent while messages m_2 and m_4 are fully indirectly fault dependent.

are no cyclic resource dependencies, and 2) it requires different means of resolution than that for deadlock resolution (i.e., removal of a *specific* fault-dependent message (or repair faulty link) as opposed to removal of *any* deadlock set message). Note that both deadlock-avoidance and deadlock-recovery based routing algorithms are susceptible to this type of fault-related permanent message blocking.

Messages which are forced to wait (possibly indefinitely) due to faults are represented in our model as *fault-dependent messages*. Fault-dependent messages can be further categorized based on whether they are waiting only on faulty resources (*fully directly fault dependent*) or are waiting only on resources owned by other messages which are fully directly or indirectly fault dependent (*fully indirectly fault dependent*). In the example shown in Figure 10, messages m_1 and m_3 are fully directly fault dependent while messages m_2 and m_4 are fully indirectly fault dependent. As with partially deadlock dependent messages, *partially fault dependent* messages are those messages whose *requests* sets contain VCs which are owned by non-fault dependent messages. These messages may resume despite persistence of the fault.

We summarize the various types of message blocking represented by our model, their behavior, and their properties in Table 1.

4 Implementing the Message Blocking Model

The message blocking model has been implemented in a flit-level interconnection network simulator called *FlexSim* (an extension of *FlitSim 2.0*). Use of this model for detecting deadlock involves maintaining a CWG, detecting cycles within the CWG, and identifying groups of messages and cycles which form knots. Each of these areas is discussed in the following subsections.

blocking behavior of message m_i \ properties of message m_i	m_i indefinitely blocked	all members of requests(m_i) owned by msgs. in deadlock set [is faulty]	all members of requests(m_i) owned by fully deadlock [fault] dependent msgs.	only some members of requests(m_i) owned by fully deadlock [fault] dependent msgs.	m_i can occur in deadlock-avoidance based routing	m_i can occur in deadlock-recovery based routing	indefinite blocking in network resolved if m_i is removed
in deadlock set	Yes	Yes	No	No	No	Yes	Yes
in cyclic non-deadlock	No	No	No	No	Yes	Yes	n/a
fully directly deadlock dependent	Yes	Yes	No	No	No	Yes	No
fully indirectly deadlock dependent	Yes	No	Yes	No	No	Yes	No
partially deadlock dependent	No	No	No	Yes	No	Yes	No
fully directly fault dependent	Yes	[Yes]	[No]	[No]	Yes	Yes	No
fully indirectly fault dependent	Yes	[No]	[Yes]	[No]	Yes	Yes	No
partially fault dependent	No	[No]	[No]	[Yes]	Yes	Yes	No

Table 1. Summary of various types of message blocking represented by the model, their behavior, and their properties.

4.1 Building and Maintaining the Channel Wait-for Graph

During run-time of an on-going network simulation, we dynamically build and maintain the CWG which reflects the resource allocations and requests dynamically occuring. The CWG is implemented as an array of linked lists. Each array element represents a message (m_i) within the network, and each linked list represents the set of VCs owned by a particular message ($owns(m_i)$), with additional links to desired VCs for blocked messages ($requests(m_i)$). Figure 11 provides an overview of the data structures used to maintain the CWG, cycle list, and deadlock list. The state of the data structures in this figure corresponds to the example given in Figure 8.

When a VC is allocated to a message, the "VCNode" data structure for the VC is appended to the linked list for that message and the VCNode is annotated with its new owner. Similarly, when a VC is released, the VCNode is removed from the beginning of the linked list and the ownership information is removed accordingly. When a message blocks, special request links are placed from the end of the linked list to the VCNodes representing each of the alternate VCs the message may use to continue routing. When a message resumes, these request links are removed and replaced with a link to the VCNode representing the newly acquired VC as described in Section 2. The direct links from the elements

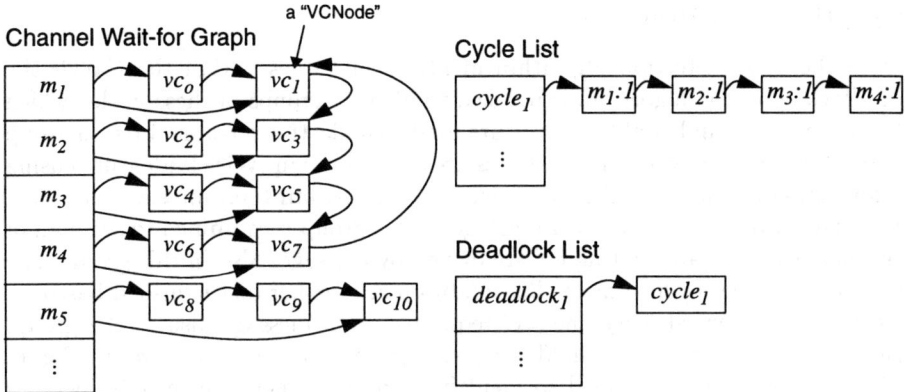

Fig. 11. The CWG, Cycle List, and Deadlock List data structures. The state of the data structures reflects the example in Figure 8.

of the array of messages to the last VCNodes of each linked list are used as an optimization for efficient traversal of the linked lists.

4.2 Detecting Cycles

Cycles in the CWG are detected by performing depth-first search of the graph with backtracking (starting with each linked list in linear order). Each node visited is marked so that the second visitation indicates the presence of a cycle. Annotations indicating visitation are removed upon backtracking. To avoid detection of each unique cycle more than once, the partial order of message IDs is used to prune the search (i.e., restrict visiting a VCNode owned by a message with a lower message ID). For example, the VCNodes in the CWG in Figure 11 are visited in the following order where '*' indicates cycle detection, b indicates a backtracking step, and p indicates a pruning measure: $[m_1]$, vc_0, vc_1, vc_3, vc_5, vc_7, vc_1, *, b, b, b, b, b, b, $[m_2]$, vc_2, vc_3, vc_5, vc_7, p, b, b, b, b, $[m_3]$, vc_4, vc_5, vc_7, p, b, b, b, $[m_4]$, vc_6, vc_7, p, b, b, $[m_5]$, vc_8, vc_9, vc_{10}.

When a unique cycle is detected, it is placed in the cycle list as shown in Figure 11. A list of messages involved and their corresponding "branches" are sufficient to uniquely identify a cycle (i.e., $m_1 : 1$ in the figure indicates the first branch of message m_1, representing the first of possibly many VCs the message is waiting for). When previously detected cycles are again detected during a different run of the algorithm, their entries in the cycle list are updated to indicate the time of their most recent detection. Our cycle detection algorithm guarantees detection of each unique cycle in the CWG during each invocation. Therefore, those cycles which were not detected during the most recent invocation of the algorithm are removed from the cycle list. Since a very large number of cycles can exist within a congested network, we use advanced indexing functions and search techniques to compare cycles in determining their uniqueness.

4.3 Detecting Deadlocks

Once the cycle detection algorithm identifies all cycles within the CWG, the deadlock detection algorithm is invoked to identify groups of these cycles which form a knot. A number of heuristics are used to make this possible. First, a group of blocked messages whose request arcs are all involved in cycles is identified using information provided by the cycle detection algorithm (i.e., messages m_1, m_2, m_3, and m_4 in Figure 11). Each message in this group is examined to see if all of the channels they are waiting for are owned by messages also in this group. The subset of messages which meet this condition are further distinguished based on whether they own at least one VC requested by a message also in the group. Note that these conditions hold for messages m_1, m_2, m_3, and m_4 in Figure 11. Cycles are then examined to identify a group of them which only includes messages from this group. A group of cycles which meets this condition forms a knot and is therefore identified as a deadlock and placed in the deadlock list, as shown in Figure 11. Detected deadlocks are "broken" by removing a single message in the deadlock set in a flit-by-flit fashion so as to simulate a progressive recovery procedure.

4.4 Time and Space Complexity

The operations to build and maintain the CWG are invoked automatically by the simulator on an as-needed basis, and each of the operations requires constant time. The deadlock and cycle detection times are invoked based on user specified time intervals. For a simulation run of length T_{sim} simulation cycles (sim-cycles), we allow the cycle detection algorithm to be run once every T_{cd} sim-cycles, $T_{cd} \leq T_{sim}$, and the deadlock detection algorithm to be run once every $(T_{cd} \times n) \leq T_{sim}$, $n \geq 1$ sim-cycles.

The computational complexity of the cycle detection algorithm can be expressed as $O((R_f/2)^{M_l} + C_a^3)$ where R_f corresponds to the routing freedom, M_l corresponds to the average hop distance, and C_a corresponds to the number of active cycles in the network. The term $(R_f/2)^{M_l}$ corresponds to the time required for full traversal of the CWG while the term C_a^3 corresponds to the time required for "processing" (determine uniqueness, record characteristics, etc.) of each cycle found within the CWG.

Currently, we are able to detect all cycles formed in networks which provide a moderate degree of routing freedom (i.e., true fully adaptive routing [5, 6] in 2D and 3D networks with as many as 4 VCs per physical channel) for up to and slightly beyond saturation loads. As an example, the execution time for a single invocation of the cycle detection algorithm on an IBM SP/2 node for a saturated 16-ary 2-cube network can take up to 3 hours. Given the theoretical worst case for C and C_a of $(R_f)^{M_b}$ where M_b is the number of blocked messages within the network, simulations can become impractical as a very large number of messages with high fanout may block within some networks at loads beyond network saturation.

The computational complexity of the deadlock detection algorithm can be expressed as $O(D \times C \times M_c)$ where D is the average number of deadlocks found during an invocation of the deadlock detection algorithm, C is the average number of cycles found during an invocation of cycle detection algorithm, and M_c is the average number of messages involved in a cycle. Thus, our simulation capabilities are not limited by the complexity of this algorithm. In comparison to the cycle detection algorithm, the execution times for invocations of the deadlock detection algorithm are negligible. However, this algorithm has been greatly optimized by using heuristics based on information provided by the cycle detection algorithm, and since it relies on all cycles being detected, it is of limited use for detecting deadlock in deep saturation for some networks. We are currently implementing an alternative deadlock detection scheme which does not require that all cycles be identified and which therefore can be used to detect deadlock behavior during network conditions beyond saturation.

The space complexity for the algorithm is also dictated by the number of cycles which can form. For example, a network containing one million unique cycles within its CWG requires approximately 75MB of virtual memory.

5 Related Work

Static channel dependency and wait-for graphs which represent connections allowed by routing algorithms have been presented in previous work [9, 10, 13, 14]. In contrast, the channel wait-for graphs presented here are dynamic and represent the state of resource allocations and requests existing within a network at a given point in time. The dependency and wait-for graphs in previous work are intended for developing deadlock avoidance-based routing algorithms whereas our channel wait-for graphs are used to 1) precisely define deadlocks and related blocking behavior, 2) model resource dependencies within networks that allow unrestricted routing, and 3) implement deadlock detection in a network simulation.

Previous definitions of deadlock within interconnection networks include "deadlocked configurations" and "canonical deadlocked configurations" [9, 10, 11]. These notions of deadlock encompass not only messages which are directly involved in deadlock, but also other types of messages which are affected by deadlock. Furthermore, these definitions do not distinguish between single and multiple instances of deadlock which may exist simultaneously. In contrast, our definition of deadlock allows identification of every instance of deadlock, and distinguishes between the causal components of deadlock and those messages which are affected by deadlock. Therefore, our definition enables us to precisely define criteria for optimal deadlock detection and resolution.

A summary of work characterizing deadlocks as knots in generalized resource graphs intended to describe deadlocks in operating systems is presented in [15]. The resource model presented here is a specialized version of this work, intended to precisely define deadlocks within interconnection networks.

6 Conclusion

This work presents an approach to modeling resource allocations and dependencies within an interconnection network. We have precisely defined various types of message blocking, described their behavior, and proposed a way of representing this behavior in a framework amenable to implementation in a network simulator. The framework correctly distinguishes between messages involved in deadlock and those simply dependent on deadlock, thus providing a means for specifying deadlock detection and resolution criteria for deadlock recovery-based routing algorithms. We have also presented an implementation of the framework in a network simulator. We have shown that the message blocking behavior of moderately sized networks can be simulated, thus demonstrating that empirical characterization of deadlocks and other message blocking phenomena is feasible and can provide useful insights for designing high-performance interconnection networks. Results of deadlock characterization performed using the framework and its implementation as described in this paper is presented in other work [1, 2].

References

1. Sugath Warnakulasuriya and Timothy Mark Pinkston. "Characterization of Deadlocks in Interconnection Networks", In *Proc. of the 11th International Parallel Processing Symposium*, pp 80-86, April 1997.
2. Timothy Mark Pinkston and Sugath Warnakulasuriya. "On Deadlocks in Interconnection Networks", In *Proc. of the 24th International Symposium on Computer Architecture*, pp 38-49, June 1997.
3. D. Reeves, E.Gehringer, and A. Chandiramani. "Adaptive Routing and Deadlock Recovery: A Simulation Study", In *Proceedings of the 4th Conference on Hypercube Concurrent Computers and Applications*, 1989.
4. J. Kim, Z. Liu, and A. Chien. "Compressionless Routing: A Framework for Adaptive and Fault-tolerant Routing". In *IEEE Transactions on Parallel and Distributed Systems*, 8(3):229-244, March 1997.
5. Anjan K.V. and Timothy M. Pinkston, "An Efficient, Fully Adaptive Deadlock Recovery Scheme: Disha", In *Proc. of the 22nd International Symposium on Computer Architecture*, pp 201-210, June 1995.
6. Anjan K.V., Timothy M. Pinkston, and Jose Duato, "Generalized Theory for Deadlock-Free Adaptive Wormhole Routing and its Application to Disha Concurrent", In *Proc. of the 10th International Parallel Processing Symposium*, pp 815-821, April 1996.
7. L. Ni and C. Glass, "The Turn Model for Adaptive Routing", In *Proc. of the 19th International Symposium on Computer Architecture*, IEEE Computer Society, pages 278-287, May 1992.
8. Andrew A. Chien and J. H. Kim. "Planar-Adaptive Routing: Low-Cost Adaptive Networks for Multiprocessors". In *Proc. of the 19th Symposium on Computer Architecture*, pp 268-277, May 1992.
9. J. Duato. "A New Theory of Deadlock-free Adaptive Routing in Wormhole Networks". *IEEE Transactions on Parallel and Distributed Systems*, 4(12):1320-1331, December 1993.

10. J. Duato. "A Necessary and Sufficient Condition for Deadlock-free Adaptive Routing in Wormhole Networks". *IEEE Transactions on Parallel and Distributed Systems*, 6(10):1055- 1067, October 1995.
11. J. Duato, S. Yalamanchili, and L. Ni. "Interconnection Networks: An Engineering Approach". IEEE Computer Society Press, 1997.
12. Sugath Warnakulasuriya and Timothy Mark Pinkston. "Implementation of Deadlock Detection in a Simulated Interconnection Network Environment", Technical Report CENG 97-01, University of Southern California, January 1997.
13. William J. Dally and Hiromichi Aoki, "Deadlock- Free Adaptive Routing in Multicomputer Networks Using Virtual Channels", *IEEE Transactions on Parallel Distributed Systems*, Vol. 4, No. 4, April, 1993.
14. Loren Schwiebert, D.N. Jayasimha, "A Necessary and Sufficient Condition for Deadlock-Free Wormhole Routing", *Journal of Parallel and Distributed Computing*, 32, 103-117 (1996).
15. Mamoru Maekawa, Arthur E. Oldehoft, and Rodney R. Oldehoft, "Operating Systems: Advanced Concepts", Benjamin Cummings Publishing Company, 1987.

On the Reduction of Deadlock Frequency by Limiting Message Injection in Wormhole Networks *

P. López[1], J. M. Martínez[1], J. Duato[1] and F. Petrini[2]

[1] Facultad de Informática, Universidad Politécnica de Valencia, Camino de Vera s/n, 46071 - Valencia, SPAIN, E-mail: {plopez,jmmr,jduato}@gap.upv.es

[2] Dipartimento di Informatica, Università di Pisa, Corso Italia 40, Pisa, ITALY, E-mail: petrini@di.unipi.it

Abstract. Recently, deadlock recovery strategies began to gain acceptance in networks using wormhole switching. In particular, progressive deadlock recovery techniques are very attractive because they allocate a few dedicated resources to quickly deliver deadlocked packets, instead of killing them. Deadlock recovery is based on the assumption that deadlocks are really rare. Otherwise, recovery techniques are not efficient.
In this paper, we propose the use of a message injection limitation mechanism that reduces the probability of deadlock to negligible values, even when fully adaptive routing is used. The main new feature is that it can be used with different message destination distributions. The proposed mechanism can be combined with any deadlock detection mechanism. In particular, we use the deadlock detection mechanism proposed in [21]. In addition, the proposed injection limitation mechanism considerably reduces performance degradation when the network reaches the saturation point.

Keywords: Wormhole switching, adaptive routing, deadlock recovery, message injection limitation.

1 Introduction

Wormhole [10] has become the most widely used switching technique for multicomputers [5, 16] and distributed shared-memory multiprocessors [19, 27], and it is also being used for networks of workstations [6, 15]. Wormhole switching only requires small buffers in the nodes through which messages are routed. Also, it makes the message latency largely insensitive to the distance in the network. See [24] for a detailed analysis of wormhole.

The main drawback of wormhole switching is that blocked messages remain in the network, therefore wasting channel bandwidth. In order to reduce the

---
* This work was supported by the Spanish CICYT under Grant TIC94-0510-C02-01

impact of message blocking, physical channels may be split into virtual channels by providing a separate buffer for each virtual channel and by multiplexing physical channel bandwidth. The use of virtual channels can increase throughput considerably by dynamically sharing the physical bandwidth among several messages [11]. However, it has been shown that virtual channels are expensive, increasing node delay considerably [9]. So, the number of virtual channels per physical channel should be kept small.

An alternative approach consists of using adaptive routing [14]. However, deadlocks may appear if the routing algorithms are not carefully designed. A deadlock occurs in an interconnection network when no message is able to advance toward its destination because the network buffers are full. As routing decisions must be taken in a few nanoseconds in wormhole networks, a practical way to avoid deadlock is to design deadlock-free routing algorithms. A simple and effective approach to avoid deadlocks consists of restricting routing so that there are no cyclic dependencies between channels [10]. A more efficient approach consists of allowing the existence of cyclic dependencies between channels while providing some escape paths to avoid deadlock, therefore increasing routing flexibility [12, 13].

However, deadlock avoidance techniques require dedicated resources to provide those escape paths. Usually, those dedicated resources are virtual channels, thus preventing the use of all the virtual channels for fully adaptive routing. Deadlock recovery strategies overcome this constraint but the cost associated with deadlock recovery can be high, specially when deadlocked messages are killed and injected again at a later time [26, 18]. Progressive deadlock recovery strategies, like Disha [2, 3, 4], are more efficient because they allocate a few dedicated resources to quickly deliver deadlocked packets, instead of killing them. Disha also uses dedicated resources to recover from deadlock. In this case, one central buffer per node is enough to route deadlocked messages towards their destination node. More recently, we have proposed a software-based progressive deadlock recovery strategy [21] thus eliminating the need for dedicated resources to recover from deadlock. Basically, when a message is presumed to be involved in a deadlock, it is absorbed at the current node and later reinjected into the network. The key issues in any deadlock recovery strategy are the deadlock detection mechanism and how often a deadlock is reached.

Progressive deadlock recovery techniques usually achieve a higher performance than deadlock avoidance techniques because they require less dedicated resources to handle deadlocks [3, 21]. However, both kinds of techniques may produce severe performance degradation when the network is close to saturation [12, 3]. This situation occurs when messages block cyclically faster than they are drained by using the escape paths or the deadlock recovery mechanism.

Performance degradation at the saturation point was studied in [12, 20]. In [12], it was shown that degradation can be removed by adding enough virtual channels per physical channel. However, this solution is expensive and may lead to an excessive number of virtual channel for most topologies. An alternative approach was proposed in [20]. It consists of limiting message injection when the network is heavily loaded, preventing message injection when the number of output virtual channels that are busy is higher than a given threshold. The main drawback of this mechanism is that the threshold strongly depends on the message destination distribution.

Very recently, the frequency of deadlock occurrence on k-ary n-cubes using a true fully adaptive minimal routing algorithm was measured [28, 25], showing that deadlocks only occur when the network is close to or beyond saturation.

In this paper we propose a mechanism to prevent network saturation. The proposed mechanism is more robust than previous proposals. It is almost independent of the traffic pattern in the network. First, this mechanism will avoid the performance degradation problem that typically occurs in both, deadlock avoidance and recovery techniques. Second, it will guarantee that the frequency of deadlock is really negligible. As a consequence, the time needed to recover from deadlock is not critical. Hence, deadlock recovery techniques that focus on making the common case fast can be efficiently used. Deadlock detection and recovery mechanisms enable the use of true fully adaptive routing.

Section 2 describes the mechanism proposed in [20] to prevent network saturation. It is the starting point for the new one. The new mechanism is described in Section 3. Performance evaluation results of the new mechanism for different message destination distributions are presented in Section 4. Finally, some conclusions are drawn.

2 Message Injection Limitation: First Approach

In this section, we will briefly describe the message injection limitation proposed in [20]. The main goal of the mechanism, as originally proposed, was to mitigate the performance degradation of the network when it reaches saturation. This problem can be stated as follows. Latency increases with network traffic until certain point, at which latency value goes up while traffic decreases. Average traffic matches flit injection rate until the performance degradation point is reached, then traffic noticeably decreases.

This behavior occurs both with deadlock avoidance and recovery strategies [12, 2]. Performance degradation is produced because these strategies allows cyclic dependencies between some channels provided that there are some escape paths or a recovery mechanism. When message injection rate becomes high, messages block cyclically faster than they are drained by the escape paths or the recovery mechanism, thus increasing latency and decreasing the number of messages delivered per time unit. It must be noticed that messages do not deadlock, but they spend a long time in the network.

Therefore, fully adaptive routing algorithms may degrade performance considerably when the network reaches the saturation point. One solution to this problem could be to increase the number of virtual channels [12], so that messages have a lower probability of being involved in cyclic dependencies. However, a high number of virtual channels could lead to a lower clock frequency [9].

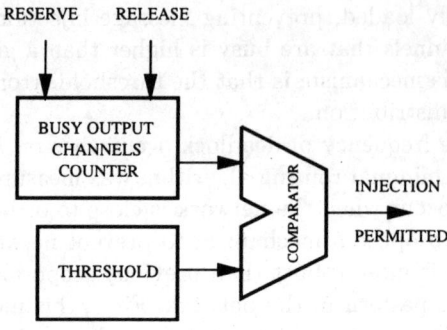

Fig. 1. Implementation of the message injection limitation mechanism

Another solution is to control network traffic, in order to guarantee that it is always under the performance degradation point. But traffic is a global quantity. Thus, it is not feasible to measure it in a distributed way. Fortunately, we have found that traffic can be estimated locally by counting the number of busy output channels at each node.

The message injection limitation mechanism proposed in [20] works as follows. Before injecting a message into the network, traffic is estimated by counting the number of busy output virtual channels at the source node, comparing it with a threshold. If traffic is lower than this threshold, the message is injected into the network. Otherwise, it is stored in the source queue. If threshold value is properly selected, it can be guaranteed that the performance degradation point will never be reached.

The implementation of this mechanism only requires one comparator and one counter associated with each router, as shown in Figure 1. The counter maintains the number of busy output channels. Its value is increased each time a successful routing is made and is decreased when the tail of a message leaves the node. This hardware is not in the critical path. Of course, this mechanism will increase the delay of those messages that are not injected into the network at once, but the average delay is lower than the one obtained by the same adaptive algorithm without injection limitation mechanism [21] because contention in the network is considerably reduced.

Let's analyze the relationship of the mechanism with deadlock recovery strategies. Recently, the frequency of deadlock occurrence on k-ary n-cubes using a true fully adaptive minimal routing algorithm was measured [28], showing that deadlocks only occur when the network is close to or beyond saturation. Thus, one way to effectively reduce the probability of reaching deadlocks is to prevent network saturation. This is exactly what the described message injection limitation mechanism does. In [21], it has been used combined with a deadlock detection mechanism to develop a new deadlock recovery strategy.

However, the behavior of the mechanism depends on the threshold used in the comparison. Although it can be easily selected for a given message destination distribution, different message destination distributions need different thresholds. If we use the threshold value that imposes the maximum restrictions, there will be a performance penalty when a looser limitation is really required. On the other hand, if we tune the threshold imposing a looser limitation than it is really required, the mechanism does not work, and the network will reach saturation.

3 New Message Injection Limitation Mechanism

The main goal of the new message injection limitation mechanism is to take into account the message destination distribution existing in the network at a given time and adapt to it.

The key idea is to dynamically update the threshold used in the comparison. To modify the threshold according to the message destination distribution we exploit the information obtained every time a message is injected. In particular, we have observed that the number of different useful dimensions that a newly injected message has to cross to reach its destination can be used to distinguish between different distributions. Effectively, when destinations are randomly distributed, the destination of a given message can be any node of the network. Thus, a set of injected messages may use every output channel at the source node. On the other hand, when a specific message destination distribution such as bit-reversal or complement is used, the destination of messages originated at a given node is always the same. Thus, messages will only use a subset of the output channels of the node. Destination distributions produced by parallel applications lie somewhere in between.

In addition, we will consider this information not only for the last injected message but for the last m injected messages. Figure 2 shows the hardware required to implement the mechanism. Each time a message generated at a given node is routed at that node, a bit set representing the physical channels that the message can use for routing is stored in a table. This history table contains information for the last m injected messages. A new bit set is obtained by computing the bitwise OR operation of the m entries in the table. This set represents the useful physical channels that have been used or could have been used (adaptive routing) by the m last messages originated at this node. The cardinal of this set is computed and used to calculate the threshold value of the message injection limitation mechanism. The threshold computation can be done by using a translation table.

An example will show how to build this table. Consider a bidirectional 3-D torus with true fully adaptive routing and 3 virtual channels per physical channel. Thus, there are 18 virtual output channels per node. For the uniform message destination distribution we have found that the optimal threshold for the injection limitation mechanism described in Section 2 was 9 busy virtual channels. With this distribution, different messages originating at each node can use any of the three dimensions. Taking into account that channels are bidirectional, there are 6 feasible physical output channels for this distribution. Thus,

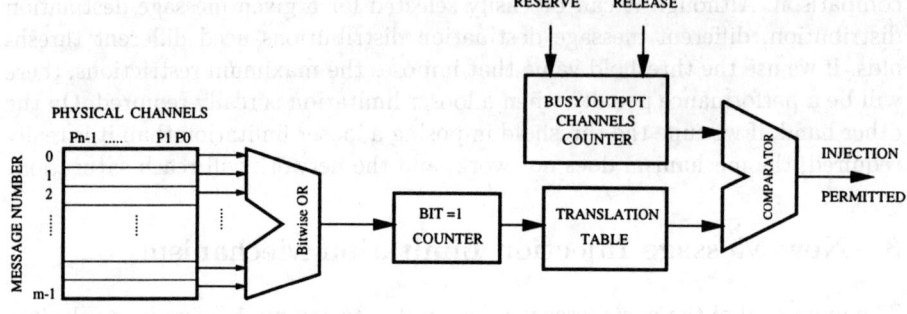

Fig. 2. Implementation of the new message injection limitation mechanism

Feasible physical output channels (POC)	Busy virtual output channels (Threshold Value, TV)
6	9
5	8
4	6
3	5
2	3
1	2

Table 1. Example of translation table to compute the threshold value.

the table should return a threshold of 9 for 6 feasible physical output channels. The returned value should decrease with the number of feasible physical output channels. For instance, in Table 1 the threshold is reduced proportionally to the number of feasible physical output channels.

The function corresponding to Table 1 is $TV = \lceil 1.5 * POC \rceil$. Less restrictive tables or functions can be employed to better match the message destination distributions that are likely to be used. In the extreme case, the number of busy virtual output channels would not depend on the number of feasible physical output channels, leading to the injection limitation mechanism described in Section 2.

Of course, the new mechanism still depends on the number of network dimensions and the number of virtual channels per physical channel, but these parameters are fixed in the design process.

When the routing control unit is reset, the first item in the history table is set in such a way that it indicates that all physical output channels are in use (all "1"). Thus, the mechanism will apply the less restrictive limitation until the history table fills out. After that, the mechanism will limit the injection according to the physical output channel usage.

Finally, it must be noticed that the update of the history table can be done after computing the routing algorithm. Moreover, the calculation of the threshold value can also be done between message routing operations. Thus, this hardware is not in the critical path.

4 Performance Evaluation

In this section, we will evaluate by simulation the behavior of the new injection limitation mechanism. The evaluation methodology used is based on the one proposed in [12]. The most important performance measures are latency (time required to deliver a message, including the time spent in the source queue) and throughput (maximum traffic accepted by the network). Traffic is the flit reception rate. Latency is measured in clock cycles. Traffic is measured in flits per node per cycle.

Taking into account the sizes of current multicomputers and the studies about the optimal number of dimensions [1], we have evaluated the performance of the new injection mechanism on a bidirectional 8-ary 3-cube network (512 nodes).

4.1 Network Model

Our simulator models the network at the flit level. Each node in the network consists of a processor, its local memory, a routing control unit, a switch, and several channels. A four port architecture [22] is considered.

The routing control unit computes the output channel for a message as a function of its destination node, the current node and the output channel status. The routing algorithm can use any minimal path to forward a message towards its destination. In addition, several virtual channels per physical channel can be used. In other words, all virtual channels in all the feasible directions can be used. This algorithm is usually referred to as True Fully Adaptive Routing algorithm [28, 25, 21]. We assume that it takes one clock cycle to compute the routing algorithm. The routing control unit can only process one message header at a time. It is assigned to waiting messages in a demand-slotted round-robin fashion (including those messages generated in the local processor). When a message gets the routing control unit but it can not be routed because all the alternative output channels are busy, it must wait in the input buffer until its next turn. The deadlock recovery strategy proposed in [21] is used. In this strategy, deadlocked messages are removed from the network at the current node, and injected again at a later time. The new message injection limitation mechanism described in Section 3 is used. Although we have not performed an in-depth analysis of the influence of the size m of the history table on performance, it seems that it does not affect significantly. We have used a value of m equal to 30 (5 times the number of output physical links). We also tried with m equal to 24 and 36, obtaining similar results.

The switch is a crossbar. So, it allows multiple messages to traverse it simultaneously without interference. It is configured by the routing control unit each time a successful routing is made. We assume that it takes one clock cycle to transfer a flit across the switch.

Physical channels can be split into several virtual channels. Virtual channels are assigned to the physical link using a demand-slotted round-robin arbitration scheme. Each virtual channel has an associated buffer with capacity for four flits. We assume that it takes one clock cycle to transfer a flit across a physical channel.

4.2 Message Generation

Message traffic and message length depend on the applications. For each simulation run, we considered that message generation rate is constant and the same for all the nodes. Once the network has reached a steady state, the flit generation rate is equal to the flit reception rate (traffic). We have evaluated the full range of traffic, from low load to saturation. On the other hand, we have considered three kinds of message distribution: uniform, with locality, and specific.

In the first case, message destination is randomly chosen among all the nodes. This pattern has been widely used in other performance evaluation studies [11, 8, 7]. For the message distribution with locality, the destination node is uniformly distributed inside a cube with side two centered at the source node, modeling short distance traffic. Finally, we have considered specific communication patterns between pairs of nodes. These patterns have been selected taking into account the permutations that are usually performed in parallel numerical algorithms [23, 17]:

- Bit-reversal. The node with binary coordinates $a_{n-1}, a_{n-2}, ..., a_1, a_0$ communicates with the node $a_0, a_1, ..., a_{n-2}, a_{n-1}$.
- Perfect-shuffle. The node with binary coordinates $a_{n-1}, a_{n-2}, ..., a_1, a_0$ commmunicates with the node $a_{n-2}, a_{n-3}, ..., a_0, a_{n-1}$ (rotate left one bit).
- Butterfly. The node with binary coordinates $a_{n-1}, a_{n-2}, ..., a_1, a_0$ communicates with the node $a_0, a_{n-2}, ..., a_1, a_{n-1}$ (exchange the most and least significant bits).

For message length, 16-flit messages were considered. This value is considered as typical in other interconnection network evaluation studies [1, 26].

4.3 Performance Comparison

In this section we compare the results obtained by the routing algorithm considering the new injection limitation mechanism with different translation tables. We will also show the results obtained with the previous message injection limitation mechanism described in Section 2 (using 9 busy virtual channels as the threshold) and without injection limitation, for comparison purposes. Note that

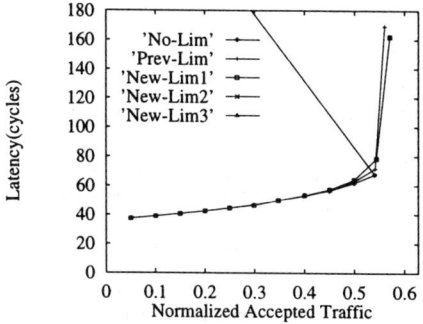

Fig. 3. Average message latency versus traffic for a 512-node 3-D torus with true fully adaptive routing (3 virtual channels per physical channel). Uniform distribution of message destinations.

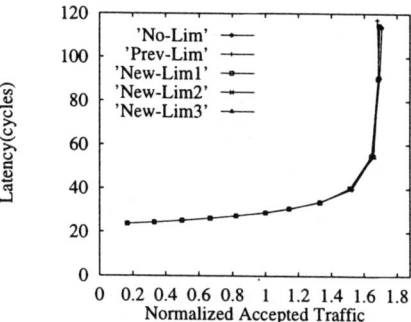

Fig. 4. Average message latency versus traffic for a 512-node 3-D torus with true fully adaptive routing (3 virtual channels per physical channel). Uniform distribution of message destinations with locality.

the average latency plotted in all the figures includes the time spent by messages at their source nodes due to the injection limitation mechanism.

For the new injection limitation mechanism we tested different functions in order to obtain the threshold value (TV). We have seen that a linear function obtains good results. In order to define a linear function, we need a pair of points. The first point is given by the TV returned for the maximum number of feasible physical output channels (TV equal to 9 for 6 feasible physical output channels). The second point is given by the TV returned when there is only one feasible physical output channel. We tried three linear functions with different slopes. The first function is the most restrictive one. It was described in Section 3. The other ones impose looser restrictions to inject messages into the network. These functions are the following:

1. $TV = \lceil 1.5 * POC \rceil$. It will referred to as *New-Lim1*.
2. $TV = \lceil 1.2 * POC + 1.8 \rceil$. It will referred to as *New-Lim2*.
3. $TV = \lceil 0.8 * POC + 4.2 \rceil$. It will referred to as *New-Lim3*.

Figure 3 shows the comparison for the uniform distribution of message destinations. As we can see, the routing algorithm without the injection limitation mechanism reaches the performance degradation point. In addition, many deadlocks were detected. On the other hand, the behavior of the previous and new message injection limitation mechanisms is almost identical. This is due to the fact that the new mechanism limits in the same way as the previous one when every output physical channel has been requested by some of the last m injected messages. There are no differences between the three functions used in the new limitation mechanism, because all of them return the same threshold value.

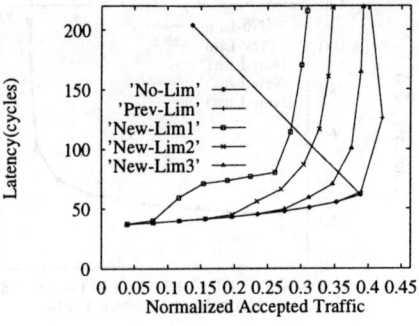 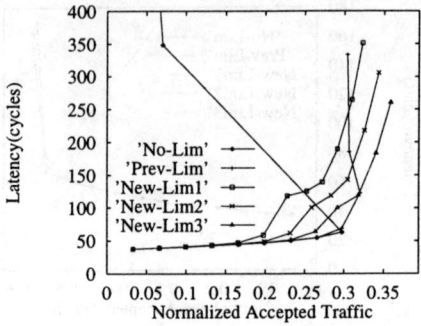

Fig. 5. Average message latency versus traffic for a 512-node 3-D torus with true fully adaptive routing (3 virtual channels per physical channel). Bit-reversal pattern for message destinations.

Fig. 6. Average message latency versus traffic for a 512-node 3-D torus with true fully adaptive routing (3 virtual channels per physical channel). Perfect-shuffle pattern for message destinations.

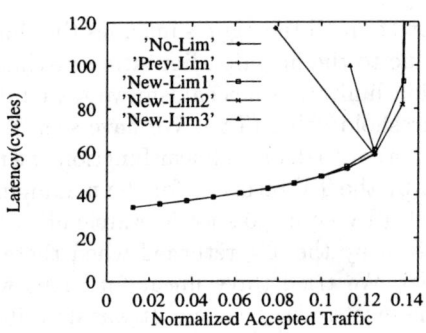

Fig. 7. Average message latency versus traffic for a 512-node 3-D torus with true fully adaptive routing (3 virtual channels per physical channel). Butterfly pattern for message destinations.

In case of uniform distribution of message destination with locality (Figure 4), all the limitation mechanisms achieve similar results. Indeed, injection is not limited even when the network reaches saturation. There is no performance degradation and there are no deadlocks in any case. Taking into account that messages traverse very short distances, the probability of being involved in cyclic dependences is very low.

Figure 5 shows the results for the bit-reversal traffic pattern. As can be seen, message injection limitation is compulsory. Otherwise, the network will suffer performance degradation and deadlocks. The previous injection limitation mechanism achieves the best results, with a small performance degradation with very high load. The new limitation mechanisms achieve worse results because they impose more restrictions to inject a message into the network. Among these, the *New-Lim3* is the best, as it is the one that limits less the injection of messages.

Figure 6 shows the results for the perfect-shuffle traffic pattern. Again, the network without injection limitation reaches the saturation point and degrades performance drastically. Although the previous message injection limitation mechanism reduces the performance degradation, the problem is not completely eliminated. Any of the new mechanisms definitively solves the problem. Again, the *New-Lim3* is the best, as it is the one that imposes looser restrictions to message injection.

Finally, Figure 7 shows the results for the butterfly traffic pattern. If we do not impose restrictions to message injection, performance degradation and deadlock are reached. With the previous message injection limitation, the problem is not solved. The problem is reduced, but not completely solved, with the *New-Lim3* mechanism. Only the *New-Lim1* and *New-Lim2* mechanisms which restrict message injection more drastically are able to prevent network saturation.

The new message injection limitation mechanism prevents network saturation in all of the traffic patterns analyzed in this section. In some cases, it is too restrictive and it achieves poorer results than the previously proposed message limitation mechanism described in Section 2 tuned with the proper threshold. However, the new mechanism is able to deal with several message destination distributions, dynamically adapting to the requirements of the traffic pattern in the network.

Among the translation tables analyzed in this section, *New-Lim3* seems to be the best choice. The small performance degradation observed with the butterfly permutation should not harm in practice because it would require a parallel application injecting messages only according to this traffic pattern and driving the network beyond saturation.

5 Conclusions

In this paper we have proposed a new message injection limitation mechanism to prevent network saturation. By doing so, the performance degradation of adaptive routing algorithms with cyclic dependencies between channels is avoided and, most importantly, the frequency of deadlock is reduced to negligible values.

The proposed mechanism consists of using a history table to keep track of the physical channels requested by the last set of messages injected at each node. The number of requested channels is converted into a threshold by using a translation table, which in turn is compared with the number of busy output virtual channels at that node in order to decide whether message injection should be permitted or not.

The main goal of the proposed mechanism is robustness. Unlike previous proposals, it is almost independent of the message destination distribution. The proposed mechanism needs to be implemented in the routing control unit but it does not affect clock frequency, because it is not in the critical path.

The new message injection limitation mechanism has been evaluated by simulation under several traffic patterns that presumably are representative of real programs. Although it does not achieve the best results for each individual traffic pattern, is able to prevent network saturation and achieve performance results very close to the best algorithm for each case.

As for future research, we plan to analyze alternative injection limitation mechanisms, looking for simpler and more effective ways to reduce the frequency of deadlock in order to make deadlock recovery really feasible. Also we plan to use traffic patterns generated by parallel applications to test those mechanisms.

References

1. A. Agarwal, "Limits on interconnection network performance", *IEEE Transactions on Parallel Distributed Systems*, vol. 2, no. 4, pp. 398–412, Oct. 1991.
2. Anjan K. V. and T. M. Pinkston, "DISHA: A deadlock recovery scheme for fully adaptive routing," in *Proceedings of the 9th International Parallel Processing Symposium*, April 1995.
3. Anjan K. V. and T. M. Pinkston, An efficient fully adaptive deadlock recovery scheme: DISHA," in *Proceedings of the 22nd International Symposium on Computer Architecture*, June 1995.
4. Anjan K. V., T. M. Pinkston and J. Duato, "Generalized theory for deadlock-free adaptive routing and its application to Disha Concurrent," in *Proceedings of the 10th International Parallel Processing Symposium*, April 1996.
5. W. C. Athas and C. L. Seitz, "Multicomputers: Message-passing concurrent computers," *IEEE Computer*, vol. 21, no. 8, pp. 9–24, August 1988.
6. N. J. Boden, D. Cohen, R. E. Felderman, A. E. Kulawik, C. L. Seitz, J. Seizovic and W. Su, "Myrinet - A gigabit per second local area network," *IEEE Micro*, pp. 29–36, February 1995.
7. R. V. Boppana and S. Chalasani, "A comparison of adaptive wormhole routing algorithms," in *Proceedings of the 20th International Symposium on Computer Architecture*, May 1993.
8. A. A. Chien and J. H. Kim, "Planar-adaptive routing: Low-cost adaptive networks for multiprocessors," in *Proceedings of the 19th International Symposium on Computer Architecture*, May 1992.
9. A. A. Chien, "A cost and speed model for k-ary n-cube wormhole routers," in *Proceedings of Hot Interconnects'93*, August 1993.
10. W. J. Dally and C. L. Seitz, "Deadlock-free message routing in multiprocessor interconnection networks," *IEEE Transactions on Computers*, vol. C–36, no. 5, pp. 547–553, May 1987.
11. W. J. Dally, "Virtual-channel flow control," *IEEE Transactions on Parallel and Distributed Systems*, vol. 3, no. 2, pp. 194–205, March 1992.
12. J. Duato, "A new theory of deadlock-free adaptive routing in wormhole networks," *IEEE Transactions on Parallel and Distributed Systems*, vol. 4, no. 12, pp. 1320–1331, December 1993.

13. J. Duato, "A necessary and sufficient condition for deadlock-free adaptive routing in wormhole networks," *IEEE Transactions on Parallel and Distributed Systems*, vol. 6, no. 10, pp. 1055–1067, October 1995.
14. P. T. Gaughan and S. Yalamanchili, "Adaptive routing protocols for hypercube interconnection networks," *IEEE Computer*, vol. 26, no. 5, pp. 12–23, May 1993.
15. R. Horst, "ServerNet deadlock avoidance and fractahedral topologies," in *Proceedings of the International Parallel Processing Symposium*, pp. 274–280, April 1996.
16. *Paragon XP/S Product Overview*. Intel Corporation, Supercomputer Systems Division, Beaverton, OR, 1991.
17. J. Kim, A.Chien, "An evaluation of the planar/adaptive routing," in *Proc. 4th IEEE Int. Symp. Parallel Distributed Processing*, 1992.
18. J. H. Kim, Z. Liu and A. A. Chien, "Compressionless routing: A framework for adaptive and fault-tolerant routing," in *Proceedings of the 21st International Symposium on Computer Architecture*, April 1994.
19. D. Lenoski, J. Laudon, K. Gharachorloo, W. Weber, A. Gupta, J. Hennessy, M. Horowitz and M. Lam, "The Stanford DASH multiprocessor," *IEEE Computer*, vol. 25, no. 3, pp. 63–79, March 1992.
20. P. López and J. Duato, "Deadlock-free adaptive routing algorithms for the 3D-torus: Limitations and solutions," in *Proceedings of Parallel Architectures and Languages Europe 93*, June 1993.
21. J.M. Martínez, P. López, J. Duato and T.M. Pinkston, "Software-Based Deadlock Recovery Technique for True Fully Adaptive Routing in Wormhole Networks," to appear in *Proceedings 1997 International Conference Parallel Processing*, August 1997.
22. P.K. McKinley, H. Xu, A. Esfahanian and L.M. Ni, "Unicast-based multicast communication in wormhole-routed networks," in *Proceedings 1992 International Conference Parallel Processing*, August 1992.
23. P.R. Miller, "Efficient communications for fine-grain distributed computers," Ph.D Thesis, Southamptom University, 1991.
24. L. M. Ni and P. K. McKinley, "A survey of wormhole routing techniques in direct networks," *IEEE Computer*, vol. 26, no. 2, pp. 62–76, February 1993.
25. T.M. Pinkston and S. Warnakulasuriya, "On Deadlocks in Interconnection Networks", in *Proceedings 24th International Symposium on Computer Architecture*, June 1997.
26. D. S. Reeves, E. F. Gehringer and A. Chandiramani, "Adaptive routing and deadlock recovery: A simulation study," in *Proceedings of the 4th Conference on Hypercube, Concurrent Computers & Applications*, March 1989.
27. S. L. Scott and G. Thorson, "The Cray T3E networks: adaptive routing in a high performance 3D torus," in *Proceedings of Hot Interconnects IV*, August 1996.
28. S. Warnakulasuriya and T.M. Pinkston, "Characterization of deadlocks in interconnection networks," in *Proceedings of the 11th International Parallel Processing Symposium*, April 1997.

Author's Index

Agrawal, Dharma P. 33

Bolding, Kevin 247
Boughton, G. Andrew 65
Byrd, Gregory T. 159

Chai, Sek M. 103, 231
Chien, Andrew A. 1

Dai, Donglai 171
Duato, J. 203, 295

Ebeling, Carl 247
Eicken, Thorsten von 185

Flynn, Michael J. 159
Fulgham, Melanie L. 21

Garcia, David 119
Garg, Vivek 55
Gupta, R. 261

Hyatt, Craig 33

Kesavan, Ram 217
Kim, Jae H. 1

López, P. 295
Lund, Craig 137

Martínez, J. M. 295
May, Phil 103
McKenzie, Neil R. 247
Melhem, R. 261
Miller, Diane 89
Moon, Sung-Whan 75

Najjar, Walid A. 89

Panda, Dhabaleswar K. 39, 171, 217
Patel, Chirag S. 231
Petrini, F. 295
Pillai, Padmanabhan 75
Pinkston, Timothy Mark 275

Schimmel, David E. 55, 231
Shin, Kang G. 75
Silla, F. 203
Sivaram, Rajeev 39
Smai, A-H 189
Snyder, Lawrence 21, 247
Stunkel, Craig B. 39, 139

Thorelli, L-E 189

Warnakulasuriya, Sugath 275
Watson, William 119
Wills, D. Scott 103

Yalamanchili, Sudhakar 231
Yuan, X. 261

Lecture Notes in Computer Science

For information about Vols. 1–1340

please contact your bookseller or Springer-Verlag

Vol. 1341: F. Bry, R. Ramakrishnan, K. Ramamohanarao (Eds.), Deductive and Object-Oriented Databases. Proceedings, 1997. XIV, 430 pages. 1997.

Vol. 1342: A. Sattar (Ed.), Advanced Topics in Artificial Intelligence. Proceedings, 1997. XVII, 516 pages. 1997. (Subseries LNAI).

Vol. 1343: Y. Ishikawa, R.R. Oldehoeft, J.V.W. Reynders, M. Tholburn (Eds.), Scientific Computing in Object-Oriented Parallel Environments. Proceedings, 1997. XI, 295 pages. 1997.

Vol. 1344: C. Ausnit-Hood, K.A. Johnson, R.G. Pettit, IV, S.B. Opdahl (Eds.), Ada 95 – Quality and Style. XV, 292 pages. 1997.

Vol. 1345: R.K. Shyamasundar, K. Ueda (Eds.), Advances in Computing Science - ASIAN'97. Proceedings, 1997. XIII, 387 pages. 1997.

Vol. 1346: S. Ramesh, G. Sivakumar (Eds.), Foundations of Software Technology and Theoretical Computer Science. Proceedings, 1997. XI, 343 pages. 1997.

Vol. 1347: E. Ahronovitz, C. Fiorio (Eds.), Discrete Geometry for Computer Imagery. Proceedings, 1997. X, 255 pages. 1997.

Vol. 1348: S. Steel, R. Alami (Eds.), Recent Advances in AI Planning. Proceedings, 1997. IX, 454 pages. 1997. (Subseries LNAI).

Vol. 1349: M. Johnson (Ed.), Algebraic Methodology and Software Technology. Proceedings, 1997. X, 594 pages. 1997.

Vol. 1350: H.W. Leong, H. Imai, S. Jain (Eds.), Algorithms and Computation. Proceedings, 1997. XV, 426 pages. 1997.

Vol. 1351: R. Chin, T.-C. Pong (Eds.), Computer Vision – ACCV'98. Proceedings Vol. I, 1998. XXIV, 761 pages. 1997.

Vol. 1352: R. Chin, T.-C. Pong (Eds.), Computer Vision – ACCV'98. Proceedings Vol. II, 1998. XXIV, 757 pages. 1997.

Vol. 1353: G. BiBattista (Ed.), Graph Drawing. Proceedings, 1997. XII, 448 pages. 1997.

Vol. 1354: O. Burkart, Automatic Verification of Sequential Infinite-State Processes. X, 163 pages. 1997.

Vol. 1355: M. Darnell (Ed.), Cryptography and Coding. Proceedings, 1997. IX, 335 pages. 1997.

Vol. 1356: A. Danthine, Ch. Diot (Eds.), From Multimedia Services to Network Services. Proceedings, 1997. XII, 180 pages. 1997.

Vol. 1357: J. Bosch, S. Mitchell (Eds.), Object-Oriented Technology. Proceedings, 1997. XIV, 555 pages. 1998.

Vol. 1358: B. Thalheim, L. Libkin (Eds.), Semantics in Databases. XI, 265 pages. 1998.

Vol. 1359: G. Antoniou, A.K. Ghose, M. Truszczyński (Eds.), Learning and Reasoning with Complex Representations. Proceedings, 1996. X, 283 pages. 1998. (Subseries LNAI).

Vol. 1360: D. Wang (Ed.), Automated Deduction in Geometry. Proceedings, 1996. VII, 235 pages. 1998. (Subseries LNAI).

Vol. 1361: B. Christianson, B. Crispo, M. Lomas, M. Roe (Eds.), Security Protocols. Proceedings, 1997. VIII, 217 pages. 1998.

Vol. 1362: D.K. Panda, C.B. Stunkel (Eds.), Network-Based Parallel Computing. Proceedings, 1998. X, 247 pages. 1998.

Vol. 1363: J.-K. Hao, E. Lutton, E. Ronald, M. Schoenauer, D. Snyers (Eds.), Artificial Evolution. XI, 349 pages. 1998.

Vol. 1364: W. Conen, G. Neumann (Eds.), Coordination Technology for Collaborative Applications. VIII, 282 pages. 1998.

Vol. 1365: M.P. Singh, A. Rao, M.J. Wooldridge (Eds.), Intelligent Agents IV. Proceedings, 1997. XII, 351 pages. 1998. (Subseries LNAI).

Vol. 1366: Z. Li, P.-C. Yew, S. Chatterjee, C.-H. Huang, P. Sadayappan, D. Sehr (Eds.), Languages and Compilers for Parallel Computing. Proceedings, 1997. XII, 428 pages. 1998.

Vol. 1367: E.W. Mayr, H.J. Prömel, A. Steger (Eds.), Lectures on Proof Verification and Approximation Algorithms. XII, 344 pages. 1998.

Vol. 1368: Y. Masunaga, T. Katayama, M. Tsukamoto (Eds.), Worldwide Computing and Its Applications — WWCA'98. Proceedings, 1998. XIV, 473 pages. 1998.

Vol. 1370: N.A. Streitz, S. Konomi, H.-J. Burkhardt (Eds.), Cooperative Buildings. Proceedings, 1998. XI, 267 pages. 1998.

Vol. 1371: I. Wachsmuth, M. Fröhlich (Eds.), Gesture and Sign Language in Human-Computer Interaction. Proceedings, 1997. XI, 309 pages. 1998. (Subseries LNAI).

Vol. 1372: S. Vaudenay (Ed.), Fast Software Encryption. Proceedings, 1998. VIII, 297 pages. 1998.

Vol. 1373: M. Morvan, C. Meinel, D. Krob (Eds.), STACS 98. Proceedings, 1998. XV, 630 pages. 1998.

Vol. 1374: H. Bunt, R.-J. Beun, T. Borghuis (Eds.), Multimodal Human-Computer Communication. VIII, 345 pages. 1998. (Subseries LNAI).

Vol. 1375: R. D. Hersch, J. André, H. Brown (Eds.), Electronic Publishing, Artistic Imaging, and Digital Typography. Proceedings, 1998. XIII, 575 pages. 1998.

Vol. 1376: F. Parisi Presicce (Ed.), Recent Trends in Algebraic Development Techniques. Proceedings, 1997. VIII, 435 pages. 1998.

Vol. 1377: H.-J. Schek, F. Saltor, I. Ramos, G. Alonso (Eds.), Advances in Database Technology – EDBT'98. Proceedings, 1998. XII, 515 pages. 1998.

Vol. 1378: M. Nivat (Ed.), Foundations of Software Science and Computation Structures. Proceedings, 1998. X, 289 pages. 1998.

Vol. 1379: T. Nipkow (Ed.), Rewriting Techniques and Applications. Proceedings, 1998. X, 343 pages. 1998.

Vol. 1380: C.L. Lucchesi, A.V. Moura (Eds.), LATIN'98: Theoretical Informatics. Proceedings, 1998. XI, 391 pages. 1998.

Vol. 1381: C. Hankin (Ed.), Programming Languages and Systems. Proceedings, 1998. X, 283 pages. 1998.

Vol. 1382: E. Astesiano (Ed.), Fundamental Approaches to Software Engineering. Proceedings, 1998. XII, 331 pages. 1998.

Vol. 1383: K. Koskimies (Ed.), Compiler Construction. Proceedings, 1998. X, 309 pages. 1998.

Vol. 1384: B. Steffen (Ed.), Tools and Algorithms for the Construction and Analysis of Systems. Proceedings, 1998. XIII, 457 pages. 1998.

Vol. 1385: T. Margaria, B. Steffen, R. Rückert, J. Posegga (Eds.), Services and Visualization. Proceedings, 1997/1998. XII, 323 pages. 1998.

Vol. 1386: T.A. Henzinger, S. Sastry (Eds.), Hybrid Systems: Computation and Control. Proceedings, 1998. VIII, 417 pages. 1998.

Vol. 1387: C. Lee Giles, M. Gori (Eds.), Adaptive Processing of Sequences and Data Structures. Proceedings, 1997. XII, 434 pages. 1998. (Subseries LNAI).

Vol. 1388: J. Rolim (Ed.), Parallel and Distributed Processing. Proceedings, 1998. XVII, 1168 pages. 1998.

Vol. 1389: K. Tombre, A.K. Chhabra (Eds.), Graphics Recognition. Proceedings, 1997. XII, 421 pages. 1998.

Vol. 1390: C. Scheideler, Universal Routing Strategies for Interconnection Networks. XVII, 234 pages. 1998.

Vol. 1391: W. Banzhaf, R. Poli, M. Schoenauer, T.C. Fogarty (Eds.), Genetic Programming. Proceedings, 1998. X, 232 pages. 1998.

Vol. 1392: A. Barth, M. Breu, A. Endres, A. de Kemp (Eds.), Digital Libraries in Computer Science: The MeDoc Approach. VIII, 239 pages. 1998.

Vol. 1393: D. Bert (Ed.), B'98: Recent Advances in the Development and Use of the B Method. Proceedings, 1998. VIII, 313 pages. 1998.

Vol. 1394: X. Wu. R. Kotagiri, K.B. Korb (Eds.), Research and Development in Knowledge Discovery and Data Mining. Proceedings, 1998. XVI, 424 pages. 1998. (Subseries LNAI).

Vol. 1395: H. Kitano (Ed.), RoboCup-97: Robot Soccer World Cup I. XIV, 520 pages. 1998. (Subseries LNAI).

Vol. 1396: E. Okamoto, G. Davida, M. Mambo (Eds.), Information Security. Proceedings, 1997. XII, 357 pages. 1998.

Vol. 1397: H. de Swart (Ed.), Automated Reasoning with Analytic Tableaux and Related Methods. Proceedings, 1998. X, 325 pages. 1998. (Subseries LNAI).

Vol. 1398: C. Nédellec, C. Rouveirol (Eds.), Machine Learning: ECML-98. Proceedings, 1998. XII, 420 pages. 1998. (Subseries LNAI).

Vol. 1399: O. Etzion, S. Jajodia, S. Sripada (Eds.), Temporal Databases: Research and Practice. X, 429 pages. 1998.

Vol. 1400: M. Lenz, B. Bartsch-Spörl, H.-D. Burkhard, S. Wess (Eds.), Case-Based Reasoning Technology. XVIII, 405 pages. 1998. (Subseries LNAI).

Vol. 1401: P. Sloot, M. Bubak, B. Hertzberger (Eds.), High-Performance Computing and Networking. Proceedings, 1998. XX, 1309 pages. 1998.

Vol. 1402: W. Lamersdorf, M. Merz (Eds.), Trends in Distributed Systems for Electronic Commerce. Proceedings, 1998. XII, 255 pages. 1998.

Vol. 1403: K. Nyberg (Ed.), Advances in Cryptology – EUROCRYPT '98. Proceedings, 1998. X, 607 pages. 1998.

Vol. 1404: C. Freksa, C. Habel. K.F. Wender (Eds.), Spatial Cognition. VIII, 491 pages. 1998. (Subseries LNAI).

Vol. 1406: H. Burkhardt, B. Neumann (Eds.), Computer Vision – ECCV'98. Vol. I. Proceedings, 1998. XVI, 927 pages. 1998.

Vol. 1407: H. Burkhardt, B. Neumann (Eds.), Computer Vision – ECCV'98. Vol. II. Proceedings, 1998. XVI, 881 pages. 1998.

Vol. 1409: T. Schaub, The Automation of Reasoning with Incomplete Information. XI, 159 pages. 1998. (Subseries LNAI).

Vol. 1411: L. Asplund (Ed.), Reliable Software Technologies – Ada-Europe. Proceedings, 1998. XI, 297 pages. 1998.

Vol. 1413: B. Pernici, C. Thanos (Eds.), Advanced Information Systems Engineering. Proceedings, 1998. X, 423 pages. 1998.

Vol. 1414: M. Nielsen, W. Thomas (Eds.), Computer Science Logic. Selected Papers, 1997. VIII, 511 pages. 1998.

Vol. 1415: J. Mira, A.P. del Pobil, M.Ali (Eds.), Methodology and Tools in Knowledge-Based Systems. Vol. I. Proceedings, 1998. XXIV, 887 pages. 1998. (Subseries LNAI).

Vol. 1416: A.P. del Pobil, J. Mira, M.Ali (Eds.), Tasks and Methods in Applied Artificial Intelligence. Vol.II. Proceedings, 1998. XXIII, 943 pages. 1998. (Subseries LNAI).

Vol. 1417: S. Yalamanchili, J. Duato (Eds.), Parallel Computer Routing and Communication. Proceedings, 1997. XII, 309 pages. 1998.

Vol. 1418: R. Mercer, E. Neufeld (Eds.), Advances in Artificial Intelligence. Proceedings, 1998. XII, 467 pages. 1998. (Subseries LNAI).

Vol. 1422: J. Jeuring (Ed.), Mathematics of Program Construction. Proceedings, 1998. X, 383 pages. 1998.

Vol. 1425: D. Hutchison, R. Schäfer (Eds.), Multimedia Applications, Services and Techniques – ECMAST'98. Proceedings, 1998. XVI, 531 pages. 1998.

Vol. 1427: A.J. Hu, M.Y. Vardi (Eds.), Computer Aided Verification. Proceedings, 1998. IX, 552 pages. 1998.

Vol. 1430: S. Trigila, A. Mullery, M. Campolargo, H. Vanderstraeten, M. Mampaey (Eds.), Intelligence in Services and Networks: Technology for Ubiquitous Telecom Services. Proceedings, 1998. XII, 550 pages. 1998.